ADVANCE PRAISE

"This is the best crime book I've ever read, fiction or nonfiction, bar none. Not only is it a great story for entertainment, it should be mandatory reading and study for anyone aspiring to be a detective, investigator, or crime writer." — *Sergeant Andy Hill, Public Information Officer, 26 years Phoenix Police Department (retired)*

"A gripping account of the Phoenix Serial Shooter case, as told by the man who led the investigation. It reads like a thriller, sizzling with vivid storytelling. You'll be hooked!" — *Robin Dashwood, Director, Raw Television.*

"Having worked these actual cases in undercover surveillance, I really appreciated reading about the investigative processes that brought these criminals to justice. Readers will enjoy how the book delves into the complexity and painstaking process it takes to investigate crimes of this magnitude." — *Steven Blasko, 32 years Phoenix Police Department, 14 years as a SWAT officer (retired)*

"A must read for any true crime junkie. An inside look at the hunt for serial murderers from the man who tracked them down. Thrilling and compelling." — *Connie Tyler, Public Information Office, Phoenix Police Department*

"An incredible thrill ride through the ups and downs of the chase for serial murderers. A unique look from inside the investigation and into the minds of the monsters who killed without prejudice." — *C. Werner, Interior Designer, ASID, IAHSP*

"Clark's book is very engaging and documents the absolute life of being a cop! His description of Maryvale rings infallible to the core. Growing up there in the 70s, I saw the transformation firsthand. Twenty years later, I worked the same grungy streets as a beat cop, investigating crimes throughout the city for 21 years." — *Detective Don Briese, 25 years Phoenix Police Department (retired)*

DETECTIVE CLARK SCHWARTZKOPF

RANDOM RECREATIONAL VIOLENCE

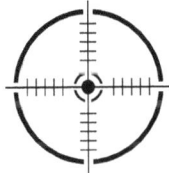

THE TRUE STORY OF THE SERIAL KILLINGS THAT TERRORIZED THE PHOENIX AREA

DETECTIVE CLARK SCHWARTZKOPF

RANDOM
RECREATIONAL
VIOLENCE

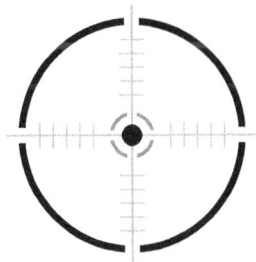

THE TRUE STORY OF THE SERIAL KILLINGS
THAT TERRORIZED THE PHOENIX AREA

PEACOCK PROUD
P · R · E · S · S
Phoenix, Arizona

First Published in the USA in 2021 by Peacock Proud Press, Phoenix, Arizona
  ISBN 978-1-7338710-6-8 Paperback
  ISBN 978-1-7338710-7-5 eBook
  Library of Congress Control Number: 2021905939

Editors:
  Laura L. Bush, PhD, PeacockProud.com
  Wendy Ledger, VoType.com
Cover and Interior Layout:
  Jana Galvan

DISCLAIMER:
This is a work of nonfiction. The information is of a general nature to help readers know and understand more about this true crime case. Readers of this publication agree that Detective Clark Schwartzkopf will not be held responsible or liable for damages that may be alleged or resulting directly or indirectly from their use of this publication. All external links are provided as a resource only and are not guaranteed to remain active for any length of time. The author cannot be held accountable for the information provided by, or actions resulting from accessing these resources.

This book is dedicated to my children,
who put up with not having their father around for three years.

It is also dedicated to the men and women of law enforcement,
who put their lives on the line every day in their communities.

CHAPTER 1

Summer came too fast once again. The end of May and the first of June in most parts of the country are a nice, warm start to summer. In Phoenix, Arizona, it comes with hundred degree days. Today would be no exception. The spring of 2006 was a distant memory, and now it was time to brace for the heat, the kind of heat that can sicken the healthiest person.

I arrived for work at the main headquarters for the Phoenix Police Department, a four-floor building at the corner of 7th Avenue and Washington Street, right in downtown Phoenix. Built sometime in the seventies, the building should have been torn down and replaced years ago. The inside had recently been gutted, but there was only so much space. Instead of offices, investigators work in space efficient "modulars" or cubicles. The whole place looks like a call center. I'm not complaining. With the new remodeling, I got an additional cabinet and a desk that my computer can actually fit on without taking up the entire work surface.

I had just finished my eighteenth year with Phoenix Police Department. Every cop I know dreams about the day they get their twentieth year in. You're finally off probation. You can take your 50 percent pension, and go find something else to do, anything else to do. The grind of the job has its way of pushing you out the door.

People often ask how I got involved in police work, and I'm still not sure how to answer. I grew up in the small, centrally located city of Casper, Wyoming, not exactly the crime capital of the world, in fact, just the opposite. I played four sports most of my childhood and high school years, did my undergrad work and played basketball at Eastern Oregon University, majoring in Business Economics. I meddled in the investment and sales world and thought about going into the teaching and coaching professions before ending up in law enforcement. The only thing I can think of is sometimes you fall into something that you're really good at, and it sticks.

Once I became a cop, I knew what I wanted to do with my career. I wanted to work on investigations. I spent the first seven years pushing around a squad car, and that was a good time. Driving like a maniac, getting in foot pursuits, and fighting like an alley cat with any perp that wanted. Vehicle Pursuit and Use of Force Policy restraints were much more lax than than they are now. We lived by one rule: hurt a cop, and you're going to the hospital, and then jail. Treat us with respect, and we'll do the same.

So in 1995, I took the test to be a detective and became a full-fledged investigator in February 1996. I was immediately assigned to what used to be called the General Investigations Bureau, now the Violent Crimes Bureau. The Bureau has five divisions: Homicide, Robbery, Night Detectives, Gangs, and the Assault Detail. Being assigned to the Violent Crime Bureau produced never a dull moment. Unfortunately, over the span of a decade, it seemed the city had blown up in violence.

First, it was the drug wars of the nineties. Mexican drug cartels fought rival American street gangs for drug territories. Bodies were littered all over the place. Neighborhoods turned into war zones, dozens of rounds fired with assault rifles; SKSs, AK47s, you name it, right in the middle of the city. It felt like Beirut.

Then came the great immigration invasion. I'm not exactly sure when it started. Probably around the time I started my career in mid-eighties, and President Ronald Reagan signed the Immigration and Reform Act of 1986, enacted to punish employers for illegally hiring known unauthorized aliens. This act also gave amnesty to over three million people living illegally in the United States. It set a precedent. Get here, and you "too" may get amnesty. I bet if Reagan could have it to do all over again, or if he'd been able to see what has happened since. . . .

Arizona has long been known as the state with the most border issues. It is literally a massive corridor for anyone who wants to seek refuge or commit ghastly crimes. Just get across the border. I watched as legal and illegal citizens were gunned down. Illegal aliens were kidnapped for ransom, and city streets shot up. All the while the open-border activists stood silently by, watching their numbers grow and then called us "racists" when we wanted to shut down the border.

It wasn't just citizens dying in these border-related crimes. I lost fellow comrades to this violence. There were many days when I wondered if the federal government was ever going to do its job and secure the border. It still hasn't happened.

May 30, 2006 was a halfway peaceful night in the city. As an investigator, every day starts out with the deluge of cases that come in overnight. With the punch of a key and the printer icon, I could see I had only three cases to review. I leaned back in my chair and started reading.

"Schwartzkopf, my office." That voice was the familiar sound of one Detective Sergeant Kenneth Laird. Kenny, as we called him, had been in the Violent Crimes Detail since 2000. He was a young guy with premature hair loss. As far as bosses go, he was a pretty good one, at least to me. He let me do my job and knew that, if a mess arose, I would take care of it.

"I need you to go to Banner Good Samaritan Hospital. We got three people shot last night, and the lieutenant wants to know what happened," Detective Sergeant Laird blurted.

"Good morning to you, too." I was busy, so I tried to get out of it. "Isn't there a summary in the ORs (operational reports) this morning, or did one of you useless supervisors forget to write one?" I shot back. The ORs were a report of exceptional incidents that occurred the night before. It was printed every day for management.

I've always been known as a smart ass, and it's easy to be one in this job. It's also easy to become jaded with all the stuff you see. Yet, criticizing management was one of my specialties. Managers laughed at themselves as much as we did. As with any organization, we had good ones and horrible ones.

"That's not the issue," Sergeant Laird said. "Patrol units took three separate random shootings last night within a couple of hours. There's no follow-up, and the reports are weak at best. Looks like somebody went target practicing with a shotgun."

"Where were the night detectives?" I asked. "Surely they would have investigated the cases or done the follow-up last night at the hospital before they went home."

"They weren't notified." He looked at me because he knew what was coming.

"What the Fu&%? How many times does this have to happen before some supervisor gets their butt demoted? That's inexcusable to have three people shot in three different incidents and for patrol officers to assume and complete the investigations. Why aren't you or someone in this chain of command ripping someone a new butthole?" I was sick of this. Some patrol supervisors didn't want to wait for investigators in the middle of the night, so they dumped the investigations on the patrol officers who responded. In this particular case, my criticism would be well-founded.

"I know, I know," Sergeant Laird continued after my tirade. "There's nothing we can do about it now. Sounds pretty simple. Just interview the victims and see if there's anything else they can add. I'll have the cases assigned to you."

"Where did it happen?" I asked.

"Maryvale."

CHAPTER 2

When Phoenix was a smaller town, back in the mid-sixties, a small community existed on what was then the furthest west side of town. I'm not sure where it got its name, but I've always heard it referred to as Maryvale. A community of small homes built for medium-income families, the streets in Maryvale were wide enough to drive motor homes down. Most of the houses built were less than two thousand square feet in size. They didn't even build garages, only carports. It was affordable housing. Schools soon popped up; nice neighborhoods were born. There were parks within walking distances, and everyone knew their neighbors.

Then something happened. As Phoenix began to grow north and east, Maryvale got left behind. It became less of a suburb and more of a central location. It was no longer the furthest west point of the city; rather, it was the "Westside." The homes that once housed middle-income families became homes for lower incomes. The yards became unkempt due to the lack of homeowner's associations. The older residents tried to stay put and hang on to their little piece of the Valley, but as the demographics changed, so did the streets. Gangs became prevalent, and shootings were a nightly occurrence. Maryvale had become the most violent part of the city.

So, on May 17, 2005, when Tony Mendez became another statistic on a crime blotter, nobody took notice. He was gunned down in Maryvale, something that happens all the time. But Tony's case would garner a whole lot more attention than the other violent crimes reported in the city's most violent section. Its significance would not be discovered until well after the fact.

By all accounts, Tony led a quiet life. He was recently divorced and had been bouncing around from one home to another. He had minor scrapes with the law, most recently an arrest for possession of dangerous drugs. But he had a family that loved him, and, like many drug users, was trying to turn his life around.

He had spent most of his adult life in and around Maryvale. He knew the streets and got around mostly by foot or bicycle. He had worked as a drywaller and lately had been doing odd jobs to turn a buck or two. A Van Halen fan, he had a tattoo of the popular eighties group on the web of his left hand. He had lived a tough life. Scars marked his body as a warrior that had seen his fair share of street life.

That evening, Tony arrived at his friend Jesse's house on a bike, pulling his two-wheel cart behind him. He had come to help Jesse fix a chain saw. It was one of the few stormy days of the year, and as day turned to night, the power went out in the neighborhood. After dinner, Tony rode off from Jesse's house. Jesse never knew why, but later would find out. It would be the last time Tony was seen alive by anyone who knew him.

As Tony rode his bike and pulled his trailer down 48th Lane, we can only guess what he was thinking. Maybe he noticed the old willow trees that hung over the street or the tall royal palms that lined the front yards of the one-story houses. With the storm subsiding, there was a pleasant breeze blowing in his face as he pedaled. Without a headlight, he kept his eyes to the road watching for any debris or anyone not paying attention for a bicyclist. Riding his bike was the only thing he was doing. Then his whole life was snuffed out in a moment's notice.

The crack, or report, of a .22 caliber rifle is almost surreal. It sounds more like the crack of a whip than the sound of a rifle. High-pitched as it is to the trained ear, it's unique. The bullet travels at one of the fastest speeds of any ammunition produced. Because of its small size and speed it causes extensive damage when it strikes the body. For years, it has been the favorite ammunition of assassins worldwide. Once the bullet enters the body, it tends to bounce from bone to bone like a pinball, tearing apart everything in its path. The skull cannot stop it, but it can keep it from exiting, as can other organs in the body.

We don't even know if Tony heard the shot; nobody else did. Pain and burning were all he felt. The flesh almost cauterized as the bullet entered the middle right portion of his back, six-and-three-quarter inches from his spine. It continued into his lung and diaphragm. Had it stopped there, he may have been able to survive. But we're talking about a .22 round.

It pierced his pericardial sac, the sac that surrounds the heart, and perforated his heart at the right atrium. It stopped in his left pectoral muscle, the last muscle of the chest with any thickness.

Tony was found slumped over his bike's handlebars in the middle of the street. At first, it was thought that he had been the victim of a motor vehicle accident. But a quick examination by paramedics discovered the small wound in his upper back. There was very little blood. It is surmised that he died almost instantaneously from the gunshot. There were no other injuries to his body.

The Medical Examiner's Office would rule Tony Mendez's manner of death a homicide. The cause of death: a gunshot wound. There was only one real piece of evidence—a tiny, gray projectile, considered to be in good shape.

CHAPTER 3

"Boy, somebody was really pissed last night," I thought to myself as I read the three departmental reports of the shootings on the night of May 30, 2006, that started at 11:00 p.m. and ended on the 31st at 1:45 a.m. Three males shot with a shotgun, three different locations, and no known motive. Two white males and one Hispanic male who does not speak English. Looks like we can rule out hate crimes for now.

As bad as it sounds, three random shootings was no record. I once had eight people shot in a three-hour time span. Patrol officers chased the suspect and his vehicle around for hours from one crime scene to another. The guy and female passenger were never caught.

My Spanish was pretty good when I was a beat cop, but lately I couldn't understand much of anything besides a Mexican restaurant menu. Before leaving for the hospital, I grabbed the first available Spanish-speaking detective I could find, and she reluctantly agreed to accompany me.

Detective Michelle Dalton had been in the Assaults Detail for a few years now. She was bright and eager to learn. I had worked with her for some time, and I liked her style and sense of humor. She was a good translator, and that's important in working violent crimes. Different parts of Mexico have different dialects. Adding to the complexity, many of the Mexicans who flood across our border are less educated, so the true meaning of a Spanish word is not what they perceive it to be.

Luckily for me, Good Samaritan Hospital was only a ten-minute drive from police headquarters. I had good luck dealing with personnel from Good Sam, as it was called. For the most part, the doctors and nurses were friendly enough, and the security folks were always helpful in locating patients. That's not always the case with hospitals and cops.

Time and time again, I would go into trauma units and stand at a nurses' station, with no receptionist, and watch multiple nurses not lift a finger to help me or point me in the right direction. I mean, I'm standing there with my gun and badge. Like, what else am I there for . . . a rectal exam? The only times cops come to hospitals on-duty is to conduct follow-ups on investigations. Sometimes I had to be downright rude.

The front entrance to Good Sam was a circular drive with valet parking. I never used the front entrance to hospitals, too crowded. I always make my way from the emergency room entrance. That's how I got to know them all. If I had to enter through the main entrances, I would be lost and walking around for days.

Good Sam's ER entrance was a steep two-story climb from McDowell Road, one way in and one way out. The walls that shoot up from the drive make the entrance extremely narrow. These walls are covered with colored bumper rubber and plastic from drivers who tried to hurry to the ER entrance. You could imagine cars careening off the walls as panicked drivers try to get their sick or injured persons inside.

The security desk was located just off the walk-in patient entrance to the ER. A rather robust security officer sat behind the desk. We greeted each other with mutual courtesy, and I gave him a rundown of the patients we were there to see. He directed us to the tenth floor, the surgical intensive care unit. All the victims had been admitted.

"That's not good," I told Detective Dalton.

"Why's that?" she asked.

"Well, if it's serious enough to admit them into SICU, then their injuries have to be pretty severe. They don't put patients up there just for the sake of available space."

"That's true. Now why didn't we get called out on this?" she asked.

I knew that she was trying to get me all fired up again. "Don't get me started."

The tenth floor SICU was broken up into pods, each one containing several individual rooms suitable for one-on-one patient care. The entrance door to Pod A was locked, and we had to be buzzed in.

All the shooting victims were listed under aliases. That was hospital regulations and a good idea. If you're dealing with gangbangers as patients, wounded for whatever reason, there was legitimate concern that, if the shooters found out where they were, they might come finish the job. Hence, the patients were given trauma names that only family would know. That would keep the thugs from finding them. As far as I knew, that policy was why none of the local hospitals had lost a patient to further violence.

We were obviously expected. A nurse in her mid-thirties came up to us as we entered the pod. The SICU staff was as curious as the victims were as to why someone would shoot three people for no apparent reason. The nurses probably knew more about the shootings than I did. Hospital staff, especially ER nurses, were great for gaining insight into why someone got shot or stabbed.

"Bet you guys are here to see some shooting patients," she said.

"That would be a big yes," I answered.

"Where do you want to start?"

"Well, let's start with Mr. James Hodge."

"Oh, good luck with him. This should be fun," she cracked. I wasn't sure how to take that.

James Hodge was living in a condominium complex just off of 89ᵗʰ Avenue and Camelback Road. Camelback, running from east to west, dissects the city, almost right dead center. This well-traveled road hosts many residential structures on its west side and many business structures to the east. The Camelback Corridor had become world-renowned for its shops and hotels, extending from Phoenix to Scottsdale. It got its name from Camelback Mountain, a small mountain that sits in the heart of Phoenix, a rock formation that juts up and appears to look like a camel lying on the ground, its two humps thrust in the air. It is one of the premiere hiking areas in the city and is simply stunning.

According to the report, at around 11:05 p.m., as James walked outside in the grassy common area that surrounds his building, he was shot. When he heard a loud blast, he didn't think anything of it, until he felt the sting of numerous pellets striking him in the back. Neighbors heard the shot, but nobody knew where it came from. James was standing just north of his condo. He was able to walk back to his place, leaving a blood trail along the way. His shoes were found in the grassy common area, along with what a patrol officer described as "a 20 gauge shotgun wadding." I sure hope he's right about the size. Nothing's worse than stating a fact or inferring something about evidence in a report and having it turn out to be different. No other evidence had been located.

Mr. Hodge's sister had been notified and was interviewed at the scene. She related that her brother had been diagnosed a "paranoid schizophrenic" and would often take late-night walks. Now I see why the nurse made that comment. Schizophrenics are tough to interview, especially paranoid schizophrenics. In grad school, I had learned a lot about schizophrenia and understood the mental illness. I hoped James wouldn't think of us as the bad guys.

According to the report, patrol officers were flagged down by a white male who directed them to the victim. This male and "his brother" were looking for their cat when they "heard screaming" and stumbled upon James. The male claimed he did not hear or see anything peculiar; his brother claimed that he heard tires squealing from a vehicle leaving the parking lot at a high rate of speed. Both of them had just happened upon the victim who couldn't tell them what happened.

Not a lot to go on. "Let's see if Mr. Hodge has anything to add, shall we?" I stated as we walked to his room. Detective Dalton stopped to summon a photo technician to the hospital.

James was sitting half upright in his bed. With his snow-white goatee and mustache, he looked like an older version of Santa Claus. His reddish hair contained a mix of white and blonde strands. It was obvious he was not comfortable, but who would be? He was lying on his wounds.

"Mr. Hodge, I'm Detective Schwartzkopf with the Phoenix Police Department. How are you doing?"

"Not too well, as you can see," he replied.

"James, I'm here to ask you some questions about the shooting last night. Do you think you can talk to me about that?"

"Yeah, some son-of-a-bitch shot me in the back!" he snapped. Who could blame him for being upset? I grew up watching Westerns as a kid and learned at an early age that anyone who struck or shot someone in the back was a gutless coward.

"Yeah, I can see that. Can you can tell me what happened from what you remember?" I didn't want him to get too riled up, but I did need to ask.

James went on tell me the same information I had read in the report. He had no idea why anyone would shoot him and really didn't have any problems with anyone. He was getting some fresh air outside.

When the photographer arrived, I asked hospital personnel to turn James over. The shotgun pattern stretched from his lower back to the base of his head. He even had a hole in his ear from a pellet. He was shot from quite a distance away. His skin had already started to turn blue and bruise from the impacts. His back had taken the brunt of the blast. He was lucky; it could have been a lot worse. Most of his wounds were superficial. The photo technician clicked away.

I told him I would get a hold of him or his sister if the case broke. "Not a lot to go on," I mumbled to myself as we left the room. Maybe we could get lucky with the shotgun wadding. Maybe the other victims could provide more detailed information.

Next on the hit parade, literally, was Miguel Rodriguez. Miguel was thirty-five years old and in the country illegally. He had been hopping from place to place and working odd jobs to survive. His sister lived in the States and several months ago decided to come across the border, and look for work. He spoke no English, and like so many other illegal aliens, he had become a victim of violence.

Miguel had been shot two and a half hours later than James Hodge. He was shot almost two miles away on another large thoroughfare, Indian School Road.

As I entered Miguel's room, I saw a large bandage on his right hip, which masked a serious shotgun wound. As I observed the X-rays of Miguel with his treating physician, Detective Dalton approached him. He was dressed in the usual embarrassing hospital gown, which covered only the front of his body. She began to interview Miguel in Spanish.

As I talked with the physician, I saw Detective Dalton look away from Miguel with a very disturbed look and frantically ask for a nurse. From the other side of the room, the doctor moved toward the side with the shotgun wound. What's the problem? Was he having a seizure, going into shock, what? A nurse came rushing in and started to work on Miguel. I stayed out of the way, and Detective Dalton stepped back. Within a couple of minutes, the doctor rejoined me at the X-ray lamp.

"Everything all right?" I asked.

"Everything's OK," the doctor replied. That was a relief.

"Hey, Doc, is there any way I can get a look at that wound? I'm seeing a high concentration of pellets here. I really need to figure out the size of that hole." I also learned that Miguel's bladder had been struck.

"Yeah, I can take the bandages off," he said.

As the doctor peeled back the bandages, I saw a gaping hole in Miguel's front hip area. The hole was so large, gauze bandages had been placed in it to plug the leak. They were soaked in bright red blood. Unlike Mr. Hodge, Miguel had been shot at close range, not quite point blank, but no more than a few feet away.

"The wound is about two inches in diameter," the doctor related. The crime technician clicked away with his camera getting as many shots of the wound as he could before they closed his bandages back up.

I began to peruse the initial police report again. Miguel was walking east on the sidewalk when a "white import car" heading west fired a shot at him. He was found on the north side of the street. A passenger could easily fire from a moving vehicle going in the opposite direction. If the car was in the curb lane next to Miguel, a shotgun would produce that kind of short-distance wound. Could a driver who was shooting do the same damage? Very unlikely, if not impossible. Almost all drive-by shootings are committed by at least two offenders. Miguel thought there were multiple passengers in the car when it went by him. Just like James, Miguel only suffered one gunshot wound.

Miguel was the only witness thus far. So it was up to Detective Dalton to get a better story. Unfortunately for us, he couldn't tell her anything further. She took down his sister's cellphone number, and I gave him my card. Besides his shotgun wound and blood at the scene, we had no evidence. Not even a pellet removed from him at this point.

Darrel Davies was the third and last victim. He had been shot just a few minutes after Miguel. Darrel lived just a stone's throw away from James Hodge, but several miles from where Miguel was shot.

Darrel reported to responding officers that he was out for a late-night stroll. I guess going for walks late at night in their neighborhood has become hazardous to one's health.

As Darrel crossed the intersection at 86th Avenue and Camelback, he too heard the loud bang signifying a gunshot. He too felt the pain from numerous projectiles striking his body. The blast was so horrific that it spun him around so he was facing the opposite direction from which he was walking. He went down immediately, didn't see the shooter, and didn't see anyone near him. He couldn't recognize if the shot came from a vehicle or not. Again, the victim was completely surprised by the shooting.

He screamed for help, just like Miguel and just like James. Some decent soul called 911. Darrel was found lying on the asphalt. Normally, in any other climate, that wouldn't be such a big deal. Except this is Phoenix, Arizona. Nighttime temperatures during the summer barely dip below 90 degrees. Once the cement and the asphalt heats up, they don't cool down until October. Darrel had the scars of the hot asphalt on his bare legs, the product of being laid out for at least twenty minutes. He too was shot only once.

As I contacted Darrel, I tried to think of something positive to say. He already knew there were two other victims shot. Everyone in trauma ICU had yakked about it. How positive and uplifting could I honestly be?

"Can you tell me anything about what happened?" I asked.

"Well, I was walking down the street from my apartment. I had just crossed the intersection." It was a vehicle, I thought to myself. Another drive-by, just like the two before it. No way had someone from the residences fired at Darrel. "As I'm walking, I hear this loud bang," he said. "Then I feel this blast of pellets hit me. Detective, it hit me so hard it blew me off my feet and spun me around."

"Did you see anyone, anything, or any vehicles at the time you got shot?" I asked.

"The only thing I remember is seeing a pickup truck that was going west. The only reason I know that is because, as I lay there, I could see the truck on the road," he said shaking his head. "Hell, I don't even know if the shot came from the truck."

"OK, bud. Anything else you remember?"

"No, I wish there was," he replied. I could tell he wanted to talk more, so I took a seat and waited for his chart and X-rays to come in. "You know my brother is in law enforcement," he said. "He's a chief of police in a town in California."

"Is that right?" I replied. I was sure I would be hearing from him soon. Wish I had better news to tell him.

"Yeah, he got the brains in the family. I just try to keep a low profile," Darrel said.

"That's not a bad thing, keeping a low profile," I said.

"Yeah, look where it got me. Shot in the street. What kind of an asshole shoots somebody who is just walking down the street minding their own business?" he asked.

"I don't know. It's very unusual, but there are two other guys that would like an answer to that," I replied. "By the way, is that something you do regularly, walk around town at 1:45 in the morning?"

"I do it when I can't sleep. It helps relax me," he said.

"Can I take a look at your arm?"

"Sure, I figured that you would want to," he said.

Darrel was right about his location. He was walking east on the south side of the street. His left arm was peppered with numerous pellets, too many to count. But it didn't take all the blast. The left side of his upper torso was also riddled, with a wound pattern that stretched from his mid-torso to his upper shoulder area. This shot was fired from a mid-range distance, not quite as far away as James Hodge, but not up close like Miguel Rodriguez.

The nurse came in with his chart.

"Jesus," I thought to myself. His left lung was partially collapsed. His colon was lacerated. His bladder was hit. He was going to have some issues down the road.

"Darrel, can you move your arm away from your body so I can see your side?" I asked. He was in a lot of pain, but he acted like a trooper. He winced as he moved his left arm away from his torso. For the first time, I saw the holes in his body cavity, lots of them. He was going to require surgery.

As I examined the wounds, the photo tech snapped shot after shot. "I know it hurts to move around, Darrel, but the better photos I get, the better I might be able to tell where the shot came from."

"I understand. My brother is a cop; he would do the same thing." It was obvious he was very proud of his brother and his accomplishments.

Darrel had probably just swung his left arm forward in a regular walking motion as the pellets hurled toward him. His arm had protected his upper body enough to keep them from striking his heart or other major organs.

"Do you think you can catch this guy? I sure would like to see him go to prison," he stated.

"Well, to be honest with you, Darrel, I don't have a lot to go on," I replied. "I'm hoping that there is a witness out there or somebody who knows a lot more than I know right now." Being honest with a victim never gets you jacked up later. Don't promise something you can't deliver.

"Good luck, Detective," he said.

"You get well, and I'll be in touch if I find out anything," I said as I left.

Detective Dalton had joined me as I exited his room.

"Thanks, Clarkster, for that experience. I'm not sure I won't be traumatized for the rest of my life," she said.

I was confused. "What are you talking about?"

"You know when you were talking to the doctor in Miguel Rodriguez's room and you asked me to talk to him about the shooting?"

"Yeah, what the heck was that all about? I thought he was going to slip into a coma and die or something."

"Oh no, that wasn't it at all," she said as we arrived at the elevators to take us back downstairs. "No, he didn't have any medical emergency at all. Well, not one that needed any real attention. "

"What was the problem, then?" I asked.

"It's pretty clear to me that he thought I was a nurse, so he decided to whip back the sheet, exposing himself completely, and show me that he needed his catheter adjusted or his bedpan emptied," she said.

I didn't know what to say. The ding preceded the arrival and opening of the elevator doors, and we moved in. A nurse and a doctor patiently waited for us to board. I could feel Detective Dalton's stare burning a hole in the side of my head, waiting for me to reply.

"I guess he thinks that every female in the hospital is a nurse. I can tell you, Clarkster, it wasn't a pretty picture seeing his unit with that catheter sticking in it." She paused for a moment. "And you better not tell anybody at the office," she said. "You owe me big time for this one."

As the elevator started to go down, I tried to choke back my laughter and did a poor job of it. My eyes watered, and I was choking through slightly pierced lips, trying not to laugh uncontrollably. I just couldn't hold it, no matter how hard I tried. I turned away from the doctor so he wouldn't think I was having a seizure.

The ride back to police headquarters was no easier. As I dropped Detective Dalton off at the front door to police headquarters, I thanked her for her invaluable translations service.

"Fu*% you, Clarkster," she said. That was Michelle, and that was all she needed to say. I didn't take it personally.

◆

After I walked the three blocks from my allotted parking garage, I plopped down at my desk and tried to put together what I knew so far.

Three shootings, starting a little after 11:00 p.m., with the last occurring at 1:45 a.m. All the victims were shot with a shotgun, unknown caliber, with different distances in all three cases. None of the victims reported seeing anybody in the vicinity. A white import car was seen at one of the shootings with possible multiple subjects inside. Two of the victims were shot next to the main streets; the other was in front of his apartment just off a main street. The only evidence recovered, besides some pellets, was one shot cup or wadding, known or referred to by most novices as shotgun wadding.

The shot cup is a more technically advanced version of the wadding. Made of plastic, this cup was created to keep the pellets bundled together longer when fired—the idea being that, if the pellets were packed together inside the cup, fewer pellets would fly astray as they headed down range. Those wild pellets, referred to as satellites, were those that you would see strike far away from the main blast pattern, which is what you would get with basic wadding. The shot cup eliminated satellites, for the most part, and kept the pellets in a tighter grouping. Most, if not all, shotgun ammunition was manufactured with a shot cup. Like a conventional wadding, the shot cup also came out of the barrel and followed the pellets as they travelled toward their intended target.

In my years investigating drive-by shootings, I had learned that the worst witness is usually the victim, especially when the shooting happens quickly, as these apparently did. By the time most victims realize they've been shot in a drive-by, it can take between five to ten seconds for them to start to organize their thoughts and look around. A car can travel a long way in that time.

These victims had nothing in common. They didn't know each other, and only two of them lived remotely close to each other. The victims were shot once with no known motive. What a piece-of-crap crime spree.

"What did you find out?" Detective Sergeant Laird inquired as I thumbed through my notes.

"I found out that these are going-nowhere cases. Thanks for asking me to look into them," I fired back sarcastically.

"Sounds right up your alley," he said.

"I'll let the LT know we got no leads," I replied.

"Good luck," he replied dryly.

As I started to bang out the reports, I felt the vibration of my pager. Most detectives quit carrying pagers years ago, replacing them with cellphones. I still carried one because I didn't want to give out my personal cellphone number to informants, victims, or anyone else.

I looked down at my belt and thumbed the button to pull up the number. I didn't recognize this number, and there was no code or serial number behind it. It's an unwritten rule for cops; always put your serial number behind your number to show who's trying to get a hold of you. Of course, that didn't always happen. I didn't recognize the number so whoever it was would have to call back later. I had too much typing to do.

In the meantime, I looked to see if responding patrol officers had taken crime scene photos. If so, they probably hadn't been submitted to the photo lab yet. Besides, the reports showed only one piece of significant evidence. What would the crime scene photos show? The same thing, maybe some blood on the sidewalk, street, or grass.

I could never have been more wrong.

CHAPTER 4

The intersection of 7th Avenue and Camelback Road had undergone a renaissance in recent years. The voters of Maricopa County had passed a proposition to allow funding for the building of a light rail system to help alleviate the congestion of traffic that flowed into and out of central Phoenix. The intersection was to be a main stop for the light rail, which would run east to Central Avenue and then south to downtown Phoenix. It was a major overhaul of the transportation system in the Valley of the Sun, one that would cause much consternation with drivers.

But on May 24, 2005 no such construction existed. 7th Avenue and Camelback was just another busy intersection in Phoenix. Every corner was full, with a strip mall or business of some kind on each one. It was also a major connecting intersection for bus service. From there, you could go just about anywhere in the city.

Lord only knows how long Reginald Remillard had been lying, sitting, or just waiting for a bus to come. He may have not known that the bus didn't come until early in the morning, starting around 5:30 a.m., or that it stopped altogether before midnight. He may not have been waiting for a bus at all.

Like a growing number of psychiatric patients in the Phoenix area, Reginald had fallen on hard times. He suffered from schizophrenia and would end up on the streets, lost and confused. He was a decorated Vietnam vet who just wouldn't take his medication. He was awaiting placement in a facility when he walked away from the VA Hospital. Sometimes bus benches were the most adequate sleeping quarters for someone like Reginald.

Reginald had a rap sheet and a drinking problem as well. He had been mandated to go to the Local Alcohol Rehabilitation Center, known as LARC. His drinking had led to depression, which had led to petty crimes. Sooner or later, he would get caught. Sometimes a jail cell was a welcome sight. At least he got two meals a day and a tent over his head at Sheriff Joe Arpaio's jail.

He had picked up a nickname, "The Duck." It was probably some confusion between his last name, Remillard, and the green-headed mallard duck. Some of his friends even called him "Mallard." But there were no friends around on this fateful morning. As Reginald sat at the bus stop, he was unaware of any evil that lurked nearby.

Just after midnight, Reginald was found lying on the same bus bench on which he'd been seen sitting upright twenty minutes earlier. Two men walking down Camelback Road found Reginald with a serious wound to his neck. The wound spurted blood in an arc because of the perforation to the carotid artery, with every heartbeat shooting another stream of blood onto the gray, dingy sidewalk where the bench stood.

Reginald's shoes were off. He had made himself comfortable. The two witnesses would later claim that, just minutes prior to them finding him, they had heard two gunshots. They described a white, older Oldsmobile heading west at a slow pace. When they heard the sound, one remarked to the other, "I'll bet you someone got shot."

As they looked upon the mortally wounded Reginald Remillard, they saw no weapon close by. This was no suicide. They had been across the street when the shooting occurred, maybe a hundred and fifty feet from Reginald.

Before dispatch could send officers to the scene, a Phoenix Police supervisor happened to pass by. He was frantically flagged down. The supervisor could see the wound and the arterial spurting of blood. Grabbing one of Reginald's shoes, he pressed against the artery to slow the bleeding. Reginald was gray and ashen. A large pool had already developed on the sidewalk, but he was still alive.

Paramedics rushed him to St. Joseph's Hospital in critical condition. He was dressed only in his shorts. His blood-soaked shoes would stay at the scene for investigators to collect later.

The emergency surgeons who worked on Reginald at the hospital were firsthand witnesses to what caused his injury. A hole in body tissue doesn't necessarily point to any specific cause, but a quick X-ray of the area would.

A bullet struck him in the left anterior portion of his neck. It had traveled through the carotid artery and into the region of his neck known as the C5-C6 vertebrae. Like a lot of bullets that strike the vertebrae, this one had fragmented, causing severe damage to the spine. One large fragment had been removed, along with all the smaller ones. Surgeons were able to graft and repair the artery and stop the bleeding, but Reginald was paralyzed. The fractures to his vertebrae were horrific. His spinal cord had been compressed. Most critically, he had lost too much blood.

On May 30, 2005, six days after he was shot, Reginald Remillard died of his wound. The autopsy report was summarized with the language that only doctors and pathologists could understand. Reginald developed anoxic encephalopathy (comatose, brain damage), acute renal failure from loss of blood (kidney failure), and respiratory failure. In short, his lungs, heart, and kidneys just quit working due to lack of oxygen. But investigators would be most interested in what really caused Reginald to die: a bullet, a lead one at that.

The manner of death was ruled a homicide. Like Tony Mendez before him, Reginald had been in the wrong place at the wrong time—shot once in the neck by an unknown assailant. The shot could have come from a car or someone sitting in one of the many parking lots within view of the bench bus.

The crime scene would yield no evidence of any substance—no shell casing, no bullet strike to the bus bench or structure that covers it. Was it possible that only one shot was fired? One shot, one kill. The echo of a rifle fired in an urban setting can, in some instances, sound like two shots. The reverberation off buildings could confuse a witness or two.

Without any evidence of a second shot being fired, the investigators would have to assume that the one shot that struck Reginald was the only shot that was fired. It could have come from anywhere east, since Reginald was shot in the left side of the neck.

The million-dollar question was, "Why?"

CHAPTER 5

In Greek mythology, the phoenix is a bird that symbolized immortality, resurrection, and life after death. It was associated with the god of the sun, Apollo. According to the Greeks, the bird lived in Arabia, and every morning at dawn, Apollo would stop his chariot to listen to the bird sing a beautiful song while it bathed.

The bird was the only one of its kind, and upon death's door, after living several hundreds of years, would build a nest of aromatic wood. It would then set itself on fire.

The bird would be consumed by the flames. And from the embers, a new phoenix would arise, embalming the ashes of its predecessor into an egg of myrrh. The egg would be deposited at the altar of Apollo. From there, who knows what happened to it?

The birth of the City of Phoenix, on the other hand, is not draped in Greek mythology.

It is believed that somewhere between 700 and 1400 AD, roving bands of Indians set up a settlement known as the Pueblo Grande, in what is now known as the Valley of the Sun. What happened to these Indians is unknown, but they created a vast canal system to irrigate the land. This system was later discovered by other Indians, and they named the ruins, "Ho Ho Kam": The People Who Have Gone. For hundreds of years, the land was unsettled. No one knows exactly what happened to the Indian settlers. Most guess that drought and an average rainfall of seven inches per year drove them away.

But, according to these same historians, in 1867, Jack Swilling stopped his horse to rest at the foot of what is now known as the White Tank Mountains. Jack saw a valley far and wide. He had ridden his horse through the soft, brown dirt. He eyed a valley with few or no rocks and a place free of cold winters and heavy snow. He recognized that, with a canal system for ample water, the valley could be a farming haven.

Swilling organized the Swilling Irrigation Canal Company. He first began to expand the canal system already in place, the ones left by Indians hundreds of years earlier. By 1868, Swilling had constructed a system of canals that would feed water to company members that started to raise crops. The colony would soon begin to grow. It was first named Swilling's Mill, after its original entrepreneur. Then it changed its name to Helling Mill, and then Mill City. Swilling originally wanted to name the colony "Stonewall," after General Stonewall Jackson of the Confederate Army. Swilling had fought for the Confederacy and thought the name was a suitable fit. But the colony's inhabitants thought differently. They settled on the name of "Phoenix," since the town would spring from the ruins of an ancient civilization. It was officially recognized as a city on May 4th, 1868.

Phoenix and its surrounding cities and towns have had a tough time shedding the "farming/cow town label," and for good reason. Urban sprawl has led to fewer and fewer orchards, but many a homeowner still plants citrus trees in his or her backyard. Horse property is still available within the city limits. Here we are, the fifth largest city in the nation, and patrol officers employed by the City of Phoenix still respond to calls of loose animals. I'm not talking about a pit bull or a cat in a tree. I'm talking about a horse or goat loose on the streets, someone's chickens have gotten out, or a rooster keeps waking the neighbors in the new subdivision.

So it didn't raise a lot of eyebrows citywide when patrol officers in the West Valley started responding to calls of injured or dead animals in the summer and fall of 2005. Most centered around the small town of Tolleson. People here understand that we live in the West. There's always some idiot with a gun, and where there's an idiot with a gun, there's a fool's idea that something or someone needs to be shot. Animals, especially larger ones like horses and mules, are easy targets.

Tolleson, Arizona is a small community wedged between Phoenix, Glendale, and the city of Avondale to the west. As you travel west on the I-10 freeway, if you blink, you might just miss the sign leading to town. The town itself rests on five-and-a-half square miles of land with little or no room to grow. It is basically landlocked with the cities that surround it and the Indian reservation to its south. Working-class families dot the landscape, trying to find affordable housing in an ever-growing metropolitan area. Although most of the lands used to be farms and ranches, the town now has more of a Mexican flavor.

Generations of horse lovers have homesteaded all their lives in and around the area. Their parents and grandparents willed down the properties to their kin just to keep the small-town feel alive. That's why the shooting of animals is so upsetting to the local folk. Horses are expensive to keep, feed, and house.

On June 29, 2005, the shooting of Sara Moon, a nine-year-old quarter horse, set the tone for the next month. Sara Moon had been boarded at a property just off 91st Avenue, a busy north and south artery through Tolleson. Sara Moon was boarded in an acre property with railed fences, rented by a judge, a Tolleson City Court judge. That brought a whole list of scumbags and lowlifes into the picture. It wouldn't be the first time someone had retaliated against a municipal judge for a supposedly "unfair" ruling. The problem was, Sara Moon didn't belong to the judge.

On July 20, 2005, the owner of an old paint called Apache had gone out to feed her in the early hours of the morning. He had found his horse bleeding on the right side. The owner had never heard a shot fired, and neither had the neighbors. Apache survived.

In neighboring Avondale, police responded to the shooting of another horse on July 26. A grey Shetland pony by the name of "Little Man" had been found dead in a pasture off 107th Avenue and Encanto Road. He had been shot two times just behind the left shoulder. The owner had discovered the pony lying in the pasture when she was going out to feed him. Neighbors had heard two shots fired. A *necropsy*, an animal autopsy, yielded two small projectiles that would later be determined as .22 caliber in size.

CHAPTER 6

83rd Avenue is the border of jurisdictions between the cities of Phoenix and Tolleson. Jurisdictions can occasionally become a nasty fight, especially if a troubled nightspot sits on a major street where one city has one side of the street and another city has the other side. Technically, the jurisdiction on the other side of the street doesn't have to respond to calls for service to the other town. They can ignore calls not located within the boundaries of the city they serve. Pettiness tends to be set aside if a cop needs a back-up, however.

But on June 29, 2005, there would be no squabbling over boundaries, no trying to juggle or ignore what had happened. A man was dead. The victim's name was David Estrada.

Unfortunately, for Tolleson Police Detective Ron Rock, the dead man had literally ended up on the wrong side of the street. He was eight feet inside Tolleson's jurisdiction, according to a boundary map. In fact, Phoenix Police units arrived at the scene before Tolleson Police.

It's taxing for Tolleson to handle a homicide, particularly a whodunit, with only a thirty-three man department and only two full-time detectives assigned to investigations. The early investigation into David Estrada's death would be perplexing. He was found lying on a sidewalk, bleeding from the head. He was barefoot, wearing green shorts and a dark blue T-shirt. Several items were found south of the body's location, including some money and a guitar. What was later determined to be David's property had been found on the side of the westbound on-ramp to Interstate 10, a usual gathering spot for hitchhikers. You can travel on the I-10 freeway all the way to Los Angeles, if you wish.

The witness who reported seeing David lying on the sidewalk thought he was sleeping or passed out. That happens a lot in a community with many transients, such as the Phoenix Metro Area. Individuals get so intoxicated with booze or drugs that they lie stiff, right where they fall. Sometimes the homeless actually make it to a shaded area, sometimes not.

The officers who arrived in the early morning hours of June 29th knew why David was lying on the sidewalk, and it wasn't because he was tired or passed out. David had been killed by a gunshot to the chest. He had obviously been coughing up his own blood. There, of course, were no witnesses to what occurred.

David Estrada was twenty years old and had spent all of his life in the Phoenix area. He had attended St. Mary's High School in Phoenix, an all-Catholic school. He had excelled in sports and was a popular kid. He also enjoyed music. He was handsome and had his whole life ahead of him. Recently, however, drugs had slipped back into his life. He had begun using in high school, but had gotten himself clean. Now his family believed that he had started using again.

In the weeks that followed, Detective Rock and his colleagues would leave no stone unturned in an attempt to find David's murderer. They followed leads supplied by family and friends. According to contacts made the day before his murder, David was seen in Central Phoenix with some less than savory characters. Investigators learned after his death that he was concerned about his mother putting him in drug rehab. He had told at least one person that he was heading for Mexico, another that he was heading for San Francisco. His bags were packed and ready to go, like the song says. His guitar, backpack, and duffle bag were found a few feet from David.

Rumors of drug debts, drug usage, and drug rip-offs filled investigators' notebooks. Numerous names were floated as to having knowledge or being involved in the fatal shooting of David Estrada. Jimmy Sands was one of those names.

A longtime friend of David, Sands contacted David's family about information that came to him via "a dream." He claimed that David contacted him through the supernatural and told him to talk to two street bums, "Psycho and Tennessee." You just can't make this stuff up. These two decided to spill their guts and told Sands about the night of the murder. Psycho told how a white car drove up 83rd Avenue and stopped where Estrada was standing. How the occupants of the car had offered David some money, and as David approached the car, somebody shot him. They had seen what occurred. It sounded legitimate.

By the time police got involved, Psycho's story began to change. He actually didn't witness the shooting; he had only heard a rumor about what happened. The story now was two white guys had been looking for David because he owed them money. Psycho refused to talk to police. He told the family member that he did fifteen years in prison and he "ain't a snitch."

Psycho was another example of the cognitive brilliance that radiates from the penal system. Forget that a kid has been murdered. Even if he did know who killed David, Psycho would be too stupid to put on the stand in a court of law.

Others would pop up with more information, claiming they knew the murderer, the motive, or where the murder weapon was located. Eric Haley would provide the latter.

Eric had been arrested by a state trooper and claimed to have information about David's murder. Eric spun a tale of how cops had shown up at his apartment and asked for a .22 caliber rifle that had been used in the murder. He had no idea what the cops were talking about. He had allowed the police to search his residence, and no gun was recovered. "Frosty," a very dangerous drug dealer, according to Eric, had the weapon and knew about the murder. During the interview, Eric admitted to smoking meth a few days prior. Investigators believed he was high during the interview.

Later, detectives would follow up at the listed address Eric supplied them. Guess what? No such address ever existed. The ones he gave for Frosty? Also false.

However, the interesting thing about crime is that it's perpetually perpetrated by the same set of dirtbags. Even in a county with over five million residents, it's amazing how small our criminal boundaries are.

It just so happened that eight days before the murder of David Estrada, I'd been called out to help reconstruct a crime scene of a shooting that had turned into a homicide in an area known as Sunnyslope. In its heyday, Sunnyslope had been filled with decent middle-class folks and residences. But lately it had become a roosting ground for rundown rentals, squatter apartment buildings, and criminals. As in Maryvale, there were pockets of holdouts and decent neighborhoods, but the area to which I was called to investigate the murder was not clean, it was not well kept, and it was far from middle class.

The apartments at 602 E. Mission had become an eyesore and filled with a veritable who's who of the criminal underground. Police were targeting the complex because of all the troubles. There were numerous felons with felony warrants being scooped up, only to see the next batch take up residence. The grounds looked like a garbage dump, with broken-down cars, abandoned furniture, and junk piled everywhere.

Although the murder I was investigating did not occur there, the major players lived there. And, what was more important, I knew Frosty.

On June 21, 2005, Diego Rojo had been in an apartment sitting on his couch with a girlfriend watching TV when he was shot. The suspect, later identified as Noel "Gordo" Escobedo, had fled the scene after firing nine rounds with a .22 caliber rifle through Diego's apartment window. Diego would later die of multiple gunshot wounds. Detective Mike Norlin would assume the investigation as case agent.

It was a complete fluke that the murder of Diego Rojo and David Estrada were within a few days of each other, that the same caliber weapon was used, and that the same players were identified. Because of this coincidence, investigators on the murder of David Estrada went on the hunt for leads that seemed extremely legitimate.

Unfortunately, Frosty was in possession of a murder weapon, just not the right murder weapon in the Estrada case.

As the investigation into David Estrada's death slogged forward, a veritable list of scumbags appeared. The family was constantly bombarding investigators with new tips on David's friends, contacts, and possible investigative leads. None panned out. But one peculiar event occurred just a short distance away from where David Estrada had been gunned down.

At 1:08 a.m., two and half hours prior to David's murder, an alarm activation was reported at a Burger King restaurant. The alarm company called the RP (reporting person) and told him about the activation. Each alarm company that monitors a business or home has a person that they phone in case of any activation. The RP then decides whether to disregard the alarm or notify police. In most cases, the alarms are false, or there's no crime committed. In this case, the alarm was a glass-breaking alarm from the play area. The alarm company was monitoring and heard no other sounds from the restaurant. The RP decided not to respond, and police weren't notified at that time.

At around noon on the day of David's murder, the general manager of the Burger King notified Tolleson Police that the front window in his play area had been shot out. He had recovered a bullet in the play area and requested detectives to come out. He believed that it may have some connection with David Estrada's murder.

This shooting at the Burger King had a purpose. It was target practice. The glass that had been shot out was painted with a two-story caricature with a big smiley face. Two holes perforated the head of the drawing.

Was this a message? Target practice before killing? Was it even related? All unknowns, and only the mind of the killer could answer that.

CHAPTER 7

On August 6th, 2005, two young women would be sexually assaulted behind a church just off Baseline Road in South Phoenix. The attack would draw little attention as the suspect pulled a small gun on the women and then raped them. He claimed to have a partner and told them if they screamed they were dead. Both submitted to the brutal attack. He told them to walk away and not look at his face.

As I started to analyze the three shotgun shootings that had occurred on May 30th and May 31st, I wondered what would piss someone off so bad that they would randomly shoot three different individuals in the same night, within a few hours of each other.

When you're diagnosing a violent crime, it's easy to separate the good cases that you have a chance of clearing and the bad ones that have little or none. It has a lot to do with the victims. Some have placed themselves in precarious situations—buying drugs, selling drugs, ripping drugs, domestic abuse, etc. Most of these victims live a lifestyle associated with violence, but not these victims. Their only "crimes" were being out late at night and by themselves.

As I looked down at the cases I held in my lap, I spotted a shadow looming over my cubicle. The shadow belonged to one Detective Cliff Jewell.

Detective Jewell was a homicide detective who had been with the Phoenix Police Department for about twenty-seven years. He had spent a few years in Homicide and before that had worked in the Graffiti Detail. I had known Cliff through a group known as the Arizona Homicide Investigators Association. I had been a member of the association for several years.

"I tried to page you yesterday afternoon, but you didn't call me back," he said. That would happen quite frequently as I've explained.

"Yeah, well I don't usually return calls to my pager without a serial number behind them. C'mon. You've been around forever, Dinosaur Boy. You ought to know better than that.

"Wait a minute, you're calling me a dinosaur? I didn't think anybody used pagers anymore in the twenty-first century. Most of us have upgraded to cellphones. You might want to try that," he said.

"No, then I would have slugs in Homicide bothering me all the time. This way I can filter out the losers I don't want to talk to. Besides, if you're bothering me, it's probably not important anyway," I said. Even though I kid around with cops from all the details, Cliff was one of the matter-of-fact kind of detectives: Joe Friday. I put down the cases. "Alright, you've got my attention," I said.

"Heard you went to the hospital yesterday doing follow-ups on those three poor bastards that got shot," he said.

"Yeah, I went there yesterday morning. The cases are being assigned to me. There's absolutely nothing to go on, so why are you bothering me?"

"Right, I have nothing to do besides come over here and bother you in your newly efficient, well-designed, ergonomically-correct cubicle," Cliff said. Everybody hated these things. I just couldn't let the comment go by without stirring the pot.

"Hey, how do you like these new digs? Pretty spacious, these cubicles, aren't they?"

"Oh yeah, they're wonderful. All my homicide books are packed underneath the desk, behind my chair, flowing into the aisle. I just love these new spaces," he replied. I had just enough leg room at the middle of my desk to be able to slide under my computer console. All my cases were packed into large packing boxes and stuffed underneath the desk. He began to snicker. "I see that you're suffering from the same space issues that we have," he laughed. "Don't you just love the fact that any Tom, Dick, or Harry could come by after hours and read your reports?" He had a point there.

"Who would want to read any of your lousy reports?" I said. "What's your clearance rate in Homicide these days? About 25 percent?" I cracked.

"Somewhere around there," he snipped.

Clearance rates for homicides were a touchy subject with management and some investigators. Homicide had been deluged with illegal-immigrant murders. And contrary to the liberal talking points or the views of people who don't work the street, these people were not coming forward and helping police track down the murderers. Most of the cases were shelved for lack of cooperation or lack of leads.

"So to what do I owe the honor of your interest in my cases?" I asked. I could tell from his sigh that this was going to take awhile.

CHAPTER 8

On August 14th, 2005, a robbery would occur at a gay bar in the area of 24th Street and Thomas Road. Two female patrons would try to take the law into their own hands and chase the robber. At gunpoint, and laid out in an alley, one of the do-gooders would be sexually assaulted.

This would begin a series of robberies and sexual assaults that would run through the end of 2005. The suspect began to move from street robberies of individuals to businesses. He hit restaurants and small shops. With each robbery the suspect grew more dangerous, and more sexually motivated. There would be numerous crimes in one week, then he would drop off the face of the earth for a month. When confronting multiple victims, he was always armed with a small, silver semi-automatic handgun.

In total, the animal would strike twelve times in the fall and winter of 2005. It would finally culminate in what was thought to be the first homicide attributed to the suspect. Tina Washington would be shot and killed in the area of 6000 S. 40th Street. She was shot once in the head with what was believed to be a 380 caliber, semi-auto handgun.

Even though some of his crimes were committed in Central Phoenix, the murderer/robber/rapist would be dubbed "The Baseline Rapist," named for the stretch of road where some of the crimes had been committed.

The lead headline in the *Arizona Republic* newspaper, one of only two official newspapers in the Valley of the Sun read, "Shots near downtown leave 2 dead, 1 wounded." The reporter was Judi Villa, a veteran crime reporter for the *Republic*.

The article started with an interview of Timothy Tordai, the lucky survivor of the killing spree that occurred on December 30, 2005. He was interviewed from his hospital bed—a damn sight better than two other shooting victims who could now be found on metal slabs. The investigation, or lack of it, was a cluster of bits of little or no information. Tordai had been shot in the back, and the bullet had exited his neck. He never saw it coming.

All these shootings had occurred in a four-block area, just two blocks away from main police headquarters. The Madison Street Shelter, one-half mile from headquarters, has housed and fed thousands of homeless people. They line the streets for blocks at a time. Nobody knows for sure how many homeless people sleep and live on the streets of this city. Government officials have no idea themselves and don't want to know.

Timothy Tordai wasn't quite homeless, but he was one step away from being there. He had been assigned to a halfway house trying to kick a bad habit and get his life in order.

On December 30th, Timothy had just stepped off a city bus. He had no car and bussed his way to and from work, a requirement to keep his current living arrangement. He had just disembarked at 9th Avenue and Van Buren Street, half a block from his home.

As Tim headed south, he cranked up the tunes on his radio and slipped on his headphones. He never heard the shot. A massive pain in his neck laid him out on the ground, and he didn't know why until he realized he had been shot. Blood poured down his chest. There wasn't a soul anywhere around him. He pulled himself to his feet with the help of a wrought-iron fence and stumbled home.

It was this police response and subsequent canvassing that would lead to the discovery of two dead bodies. Both were males with gunshot wounds to the chest. They were only two and three blocks away from where Tim had been shot. The two victims appeared to be transients.

As police responded and attempted to secure the three separate crime scenes, investigators were being awoken from their beds. The first call came a little after midnight.

What was not known at the time, but would be discovered shortly, was that additional shootings had taken place—random shootings of animals and a possible street prostitute a few miles away, all on the same night and early morning hours.

On December 29, 2005, Barbara Whitner took her black Australian Shepard, Cherokee, out on their customary walk. Barbara lived northeast of Los Olives Park, along the Camelback Corridor, on one of the quieter streets. December is a cool month by Phoenix standards, but it's great weather for walking a dog. Usually about 40 to 45 degrees in the evening, the desert somehow feels colder than its reported temperature. Tonight's walk would be at a brisk pace.

As Barbara entered the park, a shot rang out. It was 10:20 p.m. There was the unmistakable howling of a wounded animal. Barbara began to scream. Neighbors ran out of their houses to see what had happened and found Cherokee wounded with what appeared to be a gunshot to the hind legs. Barbara was hysterical. Cherokee had only been a few feet from her side when he yelped in pain.

Barbara had a tough time talking to police. "They tried to kill me and shot my dog!"

When your life or the life of somebody you care about flashes before your own eyes, it's hard to gather your thoughts. It could've been her, shot and whimpering, and she probably wished it had been. The dog was her best friend.

"It was a green Toyota-type vehicle with four doors and tinted windows. It just drove off at a normal speed," Barbara told responding officers. The car left as if nothing ever happened. A cool customer, the assassin didn't even mind leaving a witness to tend to her wounded dog. It happened so fast that Barbara didn't even get a look at the driver. She would not be able to help with any identification.

Barbara's brother had been the target of a drive-by shooting a few months earlier and had left the state because of it. "It must be the same people," she related. But how did they find out where you live and walk your dog? Why did they target your dog and not you? Was it a lousy shot that missed Barbara or a good shot that hit its intended target, Cherokee? Police needed to talk to Barbara's brother.

The dog was taken to the Paradise Valley Animal Clinic. At first, the wounds didn't appear to be that severe. But a shotgun had been used. The pellets not only perforated the hind legs, but also hit the dog's abdomen. Cherokee would bleed to death.

With no leads, officers gathered the only evidence available, a dozen or so pellets that struck the dog. The general thinking was, maybe, just maybe, police will find a gun or catch somebody in the act of shooting another animal.

A few miles across town, Ronald Travis awoke to the yelping of his two dogs. It was just after midnight on December 30th.

When police arrived, they found Ronald in his backyard, leaning over his black mix dog, Peyton. He had been shot at least once in the right rib cage. His second dog, Martin, had been struck in the shoulder and had run inside the house. Like most wounded animals, Peyton wouldn't let anyone come near it.

Ronald was getting ready to cart both of his dogs off to the vet. They were still alive. Officers inspecting the scene had discovered a bullet strike to the shed in Ronald's backyard. It was about six inches off the ground. No other evidence was found. There was no motive for the shootings, and Ronald had no idea who shot his dogs.

While officers were talking with Ronald, another shooting call came out. It was another animal down, this time just around the corner from Ronald's house. It was his neighbor, Ricardo Lopez. He stood in his backyard just like Ronald did, shaking his head in disbelief, angry, and ready for revenge. His German Shepherd, Peanut, had taken a round to the left side just behind the shoulder.

Ricardo had been awakened by the shots and his dog yelping. He too could provide no details—no suspect description, no vehicle description, no known motive. His dog had probably been targeted because of the ease of the shot. Only a chain-link fence stood between Ricardo's dog and the shooter.

But the officers recovered two valuable pieces of evidence—rim fired .22 caliber shell casings on the north side of the street, close to the Lopez residence. This was a bit of luck for investigators, but it was clearly different from the shooting of Barbara Whitner's dog a few hours earlier. As police tried to link the shooting cases, there were glaring differences, besides the caliber of weapons. Whoever shot the Whitner dog was brazen, unafraid of leaving any witness.

Back at the downtown homicides, crime scene detectives worked all three shootings. One body was located at 10th Avenue and Jefferson. The second body was located two blocks north. Police had received a 911 call regarding Tim Tordei being shot at 2339 hours. Cops were at Tim's house within a minute. Chaos ensued.

It wasn't known at the time, but police later discovered that security cameras were placed on the parking garage at 10th Avenue and Adams, right across the street from one of the murders. This garage was used by state employees of the Arizona Department of Environmental Quality, better known as ADEQ. These little buggers monitored and recorded the comings and goings of workers. The cameras caught not only vehicles entering the building, but the surrounding streets as well.

The officers completed a canvas of the entire area. Again, they could find no witnesses to any of the shootings. The wounds on the three victims were small. The victim at 10th Avenue and Adams suffered one gunshot wound to the chest, and the other victim showed a double tap to the chest. The blood had already dried around the wounds. Twenty-two caliber rounds are infamous for small holes and little leakage.

At 9th Avenue and Woodland, the officers found a .22 caliber shell casing fifty feet northeast of where Tim Tordai was shot. To hit someone in the neck from fifty feet away is a good shot with a pistol, but a rudimentary shot with a rifle. My father had taught me to shoot when I was ten years old. I could hit pop cans with my first rifle, a .22 caliber bolt action Remington, from several hundred feet. That rifle didn't even have a scope. The rifle had no kick either, which is why my old man got it for me in the first place.

The shell casing was important if it turned out the bullets removed from the bodies were .22 caliber rounds. At least police would have something to match up if they found the shooter and/or the rifle.

The officers began to have questions. Investigators could assume that Tim Tordai was shot last because his shooting triggered the phone call that started police rolling. But what was the sequence of the other murders? Who got shot first and when? These are questions that are not easily answered. It's not like those crime shows where somebody sticks a thermometer up somebody's butt, and, presto, time of death is established. Even worse are people who watch those shows and think that the crap they say they can do is real and exists. It's like the magic spray that someone pulls out of their bag. All of a sudden, blood, fingerprints, semen, lipstick, gunshot residue, the wallet that you lost when you were twelve just appears. Amazing stuff, that spray.

The truth is, it's almost impossible to state with absolute certainty the time of death. You may be able to know that it was within a certain number of hours, based on the conditions of the body and the elements in which it's found. Witnesses who saw the deceased last are the best starting point for estimating the time of death.

Tim Tordai's crime scene yielded very little besides the .22 caliber shell casing. Officers collected a Styrofoam cup, a AAA battery, and a Bic lighter.

Sometimes detectives will pick up items at a crime scene just in case it turns out later that someone was smoking, or someone had a flashlight that uses batteries, or someone was drinking while they sat in wait. It's always better to collect something and not need it than to leave it and find out later it was pertinent.

In this case, it turned out Tim Tordai was listening to his portable radio when he was shot. That's where the battery came from. The cup was also his. Who knows about the lighter?

Tim's clothes had been stripped from him by paramedics and left at the halfway house. The officers would collect his clothes to see if they contained any possible evidence. Tim had bled over a two-block area. Samples would be collected, even though investigators knew it was Tim's blood. This was another precautionary measure just in case it turned out that Tim wasn't being completely truthful about what happened.

Most people who live on the streets know other people who are in the same predicament. They know each other because sometimes it's the only way they can thrive and survive. It's important to have somebody who will look after the things in your grocery cart while you get a meal, or give you a heads-up into the crack dealer that says you owe him money, or just pass the time with you while you sit on the street hoping for a friendly handout.

These people live in a world that disgusts most individuals. In this life, people eat left-over scraps from restaurants and dumpster dive, hoping to find a piece of garbage that might be worth two or three bucks to someone. Some suffer from a mental illness, and either can't afford medication or have no idea where to get it. Most suffer from some type of addiction. Very few are homeless because they want to be. They have been kicked out of homes. Families have abandoned them due to personal issues, and shelters have turned them away because of overcrowding. We have failed miserably as a society to help them.

This is what investigators had to work with—a population that trusts hardly anyone except for others in similar situations.

It would take a few days to identify the two homicide victims from December 30. Most victims are missed within hours or a day or so. Transient victims may not have had any contact with families for months or years. Identification usually comes from fingerprints taken at the Medical Examiner's office and compared to crime data banks.

On January 5, 2006, the police revealed the identities of the two murder victims: Jose Tapia Ortis and Marco Carrillo. Both had aliases, and both were living on the street. Both of them had arrived illegally in the United States from Mexico, and both had been deported on numerous occasions. They had no priors at all—rather unusual circumstances for homeless individuals. Even if they were illegals, they were still murdered. Neither deserved what had happened to them.

When officers found Jose Ortis, he was face down on the west side of 10th Avenue, just north of Adams Street. He had fallen onto a concrete driveway. Jose had one gunshot wound to the chest. The police found a few personal items in his pockets: a watch, a black wallet with no identification, a lighter, and a meth pipe. Robbery wasn't the motive in this case.

Jose's autopsy would yield little more than what was already known. He was gunned down on the street with a bullet that pierced his chest. The bullet actually struck the xiphoid process, the small bone that hangs from the bottom part of the sternum. The bullet was traveling slightly upward and blew right through his heart. It continued on its way across the chest cavity into his diaphragm, liver, and left lung. It finally stopped when it struck the ninth lower-left rib. The bullet was easily removed and given to investigators. It was a .22 caliber non-jacketed bullet.

No muzzle to target determination could be made. It could've been fired from ten feet or two hundred feet. With the location of the bullet penetration, it didn't matter. The perforation of his heart spilled blood into his pericardial sac and lungs, basically choking the organ. Jose had no chance and probably died within a minute. His face had a few abrasions, which wasn't unusual for someone who lives on the street. Either way, it was just a footnote in his autopsy report.

Marco Carrillo was found two blocks directly south of Jose Ortis. He was on his back on the southwest corner of 10th Avenue and Jefferson Street. A stucco building was the backdrop for whoever shot Marco. His shirt was open, and paramedics had tried to save him, but the two small holes to the chest sealed his fate. He didn't make it far. The first round that hit Marco entered in the mid-chest area, puncturing his right lung, and into the heart. The path of the bullet was slightly downward, and just as with Jose, a shot of unknown distance. The second round struck him just above the right sixth rib. As the bullet moved downward, it traveled through the right kidney and the liver. By itself, the shot would have caused such a devastating injury that Marco probably would have died from that one alone if his heart hadn't already been perforated.

Based on Marco's post-mortem exam, investigators were leaning toward the same assailant for both Marco and Jose. Ballistic tests would later determine if the rounds were linked and identifiable. One thing was for sure, the rounds that killed Marco Carrillo and Jose Ortis were both fired from a .22 caliber gun.

With these two cases and the shooting of Tim Tordai, investigators now had three .22 caliber shootings within minutes and a few blocks of each other. Somebody had gone on a street hunt and found the mother lode. There were hundreds of theories that could be floated. What was certain was that the shooting wasn't over on December 30, 2005.

CHAPTER 9

In the days that followed, the shootings of dogs Peyton, Martin, and Peanut would be investigated as well. No one questioned that whoever shot Peyton and Martin also shot Peanut. Following up on dog shootings isn't the job of violent crime investigators, but these follow-ups were necessary.

There were more questions than answers. What if the person who shot and killed Marco Carrillo, Jose Ortis, and attempted to murder Tim Tordei in downtown Phoenix was the same person who shot all these dogs? Did that make any sense? Dogs to humans, and then back to dogs?

At the Travis residence, where Peyton and Martin were shot, investigators found an interesting bullet strike into the shed. The patrol officers who had taken the original report hadn't gone digging into the shed. What's more, tissue and hair, obviously from an exit wound, could be seen around the bullet strike.

Digging through a shed sucks. Such places are usually full and nasty. I've had to dig through them, pull criminals out of them, and sit in them on surveillances. It was not exactly the quintessential job.

The dogs' owner, Mr. Travis, began to think that if there's a bullet in the shed, maybe there was more evidence in and around the property. He contemplated tearing his whole property apart to help the investigation in any way he could. But before he could do so, officers found a badly deformed bullet lying on the floor of the shed: a .22 caliber bullet.

◈

In the middle of the barren desert near Yuma, Arizona, a colonel in the United States Air Force by the name of Benjamin Fly talked the federal government into leasing a parcel of land in 1935. It would become what was originally known as "Fly Field," named for its founder.

In its infancy, Fly Field started out as just a stopover for long distance flights and private airplanes. But during World War II, it became one of the busiest flight training schools in the country, graduating numerous fighter and bomber pilots.

After the war. Fly Field sat dormant for many years until the Air Force reactivated the base in 1951. The airfield's name was changed to Yuma Air Base, and then to Vincent Air Force Base, in memory of Brigadier General Clinton Vincent, a pioneer in the arena of bombing techniques.

In 1959, the facility was signed over to the Navy and ultimately renamed Marine Corps Air Station, Yuma, which is its name today. It houses numerous attack squadrons and light anti-aircraft missile battalions and has trained virtually every fixed-wing squadron that fought in Desert Shield and Desert Storm. The place is rich in honor and history.

A young private by the name of Clarissa Rowley was one of the pilots who trained there. Like most soldiers, she joined the Marines to fight for her country, but somewhere along the way, she lost focus.

Clarissa was born in Topeka, Kansas, and had always been interested in the military. She didn't come from a long line of service members, but had joined the ROTC at her high school and decided that the military was a good move for her. Not everybody associated with the military is asked to fight during a war like the one being fought against terror. Many individuals are never deployed, but are needed to run the infrastructure.

After Clarissa graduated from Paris Island basic training camp, she was deployed to Japan, one of the numerous bases around the world that the United States military keeps staffed. She would be there for a year.

After a brief trip to Yuma, she would be sent to Iraq; Fallujah, to be exact. Clarissa was a cook. That was her job. But when she was sent to Iraq, the closest she would get to the kitchen was guarding it. Her job was to guard the doors of the mess hall when the top brass decided to grab some grub. She hated her job and wanted to get out of Iraq. She would spend seven months over there, ending up back in Yuma. She got off easy.

Sometimes the military doesn't meet everyone's ideals. Pay and benefits aren't great for enlisted personnel. Clarissa was introduced to the wrong people who took advantage of her. She had no one to guide her. The military isn't a babysitter, so Clarissa fell through the cracks.

During her weekend leave, she would venture from Yuma to Phoenix, accompanied by her alleged boyfriend. At least that's how it started out. That boyfriend later turned into an abuser, and then into her pimp. She fell into the thralls of prostitution.

Clarissa ended up spending her weekends on Van Buren Street, an over-hyped hangout for prostitutes. In actuality, the street had been cleaned up in so many stings and reversal operations that all the local hookers moved to other parts of town. It became tough to find a hooker, and even tougher to find a room on Van Buren that rented hourly. The city had cracked down on those, too. Most of the owners of those fleabag hotels were forced out, sold out, or became daily rental motels.

The night of December 30, 2005 started out slow for Clarissa. She wasn't turning many tricks, much to the displeasure of her pimp/boyfriend.

Around 3:00 a.m., Clarissa spotted one last vehicle driving east on Van Buren Street. It made a slow pass by her, as most johns do. The car went up a few blocks and made a U-turn. Clarissa decided to walk across the street to make it easier for her date. The vehicle then slow rolled past her again. She was new and butterflies filled her stomach. But the car didn't stop. Here she was trying to make it easy, and the vehicle just went by her and made another U-turn. "How many times does this guy need to drive by?" she thought.

The lone driver was a male with a scruffy beard. She could see that much after several passes. He wore a hat, probably to disguise his looks in case anyone recognized him at this time in the morning. The silly things johns will do to keep their anonymity.

As she walked in the opposite direction, she noticed something a bit unusual. The car pulled into the two-way left turn lane and slowed to a stop.

That was about all she could remember. A shotgun blast would nearly take her hand off. The other pellets riddled her right side. The driver punched the pedal, now fleeing east in his dark blue sedan.

Anthony Sutton was driving on Van Buren and witnessed the shooting. He stopped to give assistance. He ended up transporting Clarissa to the hospital. Her pimp disappeared.

The police were notified as is usual protocol for gunshot victims, and Anthony actually stayed around to talk to police when they arrived. He told police he was driving home and was behind what he said was a "dark blue

Oldsmobile." The only reason he even noticed the car was because he saw a "muzzle blast" come from the car. He didn't think to get a license plate number.

After the shot was fired, Anthony noticed Clarissa running with her hands around her head. He stopped his car and was able to convince her to get in. He took her straight to the hospital.

At least Anthony gave police his correct name. Clarissa didn't even do that. Who could blame her though? A Marine on Van Buren around 3:00 a.m., walking. How could she begin to explain that?

So, she lied to the police. She lied about what she was doing out there and said she was walking to a convenience store. She told police that she had been dropped off by her boyfriend so that he could go and pick up his cousin. It was easy to poke holes through that story. A young woman on Van Buren, early in the morning, and your boyfriend just happens to drop you off on a large thoroughfare where prostitutes have been known to congregate?

The officer who interviewed Clarissa had been working the streets for a short time, but even he could tell this was bullsh@#. The story was embarrassing, but Clarissa stuck to it. She had no choice. Anything else to cops would only create more problems for her back in Yuma. It was easy to lie to the local cops, but lying to the naval investigators back in Yuma could land her time in prison. She was treading on thin ice.

It was Clarissa's pimp that had dropped her off on Van Buren and left her. The only real questions left were who her pimp was, and whether he actually witnessed the shooting. For police, it didn't really matter. Clarissa didn't seek prosecution anyway—one of the sure signs of someone trying to hide the fact that they themselves were involved in criminal activity at the time of the offense.

Clarissa was patched up, and after observation, was sent on her way. She had numerous pellets in her left arm and a few in the neck. She was lucky. The brunt of the blast missed her. But what she didn't know at the time was she was pregnant. The stress from the shooting made her miscarry. Her troubles were far from over, however.

She would face far more scrutiny back in Yuma than she did with Phoenix Police. There was no way to explain away what happened, or why she was in Phoenix. It was best to be honest with the Marines. And so she was. Clarissa told the naval investigators everything. Her interview was five hours long.

Police got the phone call from an NCIS investigator. Clarissa was actually working the streets of Phoenix as a prostitute while serving actively. Clarissa would be available for any and all interviews, including those dealing with her nighttime activities. You've got to love the Marines. Clarissa was going to set a new standard in cooperation with authorities. Oh, and by the way, she was able and ready to prosecute whatever suspect was apprehended for shooting her. Clarissa still had commitments to fulfill.

Unfortunately, as in the other cases, the leads dried up. There just wasn't anything substantive to go on. Silent Witness tips would come in but go nowhere. No pimp would come to the rescue stating that he had hired someone to off Clarissa. The case was a dead end.

CHAPTER 10

The toll for the carnage on the night of December 29 and into the early morning hours of December 30 totaled eight shootings: four dogs (three dead) and four humans (two dead).

"So what the hell have you been doing for the last six months?" I asked sarcastically.

Detective Jewell informed me they'd been pulling .22 caliber rifles that were seized or found and having them test fired. Our lab had identified some of the projectiles and shell casings as having been fired from the same gun, identified a possible gun make (a Marlin), and had behavior analysts from the FBI come out to go through all the data.

"What wisdom did those little minions from Quantico shed on this spree?" I asked.

"They wouldn't put anything in writing," he said.

"You mean anything in writing on a profile of your shooter."

"Right, a profile," he muttered. "They said something about the fact that they're leery of putting their names on profiles. You know anything about that?"

"Oh, yeah. I take it you didn't follow the D.C. sniper case."

"Yes I did, but I forgot about their involvement, at least on the behavioral end," he added.

"Well, you still haven't told me what they told you. I know they came up with some kind of profile even if they wouldn't put pen to paper." The FBI wouldn't fly all the way to Phoenix from Virginia without taking a stab at some type of profile. What if they were right? They could brag about that for years and claim they solved the case.

"They believe that it's only one guy. He's a white male, probably in his late teens or maybe early twenties. He shoots from both sides of the vehicle and has been a menace in his neighborhood since he was a child. He has probably been arrested before, but nothing that is violent oriented: theft, criminal damage, something along those lines. He never changes weapons, and the use of two different weapons is coincidence."

"Is that it?" I asked.

"That's about it."

"What about the time frame between your shootings and mine? That's almost six months! Did they happen to opine about that gap?"

"There may not be a gap as big as six months. I'm just not sure. We've had some shootings of other animals: ducks, cows, and birds. We even had a guy riding on a bicycle shot. Problem was we couldn't recover any bullets, so we can't prove they're related."

A guy on a bike was a new one. A guy on a bike brings up a new set of circumstances and obstacles. It's tough to hit a pedestrian when you're driving by, but a guy on a bicycle would be twice as hard.

"Guy's name was Timothy Bovial. He was pedaling down Camelback Road at about 40th Avenue when someone shot him in the butt. He was shot on March 10th, 2006.

"I suppose he has no useful information, like a car description or someone flashing gang signs."

Detective Jewell sighed. "Oh, he said that three vehicles passed him right before or after he was shot. He first thought it was backfire from a muffler until his rump started hurting. He got descriptions of two of the vehicles, an SUV and some type of foreign sedan."

"You can't include the bicyclist because you don't know what he was shot with, or the other animals for that matter." I sat back in my chair. "Don't you think it's a little odd that someone would switch back and forth between animals and humans?" To switch back and forth was confounding … unless.

"Obviously," he said.

"OK, back to my original question. Did the profilers say anything else about the gap in shootings?"

"No, not really. They basically think he may have gone underground or got arrested. The usual reasons for someone to stop a crime spree. But *America's Most Wanted* did a profile of the shootings and somehow got hold of the caliber of our gun. They put it out, so who knows if that got back to the shooter."

"How did that happen?"

"I don't know," he said.

"So we've got small caliber shootings, .22 caliber, to be exact, a prostitute, and another dog shot with a shotgun. And we've got my three shootings with a shotgun."

"That's right," he said.

"OK, what's the connection, if any? You've been working these cases for six months. Do you think they could be related?"

"I don't know."

"The Whitner dog and the prostitute were shot how far apart, time wise?" I asked.

"Several hours," he said. It was actually about four hours, give or take a few minutes. So the shotgun shootings started and ended the night, with .22 caliber murders in the middle. "The boys from Quantico told me that the shooter doesn't change weapons, no matter what?"

"Yes they did, but I'm not so sure. They told you that it could be pure coincidence, so I haven't ruled that out. But there's another explanation. Maybe there were two shooters: one who likes rifles, and one who likes shotguns."

The Homicide Unit didn't need this. They had all the press they could handle with the Baseline Killer being splashed across the headlines. That guy was making the whole town nervous, especially females. Nervous females make for big coverage.

There were several pieces of the puzzle that would come together later. The murders of Tony Mendez, Reginald Remillard, and the Tolleson murder of David Estrada, not to mention the horses. Regrettably, there was another jurisdiction with a homicide, one that mirrored these shootings. It was in a city that despised the words, "suspect outstanding."

CHAPTER 11

Based on the fact that a homicide was now associated with the so-called "Baseline Rapist," homicide detectives would start to work the case along with sexual assault investigators. But on February 20th, 2006, the investigation would take on new meaning.

Two women were murdered in a catering truck off of a construction site in West Phoenix. Both were shot in the head and the pants of one of the victims had been pulled down. Although these two cases were not originally linked, the investigators of the now-named "Baseline Killer" task force would have their work cut out for them.

The rapist had turned into a murderer, becoming more aggressive in each case. There would be three more murders in March 2006. Two of the victims were killed together as they closed a business where they worked. It was obvious if you didn't submit to his demands, you were killed. Both of the female victims were believed to have been sexually assaulted.

A description of the now dubbed "Baseline Killer" was put out in the media. He was a black male and wore a signature floppy hat with dreadlocks. The hair was hanging from underneath the hat, making investigators believe it was a disguise.

The City of Scottsdale lies just east of Phoenix. It is the entertainment and fun center of the metro area. As much as other cities try to boast about their developing nightlife, Scottsdale puts every other city in the valley to shame. It's where all the beautiful people go to hang out, eat, and drink at the hottest nightclubs, restaurants, and shops.

Chances are that when you're out there, you will run into a celebrity or two who lives here, or at least some sports personality. Scottsdale is renowned as a party destination, and the city doesn't like things such as crime tarnishing its reputation. Over the years, the police department has done a pretty good job of keeping the riffraff out.

Although Scottsdale's population is only a couple of hundred thousand, their violent crime rate is well below average. The police department takes violent crime personally, and they're willing to go to any lengths to solve those cases. Overtime isn't an issue.

The jurisdiction line between Phoenix and Scottsdale looks like some odd piece to a large jigsaw puzzle. Scottsdale butts up to Phoenix at only two locations, both north and south extremes. Otherwise, Scottsdale borders the ultra-rich town of Paradise Valley to the west and the college town of Tempe to the south. East of Scottsdale is the Indian reservation, which has its own unique set of problems.

Thomas Road is a heavily traveled street, and, at most times during the evening and morning hours, it is filled with Scottsdale residents commuting to and from Phoenix job sites. It is also a main road for connecting bus routes. Every day, the buses are filled with thousands of people who live on Thomas Road in the numerous apartment complexes that are scattered from Scottsdale to Phoenix.

Tuesday, May 2, 2006 would be no different. As the evening turned to night, the buses still bellowed diesel smoke along Thomas Road, dropping off its many residents.

The bus that moved Claudia Gutierrez-Cruz that night had originally started up in North Scottsdale. She had just gotten off work at Barcelona's Restaurant and Bar and had grabbed a southbound bus to get home. She wasn't even supposed to go to work that night. Someone had called her, and she had just shown up. Her usual work hours were from 3:30 p.m. to 10:00 p.m. But on this night, she left around 7:45 p.m.

Claudia didn't always travel by bus. In fact, she usually had coworkers drop her off. Her boyfriend would also share in that responsibility.

She had moved from Tempe to Phoenix for a closer commute. She had found an apartment around 50th Street and Thomas Road, an area where the rent is a lot cheaper than Scottsdale or Tempe. She shared the apartment with her sister.

Claudia had come here from Mexico and was actually working two jobs. By day, she worked at a coffee shop; her night gig was at the restaurant. She worked almost every day just to make ends meet. She was here illegally, but she had come to work and make a life for herself. She was an exemplary employee.

The bus stop located at Scottsdale Road and Thomas was a popular east/west transfer point. Any normal metro area buses would run until the wee hours of the morning, but not here. Claudia was dropped off two miles from home.

As the bus doors closed and the gagging smell of diesel smoke surrounded her, Claudia contemplated her predicament. Her sister had no car, and her boyfriend lived in Tempe, a good distance away. May nights are beautiful, so the walk would do her good. Clearing her mind of the day's ups and downs wouldn't hurt either. Then, again, who wants to walk two miles after pulling two shifts of work? But the quickest way for her to get to a good, soft bed was to start hoofing it. Claudia pulled her hooded sweater over her head, covering her flowing, black hair, and got moving.

As Claudia began to walk, somebody else had taken to watching her. She never even knew or suspected it. Why would she? As a female, she'd probably grown up dealing with male advances in her own country. American men were a lot more subtle than Mexican men when it came to that. Maybe subconsciously that was why she hooded up. It was a way to disguise herself.

But the interest she drew tonight had nothing to do with her gender. She was out, she was alone, and the street was slow with traffic and pedestrians. She had become a target and didn't even know it.

When she saw the large grocery store and parking lot, Claudia knew that she was halfway home. From the darkened portion of Thomas Road where she now walked, the lights of the store must have seemed like an airport landing strip. Was there anything that she needed? Her mind ticked slowly through the list of goods she kept on her refrigerator.

She heard the loud bang at the same time that her feet and torso jolted from the impact. Her body flew sideways as the impact pushed her from the sidewalk to a grassy area just a few feet away. She went down hard. She remained motionless for several minutes, not knowing what had happened. It was dead silent. She could still see the white and red lights of the store in the close distance.

The Bermuda grass felt warm against her traumatized body. Claudia had fallen on a small rolling hill, several feet higher than the sidewalk. No streetlight shone on the area. She was masked in complete darkness.

When Claudia finally realized she had been shot, she tried to move off the hill and back to the sidewalk. The grassy area could perhaps conceal her if the shooter returned, but no passerby would ever find her there. Claudia's blood started to mix with the sod. She pulled and tugged on the grass to get to the sidewalk. Someone needed to see her. If that happened, surely that person would stop and help. Someone had to see her crawling on her belly, a four-inch diameter hole on her side from the massive blast.

The area was empty. No one was around, and cars continued by. The street was her last option. She crawled into the curb lane, hoping to God that no one would run her over. The first witness called 911 after swerving to miss her. It was 10:28 p.m.

"911, what is your emergency?" the dispatcher asked.

The first caller began to ramble in Spanish. A female was down, and he thinks she may have been shot. The call is transferred to Phoenix Police for a translator. A green S10 pickup has stopped, and the victim is just east of the Fry's Food Store on Thomas Road.

The driver of the pickup was Daniel Brown. He pulled over right after he saw a black Chevy Avalanche swerve. That truck continued on its way. He wasn't even sure what was in the road until he climbed out and saw a body in the street.

The woman spoke only Spanish. Daniel spoke a minimal amount of Spanish, like most Phoenicians, which he'd probably picked up from a buddy or a coworker. The woman repeatedly told him "ayuda me," which he understood to mean, "Help me." He too called 911.

That night Scottsdale 911 received subsequent calls from other drivers who almost struck Claudia as well. They thought that she had been the victim of a hit-and-run. As she lay on her right side, the gruesome truth would soon be revealed. Claudia had been gunned down.

Since the first witness spoke Spanish, he began to ask her questions, and she replied slowly. Claudia asked for someone to call her boyfriend and sister. He would comply with her request later, but for now it was time to get her help.

One of the first officers to arrive spoke to Claudia in Spanish. She told him that she had been shot, which at this point was blatantly obvious. Like all good cops, he wanted to know who had shot her. She replied, "No se, no se nada." She had no idea who'd shot her.

In her final words, Claudia told him her name and that she was twenty years old. Then she went into shock. It was time for paramedics to try to save her life. They began to work on her.

Numerous Scottsdale offices flew to the scene and immediately began the task of preserving the crime scene. Flares were thrown to divert traffic, both as a precaution to officer safety and for crime scene preservation. The street was shut down at 60th Street and 64th Street. Flares were soon replaced with barricades.

As Claudia was rushed to Scottsdale Health Care Hospital, officers would attempt to separate and hold onto any potential witnesses, a daunting task.

Oftentimes, most people don't want to get involved in any part of a criminal investigation. It takes time out of a person's life, and we Americans are selfish with our time. We are a busy people, even if we don't have pressing matters.

There was no doubt that witnesses that night slipped away without contacting police. But the witnesses who were there were more than willing to help police. After all, a young woman had been gunned down.

◈

Detective Pete Salazar got the phone call around 1:10 a.m., roughly three hours after the shooting of Claudia Gutierrez-Cruz. He would be responding as soon as he could shake the sleep off.

Pete was a ten-year veteran of the Scottsdale Police Department. He had been assigned to their Violent Crime Bureau for two years. He had done his time as a patrol officer and was interested in furthering his career in investigations. Up to this point, he had no interest in promotion.

Scottsdale's Violent Crime Bureau is responsible for investigating all violent crime that occurs in its jurisdiction. It's not broken down into specific units like robbery, homicide, or assaults. It's a one-stop shop, which makes for a good overall investigative experience.

Pete's supervisor was Detective Sergeant Don Bellendier, a near twenty-year veteran. He had spent most of his career as a supervisor in the Violent Crime Bureau. He'd been around the block a time or two, and even as low as Scottsdale's violent crime rate was, he knew his way around a criminal investigation.

Detective Hugh Lockerby would also be called out. Hugh had also been assigned to Violent Crimes for a few years. Hugh had a reputation as a pot stirrer. Nothing wrong with that, but Scottsdale was a small department. Piss too many people off over there, and you can shorten the movement of your career. But Hugh, like Pete, had found a home in investigations, and they were going to have to drag him out of violent crimes.

When they both arrived on scene, they were briefed as to what police knew up until that point. There were no leads as to who shot Claudia.

After the briefing, assignments were handed out. Salazar got the case. Detective Lockerby would assist with the crime scene investigation, although it was small and insignificant. The crime scene yielded nothing spectacular—just blood-stained grass where Claudia fell and further blood where she made it to the street. As is true with many cases, Claudia's body would hold the key evidence.

The rest of the assignments were divvied up among the extra investigators. It was important in the days to come to identify Claudia's coworkers and associates. They needed to check her apartment, talk to her employers for any leads or problems that she may have had, and question other tenants at her complex.

The bus route she took home could be significant. It was important to check her exact route for any issues that may have risen on her ride home this night. Some of the buses were equipped with video surveillance, and that would have to be checked.

Who last talked to Claudia and when? Her phone records needed to be acquired. Maybe a phone call had been placed to someone who police did not know about? Detectives would also need to contact other valley agencies and see if any of them had encountered similar crimes of this nature.

The investigators also interviewed the witnesses. No one had seen the shooting. They had only seen Claudia once she had collapsed on the street. Without any significant witnesses, detectives hoped that Claudia herself could provide something to go on. Why was she shot? Right now, however, she was in surgery, and the detectives would have to wait.

With no evidence to speak of at the scene and no independent eyewitnesses, it was time to go the hospital and contact Claudia's friends and family. That's precisely what Detective Salazar would do. Motives for shootings are best developed from investigators' detailed contacts with close friends and family. It was a good starting point for this investigation, and most of them had already arrived at the hospital anyway.

Claudia's sister, Adriana, was awaiting any news of her sister's condition. Claudia's boyfriend, Felipe Romero Cruz, was also at the hospital.

But before investigators could separate them from other family and friends, before they got a chance to develop any leads from either of them, before they could talk to Claudia, who had been in surgery for hours, they noticed the somber looks of medical personnel approaching the gathering.

Claudia had fought hard. She had tried to overcome all the obstacles that life had placed in front of her. Born in Mexico to poor parents. Sneaking into America to work and provide for herself. Landing two jobs and keeping some semblance of a good demeanor. Juggling a relationship with very little spare time and sending money back to Mexico to help other family members.

But Claudia would fight no more. She was pronounced dead from internal bleeding early on the morning of May 3, 2006.

The shot that had killed Claudia could be seen in the X-rays. It was a shotgun blast at close range, with dozens of pellets littering her inside abdomen area. They were scattered through her colon and into the aorta. In and among all those pellets was a detailed piece of evidence: a shot cup.

Claudia's family, particularly her sister Adrianna, took her death hard. The wailing could be heard up and down the corridors of the hospital. The boyfriend, Felipe, was a little more subdued, but that could just have been his machismo side coming out. It did, however, raise the eyebrows of investigators.

Both Felipe and Adrianna would be transported to Scottsdale's Family Advocacy Center for interviews. These centers had become popular back in the nineties as a place that was less frightening to victims and witnesses than the standard police station. It worked especially well with children, and most communities had partnered with health care workers to help at these centers. The questioning would begin a mere six hours after the shooting of Claudia Gutierrez-Cruz.

Adrianna Cruz, along with her cousin, shared an apartment with Claudia. She told investigators of Claudia's illegal entry into the United States. She had paid a *coyote*, a human smuggler, $1,800 to transport her across the border. The coyote had been paid in full, so there was no motive for the him to have her killed.

Adrianna had come across the border two months earlier. It was a touchy subject for Adrianna. She didn't want to get deported for answering questions pertaining to the death of her sister. Investigators assured her that wouldn't happen. She provided what she could.

Claudia had gotten two jobs, and Adrianna worked alongside her at one of them, Barcelona's. Claudia never spoke of any problems at the coffee shop where she worked, and Adrianna had never seen anything unusual at the restaurant. Claudia had never been married. Her current relationship was with Felipe. They had both met him in Mexico several years before coming across the border.

Adrianna knew of no reason why Felipe would harm Claudia. She did not believe that either of them had been involved in drugs, gangs, gambling, smuggling or criminal undertakings. They rarely saw each other, and in fact, Adrianna didn't even believe they were sexually involved.

Adrianna had last seen Claudia at the restaurant. They had a conversation about why Claudia had come into work. She wasn't scheduled, and Claudia talked to the manager about it. She had left early for some unknown reason. That would be the last time Adrianna would see her sister alive.

Felipe Romero Cruz had been dating Claudia for about a year. They had met in the city of Puebla, a few hours outside Mexico City, when she was fourteen. He had been in the United States for two years.

Felipe had last talked to Claudia the previous afternoon. She'd told him that she was going to leave work early, making Felipe the only person to know this besides her coworkers. She did not tell him why she was leaving early. He also thought that she usually got off work at 2:00 a.m. instead of 11:00 p.m. Claudia had been lying to Felipe.

Felipe was not working, and the police questioning focused on his whereabouts when Claudia was killed. Were there any problems, fights, domestic issues? Felipe told the police they got along just fine.

Felipe was released, but it would not be the last time Scottsdale Police would contact him. There was a void in the time frame from when Claudia left work at 7:45 p.m., and when she was shot at 10:28 p.m. Buses are slow in the valley, but it doesn't take over two-and-a-half hours to ride the bus the roughly ten miles that Claudia traveled.

Could a simple bus ride open a window for possible contact with the killer?

In the days that followed the murder of Claudia Gutierrez-Cruz, an assembly of Scottsdale detectives fanned out over the city searching for clues in her death.

Her coworkers were interviewed, and an interesting fact came up. Claudia had received several phone calls from Felipe the night she was killed, and at least one of them turned into an argument. Felipe had failed to mention that fact during the interview. They also said that he was extremely jealous and possessive.

There were problems in the relationship, according to a coworker. Claudia would not tell this coworker anything more. The investigation began to turn on this new insight.

Felipe and Claudia were having problems, and Claudia could possibly have had other boyfriends. This became a good, logical path to follow.

Felipe would be brought in again for questioning. This time, the focus would be on him as a lead, not just an information source.

In this interview, police confronted Felipe with statements from Claudia's coworkers about the numerous phone calls on the night of her murder, the argument that coworkers overheard, and his supposed jealous rants. Felipe denied calling Claudia, and he said that an argument had never occurred.

Felipe's original story also changed. He had said that he had that day off. However, on the day of the murder, Felipe had been at work. He arrived back home around 3:00 p.m. This didn't clear him of any wrongdoing, but somewhere along the line his schedule had gotten lost in translation. Felipe stated that he didn't know of any other men in Claudia's life. She'd told him that she loved him. Claudia would get some phone calls from other friends while they were spending time together, but she'd said that these calls were just from male friends.

This lead was burned up. Felipe had nothing to do with the murder of Claudia Cruz. He was as much in the dark as the investigators.

A whodunit is somewhat of an anomaly in Scottsdale, so there was a full-court press to find Claudia's killer. In fact, calls would be made to Phoenix and other West Valley agencies, such as Tolleson, for similar crimes. Information was exchanged.

But the glaring fact was that the murders in Phoenix and Tolleson were almost six months old. They were .22 caliber, not shotgun shootings. So what if a prostitute and a dog were shot with shotguns? Besides, Phoenix and Tolleson had no leads. Their cases had gone cold, and so had their killer. It was time to unveil a new strategy. When all else failed, it was time to engage the media.

The article in the *Arizona Republic* captured the police's frustration with the murder investigation and the lack of solid leads. The article told of how Claudia had left work early, of her missed bus west on Thomas Road, of the unpleasant task that her sister, Adrianna, faced having to ship her body back to Mexico for burial. Unfortunately, no new leads came in.

A few weeks later, a second newspaper article was written to keep the murder fresh in the minds of the reading public. The story was laid out again, this time mentioning that it was Scottsdale's first homicide of the year. It was a random killing, they professed, and they needed the public's help. Still no leads.

Then they dropped the bombshell that nobody expected. They distanced themselves from the Phoenix and West Valley cases by stating that Claudia's case was not related to those unsolved murders and animal shootings. They wanted new information, and dredging up cold cases of homicides in Phoenix and the West Valley wasn't going to help them solve their murder case.

Besides, this was Scottsdale. Who would want to associate themselves with a possible serial killer who had not been caught or heard from in months? A killer who could scare the locals, the politicians, and the tourists? Crime like that was meant for Phoenix, not Scottsdale.

Even after being advised of the three other May 2006 shootings, Scottsdale Police wanted no part of Phoenix's problem. They were playing the percentages. Right now, they had a lot of investigative ground to cover. Besides, they hadn't found Claudia's possible secret lover. They still couldn't account for the hours before her murder.

Scottsdale had withheld from the media the type of weapon used. Those types of facts are best kept close at hand, just in case you actually catch the murderer. False confessions are rare, but they do happen. Not knowing the type of gun used or the type of ammunition can keep these knuckleheads from wasting your time. Police hoped the family and friends would keep this information quiet as well.

The autopsy examination of Claudia Gutierrez-Cruz took place on May 5, 2006 at the Office of the Medical Examiner for Maricopa County. The examination was conducted by Philip Keen, the head medical examiner.

The external examination showed that Claudia was a petite 4 feet 11 inches tall and weighed 128 pounds. The phenomenon known as rigor mortis was complete.

Although rigor mortis is mentioned often on TV shows, the public knows little about it and even less about how it affects the body after death. Rigor mortis usually sets in within a few hours after death, depending on the temperature of the body. It happens to all creatures, not just humans.

Calcium ions begin to permeate the muscle structure. When a person is alive, these ions are transported in and out of the muscles by the use of two fibers known as actin and myosin. These fibers help muscles contract. Another molecule, known as adenosine triphosphate (ATP), helps the muscles to expand. These molecules and fibers band together to produce the smooth muscle movement that live humans and animals use every day.

When the heart stops and the body dies, there are no calcium ions produced to go into the muscles to stop it from contracting, therefore you get rigid joints, creating the phenomenon known as rigor mortis. Maximum stiffness from rigor mortis will usually set in within twenty-four hours, again depending on the temperature of the body. The joint stiffness can last as long as seventy-two hours, but many times the contracting joints and the muscles will start to decay before seventy-two hours, thus relaxing the muscles.

A chest tube was present from the surgery that was attempted to save Claudia's life. The tubes were cut off and left in the body to show that the holes were created by surgery, instead of the holes created by a gunshot.

There was a twelve-inch surgical wound down the whole left side of Claudia's body. Surgeons had cut her open to try to repair all the damage to her insides. The shotgun wound itself was also sewn up.

The most important notes of Claudia's exam would be of her wound. The shotgun wound was one-and-one-half inches in diameter, with the pellet diameter reaching three-and-one-half inches. The wound itself was slightly to the front of her torso and on the left side. Whoever fired the shotgun was really close to Claudia, within a few feet.

There was no stippling present on the surrounding skin surfaces, even though the original surgeon had told investigators that it was there. This is the difference between a criminal examination of a body and a surgical examination. That's why I never ask surgeons for details about entrance or exit wounds. Some of them have no clue regarding the information I need.

Stippling is the bruising of the skin caused by the impact of the gunshot residue. Mistakenly called powder burns, stippling is a sign of a close, unprotected contact wound, usually left when a gun is fired within a few feet of a target.

The shot that killed Claudia could be seen on the X-rays. The pellets ripped through her abdominal cavity and struck the aorta, pancreas, duodenum, left kidney, and bowel. All of the pellets stayed inside her body. The damage was horrific. A few of the pellets were extracted for comparison purposes, but that would provide investigators with very little information.

What was more important was the shot cup that had been removed from Claudia during surgery. Each shot cup is unique in its size and amount of pellets it can hold. The one removed from Claudia was fired from a 410 shotgun. A detailed piece of evidence, it was the first real clue investigators had to go on.

Claudia's death was, of course, ruled a homicide. With James Hodge, Darrel Davies, and Miguel Rodriguez, the other poor immigrant who would be gunned down in a few short weeks, the assailant had now struck four times in May.

I read about the murder of Claudia Gutierrez-Cruz. It wasn't on my list of unsolved cases. As far as I knew, the shootings in Phoenix had no connection to the Scottsdale case. Since I didn't know the caliber or type of weapon, it wasn't my problem. That would be the last time I mumbled those words.

CHAPTER 12

On May 1^{*st*}*, 2006, one day prior to the murder of Claudia Gutierrez-Cruz, the Baseline Killer would strike again. A woman was accosted in the area of 30*^{*th*} *Street and Thomas Road, an area the killer was familiar with and felt comfortable in. As with many of the crimes, he intimidated the victim with a story of how he just committed a robbery and needed to get out of the area. The victim was forced to drive him away.*

He had her disrobe in the car. He wanted oral sex, and when she refused, he put a gun to the back of her head and fired. The gun did not discharge. The victim struggled and was able to escape with her life. She could not describe him because the assailant now wore a mask. The hat and wig discarded for fear of public recognition.

The Baseline Killer had been able to cover his tracks, or so he thought, over the course of his crimes. Being very careful about what he touched and what he left, he was aware of DNA and fingerprints. He would try to have the victims wipe themselves or smear possible evidence with other substances. It was obvious he had done time and had learned about forensic evidence.

His tally up until this point: 8 murders, 7 sexual assaults, and 8 robberies.

Forty-five-year-old Paul Patrick had grown up on the west side of Phoenix. The son of a preacher, he had tested his family values and his belief in the Almighty, which resulted in a few run-ins with the law. However, Paul had moved on from adolescence into adulthood with little fanfare. When his father passed away, his mother allowed him to stay at the house. It was good for both of them. He was able to see his mom and hold somewhat steady employment. Occasionally, he would venture out on his own, only to return to the nest.

Finding steady, fulfilling work had never been easy for Paul. He took meaningless jobs, jobs well below his intelligence level. But he was content, especially in his current one, a job stocking shelves at a local grocery store. He liked his duties, especially the fact that he could work nights. No traffic, a few customers, and a boss he got along with well.

On June 8, 2006, Paul was in the grips of a dire need. Nicotine addiction can do that. Smoking was a crutch for Paul. He had tried to quit, but decided that having only one vice wasn't necessarily a sin. Even the sweltering evening heat wasn't going to keep him from his destination, a Fast Track convenience store.

The store was only a short walk from his home. As Paul walked the few blocks, the traffic exiting from the numerous apartment buildings had mostly subsided. It was 11:30 p.m., and though traffic is moderate until the early morning hours on the weekend, it was Thursday. He could cross the main artery without worrying about being mowed down.

The fact that Paul wore a dark black T-shirt would make him difficult to see. The only light came from the illuminated signs advertising nearby businesses that were now closed, including a one-stop automotive outlet next to the convenience store. There was just enough light to reveal a lonely pedestrian.

Paul didn't concern himself with the simple details of lighting, traffic, and nighttime dangers. He just wanted some cigarettes. This would be a trip he would regret for the rest of his life.

As he walked, minding his own business, a car exited one of the two driveways to the automotive outlet. The car startled him, but not enough to prevent him from appreciating beauty when he saw it. The car was an older Chevy convertible, a real nice 60s model in pristine condition, decked and tricked out, with the rag-top up.

Paul appreciated nice things. He remembered thinking, "That's sweet." But before he could get the car out of his mind, his body lurched sideways. A gunshot struck, a startling reverberation. Paul went down immediately, writhing in pain. His body hit the cement sidewalk with a thud. He lay motionless, looking up at the Jiffy Lube sign.

The sidewalk burned from the day's sweltering conditions. But as hot as the sidewalk was, his side was hotter. "Move, damn it," he said to himself. He couldn't.

A few hundred feet away, apartment tenants had heard the shot, but for them, it wasn't anything out of the ordinary in this neighborhood. Shots were fired at all times of night. One large bang was only a reminder of all the issues they faced in a quickly growing metropolis.

However, Saul Guerrero recognized the sound as more than just a routine gunshot. He stepped outside and heard the calls for help coming from across the street. Saul could see the shape of a man lying on the sidewalk. He grabbed his first aid kit and called 911 as he ran across the street.

In a matter of seconds, police officers arrived on scene. Paul Patrick was still lying there, just a few feet away from the landscaping rock that covered the area in front of the Jiffy Lube.

Before Paul passed out, he was able to relay to officers that he had no idea who had shot him, but that a car had just passed him. The officers immediately called for paramedics as Paul's condition worsened. He was unable to give any information on a suspect or the make, color, or year of the car.

Paul was struck just above the right side of his abdomen. The hole was so large the officers could not tell what had hit him. His dark black shirt became darker with the blood that flowed from his wound.

When paramedics arrived, the grisly nature of Paul's wound became more apparent. His intestines had started to protrude from the wound, a clear sign of the sizable hole that permeated from Paul's abdomen. The race to the hospital would be crucial to saving his life.

Other than Saul and a few neighbors who heard the shot, there were no eyewitnesses. No yelling, or screeching of tires. Just a "boom." A night detective was sent out, but there was no physical evidence other than Paul's blood covering the sidewalk.

At the hospital, doctors weren't sure if Paul would live or die. He was in a fight for his life. It was obvious from the X-rays that Paul's insides were chewed up. Scattered in and among his organs were numerous shotgun pellets, too many to count. They littered the entire X-ray.

The only question that remained was why Paul had been targeted. His family rushed to the hospital. "Who would do this?" Paul's mother and brother asked. They had no clue why Paul had been shot. They just knew that he'd left to go get cigarettes.

It was a waiting game.

Paul's clothes were impounded for possible future analysis. At this point, police only knew that Paul was the victim of a possible drive-by shooting. No suspects had been identified.

It was the morning of June 9, 2006, and I had just trudged the three blocks from my parking garage. It was already ninety degrees, and I was sweating my ass off after the hike. It was a Friday, better yet, payday Friday. I had elected to work a 9/80 schedule—a five-day forty-hour week followed by a four-day ten-hour week—that afforded me every other Friday off, except payday Friday.

Fridays during the day are usually slow. Crime never rests, but even criminals need to rest to prepare for the upcoming weekend of havoc and dismay. In our work, Friday is the new Sunday.

I hadn't been at work for more than five minutes, sitting at my desk, hiding in my cluttered cubicle, when I heard the voice of Sergeant Stewart Clarke. He was going to ruin my payday moment. Couldn't he give me just a few minutes to enjoy the fruits of my labor? Nope. Then again, like most middle-class Americans, the check was gone as fast as it was direct- deposited. Who was I kidding? I didn't own my paycheck anyway.

"What's up, Sarge?" I dared to ask.

Then he said it. "Hey, you got a minute?"

When a supervisor says these words, the hair on the back of your neck will stand up. These words are muttered when something is about to happen, something that you're probably going to dislike. But maybe I was jumping to conclusions.

"I suppose. You want to step into my office?" He looked for a chair to pull up.

I had met Sergeant Clarke early in my career. We'd both worked out at the same gym, and I recognized him from my many trips with prisoners to the jail.

He had moved from patrol officer to work the Gang Unit, and we often discussed those little dumb asses that ran around, thinking they were tough guys. Some of the old gangsters (OGs) were tough and dangerous, but the young wannabes were just mouths. We used to laugh about how if you challenged them, most of them would go home and cry to their mommies.

He had been promoted to sergeant, and every once in awhile, I would see him working the night supervisor desk at the Violent Crimes Bureau. He had cut his teeth as a supervisor in Document Crimes and had transferred to Violent Crimes in 2003. Sergeant Clarke was well liked by his detectives. He was a bit of a micromanager, but he knew when to let the investigators lead with their noses, and he gave them the support they needed.

"The lieutenant wants to see you and me," he said.

I needed to check my short-term memory for any problems I may have created. Let's see. I hadn't shot anyone in awhile. Didn't wreck my city car. Hadn't told any politician to pound sand. Hadn't cursed at any victims, witnesses, or suspects over the phone, at least not this week. No false arrests, ever. I think I'm good.

"OK, do I need a union rep?"

You never know.

"Hurry up and get in there with me," he snipped, though he was still smiling about my union comment.

Lieutenant Rich Benson had come to the Assault division in 2000, fresh off the streets of Phoenix as a patrolman. He also had worked gangs as a supervisor and was one of the really nice guys in the department.

Lieutenant Benson, or LT, had taken the promotional test for commander on a couple of occasions and never made it. Nice guys really do get hosed. The LT and I had played some golf together on a few occasions, even though he was the commanding supervisor in the unit. A lot of supervisors would never do that, but golf is the international sport of anguish. Although he was my supervisor, if the situation called for it, I could laugh at LT on the course. He was the type of man I liked to be around, a higher-up, comfortable in his command.

As golfers go, LT wasn't too bad. My game, on the other hand, was up and down. My career handicap was a 10 or slightly higher. Since I only played once or twice a month, I knew I wasn't going to improve. Lieutenant Benson, on the other hand, played every weekend and still couldn't get his handicap down. I constantly ribbed him about all the golf he played, and still sucked. LT had a good sense of humor about it, and he could dish it out as well as he could take it.

The lieutenant's office was small, but at least he had a window. Some of the supervisors didn't even get that after the so-called remodeling. There were pictures of golfers and a picture of a hole from the Tournament Players Club in Scottsdale, where the most raucous PGA golf tournament, known as the Phoenix Open, is held each January.

I sat down in my customary chair next to the small file cabinet with a fourteen-inch TV and VCR on top of it. The news was on, and Sergeant Clarke had followed me in.

"How you doin, Clarkster?"

That was his friendly opening, so I knew I was going to be the recipient of something that would make my head hurt.

"Good, Rich. Yourself?"

Although he was a boss, the lieutenant was very approachable and didn't worry about titles and command authority. He was always the kind of person you could bring a problem to, and you could trust him to give you no-nonsense advice and guidance, especially when it came to the political side of policing. He had a slight smirk on his face, and I recognized that as the expression he used when he needed something handled efficiently.

"How's your caseload looking?" he asked. Sergeant Clarke stood by the door and began to slowly close it.

My caseload mattered little if something perceived as important came up.

"Why do you ask? Some politician get an email saying he's an idiot, and now wants a full-blown threat assessment done?"

This was one of my areas of expertise.

He laughed, "No, not this time. You remember those three shotgun shootings that you did the follow-up on awhile back?"

Of course I remembered. How often do you get some moron out shooting randomly at pedestrians?

"Yep, how could I forget?"

"Well, the bosses don't think they're related to the 2005 cases. They sent them back, and they ended up on Detective Dan Moncrief's desk," LT said. "The simple fact of the matter is, Clark, they have enough on their plate with the Baseline Killer, and they don't need any more whodunits."

"Ok, so what are you asking?"

"Detective Moncrief has said that he wants to work them and carry them. He'll take any other shootings, if there are any," Sergeant Clarke jumped in. "But Dan has only been here a short while, and this may became really sticky."

"Why?" I asked. "They're three random shootings with no leads, no suspects, no one that can identify anyone. Nothing to go on, nada, zippo, zero. If there were something to go on, I would have followed up on it days ago and supplemented the cases."

Benson and Clarke looked again at each other. There was something they weren't telling me.

"Well, we had another one last night," LT said. "The guys name is Paul

Patrick. He was walking to a store when someone shot him with a shotgun. Appears to be a drive-by, but nobody knows for sure because there aren't any witnesses. Just like the ones you looked at."

"Was it in the same area, Maryvale?" I asked. If so, then I could see why they called me in to look at this new one.

"Yes it was," Sergeant Clarke answered.

They both stared through me, waiting for any further comments before passing the assignment.

"So you want me to carry these first three shootings and take a second look to see if they are connected to Mr. Patrick's case?" I asked.

"That's exactly what we want you to do," LT said. "It doesn't sound like this case has anymore to go on than those first three. Apparently, the victim in the latest shooting isn't doing too well. Maybe you can get something out of him that the patrol guys didn't. Here's the case number." He handed me a sticky note. "Pull it up and get back with me if you can make anything of it."

Sergeant Clarke chimed in. "Hey, let Dan Moncrief work with you on these. He's eager to help, and if you need additional follow-up, maybe he can lend a hand."

"No problem," I said.

Detective Moncrief was new to the detail, but I had been out with him, and he seemed very competent. The question was whether or not there was anything for him to follow-up on.

The case was a day old. It was time to contact the family of the latest victim and check up on his status. As I read the report, I found that this was already starting out bad. The victim had been taken to St. Joseph's Hospital, my least favorite medical center.

◆

Just pulling into St. Joseph's Hospital was a nightmare. There was a specific parking space for police vehicles in the ER lot, but it was always taken up by some civilian's car and never available. The entrance was a drive around and had about ten parking spaces for people entering the ER, about forty less than they needed.

Crime scene photo tech Jon Kinneman met me just outside of the lobby. He was there to take photos of the injuries to Mr. Patrick. According to the report, his injuries were horrific. The photos would probably never be allowed in court because they'd be too graphic.

I had been coming to St. Joseph's for years, and the staff in Admitting was usually cordial and helpful. The doctors and the nurses in the ER, on the other hand, were hit or miss. It's not an easy job dealing with life and death issues every minute of every day. But it wasn't any different for cops. You would think that health care professionals would understand and treat cops with more respect. I mean we both deal with death and injuries.

Yet, over the years, particularly at St. Joseph's, I've had several run-ins with staff. They weren't always tremendously helpful when I wanted a diagnosis or a medical update on a patient's condition. I understand patient confidentiality, HIPAA, and all that, but we're there to help the victim. I could care less about his personal medical history. Besides, the victims wanted justice. They wouldn't want me caught up in red tape.

However, this time, a very nice assistant in Admitting told me that Paul Patrick was up in critical ICU. He was still alive, and family may be present.

While walking down the corridor and right by the cafeteria, I read Paul's original statement to officers. He knew that he had been shot by someone driving by him. He couldn't identify the vehicle, but he knew that a vehicle had driven by a man and that a shot was fired. He couldn't remember anything after that.

As I stepped onto the elevator to take me to the CICU, an orderly pushed a gurney onto the already crowded lift. The gurney carried an elderly woman with tubes to her mouth and nose, and she looked like she had been through the wringer. A long time ago, I had come to the conclusion that hospitals suck—not just because they are filled with sick people, but because of the misery that accompanies sickness or injury. God bless the people that work in these places. I have spent my career trying to stay away from being a patient in one.

The photo tech and I exited the elevator and proceeded to the security desk. The officer checked my credentials and pushed the button to open the two large electronically controlled doors. As the doors swung in the opposite direction of each other, I made my way to the help desk. After a few minutes a woman resembling some type of assistant asked, "Can I help you?"

"Yes, you can. I am looking for a gunshot victim by the name of Paul Patrick. He was brought in late last night with a gunshot wound to the abdomen."

"He's right over there, and his nurse is Jeanine. She's over there." She pointed to a short, blonde nurse dressed in green scrubs.

The assistant then called to Jeanine, who was busy reading a magazine. She looked up at us and then went back to reading.

I turned to the photographer and said, "You think she might be able to break away from the most recent issue of *People* magazine to come help us?"

"Probably not," Jon replied sarcastically.

It was obvious she was ignoring us, so I looked at the board to make sure Mr. Patrick's name had him documented in the right room. It correlated with the assistant's gesture, so I began to walk to the room.

The CICU had glass doors on some rooms, and others were just separated by curtains. As Jon and I walked into the room, I saw a middle-aged white male lying on his back. His stomach was blown up as if someone had pumped him full of air. Post-operative swelling. His color was pasty white. I turned to Jon and said, "I don't think he's going to make it."

The blanket was pulled back, exposing his upper chest cavity. A large tube with blood draining through it ran out from his right side. His body had the usual monitoring pads for his heart and blood pressure rates. He was intubated, so there would be no talking to Paul. The respirator was keeping him alive. A large gauze pad was taped to his stomach. IVs ran from both arms.

Jeanine decided to grace us with her presence and asked, "What are you guys doing in here?"

I wanted to tell her to go back to her magazine, but I tried to be nice. I introduced myself and Jon and told her I was the investigating detective assigned to the shooting of the patient.

"I'm here doing follow-up, but obviously Paul can't talk since he's hooked up to the respirator."

"Obviously," she snapped. "You guys shouldn't even be in here."

Here we go again.

I wasn't in the mood so I snapped back. "OK, we are in here! And we're going to take some photographs of the victim since this is a criminal investigation."

In other words, shut the fu#@ up.

"I need to notify the family if you're going to take pictures of him," she shot back. She started yanking on the curtain that surrounded Paul's bed.

"I don't care who you notify, but we're going to take the pictures. If you have a problem with that, get the nursing supervisor in here, and I'll have a chat with her."

What an ass.

As she stormed out of the room, Jon began to take his photos. "You think she's going to pull the bandage back?" he asked.

"Nope," I said. I'd burned that bridge.

As I checked Paul's body, I noticed a small spot of blood on his left inner ankle. It could be a pellet strike or just a blood droplet from his upper body. I'd have it photographed just in case.

The supervisor nurse and my favorite person, Jeanine, came back in.

"Hi," the supervisor said. "Sorry, we can't remove the bandage, doctor's orders." Jeanine wore a look of disgust on her face.

"Ok, thanks, I appreciate that. Do you have his X-rays around somewhere? I'd like to look at them."

"Sure, we can pull those up for you. I think they pulled some pellets out during surgery if you want to check with the OR when you're done," the supervisor suggested. At least there was one helpful person on this floor.

She placed Paul's X-ray on the viewing module. I saw that whatever pellets they pulled were insignificant compared to the numerous ones that were left in his body. Too many to count, they looked like stars in a night sky. They were too close to vital organs to retrieve. Jon photographed the X-rays.

We left the ICU after thanking the supervisor for her help and noting Jeanine had busied herself with some other task to avoid contact with us.

The hallway from the CICU led to the operating rooms as Jon and I made our way to another set of security doors. No one was here to open these, though. Just as we contemplated our dilemma, an orderly came out from the unit, giving us just enough time to sneak in. A nurse in scrubs and booties walked to the desk that sat just inside the doors. I was able to get her attention before she had to scurry back to another surgery.

"Hi, Detective Schwartzkopf, Phoenix Police. We understand that you may have some evidence for us from a gunshot victim who went into surgery early this morning. His name is Paul Patrick, and he was shot with a shotgun."

"Let me check," the nurse said. She started to look through some paperwork sitting on the back credenza. "It shows here that we did have something, but it looks like a police officer already picked it up. He signed for it this morning around 8:30 a.m." The nurse was looking at some type of release paperwork.

She handed it to me. Sure enough, one of our officer's signatures and badge number were on the release paperwork. I gave the papers back to her.

"Thanks for the help," I said.

"Oh, you're welcome, anytime."

The nurse then scuttled back toward the ORs.

There was nothing more to do here. Paul wouldn't be talking to me anytime soon, if ever. There was no family around, and they had not called police to provide any further information after they were contacted. It was time to head back to headquarters and report on what little I knew.

Back at headquarters, it was time to brief the brass on what I had learned. I also needed to catch up with Detective Moncrief and get him up to speed.

When I knocked on his door, the lieutenant was sitting behind his desk perusing the latest issue of *Police Beat*.

"Anything good in there?" I asked.

"Not really, got a decent article on some new gang intel out of Mexico. What did you find out at the hospital?"

"Well, Mr. Patrick was struck from close range with a shotgun blast. I would say by the patch over the wound, no more than five to ten feet," I said.

"Anything else?"

I could tell he wasn't in the mood for small talk.

Before I could say anything, the world's best police assistant walked in and interrupted the moment.

"Some officer brought some evidence by and said he would be doing a supplement later. I think they're your shotgun pellets from last night's shooting," Marge Mahwinney bellowed.

Marge had been our police assistant for several years. She had worked almost ten years in Homicide and several more in Assaults. She was outstanding and could remember almost any murder case or serious shooting that the Violent Crimes Bureau had investigated in the last decade or so.

Marge was the ultimate victims' advocate. She would get angry at detectives when victims or family would call and tell her that the detectives had not called them back. We didn't have to educate Marge very often. She had been around long enough to be able to separate the true victims from the pretenders. But that didn't mean they shouldn't get a call back, and, besides, she didn't want to listen to them whine either.

"Where is it, whatever was brought by?" I asked.

"I gave them to Detective Scott. He said he was going to impound them for you," she said. "I didn't think there was anything you could do with those, besides tell that they were shotgun pellets." Marge knew her evidence, too.

"We might be able to tell what size shot it is, and that's about the extent of it."

The LT was still wondering why I was sitting in his office.

"Alright, get out of here and go solve some crimes that we have something to go on," Lieutenant Benson said. "If anything breaks let Sergeant Clarke know. He'll be running everything from now on."

It wouldn't be long before I was reporting back to the LT, or I should say, before he would be reporting back to me.

CHAPTER 13

Of the ten largest cities in the State of Arizona, nine of them are located in the Phoenix Metro Area. Fourth on the list is the City of Glendale. A bedroom community, whose biggest employer is Luke Air Force Base, Glendale had pretty much been ignored in the Valley of the Sun for many years. With its population hovering around two hundred fifty thousand, it was most famous for . . . nothing.

Then, seemingly out of nowhere, Glendale became relevant. The city negotiated the building of a new arena to house the Phoenix Coyotes, the local National Hockey League team. They were able to steal the team from downtown Phoenix by building a new stadium, the Glendale Arena.

After pulling off that coup, the City of Glendale wasn't finished. They negotiated to build a football stadium for the Arizona Cardinals. The stadium was a success before it was built, landing the 2008 Super Bowl. It actually opened in 2006, and the city got its first taste of the NFL.

Elizabeth Clark never watched sports and could care less about new stadiums and fancy arenas. She lived in Glendale, but had enough worries just trying to clothe herself and find a warm bed to sleep in.

Homeless women are especially vulnerable on the streets. To stay alive, most are pushed into prostitution or servitude. Many have drug problems, which only exacerbate their situation.

Elizabeth had been given some opportunities—a handout and some hand ups. Some of the people she knew had sometimes given her a place to stay. She had minimal contact with family.

Besides her drug addiction, Elizabeth had a mental illness. She really couldn't understand why she was arrested one night for stealing Christmas lights and decorations off houses. She'd been envious of people who led normal lives, who hung Christmas lights, and who celebrated the birth of Christ. Elizabeth knew that her warrants would ultimately land her in jail, but she couldn't believe that she would be punished for stealing lights.

In order to get by, Elizabeth turned to the world's oldest profession. Prostitution and theft would provide her with what she needed the most—the small end of a glass pipe.

◈

The lights of the Quik Trip gas station are one of the only semblances of civilization at the far west end of Camelback Road and 99th Avenue, a location surrounded mostly by barren dirt and empty properties at the time.

By June 11, 2006, the dreams of many land developers had started to crumble. Phoenix and its surrounding communities had ridden the boom like no other place in the nation. Home prices doubled from 2004 to 2006, but by the summer, it was obvious the market was overpriced, and that the boom could not continue. The market would soon come crashing down.

West on Camelback from 99th Avenue was such a tract of undeveloped land. It was going to be the future for some builder, some tenant, and some owner. Now it sat vacant. A sagging, rickety chain-link fence erected along the sidewalk stood as a tribute to greed and market forces.

Elizabeth Clark pedaled her bike westbound toward her cousin's house. It was 10:20 p.m., and she had a purpose. As she rode past the convenience store and gas stop, the sidewalk serpentined from right to left. The city had put the sidewalk in to service the new neighborhood, only to have it sit abandoned.

One lone streetlight stood between 99th and 101st Avenues as she continued to pedal her Next Brand, Charger model bicycle to her destination. Elizabeth wore Tommy Hilfiger pants and a bright pink Minnie Mouse shirt that passing motorists could easily see at night.

As she passed the lone street lamp and entered the darkest area of the journey, the boom could be heard from the convenience store blocks away. The Quik Trip clerk heard it, a patron heard it, and Elizabeth Clark heard it.

At the corner of 101st Avenue and Camelback Road, Elizabeth Clarke was shot. The blast pierced her left hip and flank. She screamed out in pain and couldn't control the bike. Gravity took over. Down she went in a heap of metal and flesh.

What had happened? Had she hit something that flew up and exploded? The loud bang could have been a glass bottle she ran over. Nothing made any sense to her. She tried to think straight, but couldn't. Blood oozed from her hip.

Elizabeth was afraid to look at her wounds. She lay down on the sidewalk, her bike on its side. She began to scream and cry loudly.

One of the neighbors recognized the overbearing sound of the gunshot and looked up at the clock in his den. It was 10:27 p.m. He walked out of his house and looked to the corner of 101st Avenue and Camelback Road, but saw nothing. Within a minute, the police car's overhead lights and headlamps illuminated a female down on the corner.

Officer Cano of the Glendale Police Department had just stopped to get himself a drink at the Quik Trip convenience store. Before he even had a chance to get his soda, he was told by patrons that a loud bang had just occurred, and that a woman could be heard screaming down the street. He would have to forego the drink for now. Duty called.

Officer Cano spotted Elizabeth lying on her back with her bicycle just feet away. The Tommy Hilfiger pants had started to turn blood red. He notified dispatch of the shooting victim down at the corner of 101st Avenue and Camelback Road. Even though he was first to arrive, the shooting would fall under the jurisdiction of the Phoenix Police Department.

He tried to talk to Elizabeth, but she was going into shock. She couldn't answer any of his questions. She told the officer she needed water and that she had fallen off her bike. Nothing could be further from the truth, except for the water.

Patrol vehicles soon flooded the area as Camelback Road was shut down in both directions. Crime scene tape flew from the back of car trunks and would be attached to the chain-link fence and any other makeshift obstacle.

When paramedics arrived, they also began to question Elizabeth. Occasionally, victims will provide more information to the fire personnel than to the police. That's especially true if the victim was involved in criminal behavior, past or present. But Elizabeth couldn't provide anything that made any sense. She was whisked away.

There would be no dropping the ball on this case. A problematic trend was now apparent in the Maryvale precinct. Elizabeth Clark was number five of the random and growing list of victims who were shot by the unknown assailant. The holes in her shirt and pants were caused by the shooter's signature, a shotgun blast.

As is standard operating procedure, one investigator proceeded to the hospital for follow-up. The others would work the crime scene as best they could. Once again, there were no eyewitnesses to the shooting. Numerous people had heard the shotgun roar, but not one had been close enough to provide a description of anything or anyone.

At the hospital, Elizabeth had been given some morphine and was struggling to make sense. She was extremely emotional, understandably so. Her mental illness didn't help matters. She did not see who had shot her.

As the morphine started to kick in harder, she began to think about who would want her dead. She was advised that she may not know the shooter, that there had been other random shootings in and around the area where she was shot. She was now visibly upset about being the target of a random shooting.

"Tell them I'm not a test dummy and didn't sign up for this. It hurts!" Elizabeth ranted. That would be something investigators could pass on to the shooter if he or she were ever apprehended. Morphine is a beautiful thing.

The X-ray showed it all—shotgun pellets extending from her hip down her left leg and stopping in her thigh. Elizabeth was probably right about the shooter going in the opposite direction, though no conclusions could be drawn. The shot was fired from several feet away, unlike with Claudia Gutierrez-Cruz and Miguel Rodriguez.

Just a few short miles from the new hockey arena and the new football stadium, Elizabeth Clark had become another statistic, another notch on the shooter's belt.

◈

My pager went off at around 7:00 on the morning of June 12. I recognized the number. It was Sergeant Clarke.

I was stuck in the usual early-morning commute, but at least I was moving. As a member of a unit responsible for being called out at anytime, I was given the use of a city-owned vehicle. I had selected mine personally, a Ford F150 with a bedcover.

I continued to drive as I dialed the cellphone of one Sergeant Stewart Clarke. He answered on the second ring.

"Sarge, it's Clark. Got your page. What's up?"

"Are you in the office yet?" he asked. If I'd worked on his squad, he would have known that my day doesn't start until 7:30. I decided to cut him some slack.

"No, I'm still driving in. I should be there in about fifteen."

"See me when you get in, would you?"

Why do I have to see you? I'm on the phone with you now.

I swear, for supervisors, their whole day is filled with nothing but senseless meetings that could be taken care of over the phone.

"Is it important? I got slammed with cases last weekend and was only going to grab some files and head out."

This was a hint not to waste my time.

"We had another shotgun shooting last night."

He paused and waited to see if I had heard about it.

"Well, that's the first I've heard of one." I didn't want to go off on him without knowing all the details. All I could think to myself was, it better not have happened in Maryvale, and a patrol officer better not have assumed the investigation. "I'll see you when I get there."

Sergeant Clarke was standing just off Marge's desk and right outside the Lieutenant's office when I walked in. A simple nod acknowledged that he saw me, and we made eye contact. Lieutenant Benson was already at his desk, going over the summary of the report. He always arrived at the office at 6:00 a.m. to look over the previous night's incidents.

"Have a seat, Clarkster. I assume Sergeant Clarke informed you of what happened last night," the LT said. He, too, wasn't sure how I would react.

"He did. I would have hoped to have received a call last night about this. I thought that I was in charge of this investigation and that I was going to be informed if we had any further shootings." That was a tactful way of venting a little frustration. "Please tell me that patrol officers didn't take disposition of this case."

"They didn't. Night detectives responded and took it."

"Wasn't a whole lot to it. A white female shot while riding a bike at 101st Avenue and Camelback. Injuries were not life threatening, and she was taken to Good Samaritan Hospital," he continued.

"Any particular reason I wasn't informed?" I asked.

I couldn't wait to hear this. There was always some lame excuse for why communication between bureaus was always messed up.

"I talked to the night detective sergeant. They didn't know that we had assigned a permanent investigator to handle these shootings. They were informed that from now on you get the first call no matter what time, what date, whatever the circumstance," LT said.

Fair enough, I thought.

"Any leads or tidbits of information in the summary that they wrote up?" I asked.

"No suspect listed or seen. First witness was a Glendale cop who happened upon the crime scene," the LT related. "Looks like you got another mess with nothing to go on."

Great, I thought to myself.

Sergeant Clarke was still standing by the door as if an early exit stage right was warranted. He had nothing to add.

"I'll head to the hospital and check her condition. Maybe she'll remember something she forgot to tell the night dicks last night."

It was probably fruitless, but it was worth trying.

"Keep me posted."

As I stood up to leave the Lieutenant's office, Stewart looked at me as if to say, "Sorry, dude, you got another stinker."

He was thinking the same thing I was thinking.

When I arrived at Good Samaritan, I checked in with the security officer sitting at the desk just inside the ER. I just assumed that she would be in serious condition and being monitored since she'd been shot fewer than twelve hours ago.

The security guard recognized my credentials hanging on my left front hip. "How's it going, detective?"

"Good, bud. How are you?"

"What can I do for you?" he asked.

"Gunshot victim brought in last night by the name of Elizabeth Clark. She was shot in the area of 101st Avenue and Camelback. Not quite sure why she was brought all the way down here, but she's supposed to be here somewhere. Can you see if you can find her for me?"

The security guard began to punch the keys on the computer and strained to look at the monitor. As he scanned the information, I noticed that the ER was almost empty. It must have been because it was early in the day.

"OK, Elizabeth Clark. Brought in last night with a gunshot wound and taken to . . . . She never left the trauma room. She was released this morning and walked out of here about thirty minutes ago. Signed a release," he related.

"Are you sure? My understanding is she was injured and would be admitted."

It wouldn't be the first time someone walked out of the hospital refusing treatment.

The security guard picked up the phone and dialed the trauma area. He began to question the staff and see if they had any further updates. Whoever was helping him was going through their log as well.

"OK, thanks." He hung up the phone. "She was released this morning with her wounds bandaged. She signed herself out. Looks like she may have been homeless. Sometimes they don't like to stick around."

I could understand that. The more time she spends here, the better her chance of losing her belongings to someone else on the street, wherever they may be.

"Did she leave any forwarding information?" I asked.

He was back on the computer. "Doesn't look like it."

"Thanks for the help," I said.

No sense in burning daylight here. I would have to try to find Elizabeth and get some photos taken of her. The report didn't list any. Lucky girl. She should play the lottery. Shot with a shotgun and walked out of the hospital the next day.

As I drove back to headquarters, it was time to sit down and assess what the heck I had here. I would also need to catch up with Detective Moncrief and brief him on the new case.

◈

I plopped down in my cubicle and opened the five shotgun shooting cases I had amassed thus far: Hodge, Rodriguez, Davies, Patrick, and now Clark. I needed to see if I could develop some type of Modus Operandi, or M.O. Although a term used loosely in TV shows, M.O. is an important tool in trying to piece together stringers—those types of similar crimes committed by certain individuals or groups.

As much as some criminals try to hide their M.O., it can usually be discovered if the cases are seriously scrutinized and details are documented. Money can be a motive for robbery, but motive is far removed from methodology. A criminal's methodology is usually unique when it comes to someone committing multiple crimes. People tend to fall into a pattern that makes them comfortable and confident, and criminals are no different. Just as a worker searches for a career that he enjoys, criminals drift toward crimes where they feel dominant, areas where they feel secure, and tools of the trade that they can specifically handle well.

Detective Moncrief happened to stop by just as I cracked the folders.

"Hey, I heard we had another one last night?"

"Yep. Looks to be the same M.O. as the others. I was just getting ready to sit down and go through them. Anything on your plate?"

"No, but I went out and canvassed the area of the shooting on Indian School Road," he said.

"Which one, Paul Patrick's or Miguel Rodriguez's?" I asked.

These shootings occurred within a mile of each other.

"Miguel's, and I think we may have a lead. I was talking to the neighbor who called in, but the police didn't talk to her. She said that she saw two Hispanic males on bicycles right next to Miguel after the shooting. She thinks they were too close to not have seen what happened or have been a part of it."

This was good news—a possible witness or two and maybe even a lead on the perpetrators. It could be Miguel's case wasn't related to the other cases.

Detective Moncrief continued. "Anyway, the two guys on bicycles stood around Miguel for a minute or so and then pedaled off down the street. No 911 calls from either of them. The witness thinks they went into an apartment complex about a block down and across the street. I'm heading out that way unless you got something else."

"Go get 'em, and don't come back until you have someone in handcuffs."

Dan had a good sense of humor like most cops, and I appreciated his enthusiasm.

"You got it," he said as he bolted away.

With the cases sprawled out in front of me, I began to reread them to see if there was anything I missed. I started to take notes.

All five shootings involved a shotgun as the only weapon. They all occurred at night, appeared to be drive-by shootings, close to or on large streets. Evidence consisted of shot pellets and clothing. One "shotgun wadding to a 20 gauge" was also found by a responding patrol officer in the Hodge case. I would need to get confirmation on that.

The victims were of different races and genders. Four males and one female, four Whites and one Hispanic, although Paul Patrick was pretty dark and could be confused for Hispanic. Bias didn't appear to be the motive.

Four of the victims were walking and one was biking. And all of the victims were alone. No witnesses saw what occurred, just numerous ones who heard the shot and called police. No victim could identify the shooter. The vehicle descriptions were too vague to even mean anything.

Those were the knowns, but what were the unknowns? What was unknown was that we had no gender or race on the suspect, though you would assume it was a male. Based on the wound to Miguel and the uncanny accuracy of that shot, I would keep the two-man theory at the top of my list.

I tore the paper from the notepad and placed it in the file. There was nothing more I could do at this point, unless Detective Moncrief uncovered some type of shooting revelation.

Unfortunately, that wouldn't happen. A phone call from Detective Moncrief squished that glimmer of hope. The two bicyclists had nothing to do with the shooting of Miguel Rodriguez. They just happened up on him after he was shot. They were, of course, illegal, and didn't want to cooperate with what little they did know. The lead was a dead end.

The only thing good about the shootings was that the media hadn't caught onto them. No public information officers clamored around my cubicle asking, "Is there anything to see here?"

At this point, the shootings were flying under the city's radar, which was a good thing. I could only hope that the suspect(s) had been arrested or fled the state. Maybe he had offed himself. That was a pleasant thought. Whatever the case, there was nothing more I could do. The cases were shelved for now.

But it would be another case, or cases, that would engulf the media's attention—a set of crimes that at first seemed unrelated to anything that I was investigating. It would only be found out later, much later, how significant the circumstances of these crimes and this night would be.

CHAPTER 14

Walmart is Arizona's largest employer, with its workforce numbering around thirty thousand. That's more than Honeywell and Intel Corporations combined. Although Walmart employs more people than anyone else in the state, many job-seeking websites snub Walmart as a "top employer." The reality of the matter is that they offer products at a lower price than other retailers.

On June 8, 2006, the arson of two Walmart stores made big headlines both locally and nationally. The arson of any structure is big news, but the arson of an icon draws an enormous amount of attention. The arsons would occur less than forty-five minutes apart, and both of the stores were in Glendale.

Police departments in Arizona, for the most part, don't investigate arsons. The fire department deals with those cases, unless a death occurs. Then the local police will help out the arson investigators if leads are developed. Occasionally, police will take over the investigation, and in some cases, federal authorities are asked to assist.

The Glendale Fire Department would respond to the first fire, set at the Walmart store located at 95th Avenue and Camelback Road. Glendale arson investigator Mike Blair would head the investigation. This Walmart, affectionately known as a "big box store," was almost 290,000 square feet of discount shoppers' delight. It was built in 2003.

As it so happens, Phoenix Fire Department would be the first on scene at 9:30 p.m. Smoke could be seen filling the entire store as customers scurried from the one-story structure. The smoke and fire protection system had activated, and sprinklers had snuffed out the blaze.

This was good fortune for the arson investigators. A fire that is quickly extinguished usually leaves a good chance at evidence recovery and the discovery of the origin of the fire. The problems with sprinkler systems are that they can leave inches of water, thus flooding the floor and destroying goods. It appeared that there were no serious injuries, although numerous people suffered smoke inhalation. The exact number of potential victims or witnesses was unknown, as several just walked away.

The investigation would reveal that the fire originated on a metal shelf display in the domestics area of the store. Part of domestics is home furnishings. This particular section was filled with artificial plants, most of them made of silk. Silk plants are constructed from a petroleum-based product, making their ignition fast and furious.

Investigator Blair could not find the exact location of the plant that was ignited, but the overhead sprinklers that engaged gave away the location.

The investigators started to round up store employees and managers to see if they had any knowledge of who was responsible and why. They regurgitated the usual list of disgruntled employees to the investigators.

But the surveillance footage from inside the Walmart would be of more substantive use. That footage would capture anyone who entered or left the building and may have captured the person(s) who started the fire, if the cameras were efficiently placed and functioning.

Before Investigator Blair could even take the photos of his crime scene and begin his investigation, a mere forty-five minutes later, he learned of a second arson structure fire. Another Walmart had been torched, and another group of panicked customers had sprinted for the doors. Another arson investigator would be sent to that store.

There was little chance that these two Walmart fires were unrelated. A brief phone conversation would confirm that the second Walmart arson had occurred in the same location of the store as the first: the silk plant section. That left no doubt about the connection between the two fires.

After examining the first scene, Investigator Blair made sure that the entire store was swept for any unusual packages or articles that seemed out of place. The last thing you want to do is leave a crime scene and later have another ignition. It was too early to figure out what started the fire. Science would hopefully be able to figure out the accelerant, if there was one.

There were no eyewitnesses to the arson on 95th Avenue. The scene was photographed, and the store was closed for damage assessment. The total amount of the damaged property would not be known for a while, but it was huge.

The most important part of the scene on 95th Avenue had already been recovered. Investigator Blair was excited to find out that the second Walmart, located at 56th Avenue and Northern, had an excellent surveillance system as well. He scurried toward that scene.

As he assessed the damage, Blair noted that the fire and water damage at the second store seemed more extensive. Once again, the sprinkler system had activated and saved the whole store from ruin. The smoke had damaged everything in the fabrics section, and other parts of the store had fared no better.

The size of this particular Walmart was equivalent to the size of the other store. It was fairly new as well, built in 2004. This store also sold groceries.

In addition, it was full of customers when the smoke alarms sounded at 10:15 p.m. Thankfully, no one was burned, there were no injuries during the evacuation, and smoke inhalation injuries were minimal. The haze of smoke inside the store hung like a New England fog.

The point of origin of a fire is a key factor in arson investigation. If an accelerant is used, the origin is the best place to find what type. In this case, the middle shelf of the shelving unit was where the fire was lit. This particular shelf stood about four feet off the ground and also sat in the artificial plant aisle.

The baskets that held the artificial flowers were as black as the silk flowers that protruded from them. Only the shelving with the silk plants and flowers burned. The quick-acting sprinklers saved the other aisles.

The second arson scene was photographed and the store released back to the management. No evidence was located that day, but three days later, during clean-up, a source of the ignition would be found: an everyday Bic lighter, spotted by one of the store employees.

Once again, there were no eyewitnesses who could identify anyone acting suspiciously in the area of the fabric and floral sections of the second store.

The significant evidence would, of course, be the video surveillance tapes. Both store tapes were viewed initially for any obvious perpetrators. Walmart may skimp in some areas, but their surveillance systems, for the most part, are of very high quality. Even though these systems used VHS tapes, not digitally recorded technology, the pictures of the store's interior, as well as parking area, was clear.

Unfortunately, there were no cameras in the fabrics and silk plant sections of either store. That would be too easy. It would take days to examine the footage of all the patrons who entered the store before the fires and all the patrons that exited after.

It is labor-intensive and time-consuming to view hours of surveillance tape. Those viewing the tapes would have to assume that everybody who walked in before the fires were set were possible suspects.

The task of viewing these tapes would fall on the shoulders of the loss prevention agents, the experts who sit in the security offices day in and day out, These agents save the stores millions of dollars by thwarting shopliftings and employee thefts. They are the ones who get paid very little for what they do; who confront thieves and pay for it dearly, by injury or death; who keep prices low for their paying customers.

It would take days of research and viewing, rewinding and fast forwarding, documenting the looks of this person, or the mannerisms of that one. How long had they been there? Had they come and gone, casing the store for the right opportunity?

Chances were they drove a car to the stores. Maybe the agents would get lucky and spot the car if they could locate the criminals. License plates were unattainable with this equipment, but a color and make might be discernible.

Meanwhile, investigators would start to ask the tougher questions. What was the motive for setting these fires? Could it be that person or persons were covering up another crime? Was it an activist hell-bent on bringing Walmart to its knees, domestic terrorism? Juveniles looking for a thrill or gang member initiations? A pyromaniac? There was a plethora of possible motives.

After two days of painstaking viewing, the loss prevention employees of Walmart uncovered what they believed to be two suspicious characters. These individuals were seen at both stores prior to the fires being lit. The two males were seen on video forty minutes before the fire started at the 95th Avenue location, arriving in a light silver four-door vehicle. The vehicle was missing the hubcap off the right rear side of the car, and the back window displayed two caricatures that could not be made out.

Inside the store, the subjects shop for awhile, picking up some bedding. The two are then seen leaving the cart. Within sixty seconds of them exiting domestics, where the silk flowers are located, smoke is seen in the area. The two subjects leave the store without purchasing anything.

At 2149 hours, twenty-six minutes before the start of the second fire, the same two subjects and the car arrive at the Walmart on Northern Avenue. The two are seen entering the store through the grocery section and are observed walking through the store. Again, their path takes them to the domestics sections. One of the men is seen leaving the fabrics section, and one minute later, smoke is seen billowing from the aisle. Coincidence? I think not.

It was outstanding work by the loss prevention officer, Patricia Davies, a huge break in the case. The information and a description of the subjects were given to Mike Blair.

One more interesting piece of information was forwarded. The second subject seen at the arson sites had changed his shirt between the two crimes. Why would somebody do that? It was obvious. The shirt worn by the suspect in the first arson was bright yellow. At the second, he had changed to a black T-shirt.

The video from the recordings was good enough to give accurate clothing descriptions, hair color, facial hair, and most importantly, a tattoo worn by one of the men. The tattoo was on the person's right forearm, but the design could not be identified.

It was time to put the media to work. The still pictures from the video were released. If that didn't get the phones ringing, the reward certainly would—$20,000 for the person or persons who would identify the culprits. Money is the ultimate motivator.

It was also at this point that Glendale fire investigators decided to reach out for further help. They solicited help from The Bureau of Alcohol, Tobacco, Firearms, and sometimes Explosives.

Immediately upon release of the photos, investigators' phones were ringing off the hook. Numerous persons were identified from the photos, and all of the callers wanted to know when they could pick up the reward money.

As the investigators sifted through the calls, one that came into Silent Witness stood out. On June 20, twelve days after the arsons, a male called in. He was positive about the identity of one of the arsonists. It was someone he knew very well and had been friends with for a very long time.

Just after this call came in, another Silent Witness caller, this time a female, related the same information. She too knew the identity of one of the arsonists. She too knew the person previously, and they had dated for a short time period.

Two calls coming in within a short period of time was more than a little suspicious. It stunk of collusion. Odds are the two callers knew each other.

Whatever the case, investigators had leads to follow up on. What wasn't known at the time was how significant these June 20th calls would be, and how they would shape other investigations yet to be launched.

CHAPTER 15

June 20, 2006, the same day that calls about the arsons came into Silent Witness, was another hot day in Phoenix. But the early morning hours were cool compared to the mid-day temperatures that pushed over a hundred degrees.

It was during the early morning hours that Fredric Sena tended to spend most of his time milling about. Even though he had a place to sleep, at least for now, Fredric liked the night and early morning. It was the best time to find the items that everyone had discarded the day before.

That had become his life. Frederic was a scavenger for anything that he could find on the street, in the alleys, or in the dumpsters that lined those alleys. His leather sandals were worn down from all the time spent wandering the streets of Central Phoenix. He tried to keep to himself, but like many indigents, he was just a step away from trouble from the law.

But this had been a good week for Fredric. He had talked a liquor store owner into letting him paint the overhang to his drive-thru. It was an actual job. Unfortunately, liquor was the root of Fredric's problem.

Years before, he had become addicted to alcohol. It had cost him many a relationship. He spent most of his time in a bottle of one sort or another. It was his only release. As with so many addicts, it would cost him job after job and had taken a toll on his health as well. Fredric knew that this painting gig would get him some money, but at what cost?

Fredric also experimented with drugs, particularly meth. Sometimes it's easier, and cheaper, on the street to take a hit off a pipe than to try and buy alcohol legitimately. Frederic carried his glass pipe for said occasions. It was common knowledge that if another street person had a rock, they would share it amongst themselves. Sooner or later, it would be Fredric's turn to score the drug, and he would have to share. This was his life.

But that was the negatives. Right now, Fredric was focused on the positives. That morning around 1:30 a.m, when he walked down a back alley to the liquor store, Frederic just wanted to get started. He had nothing else to do, and if he could get the drive-thru curb and structure painted before sun-up, he could keep out of the blistering heat.

The store, A-1 Liquors, had been a fixture in the neighborhood of 9th Street and Indian School Road for years. Most of its patrons were walk-ups to the store. Cars would stop at the drive-thru after work or late at night to stock up on libations for the coming evening or weekend. But it was a neighborhood stop, and most of the traffic was local.

Fredric had been a customer at A-1 for a long time. That's how he was able to talk the owner into the painting job. He'd already purchased the paint with a down payment and left the cans at the store. He figured that a couple of cans should do it.

As he continued east through the alley, Frederic eyed the dumpsters that sat off the backyards of the residents. What would it hurt to peek in a couple of these as he meandered toward his worksite? Who knew what treasure could be found?

As Frederic pulled the big, black plastic lid up, he noticed a shiny white box. Like most transients, the smell of rotten garbage and filth had little or no effect on Fredric. If there was money to be made and it was in the garbage, so be it. The alley was dimly lit except for a few back porch lights. But the shiny box drew his attention, as it reflected just enough light to make it worthy of inspection. Fredric dove in and held the box and its contents to the light: *MSN Windows TV2 Internet Media Hardware*. Sounds impressive, but what the hell is it?

After climbing back out of the dumpster, he stuck the box and its contents under his arm. He could inspect the box later, when the light was better. The box was full of something based on its weight. He hoped he could fetch a few dollars for it.

When Frederic got to the liquor store, he set the box down. He had brought his gray all-in-one stool that doubled as a toolbox. He took this wherever he went. You never know when you might have to pull a piece of metal apart, take the legs off a chair, or need a tool. There were hundreds of uses for tools on the street. For today's job, it would work as a seat to keep his butt off the asphalt that covered the liquor store's parking lot. The stool sat high enough that the average adult could sit on it comfortably.

Fredric had hidden the paint on the property so that no one would steal it, but he'd kept the brushes in his toolbox/footstool for safekeeping. As he opened the stool, two flip-up drawers would emerge. He pulled the brushes from one drawer and closed up the stool.

The covered structure to the drive-thru had poles that were six inches in diameter and attached to a raised curb. A streetlight on the corner of Indian School Road illuminated the property. Three neon signs advertising Bud Light, Michelob Light, and Coors Light helped Fredric view the work area. Safety wasn't a big concern to this owner, unless of course it was dealing with his stock of booze. Steel bars over the windows and a steel door over the entrance gave insight into the neighborhood. It was an ugly sight, but it was a necessity to stay in business and keep insurance costs down.

Fredric read that an eighteen pack of Bud Light and Budweiser was on sale for $12.99. The sign was affixed to one of the poles he needed to paint. Cigarettes were advertised on a sign affixed to one of the other five poles, on sale for $3.95 a pack. He couldn't afford to smoke.

He perused the other signs that adorned the windows of the establishment advertising Corona, Moddels, and Bacardi Silver's three flavors: silver, O3, and Raz. Fredric didn't even know what Bacardi Silver was until he read the sign. He thought Bacardi was just a type of rum, nothing more.

As Fredric sat down and pondered whether or not he had enough lighting to get to work, a blue vehicle drove by. That was not that unusual, since Indian School Road is a large artery, and traffic can be seen on the road at all hours. But this vehicle came up 9th Street. It was almost two in the morning, and unless someone in the neighborhood got a case of the munchies … well, maybe it wasn't so strange.

A few minutes later, the vehicle came by again, this time passing by on Indian School Road. It was the same car, but Fredric couldn't make out the driver. The car's windows were tinted. The car was definitely checking him out. It wasn't speeding by, more cruising. He looked back down at the paint cans and felt he was being paranoid.

Fredric, however, had reason to be edgy. He had made some enemies on the street. Anyone who stayed out there long enough always did. He was trying to remember if any of them owned blue cars. None came to mind. It would be best to grow eyes in the back of his head for the moment.

As Frederic started to open the can of paint, a gentle breeze moved the small plastic signs attached to the overhanging roof. The string of signs had begun to sag due to previous gusts of winds. He placed his brush in one of the cans. The streetlight made the bright yellow paint reflect. His wrist and hand flexed with the deliberate movement required of brushing the raised curb.

His mind wandered, and then he remembered: There was enough light to open his street treasure. *A Windows Media* … whatever it was would be a hell of a lot more interesting than painting this curb. It was time to look inside the box.

The container wasn't as new as it had looked in the alley's dim light. As Frederic opened it, he could see there was some kind of object that looked like a computer. He pulled out an urgent letter, addressed to RCA Registration Department, and strained to read it. There was a remote controller of some type and a power cord. What is all this stuff, and can I get any money for it? Fredric was perplexed as he sat over his find.

During this time, Frederic had forgotten about his nemesis, the person in the blue car. He was too engrossed in his media player.

Fredric felt the pain of the blast before he heard it. He never saw it coming because his back was turned to the street. The shotgun blast hit him and spun him around. The pellets penetrated his upper back, shoulders, and head like stings from a swarm of wasps. He hit the raised curb. Lying on his back, he tried to arch his back and look around, but he couldn't move well enough to see who had shot him. Frederic lay next to the drive-thru stunned and bleeding over the top of his treasure box. He didn't know whether to call for help or try to run. What if they came back?

The blood continued to drip from his shirtless body onto the media box and the raised curbing of the drive-thru. He couldn't just stay there and bleed to death. Then it came to him. He knew a place to seek safe haven and get help, a place he'd been many times before to get medical assistance. The VA Hospital. It was only two blocks away.

Located at 7th Street and Indian School Road, the Veterans Administration Hospital had been a fixture in the neighborhood for as long as anyone could remember. Its big white buildings gave it the look of a sanitarium for the mentally insane in the 1900s.

Slowly, Fredric got to his feet. There was no foot traffic around, and the suspicious car had disappeared. He began the slow trek with blood streaming down his back.

It seemed to take forever, but he made it. There were armed guards in the emergency room just in case anyone came looking for trouble. As he entered the waiting room, blood was starting to coagulate in his wounds. He wasn't dripping as bad as he was earlier. He felt death creeping over him. He collapsed into a chair.

He heard medical staff personnel yell, "Hey, we got a gunshot victim in the waiting room." The pain was excruciating, and as Fredric drifted off, he thought at least he wouldn't die alone.

◈

Phoenix Sky Harbor Airport is one of the nation's busiest international airports. It services millions of customers each year and sits on a strip of land in the middle of Central Phoenix. Conveniently located for locals, the airport is easy to enter and exit, even during rush hour traffic. When building the airport, the city had understood the potential problem based on its location and constructed some freeways with access to the airport. These freeways were, of course, well traveled.

Those of us who have lived in Phoenix for a while, however, know other less used routes, one of which is 44th Street. It enters Sky Harbor from the north and ends there. You can pick it up again only on the south side of the airport. 44th Street also services a few hotels directly around the airport.

The Circle K Convenience Store sits at the corner of 44th Street and Van Buren, close to the airport, and with gas pumps ready to fill the needs of those returning rental cars. As one of the only stores in the area, the vehicle and foot traffic during daytime hours is maddening. But at night, it starts to slow, and the clerks have time to pull out and read the latest issues of whatever magazine suits them.

On the morning of June 20, 2006, the still of that downtime would be rudely interrupted. The night-shift clerk had just rung up a sale of gas when a patron stumbled in. He was looking forward to a quiet night, but it was not to be.

Tony Long had a colorful background. A military veteran with a history of blue-collar jobs, Tony was a road warrior, used to fighting to protect himself. He had grown up on the streets of various towns. Built like a middleweight boxer, he demanded respect and got it. He disliked authority, but, for the most part, he left people alone, and he didn't want any trouble.

Unfortunately, trouble seems to manifest itself if you spend enough time on the street. Tony knew that. He shrugged it off and chalked it up to being a part of the way he lived his life.

The night had started out with just him and his cousin. After a few drinks and some laughs, they split up. Tony ended up walking alone on 44th Street just south of Van Buren. The only signs of light and life at two o'clock in the morning emanated from the Circle K store just a block away.

As he trudged up the street, Tony saw nothing but barren desert to his right. Airport parking and other businesses stood across the street. What was he doing on foot at this hour?

As Tony thought about how stupid it was to be in this predicament, a deafening sound erupted. He felt the burning of his skin and turned back toward the road. He could see a white car in the distance. He looked to his left. Nothing. He then spun to look backwards at the route he had just covered. Nothing. Not a person around.

"What was it that hit me?" He began to check his body and felt blood start to ooze from his skin. He'd been shot. His whole left side started burning. He inspected the holes in his shirt.

"What the hell just happened?" he asked himself. He hadn't done anybody any wrong, at least not tonight. Somebody had just shot him for no reason, and he was pissed. He yelled, "Nobody shoots Tony Long and gets away with it." He scoured the streets for some semblance of life, someone to blame, someone for him to go after. There was no one.

Tony was hurt. As tough as he was, he needed help. He scurried toward the convenience store. Two men outside helped him in.

The clerk stood stunned as Tony walked through the store's front doors.

"I need to use the phone, man, I've been shot," Tony yelled. The clerk went to hand him the wireless phone, but instead decided to call 911.

"911, what's your emergency?" The dispatcher asked.

The clerk was in a panic. "I'm at the . . . shop, and I've got a guy here who says he's been shot."

The dispatcher could understand only part of what Steven was saying. No sense mincing words.

"OK, what's the address there? The dispatcher asked.

"427 N. 44th Street."

"And you said he's been shot?"

"Yes, he's bleeding profusely."

Tony was now standing in front of the store.

"Does he know where the subjects are that shot him?" the dispatcher asked.

There was another person inside the store who had heard the shot fired. It now dawned on the clerk that the suspect or suspects who shot Tony Long may be lurking close by. A new wave of panic set in. He asked the bystander to look for suspects.

The police arrived within minutes. Tony was amazingly coherent for just being shot. He wanted to call his cousin, or anyone who cared, and tell them about what happened. He was very upset that someone had the balls to shoot him and then drive away as if it were no big deal.

Tony's demeanor changed when officers contacted him. That authority thing, again. They could see that the left side of his shirt was full of blood, and now it was dripping on the sidewalk.

Tony became fidgety and nervous. He wasn't sure how to be treated as a victim. It was a new role for him. The officers called for paramedics and then helped Tony remove his shirt. The whole left side of Tony's body was riddled with holes. His left arm had taken the brunt of the blast.

The officers began to question Tony about what happened. But Tony didn't have any idea who shot him, and the questions had begun to annoy him. He told them what little he knew. He was walking northbound on 44th Street on the east side of the road, he heard a shot, and realized he had been hit. He'd seen a white car, but didn't know if it was related. There was nothing else to say.

When paramedics arrived, Tony became even more upset. Some coward had shot him and just drove away. He was so mad that treating personnel had to talk him into going to the hospital. He thought that if he could walk a block to the store and tell officers what had happened, he would be OK to go home. But that was not the case. He had pellets in his body. The only way to properly diagnose his injuries was a trip to the emergency room. Tony begrudgingly gave in. He was taken to Maricopa Medical Center (County Hospital to us cops), a short two-and-half-mile drive from the shooting scene.

In the meantime, officers began to walk Tony's route to see if they could find any evidence. Nothing. Witnesses, a big nothing. Security footage from the store, still a bigger nothing.

But there was something that police had learned in the hour since they had responded to Tony's shooting. There had been another shotgun shooting, just minutes prior to Tony's. The shooting of Fredric Sena had occurred several miles away, but the details were eerily similar. Both had been gunned down in a drive-by and with a shotgun.

Many years ago, I learned to keep the phone on my side of the bed. After hundreds of call-outs and responses to wanted criminals, I was conditioned to grab it after the first ring or two. Tonight would be no exception.

The phone rang and woke me from a deep sleep. On the other line was the familiar voice of Sergeant Jeff Pierce, the Violent Crimes Desk Sergeant. I looked at the clock; it read 3:00 a.m. on the dot.

It took me a few seconds to run through the few things that enter your mind when you've been woken up from a dead sleep. "Why is he calling, was I on standby, and am I dreaming?" After a few seconds, I realized that I wasn't on standby and that I wasn't dreaming. The sergeant would have to fill in the rest of the gaps.

"Are you handling all the investigations of random drive-by shootings that occur where a shotgun was used?" he asked.

The last thing you want to do is wake a sleeping investigator on a weekday if you're wrong.

"Yeah, Sarge, I am. Whatcha got?"

I tried to shake myself out of the slumber.

"Well, it looks like we may have two related shootings. You got a pen and paper?" By this time, I was moving from my bedroom to where the conversation would be more appropriate.

"OK, shoot. No pun intended."

Sergeant Pierce gave me the details of each of the shootings. 44th Street and Van Buren would be my first stop, then onto 9th Street and Indian School Road.

"It looks like they're both going to make it, but you know how that goes."

Yes, I did. Too many times I had received information from hospitals telling me that the victim was stable and going to be just fine, only to find out later that they succumbed to their injuries. The same was true of those hospital prognostications of imminent death, when I found out later the victim was easily going to make it.

"Could you call both of the patrol supervisors and let them know that I'll respond to 44th Street first, so I can release those units still there. Then I'll head to the Indian School Road shooting and take care of that investigation."

"I'll call the on-scene supervisors and let them know you are en route," he said before I hung up the phone.

I don't drink coffee, and even if I did, I wouldn't take the time to sit and brew some while officers are securing crime scenes. The ultimate goal and unwritten rule of any call-out investigator was to try to respond to a crime scene within one hour. That wasn't easy for me, living as I did in the suburb of Chandler. It was a twenty-minute drive just to get to the borders of southern Phoenix, plus another half hour to get to the northern ones. Thankfully, over the last five years, the Department of Transportation had built some freeways that connect all the cities of the greater metro area. It wasn't always that way. A shower and a quick shave would put me out on 44th Street in less than forty-five minutes.

When I arrived at 44th Street and Van Buren, I noticed two police cars in the convenience store parking lot. There was no crime scene tape anywhere, though that is usually what greets detectives in these responses. As I parked my car on the north side of the store, I was approached by a familiar face, Sergeant Dave Schweikert. Dave had been a school resource officer at a central Phoenix high school for years. I didn't even know that he'd been promoted to sergeant. I had met with him numerous times over the years, trying to assess school threats to one degree or another. He was a solid officer, and I could only hope that he was a good supervisor.

"Hey Clark, how you been?" He asked.

We shook hands and exchanged pleasantries.

"I'm doing great, except for having to get my butt out of bed," I kidded with a smile. I didn't mind getting called out at all. I looked at it as getting a firsthand look at what happened.

"Yeah, sorry about that. I was going to just have my guys take this, but they said they called you so we stood by."

He obviously didn't know about the other cases.

"I've been tasked with investigating a series of these shootings. So from now on, if you have one, you'll see my shining face." It was important for him to know this information to pass on to other patrolman and supervisors. "So I hear you got much of nothing."

"Well, we got one Tony Curtis Long, black male, says he was shot while walking north on 44th Street just south of here. Tony wasn't too cooperative, but we've got no scene, Clark. My guys walked up and down both sides of 44th Street, and we didn't find any evidence. The Circle K clerk called 911 when Tony came into the store. At this point, we're not even sure if it occurred around here." That was the suspicious side of his police consciousness at work. If something can't be explained, then the explanation is wrong. "Said he thinks he saw a white car pass him after he was shot. Not sure if it was related, though. The best part is we got no witnesses."

Sergeant Schweikert handed me the personal information on the victim and the responding officer's information. I could expect supplemental reports from everyone before I left.

This was just like the others so far. Possible drive-by, no suspect seen, no witness, and no evidence, besides the victim's wounds. He was black, so it could be racially motivated, maybe not. No confrontation either.

It was at this point that the astute cop in Sergeant Schweikert came to the forefront. "Did you say you were working a series of these shootings?" I could see he was puzzled.

"Yes," I responded. "We have had five of these so far, all on the west side of town. This is the first time I have been east of Central Avenue. But that's where this one and the other happened tonight."

"Did you hear about the one we had a month or so ago?" the sergeant asked. "It's similar to this one. Black male, just north of here, also got shot in what we thought was a drive-by with a shotgun. Patrol officers took the report. The victim was shot right in front of the Radisson Hotel up there." He pointed to the north.

This is the first that I had heard of this shooting.

"No kidding. When did you say this happened?"

Now he had my full attention.

"I'm thinking about a month or so ago. You should be able to find it. Victim survived, but couldn't give the officers any reason he was shot. Just like this one."

Sergeant Schweikert racked his brain for more information. Just then, one of the officers who responded handed me Tony's bloody T-shirt.

"Hey, I appreciate the info. I'll see if I can find anything when I get back to the office."

That was the understatement of the year. I would find that report, or the analysts would start digging until they found it.

There was nothing more to do here besides walk the scene myself. No photos had been taken because there was nothing to see. Except for the sidewalk and street, the area where Tony Long was shot was completely barren. Nothing but desert and brush. I would come back in the daylight and see if anything, like a shot cup, could be located.

It was time to get to the next scene and see if I could learn anything else, like maybe some kind of a clue as to why these two victims had been targeted.

I arrived at the second crime scene just as the sun was getting ready to come up. It was light enough to see the parking lots of the adjacent businesses, and Tuesday morning traffic was just starting to crowd the road.

As I parked just outside the crime scene, another familiar face stood out among the several officers crowded at the hood of one of the patrol vehicles. The large body of one Lieutenant John Collins shaded almost the entire front end of the Chevy Caprice.

John Collins had just made lieutenant and had been sent to third shift in the Squaw Peak Precinct, my old stomping grounds. I had worked with John as a sergeant at the police academy for years when we were both defensive tactics instructors. Once referred to as arrest tactics, they were now called defensive tactics, and we taught the techniques that are used in all situations that police officers encounter, not just ones where arrests are made. I'm sure some administrator requested the name change out of a fear from the politically-correct crowd and civil liability lawyers.

John stood about six feet four inches and weighed around two fifty. He had played some football in his youth and still looked like he could put the pads on and crush somebody. He was intimidating, and when he told recruits they needed to work on their upper-body strength, they listened. I enjoyed teaching defense tactics with John. One of the best training modules is what was referred to as the "red man" training. A fully padded uniform, the red man suit was so named because of its color. The suit was worn by tactical instructors so that the recruits could get hands-on training dealing with violent offenders. In other words, it was an all-out brawl. The suit was supposed to protect the instructor from injury, but half the time an area would end up exposed to a knee, an elbow, a kick, or even a baton. The bruises would stay around for days. It was fun for the recruits and fun for the instructors. John liked to wear the suit, and so did I. Every once in a while, we got to dish out some pain, too.

"I heard you were coming. I told everyone here that you would be dressed sharp, the same colored belt and shoes," John boomed.

He was right of course. Just because most cops don't know how to dress doesn't mean I had to follow in their footsteps.

"Hello, John. How the hell are you?" I shook his large hand. "Congratulations on your promotion. This department will promote anyone, won't they?"

The officers stood stunned around the patrol vehicle, never hearing a subordinate talk to a Lieutenant that way.

"Damn tootin they will," he fired back. "Clark, let me introduce you to Sergeant Veach. She will be briefing you as to what we've got."

The sergeant looked as new and as green as some of the officers. I'm sure having her lieutenant standing over her shoulder didn't help the situation. But she had all her notes together, and she seemed prepared.

I opened my notepad and said, "OK, Sergeant Veach, let me have it."

Patrol officers had responded directly to the VA Hospital in reference to the shooting victim, Fredric Sena. There, they had learned that Fredric had been shot at the A-1 Liquor Store, where we were currently standing. Fredric had told them about his trek from the liquor store to the VA. They had taken a look at his wound and could tell that he had been shot with a shotgun. He was listed in critical condition and had been transported to a trauma center.

She pointed toward the center of the liquor store parking lot and stated that the victim's belongings were sitting there. No shell casings had been recovered, and they'd walked the entire lot, streets, and alley around the liquor store. They had discovered Fredric's path to the VA Hospital by backtracking his blood trail.

Since Fredric had related little about what had happened to him, it was time to assess the scene. If he'd been shot in the back, he could've been standing anywhere in the parking lot with his back to one of the streets or even the alley. It was best to start at his belongings.

As I walked up to the drive-thru lane, I saw blood pools on the raised median, his property, and the parking lot. All of the blood was concentrated in this area, except for his pathway from the lot toward the VA. Although blood stains can be deceiving, they can be left where a person was initially struck, moved to after a person was struck, or stopped after being hit. Finding the person's position at the initial shooting point is important because it may yield collateral bullet strikes, or in this case, pellet strikes.

I began checking his property that was on the ground: a box, a stool, the paint cans. No pellet strikes. I checked the support poles to the covered drive-thru and could find no strikes. There were several advertisement signs around the drive-thru, so I began to check the ones in the immediate area of his property. Again, no strikes.

As I began to inspect the liquor store, I moved to a black-and-silver Bacardi sign just south of the drive-thru window. It was made of cheap cardboard, and two-cent fasteners kept it attached to the building. It didn't take long to see the numerous holes in the sign. As I squatted to bring myself eye level with the sign, I peered back toward the street. Based on the height of the sign and where it was struck, Fredric had to be sitting next to his property, probably on the stool, with his back to both Indian School Road and 9th Street. The shot had been fired from the corner of 9th Street or just a little east, say as the car turned the corner.

I began to inspect the area below the sign. Sitting right below it were three gray shotgun pellets. I recognized them immediately.

The Bacardi sign was marked, photographed, and pulled as evidence. All of Frederic's personal belongings were also marked and photographed. They would be collected later. His sunglasses, footstool, which I learned doubled as a toolbox, and his Internet media hardware.

But a big piece of the puzzle was missing. What kind of shotgun was used? The only way to figure that out would be to find the shot cup.

I solicited the help of the remaining officers. We were going to find that shot cup if it took all day. I explained to them what I was looking for, and we began to scour the parking lot.

An hour into the search, I became frustrated. What happened to it? Could it have flown off course and onto the roof of the liquor store? No way. Could it have careened off the building and disintegrated? I couldn't imagine that. These cups are made of hard plastic and fired from a gun. It might break up a little, but we should be able to find the majority of it anyway.

We continued to search. Still nothing. It was now pushing 9:00 a.m., it was getting hot, and I was growing tired. Your mind starts to wander when you're trying to find something you know is there, but you can't see it. Did somebody pick it up and throw it away, not knowing what it was? Is it stuck in the victim's clothing? Is God punishing me?

It was fruitless. The shot cup couldn't be found. It was time to pick up all the other evidence and get to the hospitals to interview the victims.

The media box was bloodstained on the top and had been opened some time prior to Fredric being shot. Blood could be seen inside the box. It was too big for a conventional evidence bag, so I grabbed a plastic garbage bag. As I lifted the box and its hardware, I discovered something that made me very happy. Hiding under the box, out of anyone's view, and the last place I would've ever looked was the shot cup. There it sat, in all its glory, just waiting to be found.

As I examined it, I could see it was skinnier than the shot cups I was used to finding. It certainly wasn't a 12 gauge, and it looked too thin to even be a 20 gauge. When I got back to headquarters, the firearms boys were going to get a visit from me. I needed to know what kind of weapon I was dealing with.

I remembered that, at the James Hodge scene, a supposed 20 gauge shotgun wadding had been located. If the assailant was using multiple shotguns, it would be unusual to say the least, but not unheard of. Whoever was doing the shooting was starting to rack up a long list of victims. Maybe a trip to the hospitals and a visit with the victims would clear things up.

I wasn't holding my breath.

✛

Walking into St. Joseph's Hospital, I could only hope that Fredric Sena was still down in the ER awaiting a bed. I was pointed to Administration and then told he had been moved to a regular floor, not ICU. My luck was changing.

As I got off the elevator, I beelined to the nurses' station. It looked like a busy morning.

"Can I help you?" a rather large receptionist/desk aide bellowed.

I introduced myself and told her I was there to see Fredric Sena. I had already pulled my flat badge and showed it to her to stop the identification runaround.

"Oh, yes. He's in room 614. His nurse is Megan, and I think she's with him now."

Megan was checking Fredric's vitals and writing something down. The room had two beds, but Fredric had the room to himself. He saw me as did Megan. I introduced myself and asked Fredric how he was feeling. Megan turned toward him too, just in case he gave her some insight that she thought was important.

"I could be doing a hell of a lot worse," Fredric said.

He was right. He could be paralyzed or dead. Megan dismissed herself from the room to give us some privacy. I asked her if I could talk to her for a minute after the interview, and she politely agreed.

"Well, Fredric, what can you tell me about what happened to you, or at least what you remember?"

Fredric began to tell me about his night, how he couldn't sleep, and that he had a job painting the liquor store drive-thru. He'd been at the liquor store for about half an hour before he got shot. He was sitting on his toolbox facing the liquor store. "I had just opened up the box that I'd found when I heard the loud bang, and the shot hit me. Man, I don't know what was going on or why anyone would shoot me. I was just minding my own business getting ready to paint. You know, the owner hired me. It was a paying job, real cash," he said.

"I'm glad that you're gainfully employed," I said.

"Thanks. I try not to sponge off people. I try to support myself. It's not easy out there on the street, you know. People always trying to take advantage of you. Look at this, I was just sitting there and got shot. I didn't deserve this."

"I know you didn't, Fredric, but can you tell me anything else that might help? Did you see anyone in the area, either on foot, or in a car who may have looked suspicious? Anyone have a reason to shoot you?" I asked.

"I did see a car, a blue one, drive by a couple of times before I was shot. I thought that was strange. I didn't see anyone around before the shooting. I did have some problems with some guys, but I didn't see them around."

We talked about those problems, and they did not seem to be related, though you never know for sure.

From what Fredric could tell me, what little he could tell me, he was obviously the victim of another random shooting. Once again, a victim alone, shot late at night or early in the morning like the others, and shot one time with a shotgun. No one was seen, and there was no known motive.

I asked Fredric to sit up from his bed so that I could see his wounds. They were uncovered and looked like most of the other victims. He was shot from a medium distance, which probably saved his life. The pellets had impacted him in the upper back, shoulders, neck, and lower head area.

I left my card with Fredric and wished him a speedy recovery. I told him to contact me if anything else came up, or if he remembered any other details. He was smiling as I left the room. It would be the last time I saw Fredric.

Twenty-four days later, on July 14th, 2006, Fredric Sena would be pronounced dead at the VA Hospital. His cause of death would be listed as "liver failure due to ethanol." No mention of his wounds or blood loss from the shotgun blast. No calls made to investigators for any input. No autopsy would be performed. Fredric died by himself.

Fredric's death would be further scrutinized later.

◆

As a matter of common knowledge, County Hospital was the preferred choice of many an injured or shot police officer. The hospital dealt with so many shootings from the city. The ER's reputation was great. Shooting victims would be brought there and pronounced dead before arrival, and then somehow miraculously be brought back to life by the ER staff. They also had the best burn unit in the state, if not in all the western states.

I took the elevator to the 4th floor, found a nursing station, and was escorted to Tony Long's room. He shared a room with three other patients. Tony's bed sat just inside the door. He was half-asleep when the nurse tapped his shoulder.

"This detective is here to see you, Tony."

All the heads of the other patients immediately jerked toward Tony's side of the room. They all hoped to pick up some kind of street chatter, something they might be able to pass on to someone. You got to love County Hospital. The information network here was almost as good as the one in County Lock-up.

"How you doin, Detective?" Tony asked as he began to situate himself as comfortably as someone could who had been shot in the side.

"A lot better than you, I guess."

Tony seemed friendly enough. I could see where he could come off as a hard-ass, if he wanted. For a guy who spends a lot of time on the street, Tony was well built. Since he appeared lucid, it was time to ask some questions.

"Tony, I'm the detective in charge of this case. I don't know squat about what happened. I know what you told officers who responded to the Circle K, but beyond that I know nothing. Think you might be able to fill in the blanks for me?" I asked.

Tony shrugged his large shoulders. "I wish I could. I don't know what the hell happened myself. I was just walking to the store when someone drove by me and shot. You see what happened for yourself."

He turned to his side to show his wounds.

"You know anyone that would want to shoot you, or did you have any troubles last night? Anything?"

He was respectful. "No sir, I didn't do anything to anyone. Got no reason for anyone to want to shoot me."

Tony related his travel direction and itinerary for that night. He was out with his cousin, got separated, ended up on 44th Street, and got shot.

"Did you see anyone around? Officers said that you might have seen a white car close by," I asked.

"No! I looked around right after I heard the bang and got shot. I didn't see nobody. The white car I was telling them about came by after the shooting. I don't think it had anything to do with whoever shot me," Tony said.

He was confident, which made me confident. No white car to start looking for at this point.

I contacted the nursing staff, and they showed me Tony's X-rays. His left side took the brunt of the shotgun blast. He was stable, but surgery was unavoidable. One of the pellets had lodged next to his jugular vein in his neck, a very dangerous place to operate on, let alone have a pellet lodged. I, of course, asked that any pellets removed be saved as evidence for further analyses. They agreed.

I was tired, and it was pushing early afternoon. I'd gotten four hours of sleep, which is more than I managed sometimes, but the heat had worn me down. It was time to get back to the office. I needed to impound all the evidence from the Sena case. The only evidence I had to show that Tony had been shot was his body and the green shirt he wore that morning.

As important as the impounding was, there was a more pressing issue: research. As in, who got shot in early May, and can I locate that victim?

CHAPTER 16

I dropped all the bags, plastic envelopes, and paper sacks full of evidence from the Sena and Long cases next to my chair and let it overflow into the aisle. I picked up the phone and called Planning and Research.

The Crime Analysis and Research Unit, CARU, had been in existence for several years now. One of the better brainchildren of the department, CARU conducted criminal research that investigators used to have to do. The unit had also expanded into such areas as crime forecasting and mapping. That entailed trying to predict when serial criminals would hit and where. It was a form of profiling, only it concerned a target area instead of a person. The secretary put me through to one of the analysts, someone I had worked with before.

Renee Brugeman had been in CARU for as long as I could remember. She had been a good resource over the years and was a no-nonsense person. She knew I was on the other end.

"What's up, Clark."

"Hi, Renee, I need you to do some research for me. I'm investigating a series of shotgun shootings on the west, and now east, side of Phoenix. I was told that there was a shooting somewhere in the area of 44ᵗʰ Street and Van Buren sometime in May. It probably occurred at night, and was around the Radisson Hotel, which is just south of the 202 freeway. Looks like the victim may have survived because patrol officers took the report. I don't think any detectives went out there."

"I heard about those shootings. So you're the lucky person doing the follow-ups? You know, Aimee Cardenas and I worked the cases of the .22 caliber shootings last year," she said.

I knew Aimee, and she was a good analyst.

"I didn't know that, but I assumed. Anyway, I don't know much more about the shooting besides that it was a black male. Wish I could be more helpful."

It was time for them to work their magic.

"That should be plenty. You're sure it was in May? I can go back further if we need to."

"Let's look at May, and if we come up empty, we can enlarge the search. How quick can you get on this?"

I didn't want to appear pushy, but I needed to find this case if it was related.

"Well, for you, I'll start looking now. I can get you something by the end of the day."

"Thank you, dear. I'll wait to hear from you." I hung up the phone.

As I looked at the bags of evidence, my head started to hurt. I'm one of those seven to eight hours of sleep kind of guys. Plus, I sweat like a pig at a barbeque. Then my clothes start to stick to my arms and legs, and that's uncomfortable. I was starting to feel a foul mood coming on. I needed to get this property logged and the reports started.

My notepad was full of information about the most recent shootings. I tried to find any dissimilarity between these two new shootings and the others. I could find none, except that they were on opposite sides of Phoenix. The earlier shotgun shootings had gotten no press coverage, so the chance of a copycat was little or none.

A copycat! The revelation hit me like a tsunami. Could it be that whoever was responsible for the rash of recent shotgun shootings had actually learned about the .22 caliber cases from 2005? What if some sorry lowlife had followed the series through the media and decided to pick it up after the long layoff? That could explain the weapons change. Of course, so could *America's Most Wanted* airing of the .22 caliber weapon. How was it that the world's best crime show would air the most significant piece of information on the case? Loose lips sink ships. I had already made up my mind that if these cases went public, there would be no comment from the lead investigator.

I grabbed my trusty notepad and added the names and case numbers of Tony Long and Fredric Sena to the ever-growing list. I also added a notation: copycat theory?

It was late in the afternoon, and I needed to brief my sergeant and lieutenant just as soon as I got this property sealed.

I had just filled out the last envelope when out of my peripheral vision I saw a hand with a report dangling from it. It was Renee from CARU. No way could she have found it that fast. She was hovering over me like a buzzard.

"See if this looks familiar."

She already knew that it was the case I'd been looking for. I pulled the report from her hand. It was dated May 2, 2006. I looked at the address. It was right at, or near, the location of the Radisson Hotel on 44th Street. A patrol officer had taken the original report. No detective had been called out.

"Oh, by the way, Scottsdale Police had a murder the same night. A female, murdered with a shotgun. It came up in our research of the 2005 cases. I have her name here … Cruz, Claudia Gutierrez-Cruz. Here's the info."

"Really," I said.

I scribbled her name down on the notepad containing my ever-growing list.

"I remember reading about her. I'll have to check with Scottsdale about that."

For now, it was back to the report burning a hole in my hand.

The victim was one Kibili Tambadu. A black male, seventeen years of age, who lived just a few blocks from the shooting. But what really caught my eye was the suspect description, or should I say, descriptions. Kibili had listed two black males as the culprits, their ages fifteen to thirty. His injuries were a shotgun wound to the back.

Before I even began to read the report, I knew that Kibili was someone I would be talking to . . . and soon.

◈

In the heart of East Phoenix sits an unusual site, at least as far as the desert goes. Proclaimed as the most advanced facility in North or South America, the Chinese Cultural Center looks like a knock-off of the famous Graumann's Chinese Theatre in Hollywood. Located on 44th Street, just a mile or so from Sky Harbor Airport, the center is an Asian gem in what many believe to be a very unsophisticated town. Its architecture echoes that of Shanghai, with its replicas of pagodas and numerous decorations.

The Chinese Cultural Center has some of the best dining in the city, and its shops are unique. If Chinese food is your mainstay, then you've come to the right place. Restaurants offer Szechuan, Cantonese, and Mandarin cuisines with the old-fashioned American establishment of the all-you-can-eat seafood buffet. Inside the center is a market, if you decide that you want to try some of their specialties at home.

It was too late for Kibili Tambadu to stop for dinner or shop on the evening of May 2, 2006. As he walked to school or the store, he would pass the center and marvel at the uniqueness of the buildings. It almost seemed out of place in the desert. He didn't know that the Phoenix Metro Area had become a haven for a lot of Asian immigrants. There weren't a whole lot of them around his neighborhood, but then again, he spent most of his time working on his English studies because he, too, was the son of an immigrant.

In 1991, Kibili's father was killed in the West African nation of Sierra Leone. He, like Kibili's grandfather, had been an international trader dealing in commodities such as gold and diamonds. When the war started and Kibili's father was killed, his mother, along with thousands of other refugees, left Sierra Leone. For six years, they holed up in a refugee camp in the neighboring nation of Gambia. His mother, Isatu, and Kibili's three siblings struggled to stay alive while living in a shack.

In 1997, the United Nations, as part of their resettlement program, reached out and touched Kibili and his family. They were told to go to the airport. Plane tickets would be waiting for them. They had no idea where they were going.

When they arrived at the airport, they learned that they were being sent to the United States. It was a good fit since all the family spoke English to some degree or another. The destination on the ticket read "Phoenix, Arizona." They had no idea where Phoenix was or what kind of place it would be. Isatu wasn't about to complain. She was happy to have a chance to rebuild all of their lives.

Upon settling in Phoenix, they realized that the landscape was mostly desert, unlike the tropical forests of Sierra Leone. Kibili and his siblings began to attend school, and Isatu found work caring for the elderly at an assisted living home. It was a field she had worked in for years at the refugee camp.

After arriving in the U.S., they owned no transportation. Kibili and his family adapted to taking the bus and walking. They flew under the radar for nine years until fate would change their lives.

It was a Tuesday night, and Isatu arrived home late from work around 8:30 p.m. Kibili and his brother Banta lived in a two-bedroom apartment, along with their mother and Banta's child.

Isatu heard the baby screaming before she even got to the apartment door. They were out of milk, and the baby needed some. Kibili was tasked with going to the store to get some. He knew that the market inside the Cultural Center closed at 9:00 p.m., so he would have to head to another store.

The closest was the Circle K convenience store, located at 44th Street and Van Buren. Kibili had made the trek numerous times before, though usually not this late. It was a around 9:30 p.m. when he left the apartment. It was a school night, and he needed to get to the store and back before it got too late.

Kibili took his usual path to the store. He would take the back streets east to the Cultural Center, then walk south to the convenience store. The one-mile walk from his apartment would usually take him about fifteen minutes, navigating through the maze of streets along the way. At this time of night, there were few vehicles on the streets.

He arrived at the store around 10:00 p.m. and grabbed the milk. There would be no conversation with the clerk tonight. He needed to get home.

As he walked up 44th Street, he could see the grand driveway to the entrance of the Radisson Hotel. It curved and circled toward the main entrance about hundred yards off the road. The sign on 44th Street for the hotel was too small, Kibili thought, it should have been much bigger The lawn surrounding the property was wet. It had just been watered, and the excess had dribbled onto the sidewalk and run down the curb. It made the immediate area a little humid, which is very unusual for Phoenix in May.

The plastic bag holding the one-gallon milk jug weighed heavy in his right hand, so he shifted it to his left. As he completed the transfer, he heard what he would later describe as a "boom." He hadn't heard that type of noise before, and it startled him. He saw a blue Honda Civic, with what he initially thought were two black males in it, drive by him going the same direction as he was walking. Instantaneously, he felt stinging pain in his back. He felt as if his shirt was on fire and spun around quickly. He saw no flames as he twisted his head around. He noticed blood on his right arm. It was hard to see where it was coming from, but the pain grew more intense.

Out of anger he yelled, but he didn't make any sense. Kibili began to question what happened. Did somebody throw something at him? Was it an explosive of some kind set off close to him? He was having a hard time assessing his injuries. He felt blood starting to ooze down his back, then his shorts. The sidewalk now painted red with drops of blood.

It took a couple of seconds for Kibili to realize he had been shot. It had never happened to him before—all that time spent in a war zone and not a real scratch to speak of. All the blood of his native country spilled, none of it his. He needed help.

He started to make his way through the landscaping and bushes that surrounded the Radisson Hotel. He stumbled over an extension cord unfurled in the rock and grass, left there by the landscapers.

The parking lot to the hotel was full of cars. Kibili hoped to find help before he passed out. He walked through the circular driveway and straight for the front doors. Four huge cultured stone columns decorated the drive. A wooden bench sat just outside the front doors, a pick-up point for travelers awaiting the courtesy van to drive them to the airport.

As Kibili walked up, the automatic sliding glass doors opened. He stumbled inside. Two large couches with a nice oriental rug decorated the lobby area. He called for help. Kibili was bleeding profusely now, and one of the registering guests called 911 for him. He was led from the registration area to the bench just outside. There was no sense in scaring all the guests and bleeding all over the lobby. Kibili hoped that paramedics would arrive soon.

Police and fire arrived almost simultaneously. Kibili was whisked away to Banner Good Samaritan Hospital. He was lucky, his wounds were not life-threatening.

Police cordoned off the scene. An initial interview would lead police to believe that Kibili had been the victim of a drive-by shooting. None of the guests in or around the hotel lobby had stayed to talk to police. Everyone seemed oblivious to what had just happened in front of the hotel. No witnesses had come forward, and no motive established.

Word would later come from the hospital that Kibili had survived. He had talked to an officer at the hospital and told him that he heard two bangs, not just one. He also told him about the blue Honda Civic that had just passed him when he was shot. Maybe the guys were Mexican instead of black, now he wasn't sure of that either. What was a fact was that he had been shot with a shotgun. The doctor told him that he was lucky.

Later, a reconstruction would show that, as Kibili walked, his right arm swung backward in its usual motion as the shot had been fired. The pellets had hit his right triceps and right hand squarely, but the pellets that hit his lower back had more or less skimmed the surface. The rest of the blast missed him completely. The shot had been fired just as the car pulled even with Kibili. He had suffered severe damage in at least two of his fingers.

Back at the scene, patrol officers and their supervisor had decided that they would take this investigation. No detectives would be called out. Photographs would be taken of the blood trail and of Kibili's injuries.

Why did this happen? Who would do this? Those were questions yet to be answered.

I put the report down on my cluttered desk and realized that serial gunmen were loose on the streets of Phoenix. With crime the way it was and the number of unsolved shootings always increasing, who really knew how many other crimes had been committed by the assailant(s)?

Renee had left me alone with my thoughts. How was I going to convince my chain of command that another serial criminal was loose and stalking innocent civilians on the streets of Phoenix?

I pulled all the other reports again and started to review them. The shootings, up until recently, had all been on the west side of town: James Hodge, Miguel Rodriguez, Darrel Davies, Paul Patrick, and Elizabeth Clark. Now I had three confirmed random shootings that were east side: Fredric Sena, Tony Long, and now Kibili Tambadu. There was no rhyme or reason for the shooting locations, except that they were all in Phoenix, with the possible exception of Miss Cruz in Scottsdale.

Theories abound when you're dealing with location changes on serial crimes. Almost all criminal forecasters say that criminals commit more crimes in areas they're familiar with, but circumstances beyond the perpetrators' control can change those dynamics. For example, extensive media coverage can cause a criminal to change their previous patterns.

Plus, criminals can be familiar with numerous areas, especially if they live and work in different locations. The serial criminals with the most success change cities and states because they know that communication between police agencies is extremely rare. If the crime or the circumstances surrounding the incident are not unusual, it's possible to commit numerous crimes in multiple jurisdictions. Sooner or later, however, serial criminals are caught because of greed, conceit, or stupidity—sometimes, a combination of all three.

In this case, it was time for me to start theorizing the possible links between the 2005 cases and the 2006 cases.

Since I had received no information from other police agencies, I had to assume that these recent shotgun shootings were a Phoenix problem. It was becoming obvious to me that the .22 cases of 2005 were related, but since we had no current record of random small caliber shootings, I had to concentrate on the weapon of choice at the moment, a shotgun.

All of the shootings were random. There were no intentional targets, and it was clearly not racially motivated—African Americans, Anglos, Hispanics had all been targeted. There had been male and female victims.

Due to the wide variety of distances in these shootings, the different traveling directions of the suspect vehicle, and the low probability of such good marksmanship, I believed there were at least two shooters working in tandem. In this way, this case reminded me of the famous Beltway/D.C. sniper shootings.

But the shooters, if there were two, had developed several unique patterns. With the possible exception of Claudia Gutierrez-Cruz, they were shooting people with a shotgun on main streets or arteries in the City of Phoenix. As far as I knew, the shooters hadn't targeted any people in other jurisdictions. That could all change if we asked the other cities to start to check with their criminal analysts and cold case files. But for now, I was going to assume that Phoenix was their hunting ground.

In addition, all of the victims were alone when they were shot. The shootists had made sure, whether by luck or skill, that the only witnesses to the shootings were the traumatized victims. All had been on foot except for Elizabeth Clark, who had been riding her bicycle. The suspects also weren't afraid to double up or even triple up their shootings. That had happened twice. These shooters weren't just satisfied with one kill or maiming. They were going to get their money's worth.

Lastly, the suspects were night hunters. The earliest shooting that occurred was at 10:05 p.m., Kibili Tambadu. The latest, Elizabeth Clark, at 2:25 a.m. I looked at the summary provided by CARU of the Claudia Gutierrez-Cruz murder.

As I looked at the time and the location, the shooting of Kibili Tambadu's shooting was twenty minutes earlier than Claudia Gutierrez-Cruz's homicide. The locations were only a few miles apart. There had been plenty of time to drive from one shooting to the other.

Scottsdale was not going to be happy. As much as anyone would want to distance themselves from these Phoenix's shootings, there was no way they could ignore this information. Both the shooting of Kibili Tambadu and Claudia's shootings were alleged drive-bys with shotguns.

It was time to contact Scottsdale . . . and share the bad news.

CHAPTER 17

"Nine! How the hell did we end up with nine shootings? The last I heard it was seven, including the ones last night."

The LT had a point. Seven looked better than nine. But nine was the right number.

I began to explain my math. "Well, when I was out investigating Tony Long's shooting, I was informed that patrol officers had investigated a previous shooting in the area, sometime in May. I had CARU research it and, sure enough, one Kibili Tambadu was shot on May 2nd, 2006, a little after 10:00 p.m. He was shot in a drive-by with a shotgun, a few blocks north of where Tony Long was shot. Same M.O."

"OK, that's eight by my math and your notes here," he said. I had handed the LT my scribbles of names and locations so he could follow along, and so I wouldn't have to recite verbatim each victim. "What's behind lucky door number nine?" he asked.

"Scottsdale," I said. "Same night that Kibili was shot. Twenty minutes or so later, a female by the name of Claudia Gutierrez-Cruz was murdered. I read about it in the paper, and confirmed it with CARU. She was also the victim of a drive-by and was shot with a shotgun. Same M.O. Scottsdale is treating it as an isolated incident, not related to any of the .22 caliber shootings. They don't know about these latest series of shotgun shootings, however."

"I can see why. Those shootings were .22s, not shotguns. Yours are the only ones with shotguns," the LT stated. "If I were them, I would try to distance myself, too. This is a nightmare."

"There's a problem with that theory, though. There were shotgun shootings at the end of the string of .22 calibers," I said. My chain of command knew only parts of the .22 caliber story, as did I, originally.

I continued. "On the night of December 29th, and into the 30th, 2005, Phoenix had two murders and one attempted murder downtown." This was going to be complicated. "Before those murders, but on the same night, there was the shooting of a dog with a shotgun in central Phoenix. Victim's name was Whitner, and her dog was killed. It looks random."

Sergeant Clarke had been sitting quietly in the corner, but pounced on the dog-shooting information. "A dog? What the hell does a dog have to do with your shootings?" A fair question from the uninformed.

"I was just getting to that. Animals and humans were shot with .22s last year, but then we have a dog shot with a shotgun. See the relationship? I believe whoever was shooting animals and humans back in 2005 has now permanently changed weapons, and is solely targeting humans with a shotgun. The M.O. fits. Plus, there was another shooting that wasn't given a lot of coverage on the same night. It's a little more complex."

"Great, I can't wait to hear this," the LT cracked.

"OK," I said, "follow along. The Whitner dog is shot early on December 29th, 2005, with a shotgun. Later that night, there are two murders of transients and one attempted murder downtown, with a .22. As we're picking up bodies downtown, a couple of more dogs are shot on the west side of town. Small caliber, probably .22s. Now it's time for the piece de résistance. Another female is shot a couple of hours later on Van Buren with a shotgun. The gunmen were using two types of weapons on the same night."

"Who's the female, and what happened to her?" Sergeant Clarke asked. "And what time was this?"

"It's a long story, but she was prostituting herself on Van Buren. She sees a car a couple of times and … blamo, she gets shot. Nothing serious, but the connection is real. So, I guess that makes ten or eleven shotgun shootings, if you want to count the dog," I said.

"I don't want to count any go*damn dog," the LT gasped. "Have you contacted Scottsdale? What do they say about this?"

"I haven't talked to them, yet. I wanted to brief you first; in case one of their supervisors called and asked what the hell we were doing, linking their shooting to our series."

"I appreciate that," the LT quipped. "What the hell is going on with those .22 caliber cases anyway?"

"I talked to Jewell. There's nothing. They're dead in the water," I said. "As far as he knows, there haven't been any other random .22 shootings since December."

"Keep me and Sergeant Clarke informed and figure out what Scottsdale is going to do."

I sat motionless for a second. I know he expected me to get out of his office, but I needed to state the obvious. "Ok, um, Houston, we have a problem."

They both looked at me as if to say, "Spit it out."

"We have a person or persons committing multiple shootings in the Valley. I am sure they're related. At some point, we may need to gather some bodies and look at how to strategically handle this. I'm not panicking, but sooner or later someone is going to catch onto this, and we need to have a response ready."

I did not want to use the word "task force." The thought of it made me ill, but it was time to broach the idea.

The LT sighed. "I hear what you're saying, Clarkster, but right now is not the time. If we had more information or some leads, that would be different. But right now, correct me if I'm wrong, you ain't got squat. We're taking this seriously, and I'll discuss it with the chain of command. I agree with you. I think you're on to something, and if I know you, you'll figure it out and make us all look good. But, for right now, this bureau couldn't even take on another task force, let alone support one. The Baseline Killer has all the eyes, ears, and money. Course that could change if you do something wonderful, or if there are more shootings. Keep plugging along, and I appreciate your hard work,"

As I walked out of Lieutenant Benson's office, Sergeant Clarke grabbed my arm and started to walk with me.

"I agree with you, that we need to get some manpower on this right now, but he's right. You got nothing," he said.

"Oh, I know, and I agree with him. I just want to make sure the chain of command knows."

Most of the time, I could care less what the managers know, but this was not the time to be selfish.

Sergeant Clarke continued. "You said 'gunmen' in there. What did you mean by that? I thought you were looking into one lone gunman."

"It's a theory I have, along with some others. I would rather not expound on it now. I'll let you know if it starts to play out." It was too early to lay my cards out on the table.

Sergeant Clarke's face wore a little sheepish grin. "I've seen some of your theories play out. Your instincts are usually excellent. Just be careful here. Soon, everybody is going to be watching."

No truer words have been spoken.

◈

"Scottsdale Police Department," the young female voice on the other end of the phone said. She sounded like a teenager.

"Homicide Bureau, please," I asked.

"One second, please."

"Homicide, how can I help you?" the male voice asked.

"Hey, this is Detective Schwartzkopf, Phoenix Police. I need to get a hold of Detective Pete Salazar. Is he in by any chance?"

"No, Pete's out of the office for the week. Can I help you with something?" The detective was courteous and sounded eager to help. That isn't always the case.

"Well, I need to talk to him about a case. I'm investigating some shootings, and I want to bounce some information off him. See if we can help each other." In a small agency like Scottsdale, this detective would probably know something about the case, but it was more important to get it from the horse's mouth.

"Let me put you through to our sergeant, Don Bellandier. Maybe he can help you out. Hold on a sec."

A few seconds later another male answered. "Sergeant Don Bellandier."

Another introduction was appropriate. Most people butchered my name anyway. "Sergeant, this is Detective Schwartzkopf. I'm with the Phoenix Police. I was calling trying to get a hold of Pete Salazar, and I understand he's gone. I would like to get some information from you or another detective about one of your murders."

"OK, Pete is out of town, but I might be able to help you."

"I'm currently investigating a series of shotgun shootings in Phoenix, and I understand that you guys caught a murder of a female in a drive-by a while back. I was wondering if you could tell me a little bit about it."

"Well, we worked with your Homicide Bureau. They should know all the details."

"Yes, unfortunately, they failed to mention your shooting. I'd like to get it straight from you guys." I paused briefly. "I'm currently looking at nine of these cases, including yours."

"Oh, I see. Well, here is what I know."

Sergeant Don Bellandier laid out what I already knew and didn't. Claudia Gutierrez-Cruz had been gunned down in a drive-by with a shotgun, a 410 shotgun. They had recovered a shot cup from inside the victim, identifying the caliber of the weapon. "We have no leads at this point. I hope your cases are going better," he said.

"Right now, I have eight of them," I said. "The last two occurred on June 20th of this year. Plus, if I take into consideration two previous ones, that makes ten." I was met with stunned silence. "By the way, don't feel bad. I don't have any leads either."

"Holy sh*%! Better you than us. Pete will be back next week. I'll have him call you as soon as he gets in the office. Maybe the two of you can get together and get some answers."

He assured me of their cooperation and hung up. I didn't tell Scottsdale about Kibili Tambadu. I needed more specifics about the time frames. It was best not to guess about a case until you get all the facts, and Detective Pete Salazar would have those facts.

CHAPTER 18

Starting in September of 2004, the Phoenix Police Department partnered with ATF to form a weapons unit. The purpose was to try to get more guns off the street and curb the violence by going after the prohibited possessors, the gun-toting felons. Everybody thought that it was a good idea and a good fit. ATF was overwhelmed with federal violations of gun cases, specifically, those involving illegal aliens. Most of those cases were being dumped for straw purchase cases, where a legal resident buys a gun or multiple guns for someone who isn't allowed to possess one.

So, it wasn't surprising that Phoenix detectives assigned to ATF would be in the information pipeline when two tips came in on the Walmart arsons. On the same day that Tony Long and Fredric Sena would be gunned down, the two tips relating the name of one of the arsonists seemed to fall from the heavens. A woman and a man had both called Silent Witness and claimed to know the identity of the "person of interest."

The media alert and subsequent release of the arsonist's photos from the surveillance videos had struck gold.

A person of interest had been named. Both the female and the male identified him from a photo that included the tattoo on his forearm. There was follow-up, including the use of GPS on a targeted vehicle that the person was known to use, all to no avail. The person of interest had vanished, even with all the follow-up provided by the tipsters. Glendale, BATF, and even their Phoenix cops couldn't locate the possible lead. The investigation of the Walmart arsons had stalled.

I had just returned from a five-day golf vacation only to find out that the shotgun shootings had taken a vacation as well. It had been eight days since the last two persons were targeted.

Detective Moncrief stopped by to tell me that there'd been no more shootings while I was gone. He cracked that I was a possible suspect since they had ceased once I left town. Cop humor.

A pile of voice mails and email messages were waiting for me. The last message on my voicemail was from Detective Darrel Smith. "Hey, Clark, can you get a hold of me? I have a shooting that I'm looking into, and I want to run the case by you, and see if you know anything about it. I'm at … Thanks I would appreciate it."

I laughed again at Detective Moncrief's joke. Nope, it wasn't me doing the shooting. As I looked at my chart, the longest time frame thus far between shootings, not including the .22 caliber shootings, had been twenty-eight days in May. And I'd been here for that whole month.

CHAPTER 19

Diane Bein could not believe how her life had spun out of control. In just a few short months, she had gone from what she thought was a loving relationship to living her life on the street. She had lived with this man, had a child with him, and loved him all the while. But he had turned out to be a bad pick. It wasn't his fault entirely. After all, it takes two to tango.

Diane was the victim of domestic violence. She had tried to work things out with her boyfriend, the father of her three-year-old daughter, but it just wasn't happening. Then she was arrested for striking him with, of all things, a vacuum attachment. It left a two-inch laceration above his eye. That was all police needed to cart her away.

It was painful losing her relationship. But that was minimal compared to what happened next. Child Protective Services opened up a case claiming Diane's daughter wasn't cared for properly, and that Diane wasn't fit to be a parent. Most of the information was supplied to CPS by her boyfriend. Soon, the child would be removed, for its safety, until a full investigation was completed.

Diana left the father of her child two days after the State took her daughter. She bummed a ride from a friend to a cheap hotel on Van Buren Street. It was all she could afford. She needed time to think, to reflect, and to get her act together. She had responsibilities, and it was time to shape up.

As Diane looked at the dingy motel room, with a pull string for the light in the bathroom, she broke down. How could she do that to her little girl? She gazed into the dimly lit mirror and saw the dark circles under her eyes. She hated where she was, and how she'd gotten there.

She grabbed her purse from the bathroom counter and fished for some relief. She poked around the package and squeezed it together: empty. Diane needed a cigarette.

The motel clerk told her of the convenience store about four blocks away. Diane took off walking, deep in her own thoughts. How was she going to get her daughter back? She needed to get a job to get back on her feet. What was her poor little girl thinking right now?

As Diane walked, she was so consumed with her own problems, she didn't notice the light-colored sedan passing her—once, then twice. It was just past 1:00 a.m. on July 1st, 2006. She was feeling sorry for herself. Who wouldn't? But, worse, she was hurting for her daughter. She sulked, walking along the sidewalk with her head down, counting the cracks like a schoolgirl.

Diane wasn't familiar with the area. It was pitch black as she walked past the Arizona Corrections Facility, a minimum-security facility built smack dab in the middle of a metropolitan city. The property was surrounded by an eight-foot chain-link fence.

The facility housed local felons who were on the way to other prisons in Arizona. If not for the State Hospital next door, it would have looked completely out of place. A lone parking lot guard stood by in a makeshift guard shack.

Diane approached the rolling exit gate to the parking lot. It stood open and was large enough to drive a semitruck through.

The street was almost empty, but a blast shattered the stillness. Diane saw a car whisk by and then felt the strikes on her face, neck, and back. The security guard jumped to his feet and peered out toward the street. He noticed a woman screaming at the top of her lungs, as blood poured down her back. The shot had hit her on her upper left side mostly, and the force had thrown her into the chain-link fence.

The night watchman stood by his post, never leaving. Was that "pop" he heard really a shot being fired? He convinced himself that it wasn't. Forget the fact that Diane was screaming. After all, this was Van Buren Street.

With blood now streaming down her upper body, Diane panicked. She looked around, unsure if it was closer to her motel or closer to the convenience market. She chose to run to the market, where there'd be a better chance of finding someone to help her.

She ran across Van Buren. The street was empty of cars. Anyone who'd been out had disappeared. She could feel her neck starting to tighten. Some of the pellets had struck her left cheek, and that area was swelling. It was getting hard for her to breathe. She was running because she needed help, but her large and small muscles all began to tighten. She wasn't going to make it. The store seemed so far off.

The Log Cabin Motel sat just east of the convenience store. Diane bent over in the driveway entrance with her hands on her knees. She saw two guys standing in the parking lot. She had run out of steam and adrenaline. She walked to them, barely able to speak. The men could see that she was bleeding profusely, and one dialed 911 while the other grabbed a towel and tried to compress the wounds.

Within minutes, police entered the Log Cabin parking lot. Diane was seated on a raised curb in the parking lot. The men who had helped her stepped back. There wasn't anything for them to tell the police. They hadn't witnessed anything besides her bleeding.

The first officer tried to talk to Diane, but she could barely speak. She pointed off to the east. The other officers who arrived began to follow her blood trail. They walked east on the south side of Van Buren for about two blocks. The darkness shielded the blood trail from its origin. Everyone out there knew by her wounds that Diane had been shot with a shotgun. The street was quickly shut down. The word filtered out over the emergency radio channels that another drive-by had been committed by the assailant wielding a shotgun.

The call came into the Violent Crimes Bureau within thirty minutes. Sergeant Pierce had been monitoring the situation from the desk. He too recognized it for what it was, another random shooting of a pedestrian. Central City Precinct was on full alert.

As he took the information down, the other line to the office rang. The night secretary answered. The supervisor on the other end needed to speak to the desk sergeant. There was a shooting of a pedestrian in Central City Precinct. They already knew that.

The secretary began to explain to the Patrol Sergeant that Sergeant Pierce was already on the phone with the on-scene supervisor, and he was gathering all the information, but thanks for calling anyway.

"You don't seem to understand," the sergeant patiently told her. "I'm not on Van Buren Street. I'm out at 16th Street and Oak. I have another one."

The phone went silent. The secretary turned to look at Sergeant Pierce and mouthed, "Pick up the other line. It's not good."

Back in 1988 the boundaries of the Squaw Peak Precinct were much different than they are today. As a young patrol officer, Central Phoenix was my area of patrol, and the precinct border went as far south as Oak Street. The northern border was Glendale Avenue.

All the field-training officers would take the young officers in Central Phoenix to the southern end of the precinct to indoctrinate them in crime fighting. Like any other part of the city, the Central Phoenix corridor had its good and bad areas.

One of those areas was 16th Street and Oak. A small apartment complex that housed eight units sat on the northwest corner. It was known to all seasoned officers as the "Hanoi Hilton," named after the infamous prison camp from the Vietnam War. The apartment complex was a haven of filth and crime. Nobody who lived there was clean, literally or figuratively. If you wanted to cut your teeth in crime fighting, this was the place to do it.

It was the best fishing hole in the precinct for picking up felons with warrants, people buying drugs, or general misfits you could intimidate into rolling on someone for something. There was always a good chance that the drivers of the cars that would pull up adjacent to the complex and park on Oak Street were driving on suspended or revoked licenses. Officers ran every license plate through the newly installed computers in their patrol cars, hoping for a stolen hit to come back, either on the plate or the car itself.

On any given night, you could find a couple of patrol cars casing the Hilton once radio traffic began to slow down, usually around midnight or 1:00 a.m. on weeknights, later on the weekends. Back then, clubs could serve alcohol till 1:00 a.m. only, and if you were patient enough, those drunks would show up at the Hilton to buy the drugs they couldn't score at the bar.

Just south of the Hilton sat a karate studio. It was dark in front of the studio, and prostitutes would hang out, hoping a john would stop by and pay the customary twenty-five dollars for oral sex. Anyone looking for anything else other than oral sex would be unpleasantly surprised. These weren't your run-of-the-mill prostitutes.

On any given night, you could find eight to ten transgender prostitutes lurking in the darkness, all of American Indian descent. Most lived in the area, and all would congregate at this corner to sell themselves. The spot became one of the biggest officer-prank locations in the city.

A field-training officer would take his new recruit to the corner and tell him to go conduct field interrogations of the prostitutes. Now, mind you, most newbies out of the Police Academy had no idea that transsexual prostitutes existed, let alone hung out at the corner of 16th Street and Oak. The unsuspecting young officer would approach the group, try to engage them into giving up their identifications, or at least their names, in the hopes of finding one or more with current warrants.

The joke was that some of the prostitutes were decent looking, and at night, it was hard to distinguish the male features. It became such a good prank that the transgenders would start to play along, hitting on the poor rookie, and flirting with him. The training officer would coax it along by saying, "I think that one likes you" or "Which one do you think is the best looking?" The rookie would invariably give in and make some comment about which one he thought was hot, or he wouldn't mind having sex with. Then much to the embarrassment of the rookie and usually in front of the other squad members, someone would tell him that they were males dressed as females. It was the ultimate in humiliation. The poor rookie would never live it down. I was fortunate enough to have spent a lot of time in Southern California before becoming a police officer, so I could spot a cross-dresser from a mile off.

As much as some things change, some rarely do. On July 1, 2006, the Hanoi Hilton at 16th Street and Oak no longer stood. It had been demolished years earlier to make room for a commercial property. The karate studio was still there, but most of the prostitutes had changed corners. Well, most had.

Jeremy Ortiz was having problems with his sexuality, enough to where he and his girlfriend were fighting about it. Jeremy had admitted to his girlfriend at the time that he was gay, yet he was jealous when other men hit on her. He also had a drinking problem. The booze, combined with the jealousy and Jeremy's own sexual confusion, made for a dangerous situation.

One night, he turned on his stove's natural gas, full blast, in his apartment and threatened to ignite it. Police had been summoned, and the adjacent apartments had been evacuated. Jeremy was sprawled out on the couch in his living room, half-conscious, not responding to police commands.

Because he was drinking so heavily, Jeremy couldn't hold a job. He began to prostitute himself. He was even prostituting himself close to where he lived, within a few blocks of 16th Street and Oak.

In the early morning hours of July 1st, Jeremy and his friend ended up getting blasted on alcohol. They had made it to their stomping grounds, a dirt parking lot behind the convenience store at 16th Street and Oak.

Just west, a small gaggle of one-story apartments used the dirt lot for parking. At one time, the lot had been paved, but not anymore. The slumlord was too cheap to repave it. The drivable cars always had a film of dust on them, and the broken-down ones were caked with dirt. Part of the dirt parking lot was a play area for the children of the run-down complex.

The commercial dumpster for the businesses overflowed with residential trash. Broken beer bottles lay strewn all around. Stupid drunks fired bottles at the dumpster. A discarded couch with its cloth barely hiding the frame, along with a box frame and mattress, had also been dumped in the lot. This, at least, was useful, serving as a bed for the homeless to sleep on.

This night, it would be Jeremy's friend who fell asleep on the mattress. Jeremy couldn't sleep. He was drunk and in a good mood. He had his headphones on and was carrying his CD player in his hand.

As he danced to the Native American tunes blasting through his headphones, a firecracker exploded. At least that's what Jeremy thought. He looked around for the scoundrel who had just interrupted his perfectly good rain dance. Earlier, a few of the residents of the apartment complex had been sitting out on their porches, but he could see none of them now. He looked for his friend who was passed out. He started to feel a stinging sensation in his face. Then his stomach, then his right forearm. Dammit, he thought, somebody threw something at me.

Even in his condition, he could see holes in his shirt. Somebody shot him.

In a panicked state, he awoke his buddy who looked up at Jeremy as if he were an idiot.

"Nobody shot you . . . get away from me."

His friend tried to go back to sleep.

"Look at my face and stomach! I'm bleeding!" Jeremy yelled.

They had no phone and knew no one. They took off walking as Jeremy blotted his face with a rag he carried. His black Diamondbacks T-shirt soaked up the blood from his stomach. It was a five-minute walk to the Circle K store at 16th Street and McDowell Road. Jeremy, gunshot wounds and all, walked up to the only clerk watching the store. She called 911.

Police found Jeremy sitting outside the store with his pal right next to him. The blood had started to dry on his face, and they could tell that he was liquored up. If the wounds hadn't been so apparent, they would have probably told them to go clean themselves up and quit drinking so much. Jeremy was in too much pain to talk. Patrol officers would follow them to County Hospital, but not before they radioed in that another shotgun shooting had taken place. They would be searching the area for the possible crime scene.

The now-familiar voice of Sergeant Pierce was on the other end of the phone that rang at my residence at 2:00 a.m. on July 1st, 2006.

"Hey, Clark, sorry to wake you, but we got two more shotgun shootings. Let me know when you're awake enough to copy the information."

Who is awake enough at 2:00 a.m. to take down anything? I rolled out of bed and tried to jolt myself from sleep.

"OK, give me just a second to get a pen," I mumbled.

Sergeant Pierce rattled off the two locations: 16th Street and Oak and 26th Street and Van Buren—one female and one Indian male shot. Another double up. The shooters were getting more arrogant by the day. They were doubling up to prove something. I stumbled toward the bathroom.

"I'll let em know you're en route. Thanks, and sorry to wake you up," he said.

"Not your fault, Lieutenant." I hung up the phone.

As I began the long trek into the city, I realized that the shooters hadn't gone away. They hadn't gotten whatever was troubling them out of their system. The eleven-day span between these shootings and the last ones on June 20th had meant nothing. They were still out there.

I was now facing the reality of seasoned veterans starting to hone their skills in my city, the city that I was sworn to protect. Maybe, just maybe, we would catch a break with these two shootings. Maybe someone had seen something. Both of the victims were alive and would want to help find these idiots.

As I approached 24th Street and Van Buren, I could see the familiar overhead lights of the patrol vehicles parked on the street. I parked my truck just outside of the crime scene and walked in. A patrol sergeant greeted me and asked if I had others coming.

"Nope, I'm all you get."

He laughed and said the usual, "Lucky you."

That line was becoming all too familiar.

The sergeant found a patrol car hood to brief on, and I opened my notebook. The victim here was a Diane Bein. She had been walking west on Van Buren when she was shot. I looked up from my notepad, and he read my mind.

"No, she does not appear to be a hooker, but we have not confirmed that," he said. "She's in serious condition at County Hospital."

She was found at the Log Cabin Motel. She contacted a couple of people who called 911. Officers had already interviewed them and realized that they were not witnesses to the shooting, just witnesses after the fact. They had released them.

"You know that we had another one about half an hour after this one, at 16th Street and Oak," he said.

"Yeah, I heard. I'm going to process this one first, and then I'll head up there and see what I can find."

The supervisor turned to one of the patrol officers and directed him to radio for a crime scene tech. I began my trek at the Log Cabin Motel. It was best to walk the scene backwards and see what I could find.

Officers took me to the beginning of the blood trail, but they had found no evidence associated with the weapon, a shotgun. The victim had bled profusely in the parking lot to the entrance of the motel. Officers pointed to where they found her. I began to follow the blood trail out to the sidewalk of Van Buren Street. The drips were consistent and separated. She had been running for a while.

As I walked about a block away from the motel, I met two more patrol officers. They had placed their vehicle in the street to block traffic and hold the crime scene tape up.

"That's where the blood trail starts," one of the officers yelled.

I was still on the south side of Van Buren. The blood trail was still consistent. No starting point for the blood drops.

The sidewalk was light gray, and the blood drops were easy to see against that background. Tougher to see were the blood drops on the asphalt street. The city lights that ran along Van Buren provided the only lighting at this time in the morning. I started to follow the drops as they wound across the street.

I yelled to the officers to accompany me with more light. They illuminated their flashlights.

No one had checked the north sidewalk. The blood trail started to stretch behind the crime scene tape. The officers looked at me, and I explained that we needed to widen the secured area. They immediately stripped down the tape and pulled their cars further east as I followed the blood trail.

As I passed the gates of the Alhambra Prison Complex, I found the origin of the crime. Only one gate led out of the prison complex, and the blood trail started, or ended, right there.

Now that I had the location where Diane Bein had been shot, it was time to look for evidence. The patrol supervisor joined us, and we began to scour the bushes, foliage, and the prison parking lot for the one piece of evidence I knew would tie this shootings to the others: a shot cup, hopefully a 410 shot cup.

Other officers approached, and I explained what we were looking for.

"What is that exactly?" they asked. "Is that like a wadding?"

I explained the difference.

An hour passed, and no evidence was recovered. Of course, there would be no shell casing in the road because only one round had been fired, just as in all the others.

I was getting pissed. Even with the crime scene being partially unsecured, nobody would have come in and taken the shot cup, and it wouldn't have disintegrated. My flashlight was starting to run down, and I didn't want to be out here till the sun came up. Where the hell is it?

"Got it!" One of the patrol officers yelled.

I was standing a hundred feet inside the prison complex looking through the parking lot. I rushed over. It had hit the chain-link fence surrounding the parking lot and dropped straight down. It took some well-trained eyes to find it. One 410 shot cup. It was sealed. My culprits had struck again.

I yelled to the crime scene tech, "Bring me the first placard."

The shot cup would be labeled "Item 1." The tech had been busy photographing the blood evidence.

I had received reports from County Hospital on both of the victims, and they were alert and eager to talk to investigators. The crime scene on Van Buren was so simple an eighth grader could have processed it. A blood sample was taken, and the shot cup was recovered. I finished a little before dawn.

I drove the four miles to the crime scene at 16th Street and Oak. A burly patrol supervisor met me there. There was literally nothing to see, other than an empty dirt lot. Officers had knocked on the apartment doors, but the few who answered either didn't see the shooting or heard something that sounded like a shot, but were not sure.

I checked the dumpster for any signs of pellet strikes and found none. There was nothing else to inspect. The cars parked in front of the apartments had no damage, and no blood trail could be located. Next stop was the hospital.

I parked my vehicle in the space marked "Police Only" and headed to the emergency room. I was lucky. Jeremy Ortiz had not yet been moved upstairs to a room.

The nurse approached me and saw my badge and gun. She was pleasant, saying, "You must be here for him."

"Affirmative," I replied. "How is he?"

"Fine. He should be out of here in a couple of hours. We just got his films back, and we're waiting for the doctor to release him."

"Any pellets removed from him?" I asked.

I hoped, at least, I could recover some kind of physical evidence.

"No. Doctor says he's not going to take any. He was hit with only six of 'em. He was lucky. The ones in his stomach did penetrate, but no surgery required. Looks like they're safe for now. He's sleeping over there."

Six pellets? The shot fired so far away that the pellets separated before hitting good ole Jeremy.

Patients were jammed into every space available in the recovery room of the ER. Jeremy was lying on his back as I pulled his curtain. I could see that blood encrusted his face, and that one pellet had penetrated his left cheek, right below the bone. There was another pellet wound to his upper lip area. Two more pellets had penetrated his upper stomach; one entered his left rib cage. The last distinct wound I could see was to the right forearm.

His attending nurse was more than happy to interrupt his slumber, and I introduced myself. I told him what officers had related and asked him if he could tell me anything else. Jeremy was still drunk, but he knew what I was saying.

He told me about drinking and hanging out in the parking lot behind the store. He had his headphones on and was dancing to make it rain. Whatever, dude.

He never saw a car and never saw anyone with a gun. He heard what he described as a firecracker go off and realized that he'd been shot. He thought he was standing by the dumpster when he was shot. He'd had a problem with some Mexican guys earlier in the evening and thought that they might have shot him. He did not see them in the vicinity at the time of the shooting.

I knew something that Jeremy didn't: He wasn't shot by the Mexicans he'd had a problem with earlier that evening. However, I could not tell him who the shooter was because I didn't know. It was through no fault of his own that he'd been shot. He was targeted because he was alone.

I told him he was lucky and gave him my card in case he thought of anything else. He assured me his buddy didn't shoot him. I knew that already.

Diane Bein had not been so lucky. She was moved from the ER to medical ICU. I was escorted to her room, where I found Diane, lying on her back, with a neck brace keeping her head immobilized. They were still waiting to see if she would be operated on.

I saw her X-rays sitting on the counter next to the bed. I asked the nurse if I could view them, and together we walked to the main desk. She put the films under the light just as the doctor walked up and introduced himself. He had seen the X-rays and explained that they were worried about the pellets in her neck. If they started to shift, she could bleed to death. As I looked at the X-ray, the doctor recognized me from the Tony Long shooting and the hospital follow-up eleven days earlier.

"You've had a rash of these shootings."

No sense in having hospital staff run to the media.

"Yeah, I've had a few. Hopefully this will be the last one."

He didn't need to know any more than that.

I left the good doctor to tend to his X-rays and went back to Diane. She was alert. The staff had told her I was coming to question her. She appeared to be in severe discomfort. I introduced myself and told her that I was looking into her case. I needed to know if she'd seen anything that might help us catch who did this.

"The only thing I really remember is a car passing by me, and someone shooting me." She wasn't even sure which way the car had been traveling. "It happened so fast. I felt the pellets hit me all along my left side."

Based on her injuries, the shot could have been fired from a car going the opposite direction she was walking, but that was doubtful. More likely, it had been a shot from a car going the same direction she was going. That's why she saw the car.

"I know it was a shotgun that was shot at me. I've heard them fired before, and I recognized the sound," she said.

"Not to mention the fact that you've got a couple dozen pellets inside your body. That gives me a clue what was used."

With the neck brace on, she could gaze only at me from the side of her eyes. My comment made Diane smile. She knew I was stating the obvious.

"The real question is, Diane, if you know anyone who wants to see you dead?"

"Well, as a matter of fact, my ex-boyfriend would want to see me dead," she stated. I had to admit that I was somewhat shocked. I'd have to explore this theory of Diane's. "I have an ex-boyfriend who has threatened to kill me in the past. We just split up."

Diane went on to explain that she and her ex were in a custody battle over their daughter. She had recently taken out a restraining order against him.

"Does he own any shotguns?" I asked.

"Not that I know of, but I haven't seen him for a couple weeks. He may have picked one up. I don't even know where he's living now, but I got a phone number to his boss. If you would like me to give it to you, I can."

"Absolutely. I'll have to look into it. Did he know where you were staying?"

She seemed to pause a second, which made me think that he might just be a scapegoat.

"I don't think so," she said.

"Do you honestly think he would gun you down from the middle of the street?"

Diane thought for a second and then replied, "I don't know, maybe, maybe not. We've had some tough times lately, and I might be assuming too much."

Whether it was an assumption, a conclusion, or a whim, I would have to look into it. The ultimate responsibility of a criminal investigator is to prove who was responsible for a criminal act. It is also just as important to disprove that someone committed the act.

In this case, I was sure that Diane was another random target. However, what I thought was now being tested by a possible act of targeted violence, this ex-boyfriend.

I asked Diane if she remembered anything else. "No, that's about it." She paused for a second. "All this over cigarettes ... I'm sorry I couldn't be more helpful."

"Don't be sorry. You didn't do anything wrong. There's no law against walking down the street to get some cigarettes in the middle of the night," I said. "But I will need some information on how to get a hold of your ex."

Diane retrieved a work number for her ex's boss, and the photo tech clicked away. I wished her a speedy recovery. I didn't tell her about the random shooters. Besides, if the shootings kept up, Diane would learn about them soon enough.

As I left County Hospital, I started to replay the events of July 1st in my head. Numerous supervisors would be waiting for me at headquarters, so I needed to get the facts correct.

The distance between the shootings was approximately five miles, give or take. The shooters had twenty minutes to drive the short distance. Both victims had been targeted because they were alone, or at least in Jeremy's case, appeared to be alone. The fact that his buddy was drunk and passed out a few feet away was moot. The shooters wouldn't have seen him anyway. No witnesses, and one shot fired in each case.

I replayed the other shootings, and they all seemed to match. Our boys had gotten away with it again.

CHAPTER 20

The only good thing about returning to headquarters on this morning would be that Lieutenant Benson was gone on vacation. I wasn't worried about any undue pressure because of the shootings of July 1st, but it would be easier to take questions from just one supervisor than multiple ones.

Sergeant Clarke met me as I walked in. "You doing OK?" He knew I had been out all morning, and it was now approaching noon.

"I'm a little tired, but at least I won't be picking shotgun pellets out of my body for the next decade." With as many as Diane Bein had in her, she would see them surface for many years to come, at least the ones that didn't penetrate too far. The others would circulate or adhere to her insides. If she was lucky, maybe she could purge them.

"Sounds like our guy again, huh," he said.

We had just entered his office, and I sat down. I was beat, and my legs were tired from walking up and down Van Buren looking for the blood trail and subsequent shot cup.

"Guys, plural," I said.

"Right, Anything to go on?"

"Not a thing. Once again, no witnesses to either shooting. Victims can't ID anyone. Shotgun used, probably a 410 in both. Drive-by's most likely."

"What's your plan?"

He looked at me as if he knew what was coming.

"Well, the first thing is to clean up this lead that Diane Bein gave me. She thinks she might have been targeted by her ex-boyfriend. I'm going to have to disprove that, just in case. Then we need to talk about getting a bunch of troops together to find these assholes."

That meant task force.

"I agree. The LT is gone this week, and he will have to approve any overtime dedicated to finding these pricks. In the meantime, start to think about putting together an operational plan that we can implement. At this point, we are going to have to use personnel from our detail. All the other undercover and plainclothes bodies are tied up on the Baseline Killer."

"I'll see what I can come up with."

As if I don't have enough on my plate as it is, now I get to devise a plan for stopping ghosts. But how? How do you stop someone from driving by and shooting out of a vehicle window? It was an act that can be completed in seconds.

I called the number Diane had given to me, and the voicemail picked up. I left a message asking her ex-boyfriend to call me. That was all I said. Over the years, I'd learned that the less information you give people, the better, and the more quickly they would respond. I also learned that some victims aren't completely truthful about the events surrounding their incident. It's something that is hard to swallow. You would hope they would be honest and forthright about the facts surrounding their case, but that wasn't always the case. Victims may have a motive to lie, and you have to look for it, or you can waste your time investigating a case that will never be prosecuted.

But I didn't have to worry about lying or less than truthful victims in these cases. They were all legitimate victims.

Within five minutes of my message, Diane's ex-boyfriend called me back. Her ex's boss had gotten him the message, and he returned the call right away. My theory was once again correct.

I introduced myself. I obtained his personal information and then told him about the shooting of his ex-girlfriend, Diane Bein. He had already heard about what had happened to Diane. He knew the call from police would be coming.

He told me the intimate details of their relationship. They fought a lot, and their daughter had to suffer through it. I could tell by his voice that it bothered him. He told me that he had been trying to get custody of their daughter, and he seemed bitter over the breakup. He even accused Diane of prostitution and severe drug abuse, although he had no proof of either. He had not seen Diane for several weeks, but knew that she was staying at a hotel down on Van Buren.

When I asked him where he was the morning of the shooting, he said he was "in bed." I asked if he had anyone who could verify that, and he said no. He owned no guns and had no vehicle. He had numerous people who could verify those facts. If he were to go anywhere, it was to work and he had to be driven there. His boss would corroborate the transportation issue. He could have borrowed a car, but that seemed unlikely.

I asked him flat out if he had shot Diane or had any idea who would have. He replied, "No way."

There was no sense in further wasting his time or mine. I thanked him for his time and bid him farewell.

I had done my job, but by doing so, it got me no closer to figuring out who shot Diane or any of the other ten victims I had stacked up.

The Fourth of July fell on a Tuesday in 2006, a lousy day of the week to celebrate the birthday of this great nation. It means that holiday plans must be curtailed somewhat, since most working adults have to go to work the next day.

Joseph Roberts had no such worries. A spry eighteen years young, Joseph could stay out all night long on any night. He was out of school, and the summer months meant fun for him. He wasn't working and really didn't need much spending money. He had his bike for transportation, and most of his friends and close cousins lived only a few miles from his central Phoenix apartment. The price of gas wasn't an issue for him.

His late nights had gotten some undue attention though. He had several minor scrapes with the law. He had been cited for possession of liquor and had been referred for marijuana possession. In his mind, those were no big deal. Hell, every kid he knew drank alcohol or smoked a little weed. He hadn't been interested in school and had probably never figured out that the combination of drinking and smoking marijuana had affected his abilities. Besides, there were plenty of odd jobs that he could do to make enough money to get by. Who needed an education?

Joseph lived with his mother but spent most of his time with his cousins. It just so happened that his cousins lived only a short distance from 16th Street and Oak, the shooting site of Jeremy Ortiz.

But in the early morning hours of July 3rd, Joseph had no idea who Jeremy Ortiz was and could care even less. It was approaching 3:00 a.m., and he had to get home. His mother would be upset that he was out this late, even if he didn't have to get up for school or go to work that morning.

Joseph's apartment sat just south of Indian School Road and 28th Street. From his cousin's place, he figured it would take him about ten minutes to pedal the three odd miles home. As fate would have it, the best-laid plans sometimes go awry. A blowout at 24th Street, right between his cousin's place and home, brought his ride to a halt. At least having a flat tire to show his mom would lessen the butt chewing.

Joseph stood over six feet tall, and having to lean over to push the trick bike with a flat front tire was excruciating work. His back and legs were aching, and the temperature was still in the upper nineties even at this time of morning. The streets were dead and peaceful. The businesses were all closed. Even the bar at 26th Street and Indian School, Warsaw Wally's, had only a few employees cleaning up the place.

With sweat starting to bead on his forehead, he pushed on past the Ever-Ready Glass Company where he could see his reflection in the large two-story windows. He thought he must look like a fool pushing this bike.

Joseph noticed more than his reflection that morning. He had spent a lot of time on the streets in his few young years of life, and he saw just about everything. He didn't know the streets the way transients might, but he watched and looked out for suspicious activity. Joseph was young, but he wasn't naïve about the ways of the street.

Right away, he noticed the car coming at him on the opposite side of the street. He kept pushing his bike, watching the car. The car started to slow down. He stopped in his tracks, gazing at the car. Joseph wasn't sure why the vehicle was slowing. Was it somebody he knew? Probably not. The headlights shut off.

He tightened his grip on the handlebars as the car came to a stop across from where he stood. He squinted in the darkness but couldn't see inside the car's tinted windows. Joseph didn't recognize the vehicle. His mind began to run through the possible scenarios. It could be someone stopping to ask if he needed assistance, or worse.

He soon realized it was worse. As Jospeh stared across the roadway, the horror of what was about to happen buckled his legs. The window on the driver's door was down. The barrel of some type of gun, a long gun, protruded from the opening. Joseph froze in fear. The barrel of the gun rested on the car door. He turned his body sideways to keep from being shot in the chest.

The blast shook the still night air. Joseph was so scared, he never even saw the muzzle flash. He felt the brunt of the projectiles strafe the left side of his body.

The white arm that held the gun pulled back into the car as it sped off. Joseph went down. He lay there, still, his legs shaking and his upper body burning.

All the businesses were closed. There was no one around to help him. As he watched the wounds seep blood, he wondered if he would ever see his family again.

A homeless transient stumbled onto Joseph first. The man could have just walked away after rifling through Joseph's pockets, maybe even taking his bike. Joseph was in no shape to fight back. Instead, the man ran to the bar and told one of the two employees that someone had been shot. They called 911.

The first officers arrived on the scene at 0315 hours, several minutes after the shooting. Joseph told them what he knew, with the fear of dying streaming through his brain. He didn't see the assailant, just the car—a silver or gray four-door type sedan. The officers put out the description over the radio. The car was long gone.

The street was shut down because all the cops knew what had happened, again. The businesses around where Joseph was shot would stay closed. Another shotgun victim lay nearly dead.

At exactly 4:00 a.m., my phone rang. It was my favorite sergeant, Paul Pierce, once again waking me during my best REM sleep.

"We got another drive-by shotgun shooting, this time at 25th Street and Indian School Road. Can you roll over there?"

Of course I would go.

It took me about fifty-five minutes to arrive at 25th Street and Indian School Road. I could see about ten patrolmen standing around talking in small groups. This shooting had drawn a crowd. There was one media pool camera set up on the north side of Indian School Road. It was the first time the media had been at any of the scenes. I could only hope that nobody had said anything foolish within earshot of the cameraman.

As I walked inside the tape, I saw something marked in the roadway. A patrol officer had placed an index card over an object sitting in the curb lane. Bending over and lifting the card, I saw the signature of my random/serial shootists: a 410 shot cup. An officer had been smart enough to recognize its importance. I could see a silver bike lying in front of a business, some type of sign-painting or design business. I saw a blue T-shirt that I assumed was the victim's underneath the bike. Paramedics had graciously left it for us to examine and collect.

I was briefed by the on-scene supervisor, who had little to tell me about what had occurred. All the information he had gathered came from the victim. And, of course, there were no witnesses. I was getting real tired of the victim being the only one able to tell me what happened. The transient that notified the bar employee to call was already gone.

The bike had a little blood on the right handle grip. There was one pellet strike to the bike's left side. It confirmed what everyone, including the victim, had related. He'd been walking on the left side of the bike when the shot was fired. There was no collateral damage to any of the businesses. It looked as if he had been shot right between two of the buildings.

There was very little investigating to do here. The blue T-shirt had several holes put there by shotgun pellets. There was very little blood. The victim must have pulled the shirt off right away to examine his wounds. That would explain its pristine condition. The shirt was bagged and tagged.

Dawn was breaking. Motorists were starting to arrive and getting impatient. I had officers open up the road to traffic and told them to tear down the crime scene tape. There was nothing left to examine here.

The media pool cameraman was long gone, and I found out that only a short interview had been conducted. There were no words spoken of the string of shootings I was now knee-deep in. The next stop was County Hospital, a place I was beginning to call home.

As I entered the fourth-floor ICU at County Hospital, I was directed to the victim's room. I saw Joseph Roberts being attended to by a person later determined to be his mother. He was sleeping when I walked in and introduced myself to the family. Joseph was awoken by his nurse, who advised me that he had been given a mild sedative for pain but should be fine to interview. Joseph looked up at me with one eye open and the other half-closed. He raised himself up slightly in the bed and winced with pain from the movement. He was dressed in a hospital gown, and the nurse adjusted the bed by pressing a foot pedal. She pulled the curtain around the bed and quietly exited the room. There was only one other patient in the ICU room.

"I would ask you how you're doing, but I think I can pretty much see that for myself," I started out. I introduced myself and told him I would be the detective investigating his case. At this point, he wouldn't have cared if I'd been the president. He was hurting.

With intermittent deep breaths and pauses for the pain to subside, Joseph laid it all out in a very intelligent, precise manner. It was not something that you usually get from a youth of Joseph's age. I could tell he spent some time on the street.

He told me about his misfortune with the bicycle tire, how it had been a pain to have to push it home, how he'd watched the vehicle begin to slow down in the opposite curb lane, and then shut off its lights. When he told me about his concern, I knew he'd been out late at night before, probably on numerous occasions. Joseph was trained to watch his surroundings. He had either been a victim of violence before, or a close friend had been victimized.

I asked him to describe the car in as much detail as possible. He was the first witness who could give me some kind of decent description of the shooter's vehicle.

"It was silver, a four-door passenger car, and it was going the opposite direction from what I was walking." It wasn't much of a description, but it was a start. "It wasn't real old, but it wasn't real new either." He had narrowed the suspect vehicle to a couple of hundred thousand cars in the metro area.

"I then saw the driver pointing a gun at me," he grimaced. He was trying to talk through the pain of his injuries. He squirmed in bed, trying to find a comfortable position. "It was a long-barreled gun, like a rifle, or a shotgun."

He didn't see the muzzle flash, just heard the roar. He tried to demonstrate how the shooter held the weapon. He sat up in his bed and put an imaginary gun to his shoulder.

"It was weird, he wasn't holding the gun right. He didn't have it at eye level. He kinda fired from the chest."

It sounded like our shooter may have been in a hurry to get the shot off and get the hell out of there. The shooter had been worried about Joseph seeing him.

"I turned my body slightly so that I wouldn't get shot in the chest. I was scared to death. I thought I was going to die."

Most people will never know what it feels like to look down the barrel of a gun and know that your fate is in God's hands. The feeling of helplessness is overwhelming. Psychologists call it "Fight, Flight, or Freeze Syndrome." Those are the only reactions that the human mind runs through when faced with the extreme stress in a life-or-death moment. The phenomenon has been studied extensively by the military over the years to try to figure out why some soldiers stay at their posts under heavy attack, and why some run for their lives. The third characteristic of freezing is even harder to understand.

Joseph froze. He thought of self-preservation first by turning his body. It probably saved his life. His mind had run through this scenario before, like people in the military or with police training. His training had come on the streets of Phoenix.

"Did you get a look at the person who shot you?" I asked.

I had anticipated the answer before the interview ever started. I, of course, had thought the worst.

"He was a white guy," Joseph replied. "I mean, I believe he was white." He needed to explain. "When I saw the gun come out of the window, I could see that the arm holding the gun was white," he explained. "That's how I know the guy that shot me was white."

"Did you get a look at any other features about this guy, like his face, hair color, facial hair, anything like that?"

"No, just his arm," Joseph said. It happened too quickly to see anything else.

I asked Joseph if he saw anyone else in the car beside the shooter. "I think he was the only one in the car, but it was dark out," he said.

There was nothing else that Joseph could provide. Well, at least it was a start. The fact that we now at least had a race on the shooter was a step in the right direction.

I told him and his family that the media had been out at the scene. There was the distinct possibility that he may be contacted now or sometime in the near future about what had happened to him. The fact that the media hadn't run with these random shootings as of July 3, 2006 was puzzling. It usually doesn't take them that long to put two and two and seven together. At this point there had been eleven shootings, including Joseph Roberts. Who was I to question their insight?

Joseph wanted nothing to do with the attention this shooting might bring. I told him I understood that, but the media can be very persuasive, especially if the shootings became more than a local story. It was already happening with the Baseline Killer case. Fifteen minutes of fame can also change the victim's way of thinking. I had seen that happen too many times in the past.

I packed up my notebook and told Joseph to call me if he thought of anything else. I left my business card with his mother.

As I exited the hospital, I knew that the undercover/surveillance plan that I had been working on needed to come together quickly. The brass would soon quit asking what happened and start asking, "What are you doing to prevent this?"

Besides, the Fourth of July was tomorrow. Lots of fireworks and gunfire to go around. What harm or attention would another shot in the night really evoke?

Sergeant Stewart Clarke was sitting at my desk as I strolled in. He wore a look of high anxiety.

"This is a working man's desk," I said. "Get out of my chair. I have work to do. The managers' offices are down by the toilets. That's where you guys do your best thinking."

"Very funny. I hope you have a plan ready!" He was actually pretty calm. The brass hadn't hammered him for answers yet. "I think I do, but I got to be honest with you, it's a shot in the dark. Figuratively speaking, of course."

"Oh, that's another good one. Have you got any more side-splitting jokes? I need to get out a pen and start writing these down. Tell me that you've got something in place that we can at least take a look at to see if it's doable."

"Yeah, I do. Get out of my chair so that I can look at my notes. I put it together in your office, the john, this morning. I'm thinking of promoting to supervisor."

"Seriously, get this put together soon because I'm going to have to write an action plan and get the overtime approved. Unless, of course, you want to run this plan by yourself … and for free."

"I don't do anything for free anymore, so I guess you'll have to get the overtime approved. Give me an hour to gather my thoughts." Sergeant Clarke stood up to leave. "Get some food, you look like sh&# … See you after lunch."

The good sergeant then left my space.

It was time to put the plan together and implement it. The last six shootings had all occurred on the east side of Phoenix, unlike the first five. It appeared that the shooters had changed their hunting grounds. That didn't mean that they couldn't change areas again, go back to the west side, or stay in East Phoenix.

I had to go with the latest trend. The surveillance units would be placed in the East Phoenix corridor.

To cover the area, I would need both fixed and roving undercover/surveillance units. The main bulk of the units would have to stay at fixed positions, while several units drove the streets looking for any suspicious driving behaviors such as cruising aimlessly around, and the following or surveillance of pedestrians by themselves.

There was one gaping hole in the plan. The shooters were probably conducting not only surveillance of their victims, but also counter-surveillance of any cars in the area. The only witness to any of the shootings was the guy who stopped and picked up Clarissa Rowley, the prostitute on Van Buren. His description of the suspect car was different from what Joseph Roberts had said.

It was maddening trying to define what these suspects were about or what motivated them. I could only hope that we could get lucky and stumble onto them.

After a quick lunch, I gathered my notes and documents, and headed into Sergeant Clarke's office. He was reading his email, most of it useless crap that the City continues to send out. He looked up and was happy to be spared the anguish of further reading.

"What you got?"

He was genuinely interested in finding these guys. He too knew that the genie would soon be out of the bottle, and that all the interest in the Baseline Killer would soon come to focus on this series of crimes.

"Before I present this, I need to know how many officers we get. This is going to take some bodies, and it's going to take some know-how."

Maybe he would forget this whole thing before I laid it out and decide that it wasn't cost efficient.

"You got all the bodies in the detail who are willing to work the Fourth of July. That gives us about fifteen at the last count. I just talked to the LT, and he is coming back in off vacation early to watch this thing run."

I explained the thought process behind the saturation of the East Phoenix neighborhoods. I told him we could stick to the main arteries because that was where all of the shootings, except one, had occurred. There was a problem, though.

"With only fifteen bodies, that means there are going to be stretches of streets where we have no fixed surveillance units. Those are going to be some huge gaps. If we do fill those fixed positions, then we lose the chance of finding the shooter through old-fashioned police work."

It was six of one, half-a-dozen of another.

We decided it would be better to cover the mobile positions than fixed ones. At least with the mobile units, we had a chance of stopping them by being a presence on the street. With fixed positions, we had no guarantee that they could spot anyone acting suspiciously in time to stop an attack. The roving units would be quicker and more proactive.

It was going to cost the city a pretty penny paying overtime on a holiday for these extra saturation units. Most of the people in my unit had surveillance experience, so it wasn't as if we were using rookies to man these positions.

I was anticipating a shooting on the Fourth of July. What shooter wouldn't take advantage of all the other bangs, pops, and gunfire on the Fourth, and then slip away as he had so many times before? Cops in Phoenix took refuge on the Fourth and New Year's so the gunfire that rained from the skies didn't strike them. Tonight would be no different.

There was one last comment that Sergeant Clarke had to make. "Boy, I sure hope this guy doesn't start shooting a day before our surveillance kicks in."

"They won't," I said.

"How can you be so sure?"

"Because they never shoot people on back-to-back nights. The same night, yes, but not on back-to-back nights."

The evening of the Fourth of July was unusually calm, with moderate car and pedestrian traffic. The LT had shown up in his Levi's and looked completely out of place. He never dressed in jeans. He began to look over the grid, and how we were going to surveil the streets.

"I don't understand your logic. Why are we concentrating on this area?"

God help us when managers start to think.

Sergeant Clarke patiently walked him through the grid and the reasoning behind the plan. The LT shook his head but decided not to tinker with what was already in place.

The surveillance was to start at 10:00 p.m. That was the earliest time any shooting had taken place. The area of the surveillance was broken down into one large grid, concentrated on the east side of Phoenix. We had seventeen volunteers to work the surveillance. We could cover all the main streets between Van Buren and Camelback Roads, plus we could cover all the main streets from 24th Street to 56th Street.

I had an open line to the communications supervisor at the radio dispatch room who was to advise me of any shootings, any type, that occurred anywhere within the boundaries of the City of Phoenix.

As the late evening turned into the early morning hours, the car traffic thinned, and the only vehicles on the road were our undercover cars and trucks. The trucks stuck out like sore thumbs. The City had fleet purchased so many Fords with bed covers that all the bad guys knew those were police vehicles.

As I drove the main roads of East Phoenix, I passed at least one surveillance vehicle every five minutes. There was no getting around it. Saturation was better than leaving a lonely pedestrian as a target.

None of the surveillance units had reported anything suspicious. A couple of drunken drivers were called in on the radio, and motor officers were dispatched to the areas to have them pulled over. There had been some reported calls of shots fired in two different areas of the city, but no hits.

We had agreed that 3:00 a.m. would be the cut-off time for the undercover units to shut down operations. As luck or God would have it, 3:00 a.m. came and went, and there were no random shootings this night.

I didn't know whether to feel relieved about no one being shot or upset that we didn't catch our shooters. Whatever the case, this would be just the first of many sleepless nights to come. Round One went to the bad guys.

CHAPTER 21

As I walked into headquarters on the morning of July 5th, I plopped down at my desk. We had been unsuccessful, but the Gun Squad had made some arrests for gunfire incidents. Detective Darrel Smith of the ATF/Gun Squad was milling about the detail when I arrived at my workstation.

"Heard you guys were out all night trying to catch the shooter," he said.

"We were out there, and they weren't. If they were, they made us or decided against doing anything."

"Sounded like a good idea being out there, especially with all the shootings that occur on the Fourth of July," he said. "We were out all night, too, trying to catch the dumb asses firing their guns to celebrate. Actually found a couple of them."

"Good for you. That pisses me off when these losers fire their guns in the air. How stupid is that, anyway? Do these idiots not understand that the bullet comes down somewhere after it's fired?"

"If they do, they don't get it. We ask them that, and they look at us like we have two heads. They've never heard of Shannon's Law."

Shannon Smith was a young girl with a bright future ahead of her. She was living in central Phoenix with her parents when she decided one day to step out of her home to talk on the phone. She was standing in her backyard when a bullet fired from some distance away came out of the sky and right down on top of her. The bullet went through her head, killing her. It was a senseless tragedy perpetrated by some moron firing a gun in the air.

The investigators attempted to plot a trajectory to where the shot may have come from and did a pretty good job isolating the area. Unfortunately, it did not lead to any arrests. The case is still unsolved.

Shannon's parents became activists for changing the current law in Arizona to make it a felony to fire a weapon in a municipality. The law is now referred to as "Shannon's Law."

"Any luck with finding your firebug?"

"Nope. We're looking for a guy of interest but can't find him. Walmart isn't happy."

It was time for me to get to work, so I brushed him off with a "Good luck and Godspeed" and turned to the task at hand.

I sat at my desk, trying to figure out my next move. Eleven shotgun shootings with no leads whatsoever. There was nothing to stop whoever was doing this. I could only sit and wait till the next shooting occurred. And I was sure that it would happen sooner rather than later.

David Perez had wasted the first few years of his early youth gangbanging on the streets of Phoenix. He had gotten busted a few times and appeared to be enjoying his status as a gang member. But that would soon come to an end.

During his time in the gang, David had met the love of his life, Patty Verdugo. She had come from a traditional Hispanic household, where her family strictly adhered to the Catholic faith.

She had met David when she was fifteen, and he fourteen. Even with her strict upbringing, she soon gave into his requests. They began having sexual relations. Like many young couples, they never thought to use birth control. Or if they did, it was just in passing. That would lead to a pregnancy. Her family would not allow an abortion, and she decided to have the child. David was definitely the father. He did not protest the birth either.

Becoming a father had not changed David's attitude. He still thought that gangbanging was more important than being a dad and providing for his child. Patty thought differently, and so did her family. They cut him off and told her not to see him. He was bad for her, and he would eventually end up dead anyway.

But Patty loved David. She was blinded by that love and wanted to be a part of his life. She, too, knew that David's present course of action would end up with him dead or in prison. She told him that he needed to get his life together and quit the street gang. He promised her he would.

Patty became pregnant, again. Her family was about ready to disown her when they found out that David was the father. With the birth of the second child, the family agreed to give David a second chance. Patty told him that it was her and the kids or the street. It was up to him. David chose Patty and his children.

David found gainful employment cleaning houses. He didn't mind working, and at this point, it was the only way that he could convince Patty he was done gangbanging. He was going to try to support her and the kids.

David moved out of the hood where he was living, away from the friends who continually tried to keep him down. Patty continued to live at home, but with any luck, David's new job could someday support all of them. He had big dreams, and he wanted to open his own house-cleaning business. He was making enough to support himself, but he needed more income to support a family.

David had moved to a neighborhood in West Phoenix a few miles from where he used to live, but none of his gangster buddies knew about the place. He kept it to himself. If his street rats found out that he had a crib of his own, they'd overrun the place. It would also become a target for violence, since David had made a few enemies of his own.

He rented a little shack off the main house on quiet State Street. It was a one-bedroom with a single bathroom. It was plenty for him. The neighborhood was one of the older ones in town. Most of the neighborhood consisted of homes built in the fifties and sixties. These homes were owned by seasoned citizens. They wouldn't put up with any shenanigans.

For the next six months, David would work, come home, and see his family. The birth of his new daughter brought new hope to his life. He soon realized that playing on the streets was a waste of time.

He'd been able to put some money aside and decided that it was time to get a bigger, nicer place, one the kids could feel more comfortable in. He had given the landlord notice. He needed some extra time to get out while working full time. The landlord had asked him to vacate by July 8th.

By July 6, 2006, David had moved most of his property. He had found a bigger place that was closer to Patty and the kids, but still away from the old hood. He'd been packing some of the last items together. He didn't have all that much stuff. The few pieces of furniture that he owned had already been moved. His bed and a couple boxes of personal items remained. He didn't have a car, so he depended on rides from family members to help him move into his new digs.

A hankering for a soda hit David around 1:00 a.m. on July 7th. The packing and cleaning had parched his throat. No respectable house cleaner would leave the home he was vacating in a mess. Besides, the homeowner might be able to refer him some business later down the line, when he opened up his own house-cleaning enterprise.

The convenience store was four blocks away from his apartment. Even though it was late and he was tired, a cold drink would go a long way toward helping him get a decent night's sleep. Nothing was worse than going to sleep thirsty.

It was only a hundred yards to the corner of State Street and 27th Avenue. But, as he made the turn south, exhaustion won out over thirst. Did he really need the soda? Four blocks was a long way. He stopped, turned around, and headed home.

He decided to call Patty. Even at this hour, she always answered her phone. She was keeping close tabs on him. He wanted her to know that even though he was out, he was still close to home.

What David didn't know was the short walk on 27th Avenue had exposed him. State Street was very dark, but 27th Avenue was well lit, like all metro thoroughfares. Someone had been driving and looking for pedestrians who were alone. He was now marked as he entered the darkness of his home street.

The headlights behind David brightened his view, but they didn't surprise him. A dirt easement along the street had once contained a pathway, but the bushes and shrubbery from adjacent properties hung so low that traversing it was impossible. He moved from the center of State Street to the left side. Patty answered on the third ring.

He knew that something was up. Not with Patty, but he felt that sixth sense you get. The car slowing behind him could only mean one thing—someone was stalking him. He'd been targeted for violence before. He concentrated on his conversation with Patty. She was excited about the new place. His mind ran a million miles an hour. Had somebody found out where he lived? Were his old banger friends upset with him since he up and left? Was he just being paranoid?

David's pace slowed, wishing he was packing a gun. In his old neighborhood, he always had access to one, if he wasn't carrying one. But he had left all that behind him.

The car was closing in slowly, and he could see his silhouette in the headlights as they lit the roadway. He slowed even more. He tried to talk calmly with Patty. At least if something happened, she would soon know about it.

He could feel and hear the presence of the car as it got to within a few feet of him. He tried not to look scared, but his body was shuddering. He stole a quick glance to his right as the car eased alongside him. He knew what to look for, but not whom.

It took only a millisecond for him to realize that the barrel of a shotgun protruded out of the driver's window. David didn't even have the time to look at the driver's face before the muzzle blast blinded him. He went down immediately, his phone blown apart as he held it to his right ear. The vehicle slowly continued on its way.

From the ground, he watched the vehicle. He had been hit, and it was bad. The whole right side of his neck burned. The blood started to fill the neckline of his T-shirt and was pooling underneath. He lay motionless, still watching the car, half the phone still in his hand. All Patty could hear was static. She hung up and waited for his return call. She had no idea what had occurred.

David never took his eyes off the car, a four-door car. He could see the silhouettes of two people in the car. Still motionless, he stayed on the ground, not wanting them to come back and finish him off. He had no idea why he'd been shot.

The car reached the frontage road of the I-17 freeway and stopped, idling, waiting to see if David rose to his feet. They were watching him. Not a muscle twitched.

After what seemed like an eternity, the car finally made the turn to go south on the frontage road. David struggled to his feet. He ran to the main house of the property, holding his neck, yelling, and banging on the door.

Jeraldo Gonzales was awoken from a deep sleep by the banging and screaming at his front door. He opened it, but no one was there. The banging now moved to the side of the house. He bolted there, only to see his neighbor, David, bleeding from the head area. He collapsed in Jeraldo's arms.

Jeraldo had grabbed his cellphone, and David called 911. How he was able to talk, let alone describe what happened to him, was remarkable.

"911, what is your emergency?"

"Yeah, I've been shot," David yelled.

"You've been shot?" the dispatcher clarified.

"Yeah, somebody drove by me and shot me."

"OK, OK, where are you?"

David was losing consciousness. Jeraldo eased him down to the ground. David gave them the address.

The police would find David in this position, on the ground with his head held in Jeraldo's lap. Paramedics were staging a block away until police had cleared the scene of any potential dangers. The responding units knew the shooter could still be in the area.

Police gathered as much information from David as they could. He had lost a lot of blood.

"It was a blue Ford Contour-type vehicle."

A guy he once knew had owned one. Victims of violent crimes tend to correlate memories of their traumatic incident with prior memories or life experiences. The incident occurred so fast that David took a piece from his memory bank, something that he thought was relevant, and gave it to police. He wasn't an expert on cars, and he wasn't expected to be. The fact that he was able to give any description of a car was a miracle.

As David was whisked away, police scoured the street for evidence. Large paloverde trees and oleanders blanketed the sides of the wide road. One lone streetlight lit the area enough for police to at least find some semblance of a crime scene. On the road sat a puddle of blood, and right next to it, the bottom half of David's cellphone.

At the hospital, David couldn't relate anything more. Calls were made to the Violent Crimes Bureau to dispatch a detective, but nobody went. The shotgun blast to David's neck was from such a close range that it was hard to tell the weapon of choice. The crime scene was small, and David's history of gangbanging made it look like a gang shooting. There were no suspects because David couldn't name one. Best of all, there were no witnesses. Unbelievably, it didn't dawn on anyone that it could be related to the random shootings occurring in Phoenix. If it did, no one spoke of it. The case would be handled like any other whodunit and handed to a case-carrying detective in a few days.

But cases like this have a funny way of dusting themselves off. In reality, the shooting of David Perez would become one of the most high-profile shootings in the investigation of this series of events. It would become that notable based on one conversation . . . a conversation that was yet to occur.

CHAPTER 22

A night out on the town for some people can be a weekly event or at least a monthly occurrence. But for Javier and Ashley Armenta, who had married young and had three children, it was an anomaly. Javier worked hard to provide for his family as Ashley had decided to be a stay-at-home mom. That meant the dollars were tight.

They had bought a house in Surprise, a small suburban enclave west of Phoenix. Their extended family still lived in the Valley, and they would jump at the opportunity to have a dinner out, with the grandchildren spending some time with Grandpa and Grandma.

One Friday night, July 7, 2006, a date was made. They would drop the kids off at the grandparents' house, which just happened to be close to one of the oldest Mexican food establishments in the Phoenix area: The Tee Pee Grill. Then they'd go off for a few cocktails at one of the local pubs.

The Tee Pee Grill has been a mainstay in the area of 40th Street and Indian School Road forever. It's a small, quaint dining establishment that does not take reservations. On the weekend, it can get crowded and seating is limited, but the Armentas squeezed in. It serves up an old-style Mexican cuisine and has a loyal clientele. The special always changes.

The Armentas ate, then ended up at the Coach House Tavern, located in old downtown Scottsdale. The Coach House Tavern is one of the few Scottsdale bars that hasn't gone Hollywood, or techno, or rap, or progressive. It played its tunes from a jukebox, has old-fashioned dartboards, and even looks like one of the old Western saloons of bygone eras. It's a pub-type atmosphere, with a mixture of local beer drinkers, yuppies, preppies, and even some sophisticates. The Armentas had arrived early enough to find seating, which isn't easy amid its small confines. They had a good enough time to stay until the bar closed at 2:00 a.m.

Javier said he was good to drive, and Ashley was tipsy but hadn't gone overboard. Upon leaving the Coach House, they headed west down Indian School Road towards the grandparents. The ride home would not be pleasant, though. As can happen after a night of having a few drinks, things are said, and adults turn into children.

Whatever the case, an argument ensued, and for some reason Ashley felt the immediate need to get out of the car. The words became heated, and she threatened to jump from the moving vehicle. Javier pulled to the side of the road, stopping in the area of 48th Street and Indian School. Ashley got out and slammed the car door. Javier felt that maybe some fresh air would cool her off. He wasn't real happy with her at this point either. A walk just might do her some good. Besides, it was only a few blocks to the grandparents' house, and it wasn't his idea for her to get out. Javier would drive there and wait for his wife.

Ashley began her walk to blow off steam. She was familiar with this section of town and knew it well. She wasn't stupid. She never would have gotten out of the car in an unfamiliar area.

But being a female out alone after the bars had closed and on a major thoroughfare gave the impression of a woman in distress. Approaching her would not be out of the question for any person driving by. Who knew why she was out there? Maybe her car had broken down, maybe she was lost, maybe she was too intoxicated to find her way home, or maybe she had a reason for being out there.

The first car that approached her had a man in it. He was by himself and driving a Jeep Cherokee. Ashley knew automobiles. Her ex-boyfriend had been a car junkie. She'd been indoctrinated to different types of cars. She knew bodies, styles, and engines. When the driver pulled up next to her, the first thing she noticed was the model and make. She was hoping it was Javier, but it wasn't. The man asked her if she needed a ride. She politely declined, and he drove off. Soon, she realized her predicament. She was alone, a female, at night, and clearly a target.

She wasn't about to grovel for Javier to come and get her, even though this encounter frightened her. Instead, she phoned a friend. Her friend, Kelly, would be a comfort on the walk home, and God forbid if anything happened, she would at least have a witness and someone to call the police for her. When Ashley called, Kelly answered.

Keeping a good pace, Ashley had rounded the corner of 44th Street and Indian School Road moving north. She and Kelly babbled about nothing in particular. Her watch read 2:30 a.m. Javier was a dog, for at least tonight. It was nervous chatter from Ashley's end. The voice of her friend on the other line was comforting.

The encounter with the driver of the Jeep Cherokee had made Ashley aware of her surroundings. Even though she was mad at Javier, his pulling up right about now wouldn't have hurt her feelings.

Just after Ashley crossed the mid-block street of Devonshire, she felt . . . or heard . . . something. It might have been subtle popping of rocks, or asphalt as rubber meets the road, or the dull sound of low-torque engine. Whatever it was, it was behind her and she felt it: the presence of a vehicle, one that had snuck up on her. Maybe Javier had finally come to get her.

With the phone still tucked next to her ear, she spun to look behind here. It was definitely not Javier. The car stood motionless, stopped at the stop sign to Devonshire Road, with its tinted windows completely rolled up.

Thinking nothing of it, she turned to continue on her way. After the fifth step, she heard the noise. In that split second, her hair flew up on the back of her head as if someone had hit her with a high-pressured air hose. The noise ringing in her ears.

"What the hell," she thought to herself.

Ashley thrust her open hand through her hair, the other still clutching the phone. The stinging sensation set in immediately. It felt as if a swarm of bees had just stung her back, neck, and shoulders. She shook her hair violently as anxiety set in. Nothing, no bees. She turned to see if the car was still there. She expected to hear laughing and taunting. She heard nothing. Maybe some jerk from the car had done it, thrown something at her. But that didn't explain the noise.

She watched as the car slowly pulled out onto 44th Street and turned left. The driver wasn't in any hurry. The calmness of the maneuver scared Ashley to death. She was still on the phone with Kelly.

"I think somebody just threw something at me," Ashley said.

"Are you all right?" Kelly asked.

By now, Ashley had felt the back of her head. Her hand was full of blood. "Oh my God! I think I've been shot!"

"Call Javier right now," Kelly yelled to her friend. Ashley hung up the phone.

Javier had already begun to worry about Ashley. He had left the grandparents and started to drive along 44th Street to find his wife. The call came to him at 2:38 a.m. His wife was in complete hysteria. Javier was only a few seconds away. Panic began to flow through his body. His mind began to fill with the horrors of letting his wife out of the minivan.

"What was I thinking?" he thought to himself.

As he pulled up to the corner where Ashley stood, he could see the pain on her face. She was crying, shell-shocked. He jumped from the minivan and ran to his wife.

At first, he wasn't sure what was wrong. She appeared to be in one piece. She turned and showed him her back. A few tiny holes spattered her back, holes that he likened to small ice pick marks. They were bleeding, but not profusely. He thought for a moment that he would be able to take care of her. Then he saw blood start to drip from the back of her head and hairline. They decided to go to the emergency room.

As Ashley crawled into the front passenger seat, all Javier could think of was how lucky they were. His wife was talking and moving as opposed to being stretched out on the street. He wasn't even sure if she had been shot or the victim of some idiot throwing an incendiary device at her. He drove to the hospital. He opted against calling the police for now.

The emergency room was full of its normal Saturday night crowd of sick and injured individuals, some worse than others. A new mother with a sick infant, a guy holding a bandage around his hand, and an elderly woman in a wheelchair, coughing into a white handkerchief.

Ashley stood, waiting to be checked in. Javier glimpsed a uniform out of the corner of his eye, actually two uniforms, the uniforms of two Phoenix police officers. Ashley was being whisked inside to get her evaluation started and to keep her from bleeding all over the ER floor. Javier wandered over to the officers.

Hospitals employ off-duty cops to make sure that people who show up shot, especially gang members, aren't bringing their gun battles into the ER. Hospitals have their own security guards, but most aren't armed. You don't want to be the only person in the middle of a gang or drug war without a gun, and drop-offs of wounded associates were common occurrences at most ERs around the city.

The officers realized that a drive-by shooting of a woman on 44th Street was not a usual event. Javier gave them a good description of the area where he believed it had occurred. The word went out immediately to on-duty officers.

Twenty minutes after Ashley Armenta had been shot, patrol officers flew to the scene of her alleged attack. The details were sketchy, but they knew that the shooting fit the mold of the others that had plagued the city. A squad of patrolmen swarmed the area of 44th Street and Indian School Road.

The road was shut down, and a line search commenced in an attempt to find the crime scene. They started walking from Indian School Road north on 44th Street on both sides of the street. After a few blocks, officers discovered the scene and what little evidence it provided. A shot cup sat just north of the corner of 44th Street and Devonshire on the sidewalk. They had found their crime scene. Now the phone calls were made to get investigators rolling. It was a little after 3:00 a.m.

But the patrolman assigned to the shooting of Ashley Armenta would have to wait. The scene would have to be held for awhile because another call would come in, another emergency call. This one would take precedence over Ashley's walk-in injuries. It was another shooting, which wasn't unusual. But the circumstances surrounding it were eerily familiar.

Garry Begay was a proud member of the Hopi Indian tribe. A native Arizonan, he had spent most of his life on the reservation.

But as a young man, he had realized that being successful in life meant leaving the reservation and heading to the cities. Even though many of the Indian tribes in Arizona had become wealthy by establishing gaming casinos on their land, Garry's tribe had yet to do so. They were one of the few holdouts. They had fought the white establishment at every turn, and their people had suffered because of it. So, leaving the reservation was more of a necessity than a desire.

Garry made his way to Phoenix, but he never forgot his roots with the Hopi tribe. He would send money from different endeavors to his parents and relatives who still lived on the reservation. It was important to keep his ties to his heritage strong. If he could make life a little easier on them by working in the big city, so be it.

With very little education, Garry found only a few things that he was qualified to do for employment. He had done several odd jobs as an adult, but he could not figure out what the world had in store for him.

Gary landed a job at a convenience market chain and found that the work was easy. His boss let him set his own hours, and Garry liked the evening shift. No family obligations kept him tied to a day shift, and he would put in as many hours as he could. Working overtime, if need be, was never a problem. This extra work gave Garry additional money for the few things he cared about in life, mainly his family.

That's exactly what happened on the night of July 7th, 2006. Garry completed his shift at 10:00 p.m. He had received a call from the manager earlier and had been tasked with some additional responsibilities. That meant overtime. His replacement had come in at 9:00. Friday nights at any convenience store, especially one in the neighborhood of 48th Street and Van Buren, would be busy until after the liquor was locked up.

Transportation wasn't an issue for Garry. He didn't own a car and lived only half a mile from the store. The manager appreciated that because he could call Garry in a pinch if one of his other employees blew off work.

Garry looked at his watch as he finished his duties. It was almost 2:30 a.m. He signed himself out, took off his watch, laid it on the white porcelain sink in the employee restroom, and washed his hands. It was time to walk home.

The walk to Garry's apartment stretched along Van Buren Street, past another undeveloped construction site. An ugly chain-link fence stood next to the sidewalk, hoping to deter trash dumpers from depositing their goods on the acres of dirt. This site was supposed to be a multi-family residential community. A construction trailer sat amidst the mounds of dirt that had been moved to make way for the project. The construction company had placed a female mannequin on top of the tractor-trailer. She stood with her arms extended upward, legs crossed, and hands toward the sky as if she had just finished a performance.

Garry had seen the mannequin before and thought it looked ridiculous. As he passed it on his quiet trek home, the absurdity of the figure puzzled him. Then he realized something else: he'd forgotten his watch at work. It was his only timepiece, and he needed it. With a big sigh, he started back to the store.

As he entered, the night shift clerk gave him a peculiar look.

"Forgot my watch when I washed my hands."

The clerk chuckled.

"Bummer, walk all that way and then have to come back. Aw, you needed the exercise anyway," the clerk joked.

As Garry took off again toward home, there were very few cars on Van Buren Street. The Saloon, at 50th Street and Van Buren, had a few cars parked out around it, but every other business was dead. When you use your feet as transportation, you pay attention to those types of details.

Garry was deep in his own thoughts when the faint sound of a bicyclist, or at least that's what he assumed, crept up from behind. He casually turned to his right to make sure that the rider saw him, and that the rider was in the street, not on the sidewalk. But he didn't see a bike. Instead, he saw a car, a white Pontiac that slowed down in the two-way left turn lane. It had snuck up on him so quietly that he'd thought it was a bike.

Garry watched the car, thinking that it was going to make a left turn or a U-turn … something. It continued to crawl by him. It didn't dawn on Garry that all the businesses were closed, and that a left turn would leave the driver in a vacant lot. Garry could make out a white male driving the car.

With the car slightly ahead of him now and looking lost, Garry continued to watch it, waiting for it to make its turn, and hoping it saw him. Even with the streetlights, this part of the sidewalk was only slightly visible, and Garry worried that he would not be seen. The next sound Garry heard was a "bang." The thunder from the blast stopped him in his tracks, scared stiff. He hadn't seen a gun, but there was no mistaking it. The light-skinned driver of the Pontiac began to drive away, normally—no screeching tires, no dust flying, no pebbles being hurled toward him.

He looked down at his shirtless torso and saw blood starting to run from wounds in his chest and stomach. With no phone, bleeding, Garry decided to walk back to work. He felt he could make it.

When he walked through the glass doors, the same clerk could only look in amazement at him again.

"What did you forget now?"

That was the last stupid question he would ask. The shot pellets that had struck Garry were few, but blood poured from the holes. The shooter had fired backward in a hurry, probably because Garry eyeballed him slowing down.

The cops who responded got a brief description of the car from Garry. They already knew what had happened. It was Van Buren: another victim with shot pellets in him.

On the ride to the hospital, the paramedics told Garry how lucky he was that he was only minimally struck. He couldn't help but think how unlucky he was. If he hadn't stayed late to finish his work, if he hadn't forgotten his watch, if he had gone home, then none of this would've happened.

Garry began to question himself. "Was that really a white Pontiac the shot came from?"

There was one thing for sure. The shooter was white and male. "God damn pale face," he mumbled to himself. Another American Indian victimized by the white man. He couldn't help but feel bitter.

◈

It took the Violent Crimes desk sergeant only a second to glance up at the sticky note with my phone number on it. He no longer looked through the roster to find my number mixed in with those of hundreds of other investigators. He decided to post it close to his computer terminal for ease of access.

I was on the road by 4:00 a.m. At that point, they were still trying to piece together the shooting of Ashley Armenta on 44th Street. Patrol officers had contacted a couple of the residents, who had wandered out to see what all the fuss was about. They were still in the preliminary stages of gathering statements, so I decided to head to Garry Begay's scene first, even though it appeared it happened after Ashley's shooting. Detective Sergeant Harry Reiter was the on-call supervisor for that weekend.

"How you doin, Clark?"

"OK, I guess, considering what I'm about to get into."

"I hear you, brother."

Harry had come to the Assault Detail about a year prior and was an excellent supervisor. He had worked as a night detective for several years before being promoted to supervisor, and he knew his way around a crime scene.

"Looks like your boy hit again and may be responsible for another shooting on 44th Street," he said.

"I'm sure they're responsible for both. Let me guess. One shot fired from a 410 in a drive-by? Right."

"Well, I'll let you take a look at the wadding, but it looks to me to be a 410. You're the expert. I'll let you make the call. By the way, the press is here, and there've been some calls placed up the chain of command this morning. They will be eagerly anticipating your summary of what happened, especially if the second one turns out to be related."

"No witnesses I presume?"

I already knew the answer.

"Nope," Harry replied. "The patrol supervisor on the other scene is asking for an ETA, and I told him you just got here. Do you want me to wake up any of the other people and get 'em rolling?"

"Let me see what we've got. If it's like any of the other scenes, I should be able to process this fairly quickly and get to the next one."

Harry and I began the walk west from 52nd Street and Van Buren to where the officers had found the shot cup. As I walked up on it, I could tell it was a 410. It was still in one piece, sitting right in the entrance to the Honey Bears Restaurant, a great barbecue place. I looked around the area of the shot cup and saw no blood evidence.

"Where's the blood?"

"Looks like the victim works at the convenience store at 48th Street. I guess after he was shot, he decided to walk back to the store. Apparently, he doesn't own a cellphone. Patrol officers found a blood trail on the sidewalk west of here."

I noticed that it was a good two city blocks from where we were to the store.

"This is getting to be the norm in these things. My victims are walking all over the place after these shootings. How serious were his injuries?"

"They told me that he was barely hit, just a few pellets. Nothing vital struck," Harry said. "By the way, your photographer is here."

"Thanks. Let me take a walk and see how much blood evidence we have. I'll be back in two hours," I said sarcastically.

"Nothing like a brisk walk in the morning to wake you up. By the way, the victim told officers the shot came from a white Pontiac."

The dark skyline was turning light orange, with a few white clouds accompanying the break of dawn. I stopped at 50th Street and talked to the patrol officer guarding that intersection. I inquired if any of the patrons or staff had seen anything.

He responded with the obligatory, "Apparently not."

I picked up the first droplets of blood just west of 50th Street, marking the spot with a fluorescent orange cone. The drops ran about every ten feet apart, indicating the victim did just get winged.

The manager for the convenience store had arrived and verified that Garry Begay was in fact working the previous night and into the morning of the shooting. Garry is a "good employee," and he knew of no reason why someone would target him. The clerk who'd seen Garry shot had already left, but he could provide nothing further. He didn't even hear the shot.

"I just got off the phone again with the patrol supervisor on the scene at 44th Street. He's getting nervous about the street being shut down for the major part of the morning. I told him that it's a Saturday and traffic shouldn't be that bad, but he is a little panicked and he still wants an ETA," Harry said.

Before I answered what I believed to be an unimportant question, I asked if he'd noticed any security cameras on the businesses.

"I looked around and made the calls and you can look yourself, but I don't see any. I'm still waiting to hear from Honey Bears. They may have video inside that I can't see," he said.

"Well, if it's inside, I doubt it's going to show the street."

I began a quick scan of the businesses on the north side of Van Buren. None of them, including a tire repair and storage business, had any apparent surveillance cameras on the outside of their properties.

"You may have to call in some more help, too. There's not much evidence, but it is going to take a while for John to photograph this scene. I'm not going to be able to get to 44th Street within the next hour," I said.

Crime Scene Tech John Kinnaman had just joined us to hear his name being thrown down.

"Who do you want me to call, the on-call detectives or Detective Udd?" he asked.

"Call Darren. He may get involved in this sometime soon if I think what's going to happen is going to happen."

Detective Darren Udd had been with the Phoenix Police Department for over a decade. Darren had actually come to my patrol precinct out of the Academy and been trained by my squad. He was a good, aggressive street cop who didn't take any crap from anyone. He had come to the Violent Crimes Detail several years back and was my everyday partner, as much as you could have a partner. He was one of the few people I trusted to watch my back when we went after the bad guys. And we did that a lot.

Darren and I had decided that it was more fun to hit the streets and chase our own bad guy, then give their names to fugitive squads and have them picked up. We gave it a shot first, and then if we couldn't locate them, we would pass it off to long-term surveillance cops. We always enjoyed placing the cold steel handcuffs on the felons.

Some detectives transferred to investigations to get off the street. They'd interview suspects over the phone and then submit their cases. What fun was that? What fun was it to sit around the office when you could be out there among them? That's why I became a cop. To see the look on criminals' faces when you nabbed them. To see their lives, as they knew it, ending. To watch them squirm as I penned out or read them the charges they were facing. How could you rob yourself of that joy? Darren hated the predators as much as I did. We made a great team.

Darren called me as he was heading to the shooting scene on 44th Street. "You doin' all right out there?"

"Yeah, I'm fine. Let me know when you get to the scene at 44th Street. I'm going to come over there before I head to the hospitals and give it a quick walk-through." I knew that Darren would take care of the scene and process it right. 'It's our boys, again." I had kept Darren briefed on the series.

"When is somebody going to do something about this?" he blurted.

"I don't think it's a secret anymore, bud. The media is all over out here, and somebody's going to make some inquiries soon. I would bet my meager salary on that."

"Good! It's about damn time."

I marked the 410 shot cup at the Begay crime scene and collected it after it was photographed. The blood trail was photographed. I took samples at the start and the finish of the blood trail. Garry's clothing had gone with him to the hospital. I packaged those few items and bid adieu to Detective Sergeant Reiter.

It was only a quick eight-minute drive to 44th Street and Devonshire, where the second shooting had occurred. Patrol officers had related they first got the call on victim Ashley Armenta from St. Joseph's Hospital. The timing of the events was still a little sketchy.

Detective Udd was processing the scene and had his measuring tapes already out. I walked up to him.

"Looks like we found the shot cup," he said. "It split into two pieces—one down here towards the corner of Devonshire and the other about 40 feet north of here."

That was odd. Shot cups usually don't separate unless they strike something hard. There was a utility pole next to the roadway, which could have caused the separation.

"Dude, I got no blood out here anywhere," Detective Udd said. "Looks to me like your vic got in the car right after being shot.

"Guys," I thought to myself. "I suppose there are no witnesses over here either," I said.

"Course not. Why would there be?"

I looked down at the two pieces of the shot cup from a 410. It was confirmed. The SOBs had doubled up again.

I bid Detective Udd adios and headed to St. Joseph's. Ashley Armenta had been taken to a nonsurgical floor. It was my lucky day—I wouldn't have to deal with any confrontations in ICU.

Two patrol officers met me in the hallway just outside Ashley's room. They'd both been present when Ashley had been brought in. They introduced me to Javier Armenta, who was visibly upset. He looked exhausted, and his eyes were puffy from crying. I introduced myself and told Javier that I would be investigating the case of his wife's shooting. I asked him to tell me everything he knew.

Javier told me about the dinner and drinks that he and Ashley had that night, how they had an argument on the way home, and how she got out of their minivan. His eyes started to water again when he told me about the fateful call he got after Ashley had been shot. He was beating himself up over what he had done.

"I should never have left her alone out there."

"Did you shoot your wife, Javier?" I asked with authority.

He looked up at me as if I had just kicked him in the balls. I could read his thoughts. "How could I think he did it?" He answered pitifully, "No! I don't even own a gun."

"Then, don't beat yourself up over what happened. People get in arguments all the time. People step out of their houses, their businesses, their cars, their yards, all sorts of places, and never get shot. Separating from a loved one in an argument is a good way to stop anything violent from happening. You didn't do anything wrong. You understand?"

He sighed and looked to the floor. He was always going to blame himself no matter what anyone said.

"Thanks. I appreciate that," Javier said.

"Javier, I need to take a look at your cellphone, if you don't mind. I'm not trying to dive into your personal life, but I need to know when exactly you got that call."

He handed me the phone, and I began to pull his call log history. He had received the call at 2:38 a.m. I verified with him that was in fact Ashley's cellphone number.

"You know, I was there within a minute of her calling me. I didn't see anyone drive past me north on 44th Street," he said.

That was an important piece of information. It put the shooters in a southbound direction toward the Begay shooting scene. Now I had to confirm a timeline between the two shootings.

"I didn't even hear the shot."

"OK, well, I appreciate that. Now, more importantly, how is your wife doing?"

Javier gave me the rundown. She would not be held for more than a day. The pellets that struck her hit nothing vital. The dozen or so pellets had struck her upper back and head.

I excused myself from the hallway where Javier and I were talking and made my way to the nurse's station. I found Ashley's nurse and asked for her doctor. He was seated just behind the desk, looking at her X-rays.

"C'mon and take a look," he said. He didn't have to ask me twice. "She was very lucky. It looks like most of the pellets missed her. Was the guy a lousy shot?"

"I don't know. I haven't had a chance to talk to the victim ... or the suspect. Any other injuries been noted?"

The doctor grabbed her chart and turned the pages of the file.

"Doesn't look like it. I'm not even sure whether we're going to remove any of the pellets. We might cause more damage than good. Besides, they'll work themselves out sometime over the next year."

Ashley was sitting up in her bed when I entered. I had asked Javier to step outside for a few minutes while I talked to his wife. I was sure that he had nothing to do with the shooting, but it never hurts to look at all the variables before tying this into the other crimes.

I introduced myself to Ashley. Many of the victims so far had been homeless, which is why they'd been in harm's way. Ashley's circumstances were different.

"Ashley, I'm glad that you're going to be OK, but I need as much information as you can give me. What did you see? Please leave nothing out."

Ashley told me about the night out with Javier, dinner, drinks, and the argument on the way home. She specifically told me about the driver who had stopped to offer her a lift.

"He was driving a Jeep Cherokee, and I don't know what race he was. But it sure made me scared. So, I decided to call my friend, Kelly, on the phone. Thankfully, she answered, and I began to tell her what had happened with Javier and me.

"May I see your phone? I'm trying to put an exact time to when you were shot."

"Sure, it's right here."

She reached for the bedside table on which her cellphone was sitting. She gave me Kelly's number, and I was able to see that she'd called Kelly at 0231 hours.

"OK, so you're talking to Kelly. What happened, and what route did you walk?"

"Well, originally, I was walking west on Indian School, but I got to the corner of 44th Street and took a right. I was just walking … and I think I crossed Devonshire and was still talking to Kelly. Then I felt it."

"Felt what?"

"A vehicle . . . behind me. It just snuck up on me. I turned around and looked, and sure enough, there was a car stopped at the intersection I had just walked through." She paused for a moment. "I was upset about the other driver trying to pick me up, so I turned around and stared at the car. It was a light blue, or silver, or metallic Toyota Camry. A 2000 model."

"How can you be so sure of the car's make and model?"

I was skeptical, to say the least.

"Well, I used to date a guy who was really into cars. He did a lot of work on them, and I learned from him. He used to work on Camrys."

"You're sure about this? The make, model, year, and color?"

I wasn't trying to offend her, but this was huge.

"I'm positive." She continued on. "So, anyway, I noticed that the car was sitting facing west on Devonshire after it pulled up to the intersection. It was stopped there as if it were waiting to pull out onto 44th Street."

"What happened then?"

She was on a roll.

"I turned around and continued to walk. That's when I heard a loud noise. It might have been a gunshot. But then I felt this stinging pain in my back and neck. At the time, I thought somebody had thrown something at me. I was still talking to Kelly, and I told her that I thought somebody threw something at me."

"Did you realize that you'd been shot?" I asked.

"No, not right away. There were a few things that flashed through my mind. Was I shot, was I hit with something, or did a bunch of bees just attack me? I wasn't sure."

"Where was the car at this time, if you know?"

Ashley continued. "I turned around after I heard the noise, and the Camry was still stopped at the intersection. I watched as it just pulled out onto 44th Street ... nice and slow, as if nothing had happened. It was no big deal."

Now for the most important question of the incident.

"Did you get a look at anyone in the car?

"No, I didn't. I couldn't see anyone or anything inside the car. It was really dark."

I cursed inside. There was nothing else from Ashley. She'd been great under pressure and duress. She was positive about the make and model, and that was good by me.

I left the room to call Ashley's friend Kelly to see if there was anything else, and she only reinforced what Ashley had said. She didn't even hear the gunshot.

I stepped back into the room and joined Ashley and Javier.

"You did an excellent job, Ashley. Thank you for your help. There is something I need to tell you about. Don't get too upset, but I need to tell you this up front."

It was time to spill the beans about her being a victim of a serial predator.

I explained to Ashley and Javier that she was the latest in a series of shootings that had plagued the city for months, that she needed to be prepared for a barrage of media coverage if, in fact, the story broke. I told her that she didn't have to discuss the case publicly and, frankly, I would appreciate it if she didn't. I especially told her to keep any information about the car away from reporters. This was a nugget I was not willing to share with the media.

"I don't like them anyway, so there's no reason for me talk to them," she said.

I hoped that she would continue to be silent. I wasn't so much concerned with her telling them what happened, just not what she saw.

John, my photographer, and I then started to look at Ashley's wounds. As John started shooting pictures, I counted eight pellet holes in her back and neck area. I could see that under her hair she had numerous others. But it was the wound on the left side of the back of her neck that caught my attention. She had an abrasion that did not resemble a pellet wound, even if it was a glancing hit. The abrasion was longer than the mark a pellet wound would leave, and there was a half-moon-shaped bruising on top of the abrasion. I would later determine that the abrasion was caused by the impact of the shot cup into her neck; the half-moon bruising was the exact size of the bottom of the cup. That's what caused it to split into two pieces at the scene.

As John and I walked from St. Joseph's Hospital to our vehicles, I began to run in my mind the scenario that Ashley had just laid out for me. A car pulled up behind her off a side street. That was unusual, but it confirmed what I believed was a major part of their M.O.: the surveillance of the victim. They had found or seen Ashley on Indian School Road but had circled around using side streets to get into a position to shoot her. They'd rolled up right behind her.

She'd been north of the intersection when she was shot. That's what she'd said, and it was what the evidence told me. That meant the passenger's side of the vehicle had been facing Ashley. The car had been maneuvered so the passenger could shoot.

When I arrived back at police headquarters, I expected media, brass, and citizens with torches and pitchforks awaiting me. Nothing was further from the truth. The only bodies in Violent Crimes were Detective Udd, who was impounding evidence from the Armenta crime scene, and Sergeant Reiter, who was writing up the crime log entry.

"What did the other vic have to say?" Darren shouted between cubicles.

I had just gotten back from County Hospital, where Mr. Begay was being kept.

"Not a lot. Besides the guy was white. Oh, and, of course, he gave me a different description of the car than Ashley Armenta did." That complicated things. "He thinks the shot came from a white Pontiac, not a blue/silver Camry."

"Who got the better look?" Darren asked.

"They both did, I think." But, my gut instinct told me Ashley was right. "I like Ashley's description better. Besides, she claims to know cars."

"Oh, that's a relief," Darren shot back.

Whatever the case, I was beat. Time to go home. Nobody was beating down my cubicle for answers. It could all wait until Monday. But Monday couldn't wait.

CHAPTER 23

There is nothing like the relief of taking off your badge, sidearm, handcuffs, and cellphones after a hot day of working in the desert sun. July 8ᵗʰ was 110 degrees, so stripping all that gear off was liberating. Besides, I had sweated through my pants and undergarments, and that's uncomfortable. I know it sounds gross, but what's the alternative? No real cop I know wears a shoulder holster, That's for Hollywood.

As I readied myself for a dunk in the pool, the phone rang. I almost didn't answer it, but I had a feeling it was someone from work ruining what was left of my weekend. It was late in the afternoon, so I knew that it couldn't be my shooters. They hit only late at night. Sergeant Reiter had made all the appropriate phone calls up the chain of command. Why did they feel the need to bother me?

"Hello," I said.

"Clark, it's Stu Clarke."

"What's up, Stu?"

I figured he wanted briefed on the two shootings from last night.

"I need you at headquarters at 8:00 p.m. tonight. You're going to be put in charge of a task force to try to find these idiots. You're going to brief everyone. Looks like you got your wish," he said.

I didn't know what to say. What task force? How many people? Was there a plan? Who do I report to? I tried to comprehend the timing and rationalize the decision making process.

"Is the chain of command aware that there have been no shootings on Saturday nights? I don't remember being consulted on shoot days and days of non-shootings. "I mean . . . what's going on?"

"I don't think they care about that right now. The word I got was that the Mayor's Office was besieged with phone calls today, wondering what the hell we're doing about these maniacs shooting people. Apparently, our detail was the only ones that were concerned. Everybody was informed, and now it's time to put the people out there," Sergeant Clarke advised.

So politics had spawned the show of force. I was happy with whatever it took to get the cops I needed to catch these guys. I wasn't going to start complaining.

"How many cops did we get?"

"Right now, it looks like you're going to get twenty to twenty-five undercover units from the Drug Enforcement Bureau, a few detectives from Family Investigations, and some hit cars with patrol officers in them. I should also tell you that they are going to run with your original plan that was set up on the Fourth of July—roving units and fixed units. The LT is meeting with Lieutenant Vermeer from DEB, and he is going to be in charge of the undercover units. Our lieutenant is going to run the Investigations side of it."

I knew Lieutenant Brent Vermeer from my patrol days. He was just the kind of guy I needed to think outside the box on these cases. He was also smart enough to realize that he didn't know everything. He would be perfect for the leadership position of the undercover units.

"How long do we have these troops?"

No sense in getting excited if this was a temporary show of force.

"Right now, sixty days, but that can be extended."

God, I thought, if I haven't caught these guys in sixty days, I had better find some place to hide. Especially since they'd become so active.

"Got any idea what you're going to say?"

"I've got a few hours to pull something together." I hung up the phone.

I wandered up to the bedroom to get dressed and drag my sorry self back to police headquarters. As I dressed, I thought about the 120 or so investigators, officers, and civilians assigned to the Baseline Killer Task Force, which had been up and running for months. That guy hadn't struck in close to two weeks. I decided that twenty-five bodies was a good start. My suspects were just coming off two shootings. The media had gotten wind of what was happening, which meant high exposure. It also meant more publicity.

Unfortunately, that was just what some craved.

The first floor at 620 W. Washington was the home of the Employment Services Bureau and the Public Relations Bureau. The latter was the bureau that housed all the media spokespeople who conducted all the briefings with the assorted media outlets. The bureau was headed by a commander, but the most notable face was that of Sergeant Andy Hill.

I had known Andy since he'd taught Criminal Law to my Academy class. He was a really nice guy and the perfect face for the TV cameras. He was sharp, educated, good-looking, and a good communicator. Andy had worked investigations as a supervisor and was smart enough to check with the detectives on cases that had high media interest. He wasn't one of those guys who just started yakking in front of a camera and ended up leaking information that might turn out to be privileged. He also didn't suck up to the media. I had seen him take some media members to task for jeopardizing investigations or reporting half-truths.

Andy was one of the first people I noticed as I entered the makeshift conference room. The room housed another unit now, and numerous long work tables made the place look like a training room center. There was one head table. The other tables fell into neat rows parallel to it.

As I looked around the room, I saw undercover drug and vice enforcement detectives with their long hair and jewelry. Some had beards, others had tattoos and piercings. Most of them I had never seen before. In violent crimes, we deal with a lot of drug-related crimes, but they were crimes of violence caused by drug sale or use. These guys and gals were undercover street buyers. Our paths would only cross if one of their marks decided to shoot up a neighborhood or get shot. Even then, their cases would just get piled on top of mine for good measure.

There were uniformed cops seated in the back of the room, trying to draw as little attention to themselves as possible. I looked at their faces, and they seemed confused as to why they would be here. In fact, I could see the consternation in all the officers in the room. I knew what was running through their minds. What the hell are we doing here? Why are we being pulled off our cases to join in this circus?

I would've asked myself the same question if I were in their shoes. Cops gravitate to the details that interest them. If these drug and vice detectives wanted to work violent crimes, they would've transferred there. Unfortunately, for them, their cases would be put on hold for awhile. Hopefully, between this task force and the Baseline Killer Task Force, we wouldn't deplete the entire investigations division.

These two sets of serial killers had sent this city into a frenzy. It was only a matter of time before the police department threw everything it had into these investigations. The city was in fear, and people were dying or getting maimed.

Sergeant Andy Hill stood up, approached me, and sat next to me. "How you doing, brother?" he asked.

"Ask me that in sixty days if we haven't caught these guys." I was sure he knew of the allotted time frame, and that it didn't mean much.

"I think with you working it with some good undercover people, Clark, you're going to catch this guy."

I had briefed Andy regularly during these shootings in case the media busted out with a story.

"By the way," he said, "the AP . . . Associated Press is going nationwide with a story that Phoenix has three serial killers at large."

I knew who the AP was, but what concerned me was the three serial killer aspect of the story.

"Three serial killers? Where the fu#@ did they come up with that?"

Andy knew everybody in the press, and he was the one they always called for information on the Baseline Killer. He'd been conducting media briefings about the case for some time now. He had also talked to the media about the .22 shootings that had stopped in December of 2005.

"Yeah, three serial killers. I know that I have been busy with the Baseline case, Clark, but I really need you to keep me in the loop about this case."

"I'll do what I can, Andy, but you have to understand that I'm going to be very tight-lipped about this case. I will not be doing any interviews or talking to any one in the media, even if we catch these jackasses. The Baseline Killer case has had more leaks than the Titanic, and I'm not going to have that happen here. By the way, it's two guys, not just one." I had decided to share that insight during the briefing anyway.

"Seriously, you think it's two guys? What makes you so sure? Can you let me in on it?"

"Evidence and shooting zones. It would take too long to explain. Just make sure you keep that to yourself. If things get really desperate, maybe we can break that to try to get some calls generated. But for now, everything in here stays in here."

"Mum's the word, brother. By the way, I hear the media has dubbed your case the 'Serial Shooter.'"

"Catchy," I thought sarcastically. The "Random Shooter" had been floated for a while. That was even worse. I decided to combine both of them. When referring to this case, I would use the term "Random Serial Shooter." It was good to be king.

I excused myself from Andy and went over to Lieutenant Brent Vermeer. I shook his hand, and we exchanged pleasantries. I told him how I appreciated Drug Enforcement's help, and he just shook his head. His guys were upset, and who could blame them? They had their own cases to worry about, their own bad guys to chase. Why were they getting thrown in here? But he knew how important it was to catch these guys.

"Lieutenant Benson tells me you think it might be two guys. Is that true?" I quickly explained my theory and told him I'd give him more details later. The brass started arriving, and Lieutenant Rich Benson signaled for me to join him at the head table. Assistant Police Chief Kevin Robinson and Lieutenant Vermeer made their way to the front. Chief Robinson was the highest-ranking manager in the Violent Crimes Bureau and was obviously very interested in the proceedings. He would lead off the briefing.

"Ladies and gentlemen, thank you for coming. I know that most of you are wondering why you are here."

The chief went on to explain about the Random/Serial Shooter case, and he relayed information that he'd obtained from my direct chain of command. He introduced everyone at the lead table and then apologized to the audience.

"I'm sorry that we have had to change some of your work hours and off days. Unfortunately, this case now takes priority over every other investigation the city has going. As you may or may not know, there is another task force dealing with the other killer known as the Baseline Killer. You will not be associated with that task force. You all will concentrate your efforts on catching this bad guy."

He then introduced the people at the head table.

Lieutenant Vermeer spoke first. "People, I know that some of you are upset that your investigations are on hold. That's normal. But you have to understand the magnitude of this case. According to Clark Schwartzkopf, and I'll let him tell you about the cases in detail in just a minute, these guys are getting more active. With his input and his chain of command, we have set up a plan to try to catch the shooters. Please listen carefully to your assignments."

Lieutenant Benson introduced himself and advised that he would be running the investigative side of the case. He also thanked them for dropping everything and threw out this little morsel: Overtime was not an issue. That eased the pain a little bit. Cops are fickle, but the only way to make a decent living in this job is to get overtime.

As Lieutenant Benson continued on about how time slips, overtime, and general housekeeping issues would be handled, I began to peruse the room. Toward the sidewall, I saw the familiar face of Sergeant Tim Bryant. Tim had worked Homicide as a supervisor for over a decade. He had recently left Homicide and had taken over the gun squad. He knew more about catching bad guys than 95 percent of the investigators on the force. He was the kind of supervisor who hung out with investigators, questioned every motive that a suspect could have, and browbeat cases to death until they were solved. He had dedicated his entire career to catching violent pukes, and I was glad he was coming to the party. I nodded when he caught me looking at him.

Lieutenant Benson finished talking and then turned it over to me. It was time to put all the cases out in front of the people who had either volunteered or been told to report to the task force. I wasn't going to leave them without the necessary information that they needed to catch these guys. No secrets here. I would give them as much as I could, without going into great detail.

"Folks, thanks for coming. You all have been handpicked for this assignment because of your outstanding ability to conduct nighttime surveillances." I paused for a second. "Alright that's bull#@^%; none of you were handpicked. You all volunteered or were volunteered, but I thought that sounded good." That got a laugh from the crowd. At least they knew I knew why they were here.

"I am currently investigating a series of thirteen shootings, all with a shotgun, all of them in the City of Phoenix." The room got real quiet. "All of these shootings are related and have been carried out by what I believe to be a team of two shooters. I won't get into those details, but I believe that we're looking for two men. I believe at least one of them is a white guy. I can't be sure about the race of his partner. I am telling you this to try to make your surveillances easier. It doesn't mean that the shooters can't be out by themselves. In fact, some of my victims only saw one person in the car. So, based on that, every male in a car is a suspect, but if you spot two of them cruising around, that should raise a red flag."

Now to the car. "The best description we have of a car is a 2000 model Toyota Camry, which is light blue or silver. That description was relayed by my last victim, who was shot this morning at 44th Street and Devonshire. She got a pretty good look at the car before they got a shot off at her. It was fired from the passenger side of the vehicle, which makes me believe there could've been two of them in the Camry."

I watched the room for responses. Nothing yet.

"I have also had similar car descriptions from other victims, but not this good. The fact is they have run the gamut of cars, but the consensus is that the shooters are driving a four-door mid-size car, white, silver, or light blue in color. I wish I could give you better intel, but that's all I got at this point."

Now to the M.O. "OK these guys are cool under pressure. They do not panic and hightail it like little gangbangers after they do a drive-by. They're cool and calm. They fire one shot and drive away. They don't say anything or yell anything. The only sound from their vehicle is a shotgun blast. They like to double up when they're out. If they hit one time, especially recently, there is a good likelihood that they're going to hit again, and it's always between the hours of 2200 to 0300. It also looks like they may be stalking their prey."

That needed to be explained.

"What I mean by stalking is that based on the shooting this morning, they are conducting surveillances of their victims. They came off of a side street and gunned down the woman. They'd always shot victims from major thoroughfares, but this morning they deviated from that plan. They actually circled in behind her off a side street and shot her. That tells me that they're taking their time, watching their surroundings. It also feeds into the reasoning as to why we have no witnesses to any of these shootings. These guys are careful, and the only witness they leave is the victim, who is either dead or too hurt to provide any useful details."

Sergeant Tim Bryant popped up with the first question. "How sure are you of the Toyota description provided by the victim?"

"Sergeant, I think we caught a real break this morning with this gal's description. Whoever fired at her missed high, but she was able to see the car sneak up on her before she was shot and slowly drive away after. She's positive it was a Toyota Camry. It's the best intel we've got so far."

He seemed satisfied. Now to the gun.

"Lastly, the gun. I believe that we're looking for is a 410 shotgun. For those of you who are not familiar, the 410 is the smallest caliber of shotgun made. It fires a small, thin cartridge, which, by the way, has never been found at any scenes. It has been used on at least half of my shootings. We also know that a 12 gauge has been used at least twice." The lab had determined the gun used in the James Hodge case was in fact a 12 gauge, not a 20 gauge, as had been reported. "So, don't be honed in on just the 410. Realize that another caliber of gun has also been used."

"As some of you may know, detectives worked a group of similar crimes last year where a .22 caliber rifle was used. Understand that at this point those cases and mine have not been linked. Do not tell anybody they have been linked. For the purposes of this task force, we are looking for shotgun assassins. There may be a time in the near future when we combine the cases."

"Folks, we do not have probable cause for an arrest. We need to locate them, identify them, get on them." I closed with thanking them again, and that I appreciated their help and discretion. "See you out there." I wanted them to know I would be on the hunt for the assailants as well.

Bill Lewis, acting Commander of the Violent Crimes Bureau, tied everything together.

"Folks, it is vitally important that we catch these people, so I am going to ask you to take your assignment very seriously. I know that you're all professionals, and I need to caution you of something. Every bit of information that you've been privy to tonight is to be kept confidential. You're not to discuss anything that you hear tonight, or any other night, with anyone outside of this task force. The information that Clark has shared with you is not to be disseminated. I don't need to tell you of the repercussions that leaking any of this information could have on the overall investigation. I'm sure that you people are smart enough to realize that."

He had witnessed that all too well with the .22 caliber cases and with the BLK. Now it looked as if the bad guys had learned from the slip and changed weapons.

"Furthermore, that means that for the purposes of this task force at present, all stops will be for intel gathering purposes only. You are not to arrest anyone unless a crime is committed in your presence. Then we'll deal with those as they arise."

In other words, forego the small-time crap and stick to your assignments.

"We understand if you feel the need to stop a crime, but we don't want your covers blown. That's why we have patrol officers hit cars assigned to this task force. They will come in and take over those incidents. They'll also stop anyone you might think is suspicious for whatever is reasonable. We'll gather intel and pass it on to Clark."

He needed to clear one thing up for sure: "Having said that, if someone shoots someone in front of you, or you think they're about to shoot someone, obviously you're cops. Take appropriate action."

Commander Lewis closed with this ardent piece of advice. "If you think that you have something, and it looks good, follow your instincts. But don't be afraid to get on the radio and ask for help or guidance. We cannot allow these suspects to know that we're out there. We need to get something on them so we can narrow our focus. We're looking for some leads because we have none. Any questions?"

The room fell silent.

I knew this plan was a long shot, but what else could we do? Having cops on the street might be the only way we get a lead in this case. Maybe, just maybe, we could be close or right on top of them when they pulled the trigger. Then we could end this thing in a hail of bullets.

Sergeant Bryant piped in with a few words of wisdom. "Hey, people, this is as serious as it gets. Make sure that you don't blow your covers going after some guy drinking alcohol in the park. If these guys learn that we're out there, they could head to another part of the city, and we would have to start from scratch. If you get tired, we have relief, right Lieutenant?" He looked at Lieutenant Vermeer, who nodded his head up and down. "If you get tired, or you have to go take a leak, let someone know. My squad will be roving units, and we can relieve you. We don't want to lose these guys because someone left an area or a post." Leave it up to Sergeant Bryant to hammer home an important point of Surveillance 101.

After the assignments were handed out, I strode upstairs to start typing up the two new cases I had just investigated. It wasn't long before Sergeant Bryant wandered to my desk. This was his first visit, but it would become a nightly occurrence for many days to come.

"How you doing, Clark?"

I kind of chuckled, and turned my chair to face one that he had just pulled up from another cubicle.

"As well as any investigator who just laid out his entire case to a bunch of strangers could be, I guess."

I wasn't being sarcastic; I was nervous. Nobody in that conference room wanted to see innocent civilians being gunned down, but on the other hand, it wasn't their case. I just hoped the overtime pay would help out.

"I've been doing some checking. It sounds like you have a pretty good feel for what these guys are up to, and it also sounds like you're not keeping a whole lot of cards up your sleeve." He was right. "That could be risky," Sergeant Bryant added.

"I know it's a big risk. But I have no choice here. They need to know what they're getting into."

Sergeant Bryant understood what I was talking about. "The problem with giving up that information is not what the cops hear. It's what they tell their buddies, neighbors, wives, kids, you name it," he said.

"Right. In an investigation like this, that could lead to trouble, and that's only one problem, Sarge. This is the most frustrating case I have ever been around. It could take off in any direction, and we could be chasing our tails going after anyone or anything because I don't have anything to go on."

"Sounds to me like this case has taken on a life of its own. Now you've gotten the brass involved, which is never a good thing," he said. "The question is, are you getting everything you need to do the job?"

"Well, now I am. The real questions are, is this the right approach, and what happens if it's not? Plus, my instincts keep getting in the way." Some of them I had never shared with anyone.

"Sometimes, those are the best … cop instincts, I mean. As long as you realize they're just instincts. It's when detectives get stuck on them and are afraid to move away that they get slapped upside the head with reality when things change."

"I understand that, but in this case, that could be anything."

He could tell I had more.

"What other instincts have you got? Maybe I can help sort through them with you," he said.

Besides the two-shooter theory, I told Sergeant Bryant that I believed that whoever was responsible was very upset with the City of Phoenix. I pulled out the map that showed the exact locations of all the shootings in this shotgun series, and a different map showing the .22 caliber cases. "They're either all in Phoenix or just off our borders. It's as if they know what the borders are."

He looked at the maps. "You talking disgruntled employee or something along those lines?"

"Possibly. It's just a theory."

I then told him that I felt whoever was doing this is good, maybe even professionals. Could be ex-military, ex-police, or someone with better than average skill sets.

"There's never a witness. They just can't be that lucky."

"Well, military training could explain that, or some type of police training," he said.

"But why use a shotgun?" I asked. "If you really wanted to kill people, and you've lost your cabbage, I would think that you'd find something a little more lethal. You wouldn't be out there blasting away with a 410 shotgun. A real professional who was hell-bent on killing would use something more powerful, like at first, with the 12 gauge."

"That's a good point," Sergeant Bryant said. "Sounds like you just talked yourself out of that theory." He was right. "See, you've taken the first step. Don't be stubborn. Beat things around a while before settling on a position."

I sighed and shook my head. What a mess. He knew that I had a lot of work to do, and he decided that it was time for him to hit the street.

"Let me know if there's anything else you want to discuss before you sound off. Sometimes a good discussion can lead to humbleness."

He arose and pushed the chair back to the desk that he had retrieved it from.

"No one knows everything, but be careful who you share your thoughts with. It may come back and bite you in the ass."

Good advice.

Before leaving, he asked, "By the way, since you're going to be out there with us, you want use of an undercover vehicle? I got an extra truck that you can borrow."

"Absolutely," I said.

"I'm sure that you don't want to be out there running around in a city vehicle that every bad guy in town can recognize from a mile away. I'll have one of my guys run you over to our facility and get you the vehicle. It's a black, raised Ford. Looks more like a cowboy's truck than a cop's."

"Thanks. I appreciate that."

As Sergeant Bryant walked away, I turned back to the task at hand: typing up the reports on the Armenta and Begay shootings. It was amazing what little information I had and what little evidence had been recovered. Two shot cups from a 410 shotgun, a condom, and a ball cap. The cap would be submitted for possible DNA processing.

It had been a long day, and it was going to be a long night.

My new, shiny, black truck was a raised piece of engineering genius. No one would mistake this for an undercover vehicle. Its pipes jetted out the side and rumbled so much it would set off car alarms when I stepped on the gas. Even cops can be obnoxious if we care to be.

Later that night, as I pulled out of the downtown area heading to the eastern part of the city, I glanced at my cellphone. It was pushing 11:00 p.m. already. The surveillance squads were busy communicating on the designated radio channel that had been set up for the task force. Patrol hit cars were already out with one guy who was either lost or driving around aimlessly. That would be a nightly occurrence as the task force weaved its current path. Stop everyone at first, and then become more adept at spotting suspicious behavior more relevant to our shooters' pattern. I didn't care how many people they stopped or who. The more intel we gathered, the more chance we might get lucky.

I had decided that I would concentrate my efforts on trying to identify how and why the shooters were hitting the east side of Phoenix. What was it about this hunting ground that gave them the opportunity to strike so frequently with such ease? What were their opportunities?

As I drove around in the dark, I realized something. I loved undercover police work at night—the sneaking around in the shadows, the spying on people who had no idea they were being watched, the thrill of the dark, and what surprises it might bring. I also realized that the same things that got my blood pumping about working under the cover of darkness were probably the same things that motivated my killers. Sneaking about, watching, lurking, and waiting for an opportunity. How they must get off on it. It was a game.

I took up a position on a two-story garage on Thomas Road, two miles east of where Claudia Gutierrez-Cruz was murdered. Traffic was busy, and using binoculars, I spied a convenience store. Our boys had to buy gas as they cruised around. Maybe I could get lucky.

As I watched the customers pump gas, I tried to put myself in the killers' shoes. It wasn't too hard. They targeted people who were alone, leaving no witnesses. They fired once and fled, never attempting a second shot, never giving the target the opportunity to see too much if they didn't put the person down. They needed to be silent, dark, and quick.

After a few minutes, I hit the road again. I circled to 44th Street and McDowell and pulled my truck to a stop. As I sat waiting for the light to change, I heard the ghastly sound of sheet metal tearing. I had heard it too many times before. Two vehicles had collided, and for a millisecond, I hoped that my world wouldn't end with that metal crashing into me.

A truck attempting to turn left at the intersection had failed to anticipate the speed of an oncoming car. The driver of the truck had realized his mistake and tried to over-correct, but it was too late. The small sedan clipped the side of the truck and went skidding past the intersection. Time stood still. Nobody moved inside either vehicle. As I reached for my radio to call for a patrol officer to come and take care of the accident, the truck revved its engine. It took off like a dragster. Dammit! Why me?

I tried to tell myself not to get involved. The cop in me took over. Screw that! The truck was flying, and I was already too far behind. I stepped on the gas, flipped a U-turn, accelerating to catch up to the truck. I had no idea if the occupants of the car were OK.

I was stuck in the middle of a situation, one that this task force had just discussed. Don't get involved with routine police functions unless you absolutely have to. I was cursing out loud in the cab of the truck. The pickup I was chasing made a quick right at an intersection and headed east. I caught the taillights as it made another quick right into a residential neighborhood. Another quick right, and the vehicle stopped. It knew I was following. The male occupant stepped out from the truck and began to assess the damage to his vehicle. I screeched to a stop and drew down on him.

The young kid realized that I was pointing a gun at him and went facedown onto the asphalt The truck's windows were tinted, and I couldn't see inside.

I had committed the ultimate sin when pursuing a suspect vehicle. I lost orientation. I started to call myself all kinds of names. I got on the radio and told the dispatcher what had happened. I was out with the truck, including the truck's license plate. I gave her the general area that I was in, but embarrassingly could not give her the exact street address. I knew that I was north and east of the hit-and-run scene. Patrol units began to fly to my location.

In the meantime, the poor victims who had been struck at the intersection stayed in the street with their car, not knowing what else to do. They were OK, no paramedics would be needed. That was good news, but I had blown my cover for a misdemeanor hit-and-run.

Chief Robinson's unit was the first to find me. He pulled up and saw me with my gun trained on the kid, who was still eating asphalt.

"You alright, Clark?" he asked.

"Yeah, I'm fine."

Together we walked up to the kid and slapped some handcuffs on him. He was alone. At least I still knew how to do that. I didn't want to ask him any questions. I already had to write a report as to what I'd witnessed. Turns out the kid was driving his dad's truck and panicked after the collision. A patrol officer took control of the kid and started in on his report.

I spent the rest of the night trying to avoid any more police actions. It wasn't surprising that my shooters didn't hit on the night of July 8th or into the morning of July 9th. They had never hit on back-to-back nights anyway. At least the night had gone smoothly. We called it quits at 3:00 a.m. I had been up for twenty four hours.

CHAPTER 24

When the task force was formed, I promised myself two things: I would stay fit, and I would keep a journal.

I had always prided myself that, in almost twenty years of police work, I had continued to maintain my physical fitness, no matter how old or rundown I got. Some cases, like my current ones, can turn out to be death marches. Try working for twenty-four hours straight on a crime scene, then grabbing a couple hours of sleep, only to start typing the report that needs to be finished within forty-eight hours for the suspect's initial appearance. Do that for several years, and that work takes its toll.

I'd always told myself that my health comes first over this job. So, over the years, I'd stayed with a ritual of hard cardiovascular workouts three times a week and weight training at least twice a week. I could rest on the other two days of the week, even if I had to put in a marathon of work on a case.

The idea of the journal was a "CYA" type of move. Obviously, anything that was case related would go into the official report. But I would document decisions made behind closed doors, just in case some manager one day tried to throw me down for a decision that was agreed upon by all my chain of command or others associated with the task force. I'm not stupid. I had seen it happen before.

The journal would contain topics of meetings, what was said, and who said it. I would keep track of who was there, just like a secretary keeping the minutes, but I was the only one who knew about it. I could also track the progress of the case, and my own thoughts about what I was doing as lead investigator. Any new theories that I conjured up would be placed in there as well.

July 9th was a Sunday, and that morning I had planned on going to church, a ritual that I had embarrassingly neglected.

I made my way into headquarters at about noon. There wasn't a soul in the office. It was quiet, and I could relax with no one bothering me, at least for the next eight hours. I printed out and began to read all of the .22 caliber cases, including the murder of David Estrada in Tolleson, plus all their animal shootings. It was obvious to me that all the .22 shootings were related, even if only a few could be forensically linked.

The tough part, if it ever came to it, would be connecting the .22 caliber shootings to the current shotgun shootings. There were glaring differences that could be tough to overcome—multiple shots fired in some of the .22 shootings, a .22 caliber weapon versus the shotguns, and the timeline of several months between the two series.

A shotgun had been used at least twice during the run of the .22 caliber shootings, specifically on the late evening of December 29th, 2005, and in the early hours of December 30th, when the dog, Cherokee, and Clarissa Rowley had both been shot. We could prove that. Still, there would be skeptics.

Once the shooters were caught, we may be able to logically explain the downtime in between the shootings. There could be numerous reasons for the silence in the six months leading up to the shotgun shootings. One glaring possibility was the destruction and havoc that all the shootings before New Year's had caused. If I had shot that many people and animals in one night, I might cool my heels for awhile, too. Chances were that if the shooters were smart, they might just assume that someone had gotten a look at them, that somewhere they'd left some trail leading back to them.

To me, the problem was the multiple shots fired. There would be all kinds of highly-paid criminal experts who would say the two series weren't related just because of that fact alone. It didn't make sense. The shooters were careful not to leave any shell casings when they fired the shotgun, yet they left casings at a few of the scenes of the .22 caliber shootings. That's a red flag. Did they not know they left casings at those scenes? Did they learn from those mistakes? Is that why they switched guns? It was time for some research.

I started by looking at all media articles associated with the small caliber shootings. Lucky for me, there were only a few. The print media had done most of the reporting on the series, culminating in a *Valley Metro* article about the bloodbath on December 29 and 30, 2005.

In January 2006, the *Arizona Republic* ran another article, this time officially linking the shootings of the animals on the west side of town and the murder of David Estrada with the animal shootings and murders of Jose Ortis and Marco Carillo. The shootings of Timothy Tordai and Clarissa Rowley were also linked.

They totaled sixteen in number. The article stated, "Police said Friday that they have no witnesses, and essentially no clue as to who is doing this."

Four of the shootings had been positively linked, meaning forensically linked. However, the article later states that "officials declined to disclose what evidence linked the four shootings, or why police couldn't definitively connect the others." Duh! Might as well just tell them if you're going to give them that much information. If the shooters were following the press and reading the newspaper, there was little wonder why they switched guns.

So, as if that weren't enough, the police further stated that fourteen of the shootings "were with a small caliber weapon, a shotgun was used in the other two shootings." It didn't mention a .22, but it might as well have. They all but laid out the case for the public and for the shooters.

The article closed with a description of a vehicle that someone had provided. "The vehicle is believed to be a 1995 or newer Honda-type sedan, dark green or gray with tinted windows." That description came directly from Barbara Whitner. It also fit closely with some of the descriptions I got.

May 7th brought a new headline: "Killers sought with sense of urgency." This article brought together the Baseline Killer and his assorted crimes of robbery, sexual assault, and murder, with the four known murders now labeled "serial sniper." He was possibly responsible for "25 shootings in the past year." Where the hell did they come up with that number? It grew from sixteen in January to 25 in May. Somebody was talking out of their butt.

When viewing the victims listed by name in the article, I saw they had Reginald Remillard on the list. That was OK, and I was aware of him. He had originally been left off for a lack of any evidence recovered in his case. A dog shot in February, another male shot, someone I had never heard of. A woman and another male I had never heard of were also listed as shot, but survived. Who the hell were these people?

I wrote myself a note to ask Detective Jewell about these other victims. If he couldn't prove beyond a doubt that they were targeted like the others, then they needed to be removed from the matrix of crimes, or I would disprove them. There is nothing worse than adding a bunch of people to a list just to create more attention, urgency, or to clear cases. If you want to lose credibility, that's one of the best ways to do it.

The article again referred to a vehicle, this time suggesting the possibility that a "light colored van" was seen at some of the shootings. Really? That, again, was news to me.

The article also contained an interview with a local forensic psychologist about serial criminals. He talked about why serial offenders commit these crimes. He ran the gamut of reasonings: financial, emotional, relational, or substance abuse. In other words, every reason why any crime is committed. No revelations there.

Then came an epiphany from an expert: it was unknown who. "Experts say small caliber pistols and rifles often are used by criminals in a city setting because they are relatively quiet when fired. The projectiles also tend to disintegrate or become so distorted upon impact that it is almost impossible to conduct ballistics tests."

Yes, some small caliber bullets, based on their construction, can get deformed upon impact. But the reason small caliber weapons are used in the city is because they're dirt cheap! It has nothing to do with ballistics. You can buy one of the thousands that float out there for less than $50.

It was time for me to conduct some serious research on serial killers. What was motivating my shooters? Pleasure of inflicting pain on strangers? Notoriety . . . through the media? Revenge? Hatred of the homeless? The possibilities were more than I cared to note.

Whatever the motive was, I needed to try to figure it out. It certainly wasn't financial gain. But what, if anything, linked serial killers and the mass hysteria they created? How many of them operated solely based on notoriety? Did they start out seeking fame, or did they just end up that way?

I still had a few hours before the surveillances started. This was going to take some time, and I didn't have a whole lot of it.

True to their word, the press ran with the story about three serial killers running loose in the Valley of the Sun. There was both a local article by one of the crime reporters and a national article that appeared in *USA Today*. Locally, the headline stated, "Police fear 3rd series of violent crimes is under way." The national headline read, "Fear in Phoenix as residents await next attack by 3 gunmen."

The local story described the Ashley Armenta and Garry Begay shootings, how they were twenty minutes apart and must be the work of the third gunman. This time the reporter listed my thirteen cases, starting with the May

2nd shooting of Kibili Tambidu. Andy Hill was quoted as saying, "I have never seen anything like this in my 22 years." No kidding. No one has seen anything like this.

As I read the local article, which also documented the Baseline Killer and the small caliber killer, the sheer magnitude of what Phoenix Police were facing was daunting. The public was stressed out. So was the mayor, and it appeared there was no end in sight. The national article also outlined the Baseline Killer, and how we had disclosed a third assailant in another unrelated series.

I could see where this was going to be a problem. There is no winner if you don't set the media straight. The fact of the matter was that I thought the .22 cases and mine were related. At some point, we were going to have to state that they were connected.

The briefing on July 9th was a breakdown of what went right, and what went wrong on the first night of surveillances. Lieutenant Vermeer had asked some of the local precinct supervisors to attend the meeting. There was confusion as to who would handle routine calls in the surveillance area, and how they would be dispatched.

We eventually agreed that uniformed patrol officers would handle all the calls, unless a call appeared to be related to the task force. The officers would be advised to get in and get out as quickly as possible.

The bigger problem was the overlapping of the two task forces. The Baseline Killer had moved areas, just like my shooters. He was now concentrating his efforts in East Phoenix also, predominantly in the 32nd Street and Thomas area, just a few miles from several of the shotgun shootings. The place was swarming with undercover cars, fixed foot posts, and the occasional patrol officer who mistakenly wandered into the area. You couldn't walk a hundred feet in any direction without being seen by a cop. It was believed that the Baseline Killer had a door in the area. Whether it was his, a girlfriend, or whoever was unknown. He had last hit on June 29th at a car wash just east of 28th Street and Thomas. Another woman dead. Our task force decided to stay clear of the area, with the exception of an occasional drive-through.

After the briefing, I went back to my desk to continue my research. I had an hour and a half before 10:00 p.m., the witching hour. I knew the city was safe for the meantime.

The night of July 9th proved to be uneventful. I hit headquarters at 3:00 a.m. and overheard the undercover officers talking about the night's events, or lack of them. Nobody on the task force could believe how many gray or light-colored sedans there were in the City of Phoenix. All of them were stopped for one reason or another. The intelligence poured in.

In the meantime, I was being informed of every shooting investigation where a shotgun or .22 was used. In a city this large, that was a pile of cases. I received word that two kids had been caught on the westside with a .22 Marlin, popping off rounds at a school. The Marlin fit, but it turns out the kids were driving a white Caddy, a far cry from a Toyota sedan. They were brought down to headquarters. I questioned them, took their gun, and booked 'em for discharging the rifle. Turns out the kids got the gun in a trade for some speakers, hardly the sophisticated pair of shootists I was looking for. These types of investigation would become a daily, and sometimes nightly, ritual.

On the morning of July 11th, I was asked to attend a meeting with Commander Bill Lewis and the Homicide unit chain of command. I had actually gotten five hours of sleep. I felt pretty good and was ready to confront supervisors with the facts about why these cases were related. There was no sense in beating around the bush anymore. The .22 caliber cases and my shotgun cases were related. Hopefully, Commander Lewis would see it that way.

Commander Lewis thanked everyone for attending. "OK, people, I have to brief the media on what we're doing to catch these guys. Right, Clark? Guys, plural?"

I nodded. The supervisors looked at me with some skepticism.

He continued. "Anyway, I have to brief the media on the status of the case. I can tell you that there are a lot of people looking for some answers, and we need to figure out some here and now. Clark has kept me up to speed on his investigation, but I want a consensus on the .22 caliber shootings. Are they related or not? If they are, we need to say so. If they're not, then we need to say so also."

A decision needed to be made. The problem was the media. Phoenix now had three serial murderers, not just two. Hell, one, or two was horrible, but three! Everyone wanted, and everyone expected answers. It wasn't the time to be wishy-washy. He looked around the room, Detective Jewell's immediate supervisor, spoke first.

"I've talked to Cliff Jewell and I've talked to Clark. I don't believe that Cliff is 100 percent sure that they're related, and I'm certainly not. Clark has made some good points, and he has convinced me that they are possibly related. I sit 40/60 against them being related."

Well, at least he thought I was 40 percent right.

He continued. "There are two troubling issues. Why did they change guns, and where did they go for five months? Five months! That's a long time for shooters who are so active to just quit. They shoot up the town right before New Year's, and then just disappear. It doesn't make sense. Maybe they were in jail. I doubt it, but who knows? That still doesn't change the fact that they switched weapons. That is unheard of in the annals of historical serial killers. These guys stick with guns that they like, that they are familiar with."

The rest of the supervisors agreed. They all said they were not as familiar with the cases as I was, but they, too, had trouble with the lay-off and the changing of weapons.

Commander Lewis looked straight at me. "All right, Clark, it's your turn. Convince us that they're related. "

I took a deep breath and spilled everything I knew. I, too, was having a hard time with the lay-off. But there could be numerous reasons for that, jailing of the suspects being just one possibility. Maybe the bloodbath on December 29th, 2005 had scared them into a lay-off. Maybe they were worried about all the media attention and the description of the car. Maybe they were concerned that we had forensic evidence tying the crimes together, which I pointed out, the media had also reported.

That brought me to the change of weapons, a smooth transition from the other point. "Look, this .22 caliber stuff has been reported. I just researched all the articles. The media knows it's a small caliber gun, and the shooter knows that too." It wasn't time to rip whoever talked about the small caliber gun, but my point was well made. "You had Jewell do a segment of *America's Most Wanted* in which the gun was identified. If they're like any other serial predators and watch TV, they know we know. They changed guns, in my opinion, because we have evidence that can link them, and they're not going to get caught with it."

I talked about the M.O., and how it was identical. The time of day and the targets were the same as well. I ended with this, "Don't forget, a shotgun was used on December 30th, 2005 also."

The room was quiet. Commander Lewis looked around the room for a few seconds. "They've gotta be related. There's just too many coincidences."

He looked down at his notepad in front of him. He had been scribbling notes while everyone discussed the cases. He looked up.

"All right. Thanks, gentlemen. I'll let you know what I decide. Clark, can you stick around for a minute?"

Everyone else rose from their seats and left the conference room. Commander Lewis spoke once everybody had gone.

"I really don't want to talk to the media, but the chief has told me to. Is there anything else I need to know?"

He was concerned, not just about us tripping over ourselves, but he didn't want to hurt the investigation.

"I've made myself very clear on what I think the media needs and doesn't need to know. The only chance we have of catching these guys is to keep some of our cards hidden. It's not going to take long for the interviews of our victims to start popping up. I've been very careful not to reveal the caliber of the shotgun being used, the 410. The damage the weapon causes speaks for itself. We can't hide that."

"Yeah, I understand that. But we need to narrow the focus. Are you sure these cases are related?" he asked with the tone of a man still trying to make up his mind.

"I'm sure."

"I hope like hell you are."

With that, he got up and left the room.

I was able to catch part of the press conference. Commander Lewis was grilled about not only the Serial Shooter case, but also the Baseline Killer. He was asked if the small caliber cases were related to the recent shotgun shootings in the Serial Shooter case. His answer was nondenial. "The cases may be related." That's playing it safe.

The mayor addressed the media and made a stunning announcement.

"The City of Phoenix, through its Silent Witness program, is offering a $100,000 reward for any information that leads to the capture of either the Baseline Killer or the Serial Shooter."

It was unprecedented. The largest reward I'd ever heard of was $25,000. The money had come from private donations and businesses, including a local radio station. If nobody had heard about the crimes before, they would now.

That kind of money gets people to turn on their mothers, not to mention acquaintances or friend

CHAPTER 25

Since the Baseline Killer Task Force had been up and running for a few months, we were going to be able to learn from their mistakes, or so we thought. They had brought in analysts from ATF to sift through their leads, document them, and put them into a database.

Because our task force was much smaller, we were given a small conference room at the east end of the Violent Crimes Bureau. It had a table that could seat about eight. There were no phones and no computers in there, so our communication and computer techs went to work to get things up and running. At this point, Detective Moncrief and I were the only ones using the room. No other investigators had been permanently assigned. I was told my partner, Detective Darren Udd, was soon to be assigned.

July 12, 2006 brought an avalanche of activity. Since the mayor's announcement of the huge cash rewards, the phones had started ringing off the hook at Silent Witness. I was also informed that Phoenix Police would hold a town hall meeting to address the concerns of the average citizen. It was to be an informational meeting, one of those public safety awareness meetings where we tell the citizens that if you don't know already to keep off the streets at night, then we're going to tell you again, in person.

For the meeting, which would be led by Chief of Police Jack Harris, the shootings and their areas were to be laid out on a life-size poster board. The police were going to hammer home the point that at least as far as the Serial Shooter went, the shootings took place between 10:00 p.m. and 3:00 a.m. Information and illustrations would also be presented on the Baseline Killer, along with the composite that had been put together: a light-skinned black male with a floppy hat and dreadlocks.

ATF had offered its services more than once during the run-up to the formation of the Random/Serial Shooter Task Force. They were itching to get inside and help. The Random/Serial Shooter investigation fit more under their expertise than the serial rapist/killer. So far, their role had been analysis only, and a few agents assigned to conduct surveillances. I was asked to brief them and see if they could provide any technical assistance. With a national database at their fingertips and the ability to bring in extra agents for fieldwork, it wouldn't be a bad idea to have them in our corner.

However, my bosses and I knew that getting a federal agency involved would bring in a whole new set of protocols, procedures, and hoop jumping. The feds can't wipe their nose without asking the U.S. Attorney's Office first. It was a source of constant frustration for the few federal agents I knew and respected. But I was told that their involvement would be as a secondary resource and that no way were they going to bully in and take over the investigation.

With those assurances, my chain of command accepted a meeting with ATF. Five agents and their supervisor caught up with us at police headquarters. I hadn't worked with any of the agents. They were all very young.

After providing a brief summary of the cases, I asked specifically what could they provide? According to them, Washington, D.C. was at our disposal. They had learned a lot from the D.C. snipers and were ready to prove it, though none of these agents had worked that case. We wanted a database like the ones the BLK task force had set up—one to track leads and follow-ups. They would check on that. The technical aspects of setting up ATF software and what the room needed were discussed in full. None of the agents had ever worked a serial offender case.

The command issues were brought up again, and we insisted that they, being ATF agents, be willing to take orders from city cops. They were fine with that. We asked them how quickly additional personnel could be brought in.

The supervisor spoke. "Yeah, let me check on that, and I'll float the idea up the line. I'm sure we can get more people to help out."

The meeting ended with an exchange of business cards.

After the meeting, I headed back to the task force command post. I'd been in the middle of checking cold cases when I had to break for the meeting. As I was looking through some 2005 cases, something jumped right off the page at me.

The summary of the case read as follows: "On November 11th, 2005 at or around 2300 hours, the victim, Nathaniel Shoffner, a transient, was shot just south of 200 N. 20th Street. The victim was found in the middle of the street with what appeared to be a shotgun wound to the torso. Subject was transported to County Hospital. No known suspects or motive for the shooting. There were no witnesses to the shooting."

The investigating detective was Bob Wenrick, a twenty-eight year veteran. Bob and I had worked on numerous cases together, and he sat directly behind me. We would bounce cases off of each other all the time. He was a good cop and a great investigator.

As I reread the entry, all the bells and whistles went off. A transient gunned down in the street with a shotgun, no witnesses, probably alone, and late at night.

I looked at the map of the shootings. 200 N. 20th Street was just south of Monroe Street, hardly a major thoroughfare. But it was only two blocks south of Van Buren, our predator's main hang out and favorite shooting gallery.

I walked over to my cubicle and saw that Detective Wenrick had left. I printed off the report and decided to spend some more of my precious time going over this case. It would not be a waste of my time.

Nathaniel Shoffner had spent most of his adult life on the street, and there were two simple reason for that: drugs and alcohol. Or maybe it wasn't that simple.

A man with absolutely no family, Nathaniel had been in and out of jail and rehab centers since 1985. He was pushing fifty years of age and had not been able to clean up or sober up. He had been arrested so many times for drinking from an open container, trespassing, and public acts of indecency that the system had become his second home.

Most of the patrol officers who worked the Central City Precinct knew him and started writing him citations to keep from having to book him into jail. This, however, was a useless endeavor. Nathaniel never showed up in court for his citations, and thus, they would always go to a bench warrant. It would only be a matter of days before he was seen drinking in public and his name run through the system. Of course the warrant would pop up. Off he would go to his second home, jail.

The clerks who worked the Circle K store at 20th Street and Van Buren knew Nathaniel by sight. He would stop in for a drinking cup for some water, and he was basically harmless. But, occasionally, he would try to steal food or beer. He had been banned from the store. Yet the clerks who worked there tolerated him. They knew he wasn't violent, but they kept an eye on him.

When Nathaniel entered the convenience store on the night of November 11, 2005, he had only one thing in mind—stealing some beer and food. It was a Friday night, and the store was busy. Thievery tonight would be made simple with all the distractions. So he was able to sneak into the store when the sole clerk was busy with numerous patrons. It was cold out, and Nathaniel was wearing his blue denim jacket. This jacket was affixed with inside pockets, perfect for concealing items.

As he walked around the store aimlessly, he waited for just the right moment. Three customers at the counter, and an open beer cooler with 20 ouncers on ice. Easy pickins! The tap of the cash register keys and the open drawer gave Nathaniel the seconds he needed. Two Mickey's Brand Malt Liquor and a Natural Light were quickly tucked inside his jacket—perfect for a cold winter's night on the street.

Nathaniel was content with the scheme. He decided that he needed some chips to fill out the menu for this evening. Again, he stood by for a moment, eyeing the clerk, waiting for just the right opportunity. The clerk turned her back, and a bag of Doritos, the cheddar cheese flavor, flew inside the jacket.

Nathaniel took another trip around the store just to make it seem he was shopping, and then he decided to make his exit. Security was lax. In fact, there was none. There were no sensors or anything like that to trip an alarm. He'd been stealing from here for years.

He went out the glass front doors and took a hard right toward 20th Street. The parking lot was full of cars, and a few people were standing around waiting for their comrades. He wanted to crack one of those cold ones, but he thought better of it. It would suck to get busted after such a clean rip.

As he made his way south from the store, he looked for the best spot to sit and picnic. The shack that he was staying in was falling apart and had no lighting. The property it sat on had been bulldozed months ago and was dark as hell. The streetlight at 20th Street and Monroe would provide plenty of light. He could sit there in peace.

Nothing like the desert cold in winter. It eats right through you and feels twenty degrees colder than it really is. So, as Nathaniel took a seat on the sidewalk, the cold bit right through his trousers. The beers sat next to him. Keeping those cold wouldn't be a problem tonight, but he wasn't sure how long he could sit. Then it happened. A car's headlights lit up the darkness. Nathaniel hadn't even been able to open a beer yet. It was probably a good thing, too. If it were the cops, Nathaniel really didn't want to lose his newly liberated treasures. That had happened before. He'd be minding his own business, trying to down a beer, and some cop would show up, confiscate it, and take him to jail, or at the very least pour out his alcohol.

Nathaniel waited for the spotlight. Sitting quietly in the darkness just off the street, he noticed that the car had slowed down about fifty feet from him. He could see, even with his poor vision, that there were no light bars on top of the car. No cops. That was good news. But he still didn't like the invasion of his privacy. The headlights on the car were shut off.

"What the hell do they think they're doing here? Don't they know this is my street?" he thought to himself.

The dog at one of the residences began to bark. Now they had done it. Not only had they disrupted the serenity of his hood, they had angered one of his favorite pets, the blue heeler mix that he called "Scrappy." Nathaniel got up from his uncomfortable position, wiped the dirt off the seat of his pants, and started to walk toward the car. The Natural Light beer was in his hand, and a Mickey was in his pocket. He could see two people in the car, both white.

"What the hell are you doin here?" Nathaniel yelled.

The driver of the car was startled and jumped. Nathaniel thought that was humorous, until he realized that the driver was holding a rifle, pointed at Scrappy.

The driver looked directly at Nathaniel with disdain. "Mind your own fu@#ing business, nigger." The passenger behind him sat still.

Nathaniel wasn't afraid, even though they were armed. He had confronted punks all his life on the street, and nobody was going to talk to him that way. He tried to pull from his memory bank a good comeback, but only one thing came to mind. "Get the fu*# out of here you Bill Clinton lookin' mother f@#*er!" He had used that line before on other white men who had ridiculed his African-American heritage.

The driver wasn't amused. The gun swung away from Scrappy and covered down on him.

Nathaniel stood there frozen and asked himself, "Is this nut really going to pull the trigger?" Maybe he shouldn't have confronted him. Maybe he should have just left them alone. "Nope," he thought to himself. Nobody shoots a dog in my neighborhood. He stood there waiting for the driver's next move.

The few seconds it took seemed like an eternity. Then he watched the driver pull the rifle back into the car.

"Yeah, chicken sh*#! Didn't have the guts to pull the trigger," he yelled.

A conversation was taking place in the car. At the very least, as much as the thought pained him, he could throw the Natural Light beer can at the driver. That would make a nice dent in his skull or car, whichever was fortunate to get struck.

But there were two of them, and he was old and tired. They would whip up on him hard if they both went at him. He wouldn't lie down, but years on the street had taken a toll. Beer can or not, he couldn't defend himself very well. The driver was fairly young, and he would assume that the passenger was the same. It was time to make a graceful exit.

As he started to walk away, he could hear movement in the car. He turned slightly back towards the last place he'd seen the driver and the car stopped. Then he felt the spray of the Natural Light beer can hit his face. Why would it explode? He then knew.

He felt massive pain in his right front stomach area. He dropped the beer and looked down at his jacket. The outside pocket was wet, and the Mickey in his inside jacket pocket was leaking. It, too, had exploded. The leaking beer was tolerable, but the pain made him double over. He could no longer stand. He fell to the cold, hard street.

Lying there, Nathaniel pulled the beer from the inside pocket. He could see small streams spraying from the can as it rolled away toward the curb. He pulled up his jacket and two shirts. He could now see the damage. Dozens of small holes littered his side. Warm blood soaked the top of his pants. He was having a hard time breathing. The car slowly pulled from the curb. It made its way past him, leaving him there in the street.

"You Bill Clinton looking mother fu#@er," he mumbled to himself. "Yea got me good."

The asphalt of the street was cold, especially on his feet. Both of his shoes had come off. All he could think of was what a good spot he had picked to be alone . . . unfortunately for him.

The police report on the shooting of Nathaniel Shoffner was twenty-six pages long. Not that unusual for a whodunit case.

The first witness to find Nathaniel lying in the middle of 20th Street was an off-duty police officer. He happened to be driving home from a basketball game downtown when he turned south from Van Buren on 20th Street. He was going to jump on the I-10 freeway and head to the suburbs when he drove up on Nathaniel. He saw beer cans lying in the street, along with vomit, and Nathanial on the side of the road. The officer, who was with his family, made a U-turn, and came back to Nathaniel. He got on his cellphone and called the nonemergency number to ask for an officer who was currently on duty to come and check on what he thought was a drunk. He didn't get out of his car. The neighborhood is dangerous, and he didn't want to leave his family unattended.

As on-duty patrol officers arrived, they walked up and began to try to arouse Nathaniel. He was barely groaning, and they, too, smelled the now stale beer in the street and the vomit that sat next to him. They rolled him over and realized this was not just another drunk who'd fallen down. His jacket was full of blood on the lower right side.

The officers tried to get Nathaniel to talk to them, but he could only groan. He had been there too long. His only hope for survival was a quick trip to the hospital and some very skilled surgeons. He was rushed to surgery. Nathaniel had been shot with a shotgun. He had dozens of pellets in his stomach. The surgeons were optimistic about his survival.

Detective Bob Wenrick pulled up on the scene at 1:00 a.m., just in time to see a dog ripping apart a bag of Doritos in the middle of the crime scene. You gotta love that. He yelled to the cop sitting in his car, "Hey, would you guys mind keeping everyone, or everything, out of the scene . . . including dogs?" They assured him they would be more vigilant. It wasn't a good way to start the investigation.

Detective Wenrick found no wadding or shot cup anywhere in the scene. No shell casing was located either. He was determined to find some ballistic evidence, so he searched, and he searched. As the scene was being photographed, he continued to search until he found a pellet; one single pellet, right on the asphalt of the street. Twenty detectives couldn't have found that pellet on the street surface, but Bob did.

As Detective Wenrick worked the scene, he kept a constant vigil for the dog. Although it looked friendly, it also had a somewhat "junk-yardish" appearance."

He noticed that the dog could get in and out of the owners fenced yard. The property's rolling gate had a separation in the bars just big enough for the dog to squeeze through.

Subsequent investigation led nowhere. Detective Wenrick ascertained that Nathaniel Shoffner had in fact shoplifted the beer and chips found at the crime scene from a convenience store two blocks from where he was shot. Surveillance video captured that. There'd been no problem at the store as far as the clerk knew, and no witnesses to the shooting, except for the dog. Numerous theories abounded.

On Sunday November 13th, Detective Wenrick got the call at home. The Violent Crimes Bureau had received a call from County Hospital. Nathaniel Shoffner had died of his gunshot wounds. He had never regained consciousness and had never told anyone what had happened. The body was taken to the Medical Examiner's Office for an autopsy.

I plopped the case on the table and looked up at the map. Gotta be related. I called Bob on his cellphone.

"Bob, it's Clark. Do you want to go chase some ghosts?"

"Sure, what you got?"

He had no idea what I was talking about.

CHAPTER 26

I hadn't been spending much time at my desk since they'd given us a command center. I had been out with the task force all night again. It must have showed. Bob took a seat at his cubicle while I was reading some information cards at my desk. I could hear him riffling through some paperwork, so I turned to talk to him.

My appearance must have told it all.

"You look like hell."

Actually, I didn't feel too bad. I had gotten four hours of sleep last night. No shootings had occurred, but that also meant that no arrest had occurred either.

"Thanks, I appreciate that. Nothing like a warm reception after sweating my butt off last night tooling around this city."

"Yeah, I heard it got to 114 yesterday. It was probably about that at midnight, wasn't it?"

I hadn't checked the temperature at midnight, but it felt like at least a 100 degrees.

Time to get down to business. Discussions about weather could wait.

"You remember that homicide you had last year, the one with the black transient gunned down at 20th Street and Monroe?"

"Yeah, I remember. The guy had just shoplifted from the Circle K before he got shot. Weird case, though. Nobody around to see anything. Didn't appear to be any motive or any fight that took place. Why?" he asked.

"Well, I was going through some cold case homicides, and I found that one. Bob, I think your guy may have been killed by the suspects I'm investigating."

I gave him a few seconds to digest the news.

"You're kidding me," he said.

Like everyone else in the detail, Bob knew the scope and reach of the cases I was working.

"It fits with their M.O.: transient, shot once, late at night, nobody around. All of it."

"Holy sh#@! What do you want me to do?" he asked.

I knew I could trust Bob.

"I don't want you to do anything. I want you to transfer the case to me. I'm going to keep it quiet. Do you have the M.E.'s report and photographs of the scene?"

"I"ll check. The guy had no family, so I haven't looked at the case for awhile."

Bob knew as well as I did that a case without any leads is seldom talked about. The murder of a transient in Phoenix with no next of kin was talked about even less, especially in the media. It's not news when somebody dies in Phoenix anymore, even if they're murdered. He began to rummage through his credenza for the autopsy report.

I had a plan for this case, and nobody needed to know about it. The press had already listed the names of the victims that had been shot. But no one would know about Nathaniel Shoffner, besides Detective Bob Wenrick and me. We were the only ones who needed to know.

July 14th would bring news that *America's Most Wanted* was coming to Phoenix to film an episode. I'd always liked John Walsh. I respected a guy who could turn the loss of a child into something that has helped take the worst of the worst off the street. It takes someone very special to turn the murder of his child into something positive. I had no problem with giving *AMW* access to the case, just not me. I wasn't going to talk about the case in public. Besides, all hell had broken loose.

Since the community meeting, hundreds and hundreds of tips had been coming in. It was information overload. Most of the tips concerned the Baseline Killer. They had a composite of the killer. But even our minority tips were keeping me busy. I needed analytical help soon. Plus my only help, Detective Daniel Moncrief, was going on vacation for two weeks. That pretty much left me alone.

It wasn't so much the fact that calls were coming in. That was good. But the quality of the tips sucked—some neighbor calling in on another neighbor he hates, no explanation of why the guy is shooting people, just that it's him.

Family members calling in from all over the country accusing their long-lost cousin of the crimes or a brother has been off his meds for awhile, and I might need to look at him.

Psychics were leaving their names and numbers on my voicemail. A call from a crystal-ball reader told me to look into a janitorial service because the guy doing the shootings is working as a night janitor. That's why they happen at night. No further information.

There was also another problem. The tips were getting mixed up between the two task forces. The tip sheet would read "Random/Serial Shooter Task Force" and would then talk about the killer having "dreadlocks," a clear reference to the BLK. This was alarming. If I was getting their tips, how many of mine were going to their command center? I could see us missing a tip or having it misplaced. All it would take was one missed tip that could break the case, and heads would roll. I immediately went over to Sergeant Clarke's office and told him about the problem.

There was an easy solution. Put Marge on it. She would straighten it out. Marge set up a box and reminded the information gatherers to forward pertinent tips and messages to the appropriate task force. It was obvious we needed a database.

Lieutenant Benson was kind enough to remind me of the meeting at ATF headquarters scheduled for today.

"And you're coming!"

It sounded like an order. I had planned on attending anyway.

The meeting at ATF was held in their conference room. I met up with Scottsdale Detectives Pete Salazar and Hugh Lockerby there for the first time. Their Scottsdale murder of Claudia Gutierrez-Cruz remained unsolved.

When we arrived, I noticed that the room was full of a bunch of suits—managers, lawyers, analysts, the kind of law enforcers who sit around and make decisions, but never get their hands dirty. In fact, I would venture to say that, by the looks of them, very few had made a felony arrest in their entire lives, let alone worked one.

The assistant agent in charge, the ASAC, began by introducing the numerous ATF people who were present. We cops all introduced ourselves and the agencies we represented.

The meeting commenced with a PowerPoint presentation. It felt as if I were at some national sales convention of some kind, trying to sell me on their product. In fact, that's what it was, a sales pitch of what ATF could provide.

The only problem I had was staying awake. The shades were drawn, and I hadn't slept much in the previous days. I noticed Lieutenant Benson pretended to get a phone call and stepped out from the room. That was always a good ploy for stepping out of a presentation if you need a break and don't want to offend the presenter.

The presentation ended, and some of the agents came up to me and reintroduced themselves. I was always terrible with names, unless it was one of my friends or someone I worked with constantly. Lieutenant Benson beelined his way over to me just as Detective Salazar and I made plans for us to meet and go over his murder case and my thirteen shootings.

"I just got word that there may have been a shooting in Glendale on July 11th, and that it may be related."

I introduced Detective Salazar to Lieutenant Benson.

"Clark, I need you to get a hold of their Violent Crimes Sergeant, who has all the details, and see what you can find out."

"Why are we just learning about this now? Don't Glendale cops read the paper or follow the news?" I asked.

"The guy wasn't hit; they missed. The victims not too happy by the sounds of it, either. Let me know what you find out."

Lieutenant Benson walked away.

I hurried back to headquarters to start the inquiry into the new Glendale shooting. But before I started that task, I noticed the message light on my telephone blinking. I decided to clear the messages off first.

"I am a lawyer in Phoenix, and a friend and colleague of mine was shot at the other night. I think I need to talk to you about what happened. Apparently, nobody out here in Glendale seems to understand the significance of this event. Could you please call me back at 602 . . . ?"

◈

Michael Cordrey was a lawyer in a county of thousands of them. Practicing law for over ten years, he had settled down with his wife and first child in the City of Glendale.

He had picked an upper middle-class neighborhood in which to live with good schools. Just the kind of place a promising lawyer with a bright future could be seen.

The practice of law can be stressful, like any career. Michael had learned a long time ago that exercise was a way to relieve stress and even take off the extra pounds he accumulated working those late nights.

In the summer in Phoenix, if you're going to exercise outside and not die from it, it's best done at night. That was what Michael did. Many times, on restless nights or even on those nights where he decided to try to shed a few calories, walking at night seemed to lift his spirits and lower his anxiety.

In the early morning hours of July 11th, Michael left his residence. He considered his neighborhood safe at night, or at least as safe as any other neighborhood in Glendale. He donned his headphones and radio. At this time of night, there were no cars or even pedestrians for that matter on the quiet street.

Half a mile from home, he made the turn and saw the lights of a car illuminate the asphalt and residential block walls that lined Mountain View Road. With his music playing, Michael couldn't hear the car coming up behind him, but the headlights gave it away.

He moved from the street to the sidewalk, just in case the driver happened to be impaired. The air was thick with the smell of honeysuckles and other various plant life. The lights of the car became brighter. He waited for it to pass and be on its way.

The sound that came from the roadway terrified him. Michael felt a rush of heat fly by his head, and the block wall adjacent to him exploded with fury. It took him a second to react. Or did he? He spun and jumped, looking to his left. A blue four-door car was parallel to his position. The car, its windows, and its interior were completely dark. The headlights had been extinguished. He couldn't see anyone insider.

"What the fu#@," he yelled.

He knew that whatever had just happened had come from the car that was almost at a standstill next to him. He took off running, backtracking along his route. A large van sat in a driveway of a house with a lone light illuminated in one of the upper windows. Michael crouched down behind the front end, able to see the car while scanning for any movement inside the house. Maybe if he yelled loud enough, the residents of the home would come out or at least call the police.

At six feet, two inches and 240 pounds, Michael was no coward. He thought about coming out from behind the van and challenging the occupants of the car. But then he realized what had happened. They'd shot at him. That was the only explanation for the rush of hot air and the block fence exploding with chips of cement flying everywhere. The blue four-door car slowly pulled away.

Michael moved out from behind the van and started walking towards home, trying to process what had just happened. Enemies? He wasn't aware of any, but he was a lawyer. He stopped as he got to the spot where the shooting had occurred and eyed a plastic object. It lay in the street right next to the curb. It had small wings that spread out. He recognized it as coming from a shotgun.

It didn't take Michael too long to get home. The more he walked, the more upset he got.

"Take a shot at me, will ya?" he mumbled to himself. "I'll find you SOBs."

He entered his home long enough to grab the keys to his car and his cellphone.

He took off, looking for the shooters. He wasn't armed, but the cops were a cellphone call away. For an hour, Michael drove around looking for any similar cars, but found nothing. The car and its occupants were gone, probably never to be found again.

He drove to the Glendale Police substation close to his home. The place looked deserted. He walked around for a minute and found no officers or staff leaving the station. It wasn't a real police station anyway, just a briefing and information center. He decided to go home. He could notify the police later, if need be.

As he pulled into his driveway, Michael was not sure if he would even bother the police with this nonsense. What were the chances of catching these guys anyway … slim to none? But that didn't make it right.

Inside the shooter's car, the conversation was not so pleasant.

"How could you miss?" the driver yelled to the passenger.

✦

I called the attorney back. He answered the cellphone on the second ring.

"Thank you for calling me back, Detective. I understand that you are working the cases of the guy going around and shooting at people from his car. Is that correct?"

Guys shooting at people, I wanted to interject, but I didn't.

"That's right. How can I help you?"

"One of my subordinates was shot at a few nights ago, and we can't get anyone from Glendale to take us seriously. We asked for an officer to come out, and they don't have anyone coming out to interview him until next week. We think this shooting is related to other shootings that have occurred, and we want to pass on the information." He seemed a little perturbed.

"Well, I need to talk to the victim. If you weren't there, whatever you say is hearsay, as you well know."

Well, if you're a criminal lawyer, you should know.

"Oh, I understand. Are you going to be at this number for a few minutes? I'll have Michael, that's the colleague who was shot at, call you. He's right down the hall."

"Yeah, I'll be here."

I wasn't going to hold my breath. Besides, I had been preparing myself for these types of calls, but not in a good way.

I had thought long and hard about the possibility of cases of false victimization. It had occurred to me that if people were willing to sell out their own kin for the Silent Witness money that was being offered, I had to consider the thought that someone could stage one of these shootings as well. It wouldn't be the first time.

This case had generated so much publicity since going national, that a person could make some bucks off staging a shooting and claiming to be the victim of the Random/Serial Shooter. Free advertising. Perhaps this is what Michael Cordrey had planned. If that were the case, I would know it when I talked to him.

When I received the call from Michael Cordrey, it was obvious that he wasn't wavering about the facts of his shooting. He had no reason to. He wasn't looking to gain anything. He just wanted to report what had happened, so that we could start to look and watch his area of town for similar crimes.

Michael told me about going back to the scene and picking up his own evidence. That sounded fishy, but again he wanted the guys caught.

I asked him why he didn't call police to the scene, and he retorted, "Why? They were gone. Why bother police that night when I could make the report the next day?"

A foolish mistake. It's not just cops responding to the scene who look for criminals. That's why we carry radios.

Police had already knocked on doors and canvassed the area. It sounded to me like they were doing their job. I assured Michael that I would contact Glendale Police and let them know that it may be related. He was good with that, and we hung up.

I gathered Sergeant Clarke, and immediately we went to the LT's office. I closed the door and laid out the Glendale shooting case. We all agreed that we would hold off adding this to the series. The media hadn't found it, so there was no reason to notify them. If we were asked, the response would be, "We're looking into it."

It was also decided that ATF would be brought on board for the sole purpose of using their analysts. Their agents would be delegated to the role of "use if needed."

CHAPTER 27

Due to the amount of tips coming in and the nature of the sources that brought them to the task force, we decided that we needed to prioritize our information. In other words, there had to be a rating system for the tips, a way to separate the good from the bad or the crappy from really crappy.

We rated them 1, 2, or 3. The Priority 1 tips were handed out and investigated immediately. We fully screened the subject of the tip for any criminal history, particularly weapons use. We checked his or her address and vehicle ownership. We looked for repetitive violent offenders who owned or drove cars similar to our shooters. We also checked employment hours. If there was a match, then the subject would be assigned an investigator or surveillance team.

Priority 2 tips indicated possible involvement, such as someone with a weapons fascination. We gave a 2 rating to someone who had made statements about harming innocent people. If the person had a history of animal abuse or was seen carrying a gun in and out of his residence at odd hours of the night, we used the 2 rating. These individuals would be run through the system and, if promising, moved up the scale for official follow-up.

All the other tips would be put in a file and kept as Priority 3 leads. These were leads where somebody would call in and say "It's so and so doing it," with no explanation why. All the psychic tips would go there as well. There would be no follow-up conducted on these leads unless further information was provided.

Silent Witness was the preferred method of reporting and recording tips. Unfortunately that wasn't always the case. Every morning my voice mail would be full of good, honest, concerned citizens who weren't interested in the reward. They just wanted to talk to me or a task force investigator personally. They wouldn't talk to anyone else.

Sergeant Andy Hill had already put out the word to the local media that the investigators weren't talking about the case, but the national media didn't care.

They left messages as well. And not only were they hitting up the police, they were running after the victims looking for exclusive interviews.

It was to be expected. I mean, how often do you have two serial killers running rampant in the same city at the same time?

The problem was, it was only going to get worse until both sets of serial killers were caught. The Baseline Killer hadn't struck in almost three weeks. The Random/Serial Shooter was active. The media frenzy was just beginning.

July 15th was a Saturday, and as usual, I was in the field. I had worked late the previous night doing surveillances of Priority 1 tips and monitoring our designated radio frequency for any shootings. There would be no days off as long as the Random/Serial Shooters were at large. I expected that with the formation of the task force. I spent most of my waking hours looking at the areas of operation, researching serial murderers, poring over cold cases, and trying to find these bastards through the tips that were still coming in. Today, I would meet the person who would become one of the most valuable assets in the investigation of the Random/Serial Shooter. Her name was Marjorie Zicha.

Marjorie was an intelligence research analyst with ATF. She was assigned to the field offices in Milwaukee, Wisconsin. She had been reassigned to the task force. I never figured out whether she was ordered in or volunteered. She had flown in on a Saturday to be ready to hit the ground running on Monday. She showed up two days early to get to work.

She was escorted back to the command center by front desk personnel. I was busy looking at a case of a shotgun found at a motel room. The suspect who left it was black, not our guys. I heard a knock on the locked command post door and put the case down.

I opened the door to find the desk sergeant accompanied by a small, thirty-something woman. I had no idea who she was, but when she introduced herself, she immediately asked how we were handling our leads.

I was taken aback. "Who are you?"

"I'm your new analyst."

She was abrupt, but enthusiastic. She was ready to go to work. I had to admit that we were doing a poor job. With so many leads coming in and two task forces running, it was nearly impossible to keep track of all of them.

"I'm going to take care of all of that for you."

She had worked on the Washington, D.C. Sniper case and knew the database like the back of her hand. I liked her right away. I showed her around the CP and explained the two different series of shootings: .22 caliber and shotgun.

As Marjorie and I strategized the leads and how they would be handled, I heard a knock on the door. The *America's Most Wanted* film crew had arrived. Correspondent Ed Miller had flown out and was ready to film and narrate the segment. They had asked me to give an interview, but I declined. Detective Jewell would do it.

I introduced myself to Ed, so he didn't think I was uninterested. He was genuinely engrossed in the story and wanted to get the word out. He wasn't one of those talking head media types that cared only about themselves or their ratings. I thanked him for all that he did and told him I appreciated *AMW*'s help. He told me that the broadcast would be aired one week from today, July 22nd. The segment would include both of the serial killer investigations. Joseph Roberts, the young man shot pushing his bike, was to be interviewed. I hoped he would be short and straight to the point.

CHAPTER 28

The Silent Witness tip came in on Sunday, July 16th, 2006 at approximately 6:49 p.m. It was recorded, and the caller was given the number of 60716. The tip had to do with the Random/Serial Shooter task force. The caller wished to remain anonymous.

Under the subject information the tip listed the following:

W/M (Sammy), 30 y/o, 6'0", 210 lbs. German-sounding last name.

Under the Information Provided section, the following was recorded:

Caller said Sammy was bragging about shooting what he thought was a man. He later found out he killed a woman. Sammy said he used a shotgun. Sammy also said that he beat a man to death by banging his head against concrete. Sammy lives in the area of 65th Avenue/Camelback in town homes. No vehicle. He has ties to biker gangs. Caller will try to get last name and call back.

On Sunday, July 16, I was in my usual spot, the CP at police headquarters, reading the previous night's intelligence reports. One of the surveillance detectives working the task force had run across a bag of ammunition at a local motel. The motel just happened to be on Van Buren. The occupants of room #126 had left a black leather bag in the room and abandoned the room in the middle of the night. Inside the black leather bag were multiple rounds, including both 12 and 410 gauge shotgun ammunition. There had been a fight and alleged abuse. The couple also had two children staying with them. She and the kids were packed up and taken to a shelter. I decided to call the shelter. Her name was Amy Johnson.

A day later, the shelter phoned back to tell me they couldn't release any information. The "guests" were confidential.

After the evening briefing, I returned to find Sergeant Tim Bryant waiting at my desk. He, too, had heard of the Van Buren incident and the subsequent findings of the ammunition in the motel room. He wanted to know if he could help.

I phoned again. "I need to locate one of the guests in one of your domestic violence shelters. She may be a material witness to an ongoing criminal matter. It is very important that I get a hold of her, and I need to get a hold of her immediately."

"I'm sorry, but we just don't give out that kind of information," a woman said. "Our patients' privacy is held above all concerns. But, I can leave her a message, and she can return your call once she gets it."

My blood pressure started to elevate.

"I'm sorry. What is your position there?"

"I'm one of the legal advocates here."

"OK. Are you an attorney who represents the shelter or a case worker?"

I wanted her to know that she may need to get a hold of one real quick.

"I'm a legal advocate, and I work here. I look after their legal affairs," she said.

That wasn't an answer, so I was going to give her one last chance.

"Look, this is a criminal investigation into an ongoing criminal enterprise where lives may be at risk, including your guest. I believe that she may have relevant information regarding a massive manhunt for a person that she knows. You need to tell me where she is right now."

"Our policy states that we cannot give out the location of our patients unless we have a court order. The best I can do for you is leave her a message, and she will get it hopefully and return your call," she said.

She was talking out of her butt. She had been told this in some b.s. training seminar or read it in one of their privacy manuals. I'd had it with this moron.

"You'd better get somebody who is higher up than you to call me back on this. I'm telling you, again, this is a matter of public safety. I want to know where she's at!"

"I told you, I will give your name and number to the shelter and get them to give it to the patient. That is all I can do right now."

She was sticking to her manual and what little she knew of the law.

Sergeant Bryant had been sitting there, quietly watching my face turn five shades of red. I snapped. "All right then, you'd better hope that whoever I'm looking for doesn't kill anyone before I get what I need, or I swear to God I'm going to find all of you who've stone-walled this investigation and arrest you for obstruction of justice and hindering prosecution!"

I slammed the phone down on the base.

I felt a little better getting that off my chest. Sergeant Bryant had a different take on the situation.

"Won't give you the info, huh?"

"You heard the conversation," I replied.

"Those mother fu#@*#s get away with that kind of sh*@ because nobody in this department has the balls to go after them for obstruction. We start booking some of these idiots in the health care industry and things would change dramatically."

He was right. We always played nice with others and got crapped on for it. Arresting some of these dolts would send a message.

"We'll see if we can find him for you."

With that, Sergeant Bryant walked away.

As I sat at my desk, the Violent Crimes desk assistant, Vicki, approached my cubicle, cowering slightly. She had overheard me yelling on the phone.

"Clark, I'm so sorry to bother you. I know you have a million things on your plate, but there is someone, a guy, on the phone. He insists on talking to the detective in charge of the Serial Shooter investigation."

I swung around in my swivel chair with what I'm sure was a completely disgusted look on my face. She was somewhat smiling, so I wouldn't bite her head off.

"Who is he, and what does he want?" I asked.

"I'm sorry, but he won't tell me. He refuses to call Silent Witness and says that he must talk to whoever is in charge. He has called three times this evening."

She was trying to relay the urgency and the fact that this guy wasn't going away. He had been a pain in the ass to her. She was hoping I could alleviate the situation.

"He claims to be some professor, or teacher, or something like that, like that is supposed to lend him credibility."

Hardly. Most academics have never viewed the real side of crime. They've only read and pontificated about it. The fact that he was in academia gave him little standing. It was obvious, though, I would have to take this call. "Put him through."

"Thank you so much." Vicki scurried away from my cubicle and back to the front desk. A moment later my phone was ringing.

"Detective Schwartzkopf," I snapped.

"Detective, my name is John … and I am a bio science engineer currently employed in the Phoenix Metro Area. How are you?"

What's it matter how I am? I could see that this was going to be a short conversation, and I was in no mood to exchange pleasantries.

"What can I do for you?" I said bluntly.

"I have been following the case of the Serial Shooter in the media, and I think I know who is responsible. Well, let me rephrase that, I don't know his name, but I know who is doing it."

He paused for a second as if I was supposed to leave my chair and break out in a chorus of "Hallelujah."

"I'm listening."

I was trying to be as short as I could with John. He, being a bio science engineer, picked up on that fact and wasn't too happy about it.

"You seem to be preoccupied. What I have is some very relevant information. If you're too busy or don't care to listen, then maybe I need to talk to someone who has more time to deal with this. This is a very complicated issue. Maybe I should speak with your supervisor."

Now he'd done it. Whatever thread of patience I'd had to begin this conversation was gone.

"I am the lead investigator in this case. It doesn't go any higher than me. I'm not going to joust with you. If you have some relevant information, you need to spill it, or I'm going to send your call to Silent Witness, and I will get the information tomorrow."

"OK, Detective, I just want you to take this seriously because I know who is doing the killing," he said. "I need your undivided attention."

What the fu@#?

"I'm still listening, and I haven't hung up on you, yet."

He began, "Detective Schwartzkopf, are you familiar with the Zodiac Killer?

The individual who was responsible for multiple deaths and shootings in the San Francisco area in the 1960s?"

I didn't know what to say, so I said, "Yes, I am familiar with the Bay Area Killer."

Who wasn't? It was one of America's biggest unsolved serial killer cases out of San Francisco. Even though I'd been a child when it happened, I remember hearing about it all through my grade school years. I once met one of the original investigators in the case, or so he'd said.

"Detective Schwartzkopf, the man responsible for the killings attributed to the Zodiac Killer is the same man responsible for gunning down the citizens of this city. He has never been identified, and he now operates here."

I'm sure I paused for a second as I thought this through. Let's see, Zodiac Killer from the late 1960's is now active in Phoenix. He would be about eighty fu*#%n years old by now, given that the Zodiac Killer was a man in his thirties or forties. He had gone dormant for almost forty years and had now just popped up in Phoenix. The Zodiac Killer not only shot people, but allegedly stabbed them as well. He was a close-up operator, shooting people in their cars with a handgun. Brilliant! Why hadn't I thought of that?

John could tell that I was processing his theory carefully, so he jumped in before letting me speak. "I know it sounds peculiar and a little farfetched, but let me tell you why."

A little farfetched? That was the understatement of the year! How about ridiculous! Idiotic! Asinine! I could think of a hundred superlatives for his theory. As he began again, I cursed myself for taking this call to begin with and for not shipping it somewhere else. Like Purgatory.

"Here are the facts. In 1969, the Zodiac Killer operated in an area of … "

It was time to stop the madness, so I interrupted him in mid-sentence.

"Sir, sir."

He paused for a moment.

I took a deep breath and calmly spoke, "There is no way that the Zodiac Killer of the San Francisco Bay Area is responsible for the series of shootings that have occurred in the Phoenix Metro Area for the past year or so. No way!"

He was upset that I'd cut him off, and no matter what I said, I knew that he was going to spill his theory to me and try to convince me I was wrong. So, I had to put an end to this conversation.

He spoke before I had a chance to end it.

"Detective Schwarzkopf, how can you be so sure that he's not involved? How do you know that for a fact? Let me explain to you why he is involved, and I will convince you that he is here and he is killing again."

The simplest answer seemed to be the best.

"Sir, the Zodiac Killer is dead," I said.

He was still listening, and I decided to take full advantage of this. I knew something that he didn't. He was all ears. I decided to expound on my knowledge.

"I know that he is, in fact, dead because Clint Eastwood killed him in the first Dirty Harry movie."

Dead silence.

The next sound I heard besides dead air and silence on the other end of the phone was the click of the receiver. I quietly put my receiver down as well.

I congratulated myself and felt that I had served a customer well with this conversation. Sometimes it's important to instruct the public in matters such as these, and for that I had done my duty. It also brought a smile to my face. A much-welcomed smile.

The male from the motel was soon cleared of being involved. He owned only one vehicle, a GMC Van, and had no access to any four-door vehicles. The ammunition? Mistakenly left at the hotel room and no gun in which to use it.

CHAPTER 29

As we pushed on into the third week of the task force, I faced some daunting challenges. I was losing detectives to much-needed vacations, and the pool of good investigators was shrinking. Crime didn't stop on account of serial murderers running loose.

My partner, Detective Udd, was leaving to go to Canada for a week or so. Detective Moncrief had just left and would be gone for two weeks. Even Detective Jewell claimed he was heading to Mexico.

Surveillance officers were watching about half a dozen targets. We had a GPS device on one in particular, a man who claimed he knew what type of shotgun was being used in the crimes. He had uttered the words "410" in public. We decided to track him with GPS instead of with constant surveillance in the hopes that if he did do something, we could put him at the crime scene.

Detective Jewell stopped by my desk to rub it in. "By this time next week, I'll be sunning myself in Cabo San Lucas while you're here slogging through these leads. Sorry, but somebody has to do it."

"Keep it up, and I'll notify the Mexican Police that you're carrying a firearm into their country. It'll take them two months just to figure out that the tip was bad, and you'll have lost forty pounds and your virginity sitting in a Mexican jail."

"Good one," he cracked back. "Speaking of tips, I found this on my desk. I thought the tips were supposed to be put in one place."

He showed me an envelope with his name on it.

"Yeah, that's why Marjorie from ATF is here. She's going to take care of the tracking and maintenance of these things. Hopefully, in the next day or two, she'll have all the kinks worked out."

I opened up the envelope and began to read the tip.

A "Sammy" person using a shotgun to kill what he thought was a man and turned out to be a woman rang no bells. At this point in the investigation, the only woman that we knew had been murdered was Claudia Gutierrez-Cruz of Scottsdale. I had seen her picture in the paper, and there would be no mistaking her for a man.

"Says he beat a man to death by banging his head against the concrete. Does that ring any bells with you?" I asked.

"No, but that doesn't mean anything."

There were hundreds of unsolved homicides in Phoenix. Blunt force trauma isn't all that rare. Unless the instrument was found at the scene, it can be a long shot trying to determine what caused the death. Maybe the guy bragging was full of it.

"There's no last name listed. It could be any of thousands of Sams out there. This gets a Priority 2."

A 2 was marked on top of the page, and it would be forwarded as such.

As I thought about the tip though, I realized that there was one possibility. Maybe Claudia Gutierrez-Cruz had worn her hair up, maybe it had been too dark to recognize her as a woman, or maybe she'd worn a hat. I called Detective Pete Salazar in Scottsdale and asked if he had noticed the attire that Claudia had worn on the night of her murder.

Pete said that he wasn't there when the body was removed and had no idea if her appearance could have been misconstrued as "male." I told him about the tip. The only significant thing he could remember about Claudia's clothing was that she'd worn a hooded sweatshirt. If she had the hood over her head, it was possible someone could have mistaken her for a man. But the temperature in May is nice, in the 70s or 80s at night; no reason to have a hood on to keep warm.

The rest of the leads were all Priority 3s. I perused the reports that had been left on my desk, most of them cold cases.

One that looked promising was an Aggravated Assault report that was filed on July 15th, 2006 in the area of 64th Avenue and Indian School Road. A white female had been walking her dog when someone drove by and pointed a gun at her. The victim, being armed and having a concealed weapon permit, grabbed her 380 handgun from behind her back and pointed it at the driver. You go, girl! The driver took off when she drew down on him. Sissy. She believed that the use of force on her part saved her life. The only problem was the vehicle: a gold Jeep Cherokee. No passengers, just the driver.

And so the reports stacked up, just like this one. If it wasn't the wrong car, it was the wrong weapon. If it wasn't the wrong weapon, it was the wrong time of day. It had been over a week since they'd struck in Glendale, and we weren't counting that one, yet. It had been almost ten days since the double shooting in East Phoenix.

The media was still hard at work, digging up all they could about past serial killers who'd run the streets of the Valley. They were also ferreting out the victims. I caught a glimpse of an interview with James Hodge, the man who'd been shot in the back at 89th Avenue and Camelback.

On July 19th, as I prepared for another briefing to tell the surveillance officers that I had little or no information to give them, I was informed of an inexcusable, bone-headed mistake.

I first received a phone call, and then I verified it through my chain of command. It was true, and the repercussions could be huge.

A local news station had asked if one of their reporters could ride along with one of the many patrol supervisors who worked the East Phoenix area. As much as I would like to throw him down for his idiocy, I will not mention his name here. This supervisor had absolutely nothing to do with the task force. He had been asked to let the reporter ride along with him so that he could show her what the police department was trying to do to catch these killers.

Now, understand that both the Random/Serial Shooters and the Baseline Killer were now believed to be operating in the same area: East Phoenix. Both our undercover operations and the Baseline Killer operations were concentrated in this area, with both fixed and moving units.

I don't exactly know what was said, but knowing who said it, I'm sure it went something like this.

Reporter: "It must be very frustrating to be chasing two serial killers with very little to go on. What are you trying to do to catch them?" Giggle, giggle.

Supervisor: "Well, we have large task forces with lots of investigators, and we have undercover units out here to be right on top of them when and if they strike."

That's all it took. One or two sentences. In one fell swoop, he'd made public that undercover operations were ongoing in the areas where the last known crimes had been committed. The reporter had gotten her scoop.

Many in the chain of command would downplay the incident, saying later that this supervisor was just confirming what the media had already assumed.

Really! But what about the killers? Did he think that letting them know about our operations was a good idea? Did he even consider that maybe they were watching the TV and reading the newspapers for any hint about the investigative procedures to gain an edge?

Obviously not. When I heard about the report, the first thing out of my mouth was, "Why was a reporter allowed to ride with this blowhard supervisor to begin with?" It re-affirmed what I had always thought: Put a camera or a microphone in a cop's face, and, sooner or later, they will act or say something stupid. That's why departments have public information officers.

I was assured that the supervisor would be chastised for his remarks. There would be no more information leaked about the investigations to anyone. No more reporters would be allowed to ride along with anyone. Too little, too late.

It didn't matter much now. If the killers were watching, they would change areas. The only thing we could do was wait and hope that they made a mistake somewhere along the way or that a tip that led us to them came in.

Although it's believed that Silent Witness tip from caller #60716 came in on July 19th, 2006, it cannot be verified. The command post would receive it on July 20th. The tip read as follows:

> *Caller called back a 2nd time and gave similar information as first call. Caller said Sammy LNU (last name unknown) bragged about using a 12-12 (double barrel shotgun). Sammy LNU residence is near the shootings. Caller said when Sammy LNU 1st started bragging about the shooting caller didn't believe him, they had been drinking. Sammy told caller to go home and watch the news. Sammy LNU called the shooting spree Rving (Recreational Violence). Caller knows Sammy's mother lives at …. Caller says he can take detectives to Sammy LNU because he does not remember exact address. Caller is 98% sure Sammy LNU is the serial shooter.*

The lead was again forwarded to Detective Jewell. The tipster again did not leave a contact number or name.

From November 2005 until May of 2006, a string of robberies of taxicabs occurred in the City of Phoenix. There had been a half-dozen of them, all at night, mostly concentrated in central Phoenix.

In these cases, the robbers targeted a specific cab company. The owner, managers, and drivers wanted these guys caught, the sooner the better. Drivers didn't want to go to pick-ups in those areas, and the cab company was losing money.

At least one of the cabs had video surveillance inside the passenger compartment. It had captured the front-seat passenger, a black male with a hooded sweatshirt and a rear passenger of American Indian descent wearing a bandanna over his face. The suspects were easily identifiable, even with the hankie.

I received the call on July 21ˢᵗ from the robbery detective in charge of the case. They had captured one of the suspects, and he was at police headquarters. He wasn't admitting to the robberies, but he was spouting off about the serial killers that now stalked the Valley of the Sun. A search warrant was being served on the suspect's home, and the detective would notify me if anything interesting, such as shotguns, were located.

This same day, I was scheduled to meet with FBI profilers who had worked the D.C. sniper case. They were in town for some type of training. Detective Jewell wanted them brought on board. I had to continually remind him that it was these FBI profilers who had said that the shotgun shootings were not related to the .22 caliber cases; that there was only one person doing the shooting, even though I had convinced him that we were dealing with two shooters, and that the individual responsible was a young white male, not older, calculating killers. It was profilers who, early on in the D.C. sniper case, reportedly stated a white guy was responsible, but two black males turned out to be the culprits.

Even still, he wanted to meet with them, so I told him I would tag along and listen. I called Pete Salazar and Hugh Lockerby of Scottsdale PD and asked if they wanted to sit in. They both decided to come along.

As I listened to some of the issues with the case, one of the agents handed me a piece of paper, a memo entitled, "Assisting in Cooperative Law Enforcement Investigations."

The memo outlined the FBI's willingness to "assist" in law enforcement investigations that require in-depth research, funding, and manpower that can be moved quickly to whatever jurisdiction is involved. It further stated that the FBI is interested in assisting only, not taking jurisdiction over the investigation. The only thing that the FBI needed was one phone call from the chief of investigations, or whoever was in charge of the case at the chief's level, to ask for help, and they would be on board immediately.

As I read the memo, a thought came leaping to the forefront. Only an agency with a history of strong-arming cases away from local police agencies would have come up with such writing. Even they knew their own reputation. But the fact that they realized their mistakes of the past and were trying to correct them spoke volumes of how much the FBI had changed since I first worked with them twenty years ago. It was obvious that they had forged good relationships with local law enforcement agencies and wanted to continue down that path. It takes a lot of guts to change, and I, for one, thought this was a positive gesture on their part.

When I finished reading the memo, one of the agents looked at me and started to talk about how they had only assisted in the D.C. Sniper investigation. He did say that he had in fact interviewed Lee Boyd Malvo, the younger of the two snipers. The fact that the FBI would conduct an interview in that case, or any other case, would mean that they considered themselves more than just *assisting*. Maybe it was one of those post-arrest interviews when all the other jurisdictions had gotten through with him.

The conversation continued, and they admitted making a slight error in the profiling of the D.C. Snipers, but they downplayed that as bad intelligence. As in all cases, you have good and bad witnesses, and profiling is based on some of that information. But the underlying fact is that profiling should be based more on the crimes, evidence, and M.O.s as opposed to witness accounts.

Most of the conversation centered around my recent cases. They were still not convinced that the .22 caliber cases were related, but they understood our point of view.

The meeting ended with the obligatory exchanging of business cards with the contact numbers listed on them. The agents again re-emphasized their willingness to drop everything and head to Phoenix. In fact, they were staying one more night and could be back in town and ready to go within forty-eight hours. I thanked them for their information.

Detective Jewell bid us a goodbye. He was getting on a plane to Mexico and would talk to us when he got back in a week. I told him I hoped he caught a case of black diarrhea. He reminded me that he has a strong stomach and had never gotten sick in Mexico.

"Well, what do you think?" Pete asked.

"I don't think they will ever get involved or will ever be asked to get involved," I responded.

Hugh Lockerby chimed in. 'I'd rather have them than ATF, any day. ATF is horrible."

Everyone has his own opinions about agencies. Hugh's thoughts were based on his experience.

We agreed to discuss it further with the task force. My guess was the FBI would not be brought in, not at this point anyway. Federal agencies don't play nice with each other.

When I got back to headquarters, I beelined to the monitor rooms to catch up with the robbery detectives. I met the case agent in charge of the taxicab robberies. I also saw Detective Alex Femenia for the first time in a few days. He was the detective in charge of the Baseline Killer investigation. He looked worn out. He probably thought the same of me.

Alex had just finished up interviewing the Indian male involved in the robberies. The information that he'd supplied, besides ultimately confessing to the robberies, was of little use to me. Whatever he knew, it didn't have anything to do with the Random/Serial Shooter case. In fact, he didn't have anything significant to add to the Baseline Killer case either.

"You can talk to him if you want, Clark, but I wouldn't waste my time. The guys full of sh#@. He's just a young punk who thinks he may have some way of talking himself out of the robbery charges," Alex said.

"Nope, I got too many other leads to look at to waste any time. I got a shift of surveillance to conduct, and tomorrow is Saturday. I plan on resting and seeing my family for a few hours," I said.

"I hear ya, brother. No rest for the weary."

Alex took off walking toward the Homicide Unit.

Working till midnight or later had become routine for all the investigators in the serial killer cases. Just for some perspective, I would occasionally meander over to their command post and ask Alex how things were going. We usually talked about the frustrations of the cases. It had been almost a month since the BLK had struck. Hundreds of leads were coming in—good ones, or what seemed like good ones, too. I'm sure that every light-skinned black male with braided hair or dreadlocks in the Phoenix Metro Area had been dimed out by somebody. They were pretty sure that the BLK's hat and dreadlocks was a disguise.

As I unlocked the command post, I realized that everyone had left for the day. As I sat down, I noticed a small group of leads with a note from Marjorie.

"Clark, you'll want to take a look at these before tomorrow." She knew that I was going to be there late, and if I got through them tonight, she could get them into the database and start the intelligence checks on any Priority 1s or 2s that were deemed worthy.

I began to read one and recognized it immediately. It was the second call identifying "Sammy" as the Serial Shooter. The caller space was still empty, meaning he didn't want any contact, and "Sammy" still had no last name.

"Sammy told caller to go home and watch the news."

Why would the alleged suspect want the caller to go home and see the news, unless the suspect was also watching? Interesting.

Caller stated he called it, "RVing," which stood for "recreational violence." OK, that's two red flags. What else have we got here?

Says the suspect used a shotgun, a "12/12." What the hell is a 12/12? I began to search for the original tip sheet for this particular caller. It took me a few minutes, but I found it in the pile of priority two tip sheets. No mention of this "12/12" in the first tip. I wondered if the caller didn't know anything about guns and meant *12 gauge*. OK, that was three red flags.

I grabbed a sheet of paper and wrote out a note to the background analyst. I wanted the address checked immediately for anyone by the name of Sammy that may have lived there or stayed there at any time in the past two years. Any longer than that and the caller's information couldn't be too reliable, especially since they supposedly had been drinking together lately.

Sammy, LNU, now became a Priority 1 lead. Since I was working tonight, I would conduct surveillance on the house to see if "Sammy" happened to show up or had any access to a silver or light blue Toyota Camry.

It was going to be another long night.

CHAPTER 30

Raul Lopez-Garcia had snuck into the United States sometime around the first week of October, 2005. He had paid his coyote in cash and was one of the lucky ones not to be held for ransom.

The coyotes who brought Raul over the border had started to get greedy. Before 2006, it used to cost about two to three hundred dollars to be guided through the deserts of Southern Arizona. Easy money for the cartels in charge.

Then the stakes got higher. The Border Patrol started increasing its manpower in places like Southern Arizona. It was getting tougher to cross the border with drugs, let alone humans. Guided trips across the border were now costing five hundred dollars or more. The organizations that had been handling the higher share of illegal border crossers now faced with tougher enforcement, plus new competition had popped up. The price increases made smuggling humans more lucrative. It now resembled the drug trade. Organizations ripped off loads of human cargo from other competitors. There were shootouts on the highways and back roads that streamed north from the border to Phoenix.

Bodies of illegal immigrants were found murdered in the desert for no possible motive except for the fact that they couldn't pay their tab. Some, it was theorized, had been executed to demonstrate the resolve and ruthlessness of the coyotes. *Don't pay, and this will happen to you or someone you care about.*

But through it all though, Raul Lopez-Garcia had made it. He had not been caught, nor had his family been extorted. He was in America, and he hoped to stay for awhile.

Raul's trip to America had taken longer than most. He lived just outside of Mexico City with his wife and other family members. He crossed through Mexico, traveling all the way to Nogales, a border town just south of the Arizona line. It was only a few days before he and another load of illegal immigrants were driven into the United States. Raul was fortunate. He had relatives who were already based in the city of Mesa, Arizona. Raul's cousin had promised him that if he got to the U.S., a job would be waiting for him. And so it was. With just a suitcase full of clothes and a few pesos, Raul moved into his cousin's apartment in Mesa.

Raul landed a job with a construction company, the same one where his cousin worked. He started as a general laborer, removing construction debris from around work sites. He soon worked his way up to the framing crew, which was a nice pay increase. Although he missed his wife and family greatly, he could never make this kind of money living in Mexico.

Raul's worksite was only six or so miles from where he lived. He had no car, but his cousin owned one. They shared the gas expense. And, for the days when his cousin didn't work, Raul had purchased a bike to transport himself to the job site.

When Raul awoke on the morning of July 22, 2006, he found that his cousin wasn't going into work that day. It was a Saturday, and his cousin was hung over from the night before. Raul was more than happy to come in and work the weekend shift. It was extra money at time-and-a-half. Who could turn that down?

At 4:00 a.m., Raul threw on his work gear and jumped on his bicycle. He was supposed to start his shift at 5:00. Construction starts early in the mornings in the summer in Arizona. Residents who have to wake up to power saws and hammers driving nails before the sun even rises have registered many complaints, but it's the only way to get a full day of work in before the sun starts to bake the employees in hundred-plus degree heat.

In the nine months that he had been living there, Raul had learned his way around Mesa. He also knew the streets that had bike paths on them. In a large metropolitan city, you take your life into your own hands if you decide to attempt to bike to work. Many bike enthusiasts, exercise fanatics, and environmentalists had learned a long time ago that biking can be dangerous to your health.

Raul had found a main street with a bike path: Stapley Drive. And at 4:00 a.m., there was little or no traffic to worry about, especially on a Saturday.

There's something uniquely odd about being out in the early morning hours in a large city. It's unbelievably peaceful. You can find yourself daydreaming and feeling as if you exist in world that is inhabited only by you. Raul felt it. The calm, hot air hitting his face as the tires whisked along the asphalt, with the only sound being the changing of the gears on his bike or the occasionally rattle of the chain as it rotated around the sprocket.

As Raul rolled up Stapley Drive, he crossed Brown Road. He was only a few minutes from his worksite. The sound of a tire blowout shocked Raul. The peacefulness of the morning ride was now gone. His bike shook as he tried to correct the handlebars, but it was too late. He went down, the bike collapsing underneath him. He hit the asphalt of the bike lane with a thud.

In just a few seconds, lying there and sprawled out, he realized he could no longer use his legs. He pushed himself to sit up. Then came the pain. Not the pain of falling and striking the pavement. Not the pain of burns and abrasions when you hit the asphalt.

Certainly not the pain of smashing one of your digits with a hammer. This pain was different. This pain brought intense burning to the muscles of his legs. He felt as if somebody were holding an iron to the whole left side of his lower body.

Raul examined his lower left extremities. There were holes in his left pants leg. Then he noticed several holes in his right pants leg, just above the knee. Then blood. Not a lot, but enough to concern him.

Raul didn't have a cellphone. He didn't need one. Who was he going to call? His wife in Mexico had no phone. He lived with the only person he had constant contact with, his cousin. He didn't need a phone.

For the first time, after his long journey from Mexico City, after the trouble of getting across the border, after struggling with the loneliness and sorrow of leaving his family, Raul wished he had never come to America. He was alone, lying on a street in a country that he didn't call home, and he wanted to see his wife.

The first person to see Raul in the street was another construction worker on his way to work. This man couldn't speak any Spanish. Raul tried to explain to him what had happened, but it was obvious they weren't communicating. Then one of Raul's friends pulled up. He could speak Spanish and called 911. His friend assumed, like the first gentleman who had left, that Raul had been struck by a car.

When the paramedics arrived, they were able to give a more accurate prognosis. As they cut off Raul's pants, they saw the numerous holes in his legs. This was no accident. Raul Lopez-Garcia had been shot.

Patrol Officer Diane Tapia of the Mesa Police Department had answered the radio call and responded to the scene. She was there in time to see Raul being attended to by paramedics. The only thing Raul could tell her was that he heard a loud "pop" before wrecking on his bicycle. He saw no one; he heard no one. The people who found him told her the same thing.

Officer Tapia investigated the case and filed the original report. The scene was photographed and wrapped up in an hour or so. Raul's injuries were not life threatening.

Later at the hospital, Raul told Officer Tapia that he had no enemies. He just kept to himself. He just wanted to go to work. I guess that was too much to ask.

I woke up late on the morning of July 22nd. It was the first night in a while where I finally felt rested.

I knew that at some point I needed to go into the office and check the leads and calls that had come in, but I also needed to spend some time at home. My son's birthday party was scheduled for early that afternoon. He and some friends were going bowling. I could attend and then drive into Phoenix.

Because I was so busy at work, the grounds around my house had gone to hell. My pool hadn't been swept down for days. I needed to mow and trim the lawns, work that I am proud to say I do myself.

As I placed the brush on the pole to sweep the pool, my work phone started ringing. I pulled up the caller ID and realized it was Sergeant Clarke calling.

I took a big deep breath and tried to imagine the purpose of the call. There were too many variables to consider, so I just decided to call him back. Might just as well get it over with. I was sure that it wasn't any good news.

"Stu, it's Clark. Did you just try to call me?"

I was hoping he'd dialed my number by mistake.

"Yeah, how's your Saturday going?"

I knew this wasn't going to be pleasant.

"I don't know yet. It just started."

I set the pool brush down as I started to walk inside.

"We may have had another shooting last night. I'm trying to confirm. It happened in Mesa, and I just got a call about it."

"Mesa? Where in Mesa?"

"One of Mesa's Violent Crimes sergeants called the front desk. They obviously have been following the cases and think this might be related. Apparently some guy got shot on a bike while riding to work. It happened at . . . let me check my notes . . . Brown and Stapley. I don't know where that is."

I did know where that was located. It was twenty minutes from my house.

"Did they say what time it occurred?"

That could eliminate it right away.

"It happened around 4:30 this morning. A patrol officer took the initial report. I'm not sure how detectives got involved, but they are now looking into it."

I looked at the clock on the wall, and it was now almost 11:00 a.m. They were a good six hours behind in responding to the crime scene. By now, hundreds of cars and numerous pedestrians had trampled through the scene. I hope they had collected and photographed what they needed during the initial investigation.

"Do you know what kind of weapon was used?"

That could eliminate our guys right away.

"Looks like a shotgun. Don't know what caliber"

Sergeant Clarke knew exactly what I was thinking. If it were our guys, and it might or might not be, they had switched jurisdictions. Shocking!

"What have you got going on today?"

He knew that was a loaded question. It would have been better to ask, "What didn't I have going on today?"

"I was going into the office later, but my son is having his birthday party, and I haven't seen him in weeks. If I can just make an appearance, I'll meet with their investigators right after the party."

My son had heard the conversation.

"I'll tell you what, I'll go meet with Mesa Police. You head into the office. Who knows? It might not even be related," he said.

The yard work would have to wait, again.

"Call me, would you, as soon as you find out the particulars? I'll be on my cellphone," I said.

"Yeah, I'll let you know." He was trying to stay positive. "I hope it isn't . . . for our department's sake."

As I readied myself, my son came into the room. He watched as I slung my gun on my hip. He knew I was heading to work. I assured him I would stop by the party and help celebrate his birthday. He walked out of the room with his shoulders slumped. I cursed and realized that right now the shooters were dictating what was going on, and we were on the defensive. I couldn't wait for that to turn around someday.

When I arrived at the office, Marjorie was already there. She had organized the leads into their appropriate folders. The ones that were already marked as 1, 2, or 3 were filed and entered. The new ones sat in the unread file. I was the only permanent detective left for the task force. Everyone else was on vacation.

America's Most Wanted was going to air the show tonight on the two different serial killer investigations. I was asked if I wanted to go to Washington, D.C. and monitor the calls that came in. It was standard practice for the case agent of the case that is featured to be in studio handling tips as they come in, which was always a good idea. They fly you out, treat you to a great dinner, put you in a nice hotel, and then fly you back. I had heard all about it. They asked for someone to come out.

I wanted to go. I wanted to meet John Walsh and shake his hand. I wanted to go to get a tip on who was responsible for making my life a living hell. But I couldn't. There was no one home to man the ship. In a case like this, things can happen quickly, and I knew if I went back to D.C. that something would break. It already had. There was a possible shooting in Mesa. I stayed in Phoenix.

As I began to read through the intelligence reports and Silent Witness tips, I found three more Priority 1 targets who would need surveillance. We were running short of manpower, and three more targets would be tough to cover.

I was also running short of analysts to do background checks on the Priority 1 targets. Because of that, I had asked Lisa Ruggeri to join the task force.

Everyone wanted Lisa to be a part of their background criminal investigations. She was an expert in criminal intelligence analysis. She could find almost anyone, anywhere, at anytime. If she couldn't, she could give you the best ten people to contact to find out where the person you were looking for was.

Lisa was assigned to ACTIC: the Arizona Counter Terrorism Information Center. There she was asked to find the bad guys, those who would want to destroy this country and its citizens. To get her pulled away from her job took a lot of string pulling. We touched base today. Even though it was a weekend, she gladly took on the responsibility. She, too, would be leaving soon, but not for a vacation. She was heading back east to train others in her field of expertise. She assured me that I had her full attention until then.

"I guess we need to catch these guys before you go then, don't we?"

"Yes you do," she said. She wouldn't be leaving for ten days.

As I was devising a quick route to stop at two of the Priority 1 targets' homes not under surveillance, I received a call from Sergeant Clarke.

"What'd you find out?" I asked.

"Not a whole lot. The only evidence at the scene was a shotgun wadding, unknown caliber. The bike rider is stable, and he will survive, but he is Spanish speaking only. The detectives are out with him at the hospital as we speak. They're going to try to get pellets from the victim to see if we can determine a shot size." That didn't clear a whole lot up. "Let me see, what else? Oh, ... they have no witnesses, and their exact time of the shooting is closer to 4:45 a.m."

"Great," I answered. "If it's our guys, not only have they changed the area of operations, they've also pushed back their time of operation. By almost two hours!"

This was a nightmare, if it was related. It would mean that the task force would need to shift our hours, making the surveillance units work longer into the morning. I could see that going over like a lead balloon.

"I told them that you would meet with the investigative team on Monday, when their upper chain of command was present. Go down there, brief them, and ask 'em for whatever information they have. Be ready for some tough questions. I'm sure they don't want these guys to have switched areas."

I already had my own plan devised. I wasn't saying anything until I figured out what the bicyclist had been shot with, then I would brief them. If it wasn't our guys, there was no need for more information about what we're doing out there.

Somehow, I knew that it would be. I looked down at my phone. I was already late for my son's party.

It didn't take long for the media to sniff out the Mesa shooting and immediately try to link it to the Random/Serial Shooters. There hadn't been a confirmed shooting in two weeks. This was big news. It was important for me to reach out to the Mesa investigators involved to try to keep a lid on any premature talk about the shooters being responsible.

Nothing had been definitively reported as of Sunday, July 23rd, so that was good news. But there were questions being forwarded, and numerous pundits explaining the two sets of serial killers' actions and why was it so tough to catch them.

Experts from all over the country were being interviewed, which led to some fairly good analysis. The problem was no one that I'd heard of, or from, had ever had to deal with two serial killers in the same community at the same time. The press was asking tough questions of these experts, and they really had no answers other than the basic motivators of renowned serial killers.

They discussed the exploits of Ted Bundy; Son of Sam killer David Berkowitz; and Robert Pickton of British Columbia, who murdered dozens of prostitutes. All of them were later to be categorized into one of many motivational aspects, such as Hedonistic or Power/Control murderers.

As I read and studied papers, reports, and research, I learned that most of it was done by faculty members at universities or media folks. The police who had worked the cases had seldom written about them. I guess they decided to leave the whys to the scholars. That was unfortunate. I would have felt better reading about what the cops said.

As I sifted through the leads at the command post, I noticed a drop-off in the number of tips coming into our task force. With as much media attention as the Random/Serial Shooters were getting, there was no logical explanation for the drop-off. The reward was still a hundred thousand clams to the person who fingered these guys.

If, in fact, Mesa's shooting was the work of my guys, renewed interest would be bountiful. I hoped that it wasn't their work. I hoped that the shooters were still lurking in East Phoenix, soon to be pulled over, and interviewed with the Toyota Camry identifying the registered owner, and perhaps they'd be carrying a concealed gun, like a 410 shotgun. I hoped they hadn't moved to Mesa. I hoped they hadn't moved for the sake of all the residents, especially the ones living in Mesa. The residents had no idea what they were in for.

I packed up my gear and headed out to conduct surveillance. Tonight's target for me had been fingered by a coworker. The tip had come in that James Moore had an interest in guns, had a violent past, worked late at night, and was overheard talking about gunning down people.

Moore's background check was even more interesting. He did have a violent background and had been arrested twice for concealed weapons, both handguns.

However, he had threatened an ex-girlfriend with a rifle several years earlier. The ex had made a police report, but nothing had come of it.

The neighborhood where Moore lived was a stone's throw away from where I'd purchased my first house in Phoenix. I knew the area well—middle-class incomes, mostly blue collar, but lately, a lot of white trash. In fact, I had left the neighborhood after two shootings a mile from my house, involving outlaw bikers.

Moore's house sat on a street that ran east and west, and it was two up from the corner on the north side. I tactically parked about four houses away and could see the front yard area. There were six or so vehicles parked in the driveway and the street around the home. One was parked in the yard. Yep, white trash.

I had been given night vision binoculars. They were great until someone drove up on you with their headlights. It took a few seconds for the blindness to go away.

The Moore house was jumping for a Sunday, and I could see numerous people in the front yard area. Word on Moore was that he liked to party and was using drugs. That accounted for the vehicles and the milling around of several individuals.

As I watched the house, I noticed a neighbor two houses to the east standing in his driveway. He was looking at me, but I couldn't tell if he had seen me. The street was dark, but if a car drove by, it would light up the interior of my truck. Even with its tinted windows, there was no hiding from view through the windshield.

The neighbor then started to throw a rubber ball down the street, and his short-haired golden retriever ran after it, sucked it up, and sprinted back to the owner. He repeated this several times. After each throw, he stared toward my truck.

Surveillances are mastered through years of experience. Conducting them by oneself is not recommended. The key to success is knowing when you've been identified by someone: the target, a neighbor of the target, or just someone out walking around. Once you've been marked, you have to move or risk being blown. Most people will just call the police on a suspicious vehicle. That can be handled. But once you're made and your vehicle is made, it can be very tricky to continue the surveillance. It can also be dangerous. If the neighbor is a friend of the subject you're surveilling, he may call him. They may plan an ambush. I've seen guys dress up to look like the suspect and even leave in the suspect's car in order to pull officers off the real suspect, allowing him to take off later.

I wasn't sure if I'd been made, so I began to try to figure out where to go. The big black truck would be noticeable anywhere in the vicinity, and there were only certain spots I could sit in and be able to see the house and anyone who left.

As I planned my next move, the neighbor and his dog decided to call it a night. He turned around and walked inside his house with his trusty pet following. I decided to stay put. Maybe they hadn't seen me. There were no calls into police.

About fifteen minutes later, the garage to the ball thrower's home opened, and an SUV backed out. It, of course, turned right toward me and lit up the interior of my cab like an airport landing strip. The SUV rolled by slowly, with the driver, a woman, staring at me the whole time. I had been made.

I watched the SUV go to the end of the block and make a U-turn. It was coming back my way, again lighting up the interior of my truck. This time, it stopped right next to me. As I looked out my driver's side window, I saw the front passenger window in the SUV sliding down. Now I was getting irritated. It's one thing to check and see if a stranger was lurking in the neighborhood and to phone the police, I understand that. It was something else to confront the stranger.

I didn't roll my window down right away. I left it up for a few seconds to add to the tension the driver must already be feeling. I then slowly rolled my window down. I didn't say a word.

She spoke first. "Can I help you?"

What an idiot. Do I look like I need your help? It's 9:30 at night, and it's dark out. Who are you to be asking if I need your help? What if I were a bad guy, or God forbid, our shooters? What would stop me from blowing your head off?

I wanted her to know I didn't appreciate her confronting me, so I gave her an ugly look and stated simply, "No thanks."

Her once-helpful look changed to a look of anger, and I could see her scrunching her face up. She was not happy with my answer. I could tell she was straining to come up with something clever.

"Smart ass," she yelled, and then gunned her SUV back to her home. She ripped into her driveway and parked.

The vehicle lights turned off, and she jumped out of the driver's seat and walked to the rear. She stood there staring at me with her arms crossed. Good. She was upset now, too.

About a minute later, her husband, the ball thrower, walked out from the house and stood next to her. Coward! If anyone was going to confront me, it should have been him. They were talking, trying to figure out what to do with this shady individual parked down the street who had been so rude. I was hoping they would just call me in. I had my radio next to me, waiting for the call about my surveillance being burned, but it never came. Minutes went by as the two stood in their driveway, staring at me. I couldn't even divert my attention from them to my target. I couldn't even raise my binoculars because they'd know who I was watching. So they stood there and I sat there, each glaring at each other.

It was obvious I could never return to this target. The snoops would tell everyone about the black truck that sat on their street with a lone occupant, about the "smart ass" who wouldn't tell them what he was doing.

I did understand their concern. The city had two serial killers on the loose, and people were panicked. A stranger in the neighborhood smelled of trouble, if not for killing, possibly burglarizing cars or homes. I understood all that. But you still don't confront complete strangers. You call the cops, and they do that.

It was painfully obvious that I had to leave, but before doing so, I was going to let the snoops know what I thought of their tomfoolery.

I made it as dramatic as possible. I started my truck, which roared loudly anyway. I pulled up to them slowly, giving them time to feel great anxiety. I kept my headlights off, for effect, until I was almost upon them; then, I lit them up. They both stiffened.

I could see the angst in their faces as I rolled my passenger window down. My badge was out, and I flipped it up. I then let them have it.

"Next time you decide to confront somebody, you'd better realize who it is you're confronting."

My badge reflected what little light came from outside my truck. Both of their mouths dropped opened. They didn't know what to say.

I needed to add one more caveat. "You're lucky I'm a cop and not a lowlife with a gun, lady, or you might not be standing there now."

I floored the truck and ripped out from in front of their house.

I looked back through my rearview mirror, and they were still standing there with the same stupid looks on their faces.

As I drove away, I justified my actions and words as conducting a public service. Never again, I hoped would Ball Boy and his wife confront a complete stranger anywhere, even on their own block.

Lesson learned.

CHAPTER 31

My meeting with Mesa Police commenced at 10:00 a.m. I'd never been to their main police station, located right in the middle of their downtown district. Like Phoenix Police, they housed their Violent Criminal Investigations division in the main station.

As I walked into their building, I wasn't even sure whom I would be meeting with that morning. I was told that the lead investigator from the bicyclist shooting would be present and maybe her supervisor. Beyond that, I had no idea. I was told to ask for Sergeant Mike Collins. I flashed my badge to a civilian behind the bulletproof glass in the main lobby and asked for the sergeant. I would have to wait in the lobby with the seedy elements that were floating around. I decided to stand in the corner, keeping my back to the wall and my face to the crowd.

After a couple of minutes, a linebacker-looking guy walked through the secured door from inside the building. He came up to me and introduced himself. Sergeant Mike Collins, Homicide Bureau. I didn't know if that was good or bad. I hoped that our victim hadn't punched his ticket to the afterlife. I was assured he was OK. He had taken most of the bird shot in his legs. That was the good news. The bad news was that in the forty-eight hours since the shooting, they had no leads. Not one person had come forward.

We rode the elevator to the second floor and took a stroll to one of their briefing facilities. As we entered the room, an individual, who introduced himself as Lieutenant Wayne Pew, sat at one of the rectangular tables that had been placed together at their ends to make a horseshoe. I took a seat at the middle table. Sergeant Collins excused himself to gather the other members for the meeting. Lieutenant Pew and I made small talk. He was a veteran of Mesa's Violent Crimes Bureau, and I told him that I had spent the last ten years doing the same.

Sergeant Collins returned with three more gentlemen. They introduced themselves, including the commander of the unit, Mike Tolan. We were waiting on the lead investigator, Vicki Hixson. She entered just a minute later, and we were introduced. She carried a small yellow evidence envelope. I told them to call me Clark.

I got straight to the point, telling them that I may be able to save us all a lot of time by examining the shot cup from their scene. I didn't want to cause them any undue stress, and at this point in my investigation, secrecy was of the utmost importance.

They all understood. Detective Hixson slid me the envelope. As I opened it, my heart sank, and I'm sure a look of deep frustration overtook my already tired face. I was holding in my hands what I was 100 percent sure was proof of the latest shooting in the Random/Serial Shooter case: a 410 shot cup.

Before I blurted out my belief, I asked them to explain the circumstances surrounding the shooting of the bicyclist, Raul Lopez-Garcia.

Sergeant Collins and Detective Hixson narrated what they knew. Garcia had been riding northbound on Stapley Road, probably in the bike lane, when he was shot. He was riding to work and had no enemies. There was no motive for the shooting. Garcia described hearing a "popping sound" just before going down. He did not see who shot him, nor did he have any idea from where the shot came. He was alone.

As I looked around the briefing room, I didn't really know how to express my regrets to them. My shooters were now operating in Mesa. They were all going to be pulled into the largest criminal investigation in the history of this state. A tornado of press, meetings, and tactical planning awaited them along with countless hours of asking themselves for some reason as to why these things were happening. There would be plenty of hoping and praying for one break to solve their case before somebody else got shot or dies.

The worst part was telling them there would be more. They all stared at me. I needed to choose my words carefully. I took a deep breath.

"Gentlemen and Detective Hixson, I wish I could say that I had good news for you, but I can't. It looks to me, at least at this point, the Random/Serial Shooters may have come to Mesa." *May* was too delicate. "What I'm holding in my hand is a 410 shot cup, the same type of ammunition used in at least six of my shootings." I paused for a few seconds. "I'm sorry. I wish I had better news."

I looked from one face to the other. I could see Commander Tolan digesting what I had just told him. I could tell he was trying to figure out how to report this to their chief of police, who happened to be an interim chief.

Lieutenant Pew was quick with a response. "Clark, what do you believe we should do next, and can you explain to us your reasoning behind your assessment?"

"Sure."

It was only fair that they knew what I knew. They were in it now, a chip in the big game, whether they wanted to play or not.

Over the next hour, I explained in great depth the shotgun shootings that had plagued the city of Phoenix, and how the M.O. of their shooting matched the thirteen I was currently investigating. I briefly touched on the .22 caliber shootings. I hoped they didn't have any of those, but I told them they needed to research those shootings, along with any other random, unsolved cases that they might have. This may not be their first shooting.

Lastly, sarcastically, I told them that the media would be all over them. Be ready and be forewarned. This story is huge, and it has gone international.

I could see the stress starting to build in their faces. Sergeant Collins looked especially tense. He was sharp. He knew that backtracking cases took time, and who knows what can of worms you can open if you look hard enough.

Commander Tolan, a man with over thirty years of experience, seemed to take it all in stride. He asked the next question.

"Clark, we have media calling already. That was one of the reasons we asked to meet with you. Do you have any suggestions as to what to tell them?"

His public safety mode had kicked in, but not at the expense of jeopardizing the investigation.

"Well, at this point, the only people who really know that this is the calling card of the Random/Serial Shooters are sitting right in this room. You all control what, if any, information gets out." That was the truth. They did control tying the cases together, plus there was always the slight possibility that this was a copycat. "The fact of the matter is, nothing is certain. The only tie right now evidentiary wise is that shot cup, which I'm sure will be inconclusive forensically."

They understood where I was coming from, and they didn't want to cause a panic in their city. If, for some reason, the case came back as unrelated, then it would look like they'd cried wolf too soon. On the other hand, if they didn't inform the public, and another shooting occurred, and this bicyclist case was related, their liability could be huge.

"What do you suggest?" Commander Tolan asked.

"Can you hold off on any announcement until I can get the task force informed? Say, twenty-four hours? I know that it has been forty-eight hours since the shooting, but it would give me time to brief my chain of command and figure out how to respond to the possibility of changing our surveillance grids."

This was a nightmare. If the shooters had moved, as I suspected, it would render the surveillances of East Phoenix useless. All that manpower sitting, watching, waiting, and hoping to catch these guys in the act would be all for naught. We would need some time.

I continued. "The fact of the matter is, folks, that you're going to need to join the task force. It's going to take a coordinated effort by your department and the task force to put some plan in place if our shooters have come to your city."

"Did you say shooters, plural?" asked Lieutenant Pew. "You mean, you think you have more than one?"

"Shooters, plural, as in two shooters in the same car. As far as I know, I have not confirmed any copycat shootings. God help us if that starts."

They all agreed. Commander Tolan then spoke again.

"I think I can convince our chiefs to sit on this for the time being. From what you tell me, this sounds like a massive undertaking. I think the least that we can do is sit on it for twenty-four hours, until we can at least get something together on our end and figure out how to handle this."

He looked around for anyone who disagreed.

Sergeant Collins had his head down and looked as if he was suffering a stroke. Lieutenant Pew was the first to nominate Sergeant Collins as the go-to guy.

Sergeant Collins lifted his head up and acknowledged, "Thanks a lot."

Mesa Police had yet to canvass the neighborhood. Detective Hixson informed me of a bank that sits across from the shooting site. She would attempt to obtain any surveillance the bank might have. Any leads or tips would be fired to me immediately for tracking and storage in the data bank. As Detective Hixson, Sergeant Collins, and I began to discuss semantics, Commander Tolan arose from his seat. "I'm going to take off and brief our bosses. Is there anything else that you think I need to know, Clark?"

"Yes, there is." I didn't want to say it, but I felt obligated to tell them everything. "If it is our guys, and I believe that it is, they will hit again. They tend to stay in the same area for awhile. They get comfortable if the hunting is good."

"I see," Commander Tolan said.

"One other thing. I believe that they follow the media and the attention it brings. If they don't get their press, they may strike again, quickly."

A smile of raw disgust formed on commander Tolan's face. He knew what I was talking about. That would make the decision to sit on the case even harder. Feed the public safety aspect, or feed the egos of two maniacs.

Neither choice was very appealing.

He had just left work, and the idea of a trip to Las Vegas sounded pretty good. He loved Las Vegas. He was even treated with some comps when he went there, even though he was really a nobody.

But Vegas didn't know that, and neither did his partner. Since they had started living together, he believed that his partner had never been to Vegas. It would be a good time to go. Flying was expensive on short notice, and he didn't want to put the miles on his personal car. He'd been doing a lot of that lately. It's over six hundred miles miles round-trip from Phoenix to Las Vegas. Besides, he knew people at the airport that could give him a discount.

Thrifty Car Rental sat in Terminal 3 Sky Harbor Airport. When he and his partner arrived at the counter, two service agents were working the desk. It was Monday, and most of the business travelers had already rented their cars for the day or the week.

"I need a mid-size for two days."

"OK, I need to see a driver's license and a credit card please," the clerk said.

The man dug into his wallet and pulled out his license and U.S. Bank credit card. He couldn't remember the last time he had even used his credit card for a purchase. His debit card was his usual mode of payment for most, if not all, of his financial transactions.

"I won't need any insurance or anything like that."

No sense in wasting money on trivial insurance needs, he thought to himself. That money would be better spent at the casinos.

He loved casinos. The gambling, the atmosphere, the adrenaline rush when you win money. It all fed one of his many appetites. The same way gunning people down fed him.

Gambling in Arizona had been legal for years at the Indian casinos. He and his partner had made their way out there numerous times. They probably wouldn't even be going to Las Vegas except for the fact that they'd been eighty-sixed from one of their favorite casinos the night before.

Someone had spotted them slashing tires, which of course they did on numerous occasions in the parking lots, after losses. Whoever had spotted them had been quick enough to write down the car's license plate. Last night, they'd been confronted as his car sat in the same casino parking lot. They were detained and questioned. But he and his partner weren't going to admit to anything.

The interior of his car was searched, by his consent, and the cops found some sharp objects that they did in fact use to puncture tires. But he lied his way out of it. The knife, he said, was used for cutting limes. He was a bartender by trade. The center hole-punch was his partner's and was used to stamp metal. The ice pick was also used for bartending. He had an answer for everything.

He was cooperative and cordial. But he wasn't going to let them search his trunk. In it hid a weapon of destruction. Who knows what these crazy Indian police might do with his baby? There might be some tribal law about guns on the reservation or some other BS. He wasn't about to be stripped of an appendage.

When the police and security had had enough of their denials, they were sent home. "Never return to the property of this casino again or any of the Salt River Indian gaming sites. Do you understand?" The security and police had made it clear. Come back, and you'll go to jail for trespassing.

They both understood, and he gathered up his tools of the trade, ones he occasionally used for bartending, but more importantly the ones he used to wreak havoc.

The casino's customers would be spared any more destruction. Others would not be so lucky. He'd promised himself that.

"The rental contract is in the envelope. Head out these doors to the left, and follow the signs to customer car pick-up. Thanks for renting from Thrifty," the clerk concluded.

As the two walked to the rental area, his partner announced he needed a drink. Nothing like starting out with a little belt. But the partner would wait until he drove the rental car to their apartment. His buddy drove his car. He didn't want any trouble before they left town. Driving the rental was cool. He never got to drive.

$$\diamond$$

Trying to figure out what to say to my chain of command about the latest shooting perplexed me. I could blame the announcement of our undercover operations as the reason for the change of areas. It was logical. If the shooters were following the media, then they had likely picked up on the report. Maybe they figured that, with all the media attention, it was time to pick up and go somewhere else besides East Phoenix. Why not keep the cops guessing? There was also the possibility that they were trying to scare the entire Valley. Start on the west side, move to a central location, and then move way east. If you truly wanted to cause panic valley-wide, that would be a way to do it. If that were the case, then no city was safe.

I had called Sergeant Andy Hill and asked him to attend the meeting. We truly needed cooperation between both police departments. If both Public Information Officers shared information, maybe together we could make a smooth transition into the release of the latest shooting. If not, then the task force and its surveillances would be thrown into disarray.

The meeting with my brass lasted about one hour. Commander Lewis had been promoted to Assistant Chief and would no longer be in charge of the investigation. I told them everything I knew about the newest shooting, and that it was clearly related. I told them I had asked for twenty-four hours to get our ducks in a row. No one in the room seemed to grasp what had happened.

There were far more questions than answers. One thing was certain. Mesa could not afford to sit on this shooting forever. Sergeant Hill excused himself to take a phone call. He was gone about ten minutes.

As the meeting wrapped up, Sergeant Hill returned with a press release in his hand. "Mesa's PIO just sent me this. This is their press release they're going to put out tonight."

So much for giving us time. In essence, if it didn't hit the newsstands until the following day, that would be almost twenty-four hours. Again, I understood their predicament.

He handed me the press release, which was fairly generic. It didn't tie the Mesa shooting to our series, saying just that "police were trying to determine whether a series of random shootings in Phoenix have spread to east Mesa." Investigators were "comparing notes" with Phoenix Police.

"There are some similarities, but we're not sure," said Mesa Police spokesperson Sergeant Chuck Trapani.

Andy Hill chimed in that Chuck was a good guy, and that he could talk to him to see if Phoenix and Mesa could do a dual agency release.

Nobody in the room doubted that the shooting of the Mesa bicyclist was related. The only words that had not been uttered were "officials have linked the shooting to a string of other shootings throughout the Valley."

With all the ups and downs of the investigation, mostly downs, I'd been shucking my usual fitness routine. Tonight, I would hit the treadmill and clear my mind. All of the targets were covered, and I wouldn't be needed for anyone in particular. I was going to stop at my gym for a little stress break.

This new shooting, once released to the media, would start a whole new run of leads, most of them coming from the East Valley: Mesa, Chandler, and Gilbert areas. Mesa would need a lot of assistance.

I arrived at my gym just in time to see the 9:00 p.m. news. As I climbed on the treadmill and dialed up the gauges, I began to watch as the lead story flashed "Serial Shooter." I couldn't hear the newscast because I had forgotten my headphones, so I jumped off the treadmill to read the closed captioning.

The newscast talked about linking the Mesa shooting to the Serial Shooter. A joint news conference was going to be held the following day, July 25th. It didn't even take twelve hours for the press to get the story. They even revealed that Phoenix Police had just met with Mesa to determine if certain criteria had been met to join this shooting as part of the series. There were no interviews, just a closing statement that invited viewers to "tune in" for further developments.

I climbed back on the treadmill, realizing our shooters had gotten just what they wanted—immediate press coverage and more anxiety created. As the rubberized tread began to roll and the hum of the electrical controlled rollers sang, I couldn't come up with any solutions to the new dilemma now facing the task force.

My shooters' move to Mesa, a city of a two hundred thousand residents, was not good news, except for maybe the rest of the Valley. No one would be cheering tonight.

I opened my gym bag, fired my sweaty clothes into the laundry basket, and headed upstairs. They were already asleep, which is the only time I saw them now. I had promised myself the same restful bliss after my workout. There was nothing more I could do tonight.

I had just walked into my closet to grab some clothes when I could hear my phone. It had been ringing since I'd left it in the kitchen. There were two voicemails. I didn't recognize the number, but it was an East Valley area code. Before I had a chance to listen to the messages, the phone started to buzz again. The stupid thing rang all the time, so I'd decided for my own sanity that vibrate would be its permanent operating mode. I didn't recognize the number, but it was another call from the east side of town.

"This is Clark," I answered.

It was Sergeant Mike Collins of the Mesa Police Department.

"Hey, Clark, it's Mike Collins. I'm sorry to bother you, but I thought you might want to know what we discovered. We may have video and audio of the shooting incident."

I immediately started shaking. "You're kidding me, right?"

It was a stupid response, but I was too dumbfounded to think of any quick comebacks.

"No, I'm not," he said. "We were conducting some canvassing, and apparently one of the neighbors in the vicinity of the shooting has a video and audio surveillance system. He claims to have heard the shot on Saturday night. In fact, it woke him up. He was watching the news and realized that the shooting had happened right behind him. He told our dispatcher that he may have recorded the whole thing. Detective Hixson is on her way out there, and we have one of our techs headed there, too. Would you care to join us?"

He didn't have to ask twice.

"I'll be right there. Tell me where I'm going."

Sergeant Collins relayed the address, and as fast as I had undressed to get into bed, I was dressed and out the door. The heck with a good night's sleep. Sleep is overrated. Could this be the real break in the case that we needed?

In fewer than five minutes, I was headed to Stapley Drive and Brown Road. Sergeant Collins would guide me into the neighborhood when I got close. The house with the surveillance system sat at the end of a cul-de-sac that just so happened to back up to Stapley Drive.

I quietly knocked on the door, hoping not to disturb any sleeping children. A very pleasant woman answered the door, and I identified myself as a police officer. She smiled and let me in. As we walked from the foyer toward the living room, I saw big Sergeant Mike Collins taking up most of the living room. Detective Hixson was present, as were two other detectives, and the male homeowner. They were all peering at a television screen sitting on a shelving unit.

Sergeant Collins gave me a nod, acknowledging my presence, and moved his head to the side in a gesture to step out to the backyard. I followed the lead, and together we exited the living room to a back patio area.

"Looks like I was a little premature. The homeowner has video and audio, but only video of the front of the house. As you can see, the backyard backs up to Stapley Drive, and he doesn't have that covered with a camera. Sorry about that."

There was nothing to be sorry about. It was just another unlucky break in a case that was full of them.

He continued. "The tech guys are trying to download the shooting. Looks like he recorded it on some type of system, maybe a DVR. We have audio of the shooting, but the video only captures the front street."

"We're ready in here," one of the forensic techs said. Sergeant Collins and I proceeded back inside the home, with the anticipation of a great lead now greatly diminished.

"Cue it up, and let's see what we've got."

The homeowner worked for a security company. The video was state-of-the-art. He had three cameras stationed around the home. One in front covering the cul-de-sac, one covering his front porch, and one covering his back porch. All of them were wired for sound.

We skipped over the front porch and street recording and went to the back porch camera. We turned up the audio. Together, we all sat and listened as the humming of tires to pavement was recorded. You could differentiate between the sounds of traffic on Brown Road and traffic on Stapley Drive. It was a great system.

At around 0441, the recorded time on the DVR, you heard the sound of one last set of tires and then a "bang." No mistaking it, the shotgun blast was captured on the audio system. It startled everyone in the room.

"Play it again, please," I requested. I was listening for the screeching of tires or any sign that our shooters panicked after the shooting. We all listened. Nothing but the small echo of tires on asphalt, and then, "ca-bleweey." The sound startled some of the people again. It was loud. No wonder the poor homeowner had been awakened by the shot.

But what you didn't hear was panic. No screeching tires, no jamming on the gas pedal, or the roar of an engine. Just a quiet getaway. These guys shot and didn't have a care or worry in the world.

I looked at Sergeant Collins and asked him to take a walk with me out to the shooting scene.

We both jumped in our vehicles and drove to the bank situated just across the street from where Raul had been gunned down. Sergeant Collins had made a call to have the originating officer meet us at the scene to explain where the victim was found. She arrived a few minutes after we did.

Standing in the gravel easement was what used to be a green electrical box. It was either a local phone or a cable box. It had obviously been there a while, since the green color had turned to faded blue. The bottom was rusting out as well.

"Right there is where we found the shot cup," Officer Tapia said as she pointed to the gravel just in front of the box.

I looked at the electrical box and could see that it had suffered numerous pellet strikes.

Detective Hixson then joined us. "Where did you find the bicyclist?" I asked.

Officer Tapia pointed to an area about twenty yards north of the box. "I found him lying in the bike lane."

I directed my next question to Detective Hixson. "Didn't you say the victim took most of the shotgun blast in his legs?"

Nobody knew where I was going with this.

"Yes, he did. Most of it in his left leg. But he also sustained wounds to his right leg as well," she said.

"Was the blast directly in the side of his legs, more back, or more frontal?" I asked.

She had just returned from the hospital, so the strikes would be fresh in her mind. She pulled out her notepad.

"I documented twenty-four pellet strikes to the front of his upper left leg, same amount to the inside area of the upper right leg, four exit wounds to the back of the upper left leg, five exit wounds to the back of the upper right leg, two pellets to the inner portion of his right calf, and one pellet in the inside portion of his right ankle."

Based on the wound pattern, the shot came from in front of the bicyclist. That would be a tough angle for the passenger to pull off, if the car was traveling the same direction as the bicyclist. It would be not so difficult for the driver to shoot the victim, if they were going the opposite way. There was no side road to ambush and fire from.

The homeowner had agreed to turn over his hard drive to Mesa Police detectives for the purpose of downloading the shooting audio. They promised a quick turnaround. I was assured that I would have a copy of the tape for task force listening by the following day. That was good enough for me.

As I got in my truck I looked at my phone. It read 2:30 a.m. Who needs sleep? I yawned the whole way home.

CHAPTER 32

The audio of the shooting of the Mesa bicyclist created quite a stir, though there was no reason to get our hopes up. It would make for interesting chatter. The Internet was abuzz with the Mesa shooting. A press conference was still scheduled for that morning. Both Mesa Police and Phoenix police would conduct it.

Sergeant Andy Hill had heard about the audiotape, but he had been misinformed about its content. I gave him the straight scoop and reminded him not to release any of that information just yet.

Whatever the case, the serial killers were making national news every day. Vans sat outside Phoenix Police headquarters for weeks, all hoping to get an exclusive on any new information about either the Random/Serial Shooter or the BLK. Nobody knew what I looked like, and I had asked that no names be released. The media had only been given "investigators and detectives" in charge of the case.

Today would be the first get-together of all the jurisdictions now involved in the case, except for Glendale. We still hadn't added Michael Cordrey's shooting to the matrix. The jurisdictions now totaled six. We had hijacked the downstairs conference room.

Commander Mike Tolan from Mesa P.D. saw me sitting alone and plopped down next to me. "I saw the news report last night," I said. "It was a good idea to release it. Safety trumps anything that we might have uncovered. Only problem is now, the spotlight is on you. Any plans in place?"

"We're working on it. Our budget is always tight, and getting extra manpower is a fight. If you have any suggestions, please let me know."

"Tell whoever pulls the purse strings to get on it now before one shooting becomes thirteen. Scare the hell out of 'em. Let me know if you need me to talk to anyone."

"Actually, I would appreciate you briefing our chief's office and our PIOs. You're the expert here. We're in uncharted waters. Their meeting is this afternoon, if you can make it. "

"I'll be there."

It was the least I could do.

Detective Vicki Hixson took a seat beside me and handed me a manila envelope. "These are the crime scene photos and the victim's photos. I think you'll see that you have everything you need. I should have a copy of the audio of the shooting this afternoon."

I opened the envelope and began to look at the victim's wounds—definitely frontal on the left thigh and more inner on the right thigh. The shot was fired from a medium distance. There were no pellet strikes above the waist.

The shot pattern on the victim showed that he'd been in motion when the shot was fired. His left leg was almost completely extended with the downward motion and bottoming out of the bike pedal, while the opposite leg had risen to a bent position, supported by the other bike pedal. Thus, both legs were susceptible to the shot as it streamed toward him.

It appeared that our shooters hadn't changed their pattern. They were still firing from the street, probably slowing just enough to get off a shot. Accuracy was waning though. The bicyclist had been struck low.

Lieutenant Benson called the meeting to order and asked everyone to introduce themselves. He had been waiting patiently on our new commander but decided to start late without him. We couldn't sit around all day.

After introductions, Detective Hixson gave a brief summary of the shooting of Raul Lopez-Garcia, the bicyclist. The fact that a 410 shot cup was recovered, not to mention the other similarities, supported the notion that this case was related to the other shootings.

Lieutenant Wade Pew then spoke of their plans for follow-up, and what at their command staff intended to do. It would take them a little while to be up and running with a permanent plan. All leads for Mesa's shooting would be funneled through Detective Hixson for dissemination to Mesa detectives. They had enough people to deal with those leads and might even be able to spare a couple detectives. The meeting was adjourned.

The third and final tip from caller #60176 was believed to have been called into Silent Witness on July 25, 2006. The reason for the confusion was simple: Whoever took the original call and the second call added this additional tip to the already generated tip sheet.

The tipster now had a name. Ron Horton. He listed his phone number for contact, and he was willing to speak to an investigator.

The additional information provided by Ron Horton read as follows:

Caller called back a 2nd time (actually 3rd) and gave similar information as to the 1st call. Caller said Sammy bragged about using a 12 12 (double barrel shotgun). Sammy's residence is near the shootings. Caller said when Sammy 1st started bragging about the shootings, caller didn't believe him. They had been drinking. Sammy told caller to go home and watch the news. Sammy called the shooting spree Rving (Random Recreational Violence). Caller knows Sammy's mother lives at … . Caller says he can take detectives to Sammy because he does not remember exact address??? Caller is 98% sure this is serial shooter. He believes Sammy may live on the eastside of town now, possibly Scottsdale.

◉

With Mesa as the new target area, nobody knew exactly how to handle the switch in locations. If in fact the shooters had changed areas, the question everyone was asking themselves was "Is it permanent?" I was confident that if they kept up their antics in East Phoenix, we would catch them. Moving to Mesa changed the odds greatly in the shooters' favor. It was actually smart, even if they hadn't heard the supervisor from Phoenix Police give up our undercover operations.

Detective Hixson had been kind enough to provide me a copy of the audio of the Raul Lopez-Garcia shooting. So I decided to spend the day going through leads and listening over and over to the shooting to see if I could pick up something, anything, to give me some kind of lead into how they operated.

The microphone that had picked up the shooting was phenomenal. You could distinguish the sound of the tires and engines of the vehicles that passed behind the house. You could tell the difference between cars and trucks just by the volume of the tires rolling on the pavement.

Just seconds before the shooting, you could hear the faint sound of tires to asphalt and then a brief pause. The gunshot was heard, but no sound of tires rolling after the shooting. There was no sound of the bicyclist hitting the road, either.

As I prepared myself for the 9:00 p.m. surveillance meeting, Sergeant Timothy Bryant scooted over to my desk.

"Clark, have you been listening to your police radio at all?" he asked.

"No, why?"

"There's a reported shooting that just came out."

"What! Our guys?"

I was stunned. I swung around from my desk as if I had been sucked up in a tornado.

"Yeah, I just heard it coming in. I was monitoring hot traffic on the radio, and the call came out. Someone reported being shot in the area of 40th Street and Thomas," he said.

I looked down at my cellphone. It was a little after 8:00 p.m. I jumped from my chair and ran to the Sergeant at the Violent Crimes Bureau desk.

"I'm pulling it up for you now," he fired off before I had a chance to say anything. "Looks like a bicyclist is reporting being shot in the back. He's at a convenience store. No weapon seen. Officers are describing the wound as a single gunshot wound to the back. Fire is responding."

"What kind of weapon?" I asked.

"Doesn't say. Let me see what I can find out," the desk sergeant said.

Before Sergeant Bryant could say anything, I looked at him and said, "I'm starting that way."

"It's going to be a fu@#*n zoo out there. You're right in prime time for news coverage," he blurted out.

"I know. Maybe I can get there before they do."

My undercover truck was parked across the street from police headquarters. Seconds later, I screeched out of the parking lot. Without lights and sirens, I could be to 40th Street and Thomas Road within ten minutes. I wouldn't be driving the speed limit.

As I flew up 40th Street, I could see in the distance that the entire intersection had been shut down. All traffic going north on 40th Street had been diverted. The boys in blue had done their jobs.

As I pulled in across the street, I noticed, much to my chagrin, no fewer than six news trucks parked right next to the store. They were already setting up for their remote broadcasts.

This shooting came out over the regularly monitored police channel that any yahoo, including the press, can intercept with a police scanner.

There were patrol cars everywhere. I stood across the street for a moment and gathered it all in. This is what it had come down to. A city under complete siege. Sergeant Bryant was right. It was a zoo. But it was more than that. It was out of control. It's just what the shooters wanted. People who were panicked, news personnel scurrying, and police clueless.

I walked up, and the on-duty sergeant looked completely overwhelmed. Who wouldn't be? He had to deal with all of this attention on a Wednesday night. I smiled at him as I stood by the trunk of his car. He was on the phone with his boss. He was trying to write down information while squeezing the phone against his ear and shoulder. I recognized him. His name was Sergeant Mike Lanning, and he used to work Violent Crimes as a detective.

He saw me and nodded, then hung up the phone.

"Are you all right?" I asked.

I wanted him to know that I wasn't panicking, and neither should he.

He looked at me and smiled a little. "I am now that you guys are here. This is unbelievable."

Lieutenant Benson and Assistant Chief Bill Louis arrived. News helicopters, at least three, circled overhead. Sergeant Lanning would have to yell during the briefing.

The victim was a Daniel Suarez. He'd been riding his bike on Thomas Road when he was shot once in the back. He realized immediately that he had been shot and pedaled a block or so to the convenience store. A maroon Toyota 4Runner passed by him immediately after the shooting, going the same direction. He described hearing a "whoosh sound" right before impact. Currently, there were no witnesses. He was transported to Banner Scottsdale Osborn Hospital, and the lone projectile was still inside him. This was no shotgun shooting.

As I took notes, I was sure it wasn't related. Shooting victims in the back was our boys' trademark, but unless they added a silencer to their small caliber gun, this wasn't our guys. The shooting was too early and the streets too crowded. A copycat screwing with us?

I made my assessment, and we all agreed it wasn't related. Lieutenant Benson called for another detective to respond and take disposition of the case. I made my way to the hospital.

Daniel was resting in a hospital bed in a recovery room, having a little trouble understanding all the fuss over him. I told him that people are a little curious when bicyclists and pedestrians are unexplainably shot. Then it dawned on Daniel. He understood all the hubbub. He had heard about the Serial Shooter and looked at me with some curiosity. "I thought they shot people late at night?" He was also in discomfort. The projectile had punctured a lung. No laughing matter.

"They do. That's why yours may not be related. I'll know more when I see what type of projectile struck you." He seemed a little relieved with those assurances.

Daniel's MRI showed it all. As the doctor put the picture on the light for me to examine, I could see the projectile perfectly. It was the size of a small caliber bullet with one significant difference. It was cupped and crimped toward one end.

It was a pellet, probably fired from some high-powered pellet gun. They were dangerous, because they can cause serious injury, just like in this case. Most pellets of this kind don't penetrate quite as deep as this one did, however. It wouldn't be removed.

Upon leaving the hospital, I drove toward East Phoenix. I decided that the only way for us to catch these guys was to play like these guys. So that's what I did. But I didn't like it.

I'd park my truck off one of the main streets in our surveillance area. I would shut off my engine and sit there and observe. I would monitor traffic and watch pedestrians walking up and down the streets, to and from convenience stores or apartment complexes, without a worry.

Countless times we'd warned the public about the shooters' method of operation, the hours they operated, and how they targeted individuals. Yet the people I watched walk up and down the street that night were completely oblivious or indifferent to what was happening in their community. There were dozens of them, perpetually alone. They were either ignorant or stupid. No wonder the shooters were so successful.

As I sat in an empty, one-story office lot, I watched with amazement. The more I sat there, the more upset I became. Here I was sitting in my truck, sweating my butt off because my motor was off with no air conditioning. And what were these people doing? Walking around like sitting ducks. Fish in a barrel.

With so many targets, I began to wonder if this case would ever come to a conclusion.

It was becoming the norm to get only three or four hours of sleep a night. Marjorie had basically become my mother. Whenever I misplaced something in the command post, she would ask, "OK, Clark, where was the last time you had it?" It was embarrassing. I was looking for all the news articles on both serial killers. She was able to track down the file.

Notoriety seemed to me to be as good a motivator as anything else. I kept clinging to this theory. As I started to go through the articles though, I realized that the BLK was still getting as much or even more press than my guys. The BLK hadn't struck in over two months, yet his composite drawing usually accompanied any press of the Random/Serial Shooter.

Even after the recent Mesa shooting, the length and depth of the articles were still equivalent in size and scope. I wondered what my shooters thought of that.

If they were shooting for notoriety's sake, they may get a little upset with all the newspaper ink still flying about the BLK. If it were a competition, then there was a good chance they would increase their activity. They would want more ink than the BLK.

As I finished reading the articles, Lieutenant Benson walked into the command post. "Hey, the Mayor and Chief Harris are in the building and are coming down. They want to talk to you and see the command post. Can we try to make this place look organized?"

I looked around, and the place looked like a command post. Logs, photos, files, and notebooks filled the tables. Maps were on the walls. The place looked like an information center. I thought it was pretty organized. I looked at Marjorie.

"You want me to get a dust rag out?" I asked. "This is as good as it gets. We don't have closets or a chest of drawers to put everything in." I looked at Marjorie. "Does this look organized to you?"

"Yes, it does," she said. "I could, however, put the fifty or so notebooks in a corner and throw a blanket over them to hide the contents if you wished."

She smiled wryly at the LT, deciding to jump on the bandwagon.

He looked at both of us, and smiled. "Smart asses. Just be ready, Clark, and watch what you say." He looked Marjorie's way. "You too . . . analyst."

He turned and left the room.

Most of the time it was just Marjorie and me in the CP. We had grown to appreciate each other's sense of humor, and I had grown to appreciate her sense of duty and integrity when it came to working this case.

As I sat looking through the tip sheets, the door opened and in walked Chief Harris, Assistant Chief Kevin Robinson, and Mayor Phil Gordon. I knew the chiefs but had never met the mayor. I stood up and introduced myself. I also introduced Marjorie to the trio.

They all looked around the command center, and the mayor began to ask some basic questions. Marjorie talked about the database, and how we tracked leads. She opened up one of the many files and showed them the tip sheet that was created to follow each lead and how it was tracked.

Mayor Gordon told me how the city had just been donated a dozen billboards to be used as an ad campaign to get the word out on the two sets of serial killers. That was good news. The more information, the better.

"We are going to give you what you need to catch these guys," he said.

I thanked him for that.

Chief Robinson broke in and asked me if they could listen to the recording of the shooting in Mesa. They all wanted to hear what had been a secret the press hadn't picked up on.

I escorted the three to the Forensic Imaging Unit. The supervisor saw me coming and was hoping that I wasn't coming to his section. There's nothing like an unannounced visit from the chief and the mayor. I could see the panic setting in. I just smiled at him as we walked in the cramped two-room workspace. The door closed behind the four of us.

"How you doing, Greg?" I introduced him to the mayor and the chiefs. I wasn't sure if he had ever met them. "These gentlemen would like you to cue up the Mesa Police audio of the recent shooting, along with the images captured on the video." I handed him the DVD.

Greg knew which one I was talking about. "Oh, sure, come right over here, and I'll put it up on the bigger monitor."

Within seconds, we could see the back porch video projected on the larger monitor. The video showed a tricycle and a few toys. We heard the sound of the cars rolling by, and then the shot that startles everyone the first time they hear it. Then came the silence. This DVD had been edited for just the important part. They all asked to hear it again.

Before they had a chance to ask any questions, I offered up some information. "Whoever did this shooting conducted themselves in a very efficient manner. No panic, no screaming at anyone, just the shot, and a cool getaway. They're very comfortable doing what they're doing."

They all looked at each other.

The mayor was the first to ask a question. He looked at Chief Robinson, the leader of the task force. "Why would somebody do this?"

Chief Robinson turned and looked at me and stretched his arm out in my direction. He simply said, "Clark."

All three of them looked at me. I stood for a second, remembering what Lieutenant Benson had said. "Be careful what you say."

"We don't have any witnesses to these shootings because there are two of these guys. They operate as a team. One works as a lookout while the other fires. They change up who shoots." All three of them stood quietly. I continued. "They have become more active because they enjoy the press. I believe they're competing with the Baseline Killer for notoriety. They know we are looking for them, so it doesn't surprise me that they changed areas. But if we don't catch them, they will return to Phoenix. There are too many targets to stay away."

The three leaders asked no questions, instead digesting the sober reality of what was happening. None of them disagreed with what I said. I went on. "I am positive that the earlier .22 caliber shootings are not only related to these shotgun shootings but were perpetrated by the same individuals. They changed guns because of their know-how of weapons and ballistics. Whoever is doing this knows that shotguns are almost completely untraceable. There are no copycats operating in Phoenix or now Mesa."

The mayor shook his head and looked down. The chiefs stared at the monitor depicting the backyard images adjacent to the Mesa Shooting.

Chief Harris turned to me and we shook hands. "Thanks for the information."

Chief Robinson gave me a nod and said thanks.

Mayor Gordon extended his hand and said, "Good luck. I know you'll get your men."

I thanked him for his support. They thanked Greg for letting them view the DVD and together walked out of the room.

I looked at Greg and before he could say a word, I said, "I had no idea they wanted to view the DVD."

He wasn't buying it. "Yeah, sure. Next time, give us a few seconds heads-up, please."

Like I had a choice in the matter.

CHAPTER 33

With Detective Pete Salazar from Scottsdale on board full time and my partner, Detective Darren Udd, back from Canada, Friday July, 28th was turning out to be a day fat with investigators. That was something I hadn't seen in awhile.

Pete took the tips that came from Scottsdale. Darren had started to re-associate himself with high-priority targets, and I was busy looking at shotgun-shooting silhouettes—paper targets fired at from two to fifty feet.

There were many variables to this testing, the first being the length of the barrel. The shorter the barrel, the wider the shot pattern would become as the distance from the target increased. If you think of a megaphone, the kind you see cheerleaders yelling through, the circles created at the mouth and end somewhat simulate a shotgun pattern if a shot is fired directly at a target. The pattern starts out small and then gets larger as it heads down range, just like the megaphone. If the shotgun is tilted down, up, or sideways, it can change the pattern and direction when it strikes a target.

Other factors affect the pattern as well. The target itself, such as a human, can be very dynamic. Unlike a silhouette, a person can move, bend, and turn. The load of the cartridge fired can also affect its velocity and pattern. All the variables needed to be considered.

As I was going through the photos of the victims' injuries, I could see that there were only a handful of shot patterns that struck enough of the victims to reconstruct. The other ones, where only a few pellets had hit the victim, could not be reconstructed. I was making notes when Sergeant Stu Clarke came walking in the command post.

"I need to talk to you right away. Let's head over to the LT's office."

I was busy, but the first thing that went through my mind was that I'd said something I shouldn't have to the mayor and chief the other day. I tried to remember if I had misspoken.

Lieutenant Benson was sitting at his desk reading what appeared to be a tip sheet. "Close the door and come on in." Both Stu and I sat.

"Chief Robinson called me this morning and wanted me to pass on to you from Chief Harris and the mayor that they think you're doing an excellent job. They have full confidence in you solving this case, as do I."

That was reassuring.

"Thanks, I appreciate that, but you didn't call me in here for that."

I knew something else was coming down the pike.

"No, I didn't. Something has come up that you need to be aware of because we're going to have to deal with this right away."

He then handed me the tip sheet.

The tip was from a current police detective who'd been contacted recently by an ex-cop. There were some suggestive comments made by the former police employee, who had happened to leave under poor circumstances.

In the tip, the former employee had stated that the task force would never figure out who was responsible for these shootings. That the killer *would continue until he decided it was time to call it quits.* This ex-employee was evidently following the case closely based on some of the factors explained in the tip. The rest of the information I will keep private.

I was familiar with this particular employee. He had left very disgruntled and was considered a time bomb ready to go off. I took a deep breath and looked up at Lieutenant Benson, who was staring at me, awaiting some kind of response. Based on the intel in this tip, I had no choice but to make this person a priority target.

What next? "I can't tell you how bad the press would be if that tip got leaked. The damage would be substantial," he said. He was right, damaging to the individual, and the department, if true, or not.

"I'll take this one personally. I don't want anyone in the task force having to deal with this. It could be clear coincidence, or it could be something more," I said.

"I agree. I don't want anyone to know about this. You're to brief me, and me only, about anything you find. The last thing we need right now are a bunch of rumors flying around that an ex-employee may be the Serial Shooter," Lieutenant Benson added.

"Lisa Ruggeri is getting ready to go back east on some training. I'll get her to do all the background checks. She won't say anything. She's used to dealing with delicate matters like this," I said.

"I know you've got a lot going on, but get on this right away. I don't want to reallocate any manpower to this unless I absolutely have to," Lieutenant Benson stated. "Now, get out of my office." I stood to leave. "And put in a decent day's work for that huge overtime bill you keep sending the city."

I left the office with a nod from Sergeant Clarke. It wasn't as if I didn't have anything else to do. I started mumbling to myself as I walked back to the command post. I must have continued mumbling because Marjorie asked, "Are you OK?"

The question woke me up and brought me out of my funk.

"Yeah, I'm fine."

I plopped down in a chair and started thinking of all the horrible scenarios an ex-employee could bring to the case. Weapon experience, tactics, training, knowledge, and a lethal mentality. If it was an ex-employee, he had to be working with someone. It would explain a lot of things.

I looked up at Marjorie. I decided to bring her into the loop.

"I need to make you aware of something."

I handed her the tip sheet. She had no idea who the person was and didn't really care until she got to the bottom of the page.

She looked at me with a blank stare. "How do you want me to handle this?"

"Discreetly. No one is to know about this besides me. Lisa Ruggeri will handle the background intel. Anything else we find comes right to me. Do you understand?" She nodded. "Any other tips that come in with this name, I want flagged. In fact, any current or ex-employee that gets named as a tip is flagged and sent to me only, OK? This is a nightmare. The quicker we put this behind us, the better."

"If we can," she added.

At this point in the investigation, I counted almost two dozen high priority targets that the task force was either actively surveilling or monitoring for further follow-up. Two had GPS tracking devices attached to their cars. The information gathered from those had been compared with the latest shooting, and neither of those individuals vehicles had been anywhere around the last shooting in Mesa. It was decided to leave them in place for now, in case the Mesa shooting was not related. I knew it was, but that was a command decision.

As I began to browse the two dozen targets, I received a call from a number I did not recognize. It was Detective Darrel Smith of the ATF/Gun Squad.

"Hey, Clark, it's Darrel. I just got off the phone with a guy who wants to come forward with information on the Serial Shooter. He says he's called Silent Witness a couple of times, and no one has called him back."

That sounded odd. If he had called Silent Witness his name and number would be logged. If the information was specific, he would have been contacted. But that didn't matter. I was busy, and I needed to get back to the task at hand.

"What did he say?" I asked.

"He says your shooter is Sammy Dieteman, our possible arsonist. The guy I told you about that our informant says was responsible for shooting a man on a bike on the west side of Phoenix."

He was rambling, and I needed to understand.

"OK, slow down. The guy that you're looking for, the one that committed the Walmart arsons, this guy says is the Serial Shooter? Is that what you're saying?" I wanted to understand what he was talking about in the simplest of terms.

"Yeah, he says this Sammy guy was talking to him in a bar and has information about one of the shootings. But I didn't know which one he was talking about. So I just let him ramble, and I recorded the information. I don't know what he knows, but he's positive that Sammy is your guy."

"How did you come to this information, and why did the tip come to you?"

Detective Smith was out of the pipeline as far as tips go, so he should never have been given a heads up.

"I put a file stop on Samuel Dieteman. I got a call from one of the analysts over in the task force because of the file stop, and she gave me the phone number to the tipster. I called the tipster. I don't know what he knows, but we should meet with the guy. The guy's name is Ron Horton."

My head was swimming with this information and the ex-cop's new lead.

"Let me get back to you. I need to track down the original Silent Witness tip sheets with this guy Horton's information on it and see if it has been looked into. I'll call you back when I find it." We both hung up.

I yelled for Marjorie. "We have a tip over here somewhere from a guy by the name of Ron Horton. He says he knows who the Random/Serial Shooter is and claims he's called, and no one called him back. Find his tip sheet, please, so I can figure just what the hell is going on here."

"OK, that name doesn't sound familiar, though" Marjorie said.

Her fingers began to busily punch the keyboard of the computer.

In a few seconds, she had an answer.

"Got it! Ron Horton. Called originally on July 16th, tip number 76. Says 'Sammy bragging about shooting what he thought was a man, and turned out to be a woman. Later called back and had more details. Sammy has no vehicle, ties to biker gangs.' No name or phone number listed on either of the first two tips. Says it was assigned to Detective Jewell."

"I know that tip."

It was coming back to my cluttered mind. Without a name, there would be no one to contact, and without a phone number, there wouldn't be any way to get a hold of the tipster. Marjorie continued on.

"This other tip just came in today. It was just entered by an analyst. He gives his name, Ron Horton, and his phone number is listed on it. He provides an address for Sammy D. No last name again."

"Print that up."

"Second tip was also forwarded to Jewell. Isn't he on vacation?" She asked.

She handed me the tip.

I said, "It says, 'assigned Detective Schwartzkopf.' I've never seen this part of the tip before. I did the follow-up on this case. I sat up on this residence." I realized what had happened. "Where is the follow-up sheet on this case?"

Marjorie pointed out it was attached to the lead sheet. Sure enough, it was one of the surveillances I had conducted myself and noted. My case notes read, "No Sammy found associated with this residence after background check. Surveillance showed no car similar to possible suspect vehicle. No further follow-up at this time."

Marjorie was getting upset.

"I don't understand this. It says Jewell got the initial two tips, Priority 2, no follow-up." That sounded right. "But then this only shows two tips in total, but there are three entries. This doesn't make any sense."

I could care less how the information had gotten to us. What was important was that we had it, and somebody wanted to talk about Sammy Dieteman being the Random/ Serial Shooter.

I called Detective Smith on the phone and told him to make an arrangement for us to meet with Ron Horton. Since he had already made contact, I would let him continue to be the go-between for now.

When the tips had started flooding in because of all the publicity this case had received, I considered that someday a real smart guy might try to come to the task force with a tip. Money might not be important to this guy, but information would be. This smart guy might try to fish for information because he's a part of what's going on. Because of that, I trusted no tipster. Ron Horton and anyone else was going to have to prove himself trustworthy. I wasn't jumping on anyone's information bandwagon.

But there was a bigger question looming. Who is Ron Horton?

◈

The meeting with Ron Horton would take place at 6:00 p.m. at A Taste of Mexico. Horton had picked this Mexican restaurant, saying he felt comfortable meeting with police at this location. I arrived an hour early to conduct counter surveillance to see if anyone would be watching us. A small shopping plaza sat across the street, so it was a perfect place to see any traffic coming in and out of the area. Since it was a Friday, all the businesses along this stretch of road were hopping. I had arranged for two task force members to circulate and report to me by cellphone any suspicious activity. In addition, some ATF agents were standing by.

Ron had told Smith that he would be arriving on a motorcycle, an orange Harley, and he'd given a general description of himself.

At a few minutes before 6:00 p.m., Smith and I walked across the street to the eatery. We hadn't seen any activity that would lead us to believe we were being watched. Shutting off our radios, we would be available only by cellphone, which we would use from a bathroom if we became wary inside the place.

I noticed a white male with loud pipes on his motorcycle pulling into the parking lot. He was wearing no helmet, of course, rebel bikers seldom do, and his long hair flowed off his shoulders. Ron Horton got off his bike and ambled toward the front door.

I had learned long ago in police work not to judge an informant/witness by his looks. Ron Horton looked like every other biker I knew, except he didn't have the rap sheet to go along with it. He'd had a DUI a few years back, but so do a lot of ordinary citizens. He had been a witness in a domestic dispute of some type and had actually provided good information to the police upon contact. From everything I could find, Ron Horton played the role of biker, but without the attitude and the criminal record to go along with it.

We introduced ourselves, and I pointed out that we should enter the restaurant before starting to have any in-depth conversation. A small bar greeted customers as you entered the front of the establishment. The place reminded me of an old-fashioned diner, with aluminum tables and chairs. We waited for the hostess, and I asked for a table that was away from everyone else. I didn't want any ears in the cornfield to overhear our conversation.

We moved to a table that stood up a couple of stairs on a raised floor. There was one guy eating alone, so we settled a couple of tables away. I sat with my back to the door, which I hate, but Detective Smith sat across from me. I could see everyone behind him, and he could see everyone behind me.

The waitress came by immediately. Ron ordered a beer, iced tea for Smith, and I ordered lemonade. Anyone watching closely could pick out the cops. Normally, I would have had a beer on duty, just to keep up appearances, but I had a long night ahead of me. I still had an ex-employee to investigate.

"So, where do you guys want to start?" Ron asked.

"Why don't you give me some background on Sammy Dieteman and your relationship?" I said.

"OK, I'll try, but I have to warn you … I'm not real good on time frames."

Not the kind of answer I wanted. This could be a short conversation.

Ron started slowly. "I met Sammy, everyone from the bar calls him Sammy, about a year or so ago. He was working and drinking at a place called Pollock Joe's. That place has since shut down."

The waitress had returned with our drinks, so Ron waited until she left.

"When I first met him, he seemed nice enough, but he acted depressed. I knew he had some family issues. His mother kicked him out of her and his stepfather's house, and Sam never got along with her husband. When he got kicked out, he really didn't have any place to go. So I let him stay at my house for about a month. I've got three boys, and I'm raising them on my own. The rooms are filled, and I have a full-time job, but I felt bad for the guy."

I liked the fact that he was raising boys on his own. That showed character.

"So when was this, the time he was living with you?" I asked.

Maybe it was during the times of one of the shootings.

"Remember, I ain't too good with time frames," Ron said. He paused for a moment. "I believe it was some time in October of 2005. Sammy was drinking a lot then, and I couldn't have that around my boys. I asked him to move out after about a month."

"Where did he end up, do you know?"

"Well, he ended up back at my house because he was basically living on the street, staying in dumpsters, boxes, and such. I wanted to help the guy out. In fact, I was pissed at him for not coming to me sooner. But he knew I had my hands full, and he didn't want any handouts."

This didn't sound like my guy or one of them. Living out of dumpsters? This team was too good to be down and out bums. Besides, they were gunning down homeless transients. It didn't make any sense. I needed more background information.

"Tell me about his personal life, besides being an alcoholic."

"Sammy told me that his dad had been in prison and was just recently released. I even met the guy one time. He came to Phoenix, and Sammy introduced me to him. I gave him a bunch of crap in front of his old man. You know, like, 'This is really your kid? I'm sorry.' Good-natured ribbing. Sammy didn't like it at all, though. I saw him in the bar a few days later, and I asked if his dad was still around. He said he didn't care."

It sounded like family dynamics were a troublesome area that needed to be explored if Sammy was involved.

"He had a real good job as an electrician. He worked for Motorola or somebody like that, but got fired. He threatened to kick his bosses' ass or something. Anyway, that's how he ended up at Pollock Joe's as a bartender."

Ron took a gulp of his beer. It looked inviting, and I considered having one.

He continued. "I tell you, though, the guy was hosed at every turn. I mean, his ex-wife took him to the cleaners. He has a couple of kids. They live out of state. Matter of fact, I think they just came to visit. Anyway, Sammy had a good paying job, but he was only clearing about 150 bucks a week. The rest he was paying in child support. I mean, how can a guy live off of that a week?"

Negative family dynamics, again. I was starting to feel sorry for the guy myself. "Tell me a little more about his violence potential. You ever see him or hear about him doing anything violent?" I asked.

I knew that Sammy Dieteman had a criminal record that showed assault, but no weapons. I needed to know if weapons were involved in something that hadn't been reported.

"He's been eighty-sixed out of a couple of bars for fighting, so he likes to fight. He'd been bragging a while back about how he and some friends, who

I don't know, would drive around and jump people on the street. He said they'd pull up to somebody on the street, jump out, and beat the guy's ass. He even told me about a time where he beat this guy up, and as the guy was sitting on the side of the road, he started to console the guy. Rubbing his head, like he genuinely felt bad for the guy. Then he proceeded to slam the guy's face on the concrete. I don't know if the guy lived or died. You should be able to find that out."

"Who were these people that he beat, did he say?"

This was a huge red flag if it turned out they were transients.

"He didn't really say. Just people he would see on the street."

Now it was time to get to possible weapon usage.

"Have you ever seen Sammy with a gun?" I asked.

"He talked about owning a handgun, a 9mm I think, but I never saw it. Course that's the reason I called Silent Witness in the first place . . . what he told me about the shooting."

"Yeah, I read your statement about him talking about shooting someone. A woman he thought was a man. Tell me about that."

Ron stopped for a second as our food arrived. I was starving, but I'm really finicky when it comes to eating Mexican food. But, for the sake of the investigation, I would at least try the food.

We shooed the waitress away, and Ron began. "We were sitting in a bar called The Ditch, when Sammy started in by asking me if I'd ever killed anyone. I looked at him like that was a stupid question, of course not. He said that he had. That he had actually killed somebody. I thought he was bullsh*^#ing so I played along. He told me that he killed some woman that he thought was a guy. Said he used a 410 shotgun."

A 410 shotgun!

I didn't want to get too excited, so I calmly asked, "A 410 shotgun. He told you specifically a 410 shotgun was used to kill a female that he thought was a male?"

I wanted to make sure of his facts.

"Yep. Then he began to talk about shootings that were occurring in his neighborhood. At the time, I knew that he was living with some guy by the name of Jeff, but I didn't know anything more. I do know that Sammy lived on the west side, somewhere around 91st Avenue and Camelback. At least he did. Now I hear that he moved to Scottsdale somewhere."

I looked at Smith who hadn't uttered a word, and he nodded without saying anything. They had been trying to find Sammy through this Jeff guy. Even though Ron wasn't good with time frames, I needed more specifics.

"When did this conversation about the shooting of the 410 shotgun and the other claims about different shootings occur?" I asked.

"Must have been in May, I think. I'm not sure. Like I said, I'm terrible with time frames."

As I spoke with Ron, I became more of a fan. I watched his demeanor and mannerisms. Besides moving his long hair back from his mouth so he could eat, he wasn't nervous about telling the cops what he knew. He was the three Cs: cool, calm, and collected.

I wanted to see if I could get him off his game.

"Ron, if you knew about this in May of 2006, why did it take you until the end of July to call the police?"

It was a legit question, and one he would hear again if his information turned out to be corroborated.

"I don't keep up on current events. I'm too busy working and raising three boys. I don't read the paper, and I don't watch the news. The only way I heard about what was going on was through a pool league."

"A pool league?" I asked.

Bikers love to play pool, billiards. Go to any biker bar, and you'll see that it has pool tables and dartboards in it. No skeet-ball there, no pop-a-shot. They'd use the basketballs to throw at each other.

"Yeah, I play pool in a pool league that meets every Wednesday night. We play at different bars. So, I'm playing in my league, and some of my friends start to talk about the shootings that are going on. I got no idea what they are talking about, so I ask them to fill me in. They start to tell me about some guy going around shooting people on the street, randomly. As I'm listening, I start to think about what Sammy told me. They tell me how the media had been reporting that the guy was shooting people on the west side, and now they think he may be shooting people on the east side of town. I went home after that and started to watch the news myself. I saw they had a shooting in Mesa, and I figured that Sammy was involved because he lives over there now. I put two and two together. That's why I phoned you guys a couple of days ago. It's gotta be him."

I wasn't as confident as Ron was, but he was making a compelling case.

"Oh, yeah, and he calls what they do 'RVing' or 'RRVing.' It stands for 'recreational violence' or 'random recreational violence.' One of the two."

I set my fork down. The food wasn't half-bad.

"You say *they*. Do you have any idea who *they* is?"

I liked the fact that he was putting at least two people as being involved.

"Well, he didn't name names. And I say *they* because of the beatings. He always talked about them as if there were a couple of them doing it. The shootings? I don't know for sure. He only talked about himself shooting someone."

"When's the last time you talked to Sammy?"

It was time to locate this guy and figure out just what he was up to.

"I talked to him about a month ago. Sometime at the end of June. That's when I heard that he had moved to Scottsdale."

Ron had finished his food, and the waitress returned to clear the plates. I ordered more lemonade to keep the conversation going.

"What else can you tell us about him? Anything else of a violent nature?" I asked.

"One night, we're at a bar called the Westwood Tavern. I was there drinking with Sammy and some other friends when Sam left the bar and went outside. He was gone for a while, so I went out to check on him. I see him coming from behind this wall, a wall that surrounds this dumpster. All of a sudden, I see flames shooting out of the dumpster. The damn thing is on fire. Sam starts yelling to call 911. Someone started the dumpster on fire. So I get on the phone, and the fire department comes out. After we left the bar, I start asking him about the fire. At first, he denies it, and then he admits to it. He started it. I told him he was a dumb fu*# for doing that. He just laughed."

I needed Ron to tell me why he had called.

I asked him, "Why are you coming forward with this information?"

I already knew why, or at least partly why: the reward of up to $100,000. That was a good reason, even if he didn't admit it.

Ron sat back for a moment, and I could tell he was struggling with a reason. "I ain't a snitch. Never have been. But dammit, it's not right going around shooting people you don't know. I mean, if you got a beef with somebody, handle it like a man. But what he's doing, it's not right. I thought to myself what if that was someone I knew that was walking down the street and got shot, like one of my friends or family. I'd be upset."

I left it at that. The money wouldn't hurt either, but I think he was sincere in his reasoning. He was, of course, right. Shooting people like a coward from a car is despicable.

When the check came, Smith grabbed it. This meal would be on the Feds. I popped another question as Smith put down his credit card.

"I know the biker creed. No snitching. But would you be willing to come in, and give a statement on the record? In other words, a taped interview?"

I really didn't need his recorded statement. I could subpoena him just based on our conversation. But a cooperative witness would look much better than an uncooperative one. Silent Witness or not, by meeting us, he was not protected anymore.

Ron wasn't quick to jump. He figured that he could fall under the protective umbrella of Silent Witness, but he was wrong.

"I'll have to think about that."

That was fine for now. As we all got up to leave the restaurant, Detective Smith asked Ron if he would look at a photo. He agreed, and we all walked over to our ride. Smith pulled out a composite photo from the Walmart surveillance camera, depicting the two individuals wanted for questioning.

Ron looked at the photo. "That big guy right there," he said, pointing at one of the two images captured in the photo. "That's Sammy. The other guy … I'm not sure."

But the photo jogged Ron's memory.

"Oh, I forgot to tell you one thing. There was a night that Sammy and I were drinking in a place called the Rib Shop. It's over off of 83rd Avenue and Indian School … a real dive bar. Anyway, we were drinking, and Sammy tells me that Jeff and he had a fight, and that he couldn't go back there. As we're talking, this guy comes walking in the bar, this *crazy-looking* guy. The guy was there about three minutes, mumbled something, and asks Sam if he was ready to go. The guy then storms out of the bar like he's pissed off. Sammy leaves a few seconds later. It was bizarre. He caught a ride with the guy because Sammy's got no vehicle. The reason I'm telling you this is the second guy in the picture, he kind of looks like the guy that came into the Rib Shop that night."

Well, now we have two individuals: one identified as Sam Dieteman in the Walmart arson photos and a possible co-conspirator. Smith had other witnesses to identify Dieteman from the surveillance cameras. But what I had was much more. I had a second subject to tie to Dieteman. That is, if Dieteman was involved in the Random shootings. I was a long way from there. But one thing was for sure. We needed to locate Sam Dieteman.

"Ron, I need to ask you something. In order to prove your theory correct, and, by the way, you're very convincing, I would need to find Dieteman. I know that you don't know where he lives, but do you have a cellphone number for him?"

He looked down at the ground and appeared to be trying to recall one.

"I'll have to get back with you on that." I didn't know if he knew and wasn't going to provide it to me, or if he didn't know, and was going to check around. "I need to talk to somebody first about this whole thing. Besides, he changed cellphone numbers a while back. I don't think I have his current one."

"OK, I'd appreciate that. You can understand we're under time constraints. I would hate to see anybody else get hurt," I said. If he did have a conscience, which he appeared to by coming forward, a nudge in that direction couldn't hurt. "Also, if you have to ask around for a phone number, please do it discreetly. I wouldn't want Sammy blowing town by thinking that we're on to him." I closed with this deadline. "If you can, I need it by tomorrow."

That wasn't too much to ask. Twenty four hours was a world of time. If Ron didn't know the number himself, he knew people who could get it. He could move in those circles with little or no suspicion, unlike us. If we started asking questions about Dieteman, he would find out in minutes.

We bid adieu, and I thanked Ron for coming forward. Smith and I stood there and watched him walk back to his Harley, push the electric starter, and zoom off toward his home, which, by the way, wasn't too far away. I'd done my homework, too.

"What do you think? It sounds pretty good to me," Smith said.

"Of course, it does. He helps with your arson investigation. But I'm a long way from proving Sam Dieteman is involved in the Random/Serial Shooter case."

It wasn't time to point fingers, but I needed to know.

"Now, why haven't you and the guys at ATF been able to find Dieteman?"

It was 10:00 p.m. by the time I finished with the notes on my meeting with Ron Horton. Three full pages documented every important aspect of our conversation. The night was still young, and I had more work to do. I had to make one more stop tonight, one that I hoped turned out to be nothing.

I drove from police headquarters to a middle-class area of Scottsdale. No million-dollar homes here, as is the case in some parts of this city. Just a small subdivision with a circular road that would take me to my destination.

I didn't slow down on my first pass, but I noticed cars sitting in the driveway. I'd run a motor vehicle check for all cars registered to this ex-employee, and I'd found something extremely disturbing—the ownership of an imported four-door sedan. The only thing I didn't know was the color.

I had to be especially cautious, for the person I was now about to check on knew all the tricks. He would notice anything unusual. If he were involved, he would be paranoid and ready.

I pulled my truck to the end of the street and turned around slowly. On my next pass, I'd go by a little slower, slow enough to get the license plate numbers of the cars in the driveway. There were two cars registered to this household. I verified the four-door sedan in the driveway, along with a smaller truck.

Even though the house sat where there was little lighting and no porch lights were on, I could easily see the color of the four-door sedan: silver, just as some of the victims had stated seeing right before they were shot. I took a deep breath, cursed, and pulled around the corner.

It was just my luck. I'd have to find a surveillance team to watch this house, this person, this silver car. It would take a team of five or maybe more surveillance people to watch the comings and goings of this individual—a great team, skilled beyond belief, ready to act, ready to report, ready to shoot someone perhaps they knew or had heard of.

I shuddered at the thought.

CHAPTER 34

"So what do you think? When is this guy going to strike again?" Commander Tolan asked. We had met in the early hours of Saturday, July 28th, to use the DVR recording to try and reconstruct the shooting of the bicyclist. Several vehicles would be used in an attempt to simulate the same sound the vehicle made right before the shooting.

I corrected him immediately. "You mean when are *they* going to strike again?" I said.

"Sorry, when are *they* going to strike again?"

"Well, Commander, they never strike on Saturday nights into Sunday mornings. No reason to think they'll hit tonight. It's a good possibility that it will be soon, maybe even tomorrow."

He looked at me as if he knew what I was going to say. "I think you're right. Tomorrow or the next day. I don't know a tenth of what you know, but I just have a bad feeling about the next couple of days."

"Our boys like the ink. They're due. In fact, they're overdue. It's been six days," I said.

"We have undercover units out there, and all our patrol officers have been briefed on what to watch for. Hopefully we'll get lucky."

I hoped so too. For all our sakes.

◈

I had arranged for Lisa Ruggeri to meet with me at police headquarters. I knew that it was Saturday, and that she didn't usually work on those days, but this was urgent. She was at the command post, gazing through one of the files, when I sauntered in.

"Here you go," she said, handing me a notebook. "All the background on you know who. There wasn't a whole lot there. You do want to look at what

I dug up on other police contacts. The person has had a few since leaving the department."

"Thanks dear," I said as I put the notebook down. I could tell she was irritated.

"Don't you want to look at that? That's some interesting reading."

"I'm sure it is. But I have another task for you that I need before you leave."

Lisa put one hand on her hip and tilted her head off to the side like this was going to cost me. I handed her Ron Horton's tip file.

"I need a full background on this guy, Sam Dieteman, including any photos from any state that you can drum up. This came in last night, and it's just as promising as the notebook you just handed me."

Lisa looked at me in a stunned fashion. "You're not kidding."

"No, I'm not." She thumbed through the information.

"When do you need this?"

"Yesterday," I said.

"I'll get it to you by this afternoon. Is that quick enough?"

She was being sarcastic; of course it was.

"Thanks, you're a lifesaver."

She flew out of the room to copy the file.

Marjorie was already in and had listened to our conversation.

"How did the driving thing go?" she asked.

I tried to explain to her what the goal of the reconstruction was, but she looked at me as if I were speaking Chinese.

"OK, I guess."

I needed to change the subject.

"Did we ever figure out where the additional tips from Ron Horton were, and do we have them all?"

I was tiring of this saga.

"I can't figure it out," she told me, "but yes, we have them all. The only problem is, I can't tell how many times he called. It looks like the second and third calls were added to the original call, but with different dates."

"OK, as long as we have them all. I need to go through those to see if they're consistent with what he told me last night."

Lisa came back from the copy machine and handed me the Horton file. I sat down with my notepad and started going through the information. I noticed immediately there were a couple of problems.

During our conversation the night before, Ron had told me that Sam said he used a 410 to kill a man who later turned out to be a woman. In his Silent Witness tip, he'd said that *Sammy bragged about using a 12 12 (double barrel shotgun)*. There was also the first call, where he said *Sammy lives in the area of 65th Avenue and Camelback*. Yet, Ron said Sammy lived at 91st Avenue and Camelback. Not a huge discrepancy, but one that would need to be cleared up. In the last call that was logged on July 25th, Ron stated *he has three children and fears for his life. Sammy may hurt him if he knows he called so he begs we do not give his name out.* He never mentioned anything about being in fear for their lives. If he was in fear, then that could create logistic problems for us and his family. This would need to be explored further.

After reading through my notes and rereading the tips, I was going to have a hard time waiting until that afternoon to get my book on Mr. Sam Dieteman.

◈

The lead article in the *Mesa Tribune* outlined a community meeting that had been set for Monday, July 31st, at a local elementary school. Of course, there would be Spanish translators on hand for anyone who couldn't speak English. The main objectives of the meeting were to *raise awareness and enhance personal safety.*

The Internet was hopping with personal blogs that people had posted in response to the killings. There were encouraging stories about how not to let the serial killers dominate your existence. Vigilance was the key. And, of course, there were the cop haters. Those who took the cases as a chance to spew about how incompetent police are, and how criminals in the Valley must feel safe because you don't have to worry about being caught here for any violence you commit.

People were upset about how their way of life had changed. I read those particular stories with interest. Although these citizens hadn't been shot or even shot at, they were victims nonetheless. They talked about how they missed the freedom of jogging or taking their dogs for a late-night stroll. How the summer heat is too unbearable during the day or even the evenings, and how their pets had become disgruntled as well.

The very freedoms that had made this country, this state, and these cities safe were being torn away because of a serial rapist/murderer and two serial shootists. Those stories tore at me more than you can imagine. These maggots had taken the cities of Phoenix and its surrounding areas hostage.

As the afternoon wore into the evening, I finally got the call I had been waiting for from Lisa Ruggeri.

"Your book is ready," she told me.

We agreed to meet at the command post so she could go over some of the finer details with me.

Samuel John Dieteman was born on October 17, 1975 in Mankato, Minnesota to a Scott and Mary Dieteman. He was an only child with a half sister through his mother.

According to his history, it appeared that Samuel Dieteman lived in Arizona for periods of time and then Minnesota for periods of time. He had addresses in St. Peter, Minnesota, and Phoenix, Arizona, overlapping the same time periods. The scan showed a Dorothy Dieteman, who appeared to be his wife at one time. She showed a different address after 2001. So this must have been the divorce that Ron Horton had spoken of, where Sam was milked to death. It looked as though they had a daughter as well.

FBI records showed that he had been arrested several times in Minnesota for crimes that ranged from criminal damage to DUI. He had been popped with drug paraphernalia and marijuana. There was also one charge of burglary of a dwelling. This was a felony that looked to have been reduced to a misdemeanor, probably based on the completion of probation. He had spent about ninety days in jail and had no convictions for a violent offense. It was not the kind of record that you would associate with a serial killer. On the other hand, serial killers like Ted Bundy had little, or no, previous criminal history as well.

Locally, in Arizona, it looked as if Samuel had decided to get a little physical a couple of times. He was listed as a suspect in a bar fight on June 30, 2006. He was accused of sucker punching some guy who the bartender later told police had been minding his own business. The victim wanted prosecution. He was left with a swollen left cheek and a cut to his lower chin.

I could find no history of gun ownership for Samuel Dieteman, particularly no shotguns or .22 rifles. His pawn history was limited to some household items. He did currently have a misdemeanor warrant for his arrest on a failure to appear in Glendale City Court. The charge was for shoplifting. That was good news for us. If we did need to bring him in to talk to him, we could always arrest him on his misdemeanor warrant. Of course, we would have to find him first.

Speaking of Ron Horton, nightfall was fast approaching, and I had not heard from him. He either had decided not to give up Sam's cellphone number or hadn't had a chance to talk it over with whomever he needed to confide in. I decided to give him until the following day before pressing him. I had plenty to do at the moment anyway.

As I awoke on Sunday, July 30th from another short night's sleep, I decided to place divine intervention into the matrix of possible solutions to bringing this case to a close. As a true believer, I have never read the entire Bible, but I have attended church services most of my life.

I was raised in a Presbyterian church as a youth and found prayer and belief a solid structure under which to house my spirit. I have always had a unique relationship with God. So, on this Sunday, I came to my church, the one I had been faithfully attending for years. I came that morning to pray that the destructive wrath in this case would stop, that I would be shown the way to catch these individuals and put an end to their crimes.

I only hoped that I wasn't asking too late.

◈

Since I was sure the killers were following the media blitz over the case, I continued to monitor print, TV, and the Internet as well.

Sunday's big news story was the arrival of the Guardian Angels to the Valley of the Sun. The Angels, a citizens' watchdog group, were going to be conducting foot patrols in the areas of the last known attacks. Chapters of Angels were flying in from all over the country. They had come to dispel fear and take back the streets. They wore red berets and white T-shirts that read, "I support the Guardian Angels." There was even talk of their leader, Curt Silwa, coming into town.

Other news stories were interviews with residents. Young girls were scared into staying put at night, instead of going out. There was an uptick in the sale of firearms, stun guns, and pepper spray.

The blogs were more interesting to read than the hypotheses spewed by the talking heads. There were those people who just didn't get it, and those who clearly did. One such writer was a man from Sun City West, a retirement community situated in the northwest metro area. In summary, he wrote, "The Valley is a large place, and Phoenix a major city. Were we gullible enough to believe that we would be spared the kind of serial violence that now plagues our city? It happens in every large city at one time or another. Use common sense for crying out loud. Don't go out at night by yourself if you're a woman, and stay off the streets if you're by yourself of either sex. Oh, and that exercise thing that you like to do when it's cool out? Stop it. Which is more important, working out or staying alive? No one will care how you look if you end up dead!" That was good advice.

As I made my way back to the command post, I received a call from Detective Smith of the ATF task force. He and the other agents had been talking about Ron Horton and how to approach the arson cases without screwing up the Random/Serial Shooter case.

I thought for a second and wasn't sure if I had heard what I thought I had heard. I asked him to repeat it and he did, word for word. It deserved an answer, but not the one that they wanted to hear.

"Well, the shooting cases will take priority over the arsons. So anything that you guys decide to do should be brought to the task force before being implemented."

I thought that was gentle, but clearly direct.

"Yeah, that's what I thought, but we need to sit down and talk to you about the arson cases and how to proceed. I don't want to see the shooting cases compromised, but people over here want to move on the arsons. They think that is the best way to clear all the cases," he said.

I got the feeling that the managers at ATF were getting antsy for some press. But I didn't care about their glory. I cared about solving the cases and getting these guys off the street for murder, not just for arson.

I decided it was time to talk to the agents and set them straight. They were putting the cart before the horse and jumping to conclusions that had not even begun to play out. If Ron Horton's information could corroborate their other informant, so be it. The arson cases could be cleared, but that would be after the shooting cases were cleared. I needed to find out who was pushing this new agenda.

As afternoon approached I still had not heard from Ron Horton. It was almost two days since we met, and it was time to find Samuel Dieteman. I left a message for Ron on his cellphone. He needed to call me, and we needed to meet again.

I then called my supervisor, Sergeant Clarke. I told him about the conversation I'd had with Detective Smith of the ATF task force. I could tell that he was irritated.

"It was made very clear to their chain of command that the shootings take priority over anything else," he said. "They agreed, and that is not supposed to be a problem. Our chief made it very clear. Don't screw with the shooting investigation."

"I'm heading over to brief some of their agents," I said. "I get the feeling they're getting itchy trigger fingers, so to speak."

"I'll call the lieutenant. You tell them to back off and calm down. Everything goes through the task force."

That was simple enough.

Upon arriving at their headquarters, I was troubled about what to say to these agents. After all, we were on the same side, at least I thought we were. Smith had no doubt told them what Ron Horton had said during our encounter. But identification wasn't the issue, even in the arson cases. We needed to corroborate Ron Horton's statements in regard to the Random/Serial Shooter case, and we were miles away from tying Dieteman to those cases. It was all hearsay that Dieteman was even involved in the shootings. At this point, there was no evidence to support anything that Horton said. This was just one man talking to another. Even these young guys would see that.

I had decided to shock them into reality. Catching these guys would be much more difficult than they ever imagined . . . and it would be downright dangerous.

Detective Smith met me in the lobby of the building. No one was around, as the building was obviously closed for business on Sunday. Smith had been around a long time, so I decided to talk to him first.

"Darrel, you and I have to talk before I go upstairs to meet with these guys."

We sat in the lobby.

"Here it is," I said. "Let's say that Ron Horton's information turns out to be good, and that besides being a Walmart arsonist, Sammy Dieteman is one of the Serial Shooters. We're a long way from there, but for the sake of argument, let's say he is, OK?"

"OK," he replied.

"You've been around for awhile. How do you think this is all going to end? Do you think if you guys find Dieteman and question him about the Walmart arsons that he's just going to roll over and admit to half a dozen murders or so and a dozen or more attempted murders? I mean, c'mon, would you? You don't even have the arsons solved. He's just a strong investigative lead. But he isn't on tape doing it. He's just there in the store or both stores. He and his buddy. I read the reports."

"Yeah, you're right. But we have to find the guy and at least question him," he replied.

"I understand that. But if you guys start poking around and start making inquiries into the shootings, you've just unzipped our fly. All the work the task force has done will go for nothing. They'll know that we're on to them before we get on to them. And that's if he's even related, which is yet to be determined."

"I see your point," he said.

He looked down at the carpeted floor while he processed what I was saying.

It was time to re-ask the question I'd just asked.

"How do you think this is all going to end? Forget Samuel Dieteman. How do you think we're going to catch whoever is responsible for these shootings?" Smith had been out there beating the brush trying to find Dieteman. He should know how hard it is to find someone who doesn't want to be found. "These guys leave no witnesses. Think about it."

He gazed up from the floor, and the statement hit him like a hammer in the head. "It could get ugly," he said.

Violence versus the violent—an ugly thought.

"Yeah, it could. You . . . I . . . maybe one of our undercover units spot them shooting someone or worse. I hope it doesn't come to that, but it might very well. Now do you think these agents upstairs can handle that dilemma if Dieteman turns out to be involved and calm down about these arsons? Nobody died in the fires, and whoever is pushing this needs to back off."

He thought for a minute. "Yeah, I think the agents can handle the reality of the situation. I've worked with them for awhile. I owe them the benefit of the doubt."

He seemed convinced. We both got up and headed for the elevators that would take us to ATF's hideaway.

A couple of passkey doors later, and Smith was gathering all the five agents for a meeting. It was time to get them straightened out or at least get them to get their bosses straightened out. We moved to an empty room with a few chairs scattered about and no table. It was uncomfortable, and I was tired. I had decided in the elevator to level with these guys. I hoped they would understand.

Detective Smith started by explaining why I was there, that I needed to share some information about the shootings, and that if Sam Dieteman was involved, they had to tread lightly in what they were doing so as to not undo the task force's work. He was spelling it out for them in the simplest terms possible. Cops who had worked hundreds of cases would understand it immediately. They, on the other hand, appeared to be struggling. I decided to clear it up for them.

"There is no probable cause to make any arrests in the shooting cases, nor your arson investigation, from what I've been told and read. We have no one that can I.D. the shooters. If you go grabbing people, you could risk the entire investigation. These shootings take precedence over anything else. Period." I was getting irritated.

One of the agents then asked, "Well, we got a taped interview with Ron Horton where he's talking about Dieteman, telling him about a shooting. That sounds like pretty solid evidence to me, at least enough to grab him up and talk to him about the shootings." I looked at the agent and then glanced around the room. They all seemed to agree.

"So what? That's a far cry from PC to make an arrest. Ron Horton didn't witness anything, besides Dieteman saying he was involved. If Sam Dieteman is behind what's going on, and if we can somehow prove it, then Horton becomes valuable for court. But only then. We're miles from there now."

They seemed to comprehend what I was saying, but then another question arose. "Well, what about the tape of Horton's interview with Darrel?"

Maybe it was because I was tired. Maybe it was because I was tired of answering "what ifs." Whatever it was, I snapped. "I don't care about the recording. Bury it, shelve it, it doesn't matter. I talked to Ron Horton in person, and he'll be asked to come in and give a full statement . . . soon. But for now, you guys need to understand something. What he said matters little unless I can get more on whoever is shooting people."

It was quiet as they all looked around at each other. I decided to make them put on their thinking caps.

"Look, if we find whoever is responsible for doing this, we're going to have to follow them. We're going to have to watch wherever they go, watch whatever they do. Do you know what that means?"

I looked around the room, and it was obvious that they didn't.

I continued. "We might get lucky and somebody sees them shoot someone, or we're right there after they do it, but I doubt it. Instead, there's a really good chance that we may catch them in the middle of a shooting, that they may gun down somebody right in front of us, and we may not be able to stop it! Do you understand that?"

They looked at me like deer in the headlights. They wanted so badly to be involved in this high-profile case that reality had never occurred to them. We weren't dealing in absolutes. Gray was the appropriate color.

As I looked at them, no one said anything. I knew what they were thinking. The same thing that I had been thinking for months. The same thing my bosses feared. This is a terrible situation. Just then, my cellphone buzzed, and I excused myself from the room. It was my partner, Detective Udd. I answered it.

"Hey, bro, where you at?" he asked.

"Wasting my time over at ATF."

I was upset at myself for spilling the beans.

"Sorry, dude, get out of there and back to cop land before you become part of the federal bureaucracy." That was a good one. "What's on for tonight?"

I could tell he was in the mood to go stir up trouble, and frankly, after this meeting, so was I.

"Let me get back to you."

I then closed the phone.

Detective Smith then escorted me out. As I walked by the desks, I saw two of the agents quietly talking. I knew what they were talking about, and I didn't care. They needed a dose of reality. Not everything plays out in the real world as it does in their world. Not every crucial decision is made by a bunch of suits back in Washington D.C.

This was street work. And, sometimes, street work can get dirty and ugly. I needed to talk to Ron Horton again and figure out for sure which side he was on. No more game playing, no more sitting on the fence. Time to man up or be run over.

As I drove back to police headquarters my cellphone buzzed, again. I heard the rather distinct voice of Ron Horton.

"Hi Detective, I got your message, and I'm calling you back."

"Ron, we have to meet and we have to meet right now. Are you available?"

I think he could tell the sense of urgency in my voice.

"Yes, I am. Where do you want to meet?"

"Same place as Friday, in thirty minutes."

"OK, I'll see you there."

He didn't even hesitate to meet. That was a good sign.

I got on the phone to my partner. "D, meet me at 35th Avenue and Dunlap as soon as you can. I need back up. I'm going to meet with Horton again."

"I'll be there. I'll phone you when I'm in the area," he said.

What I didn't know was that somebody else was talking to Ron Horton. Somebody with a different agenda.

<hr />

I arrived at the same Mexican restaurant a little before 7:00 p.m. Ron was already there, sitting at the bar, having a cold draft. We moved to our same section of the room.

"Thanks for meeting with me on short notice, Ron," I began. "I have to clear up some things about the last time we met. You up for some frank discussions?"

"You bet. I got nothing to hide, and I'm more than willing to help out."

I asked him if he wanted anything to eat, and he declined. I asked our waitress for some chips and salsa.

"Give me a draft beer, also."

I deserved a cold one, too.

"I just want to tell you, Detective, I've been thinking about what you said and whether or not I'd be willing to come forward. I decided that I got no problem coming forward. I'll be there for anything you need. Court . . . or whatever."

"Thanks, Ron, I appreciate your willingness to help, and one day, you and I will sit down and discuss all you know on the record. But for right now, I got a lot of questions that need to be answered before I go off running on some wild goose chase. You know where I'm coming from?"

"Yes, I do. I'm sure you're a busy man. Fire away with whatever you need to ask."

I began to appreciate his candor.

"Tell me about Dieteman and his personality."

I needed to know if this was a guy who could run around and kill people.

Ron stated that for the most part Sam's demeanor was calm, but he could explode at a moment's notice. He would get into bar fights with patrons who just looked at him the wrong way. And if you were ever ugly or physical with a girl in front of him, he'd kick your ass all over the place. He hated guys who put their hands on their woman.

"I told you about him being depressed. But, besides that, he was always calling himself worthless."

Dieteman would talk to Ron about how Ron had his act together, had a job, and was raising three boys on his own. How Sam couldn't even get his own kids to come see him. They wanted nothing to do with him. Sam had a stepdaughter as well as his own daughter.

I looked down at my vibrating phone. I flipped it open to read that my partner was outside watching my back. No sign of anyone else around.

"Ron, if Sammy was out shooting people for fun, why would he confide in you about what was going on? Why would he trust you?" They had known each other for only a little over a year.

"I think he was bragging. I think he needed someone to think he was important, and, for some reason, he picked me. He trusts me, and I'm about the closest friend he's got, besides somebody we both know. I think he likes the notoriety."

That was an interesting perception. It was obvious that Ron Horton knew Samuel Dieteman well enough to make that jump. It was just the sort of bridge I needed to pursue Dieteman further.

"When we first talked, I think you mentioned that Sammy never had a vehicle, that he always had to walk to where he was going or get a ride. Is that right, or did I misinterpret those facts?"

"No, that's right. I never saw the guy drive a car. He was always bumming rides off people. I gave him rides home from the bar to Jeff's place a couple of times. I don't even know if he had a driver's license," Ron said.

Dieteman without a car put a minimum of two people into the conspiracy.

RANDOM RECREATIONAL VIOLENCE **291**

"Any reason to believe that he would have gotten one from somewhere or is using one now?"

"Nope. He was living from place to place without one. Unless he stole one, or someone gave him one, I would have to say no. The guy had very few possessions. I think I would have heard if he had a car. Besides, when I met him a month or so back, he was dropped off at the bar and picked up there by that crazy-looking dude."

It was time to change subjects.

"Ron, when we first talked, you told me about Sam telling you specifically that he used a 410 shotgun to kill someone, a female that he thought was a male. Now, I looked at your Silent Witness call sheets, and they mention a *12/12 double barreled shotgun*. What the hell is a 12/12 shotgun?"

Ron started to laugh. "I'm sorry, Detective, I just don't know weapons very well. When I was talking to a buddy of mine about Sammy, I told him that he used what I thought was a 12/12 shotgun. My friend laughed his ass off and told me there was no such thing. I told him that it had two numbers in it, but I knew that it wasn't a 12 gauge. My friend mentioned a 410, and that's when it dawned on me what Sam had said he used. It was my fault. They didn't report it wrong. I just didn't know any better."

That story even brought a smile to my tired face. A 410 did have two numbers in it. I guess he was at least half-right. A defense attorney would have a heyday with that.

"I take it this friend that you confided in is the same friend that you needed to talk to before you gave me Dieteman's cellphone number."

I didn't want Ron to forget that I have an unusual knack for details.

"It's not that I didn't want to give it to you," Ron said. "I just didn't want to give you the wrong one." He slid me a small piece of paper with numbers written on it. "You'll find that is his current one. My buddy just talked to him last week."

Getting the phone number was huge, but it would take time to track Sam down by its usage. I needed something more time efficient.

"Ron, I need you to call Sammy and set up a meeting. I need you to agree to meet with him so we can find him and track him."

That would cut to the chase.

Ron paused a minute.

"It's not that simple," he said. "I can't just call him. These guys only text message each other. They rarely talk on the phone. Paranoid sons-a-b*^#@es. They think the cops are listening to every phone call, so they text each other. I would have to text him to get him to meet me."

"Whatever you have to do. Text him or send a pigeon with a message tied to its leg. I don't care. We need to find him right away. I need to find him right away."

The clock was ticking.

"I understand." Ron paused for a moment and then spoke. "Detective, I know it may be hard to believe, but I know he's involved. The minute those shootings moved to the east side from the west side, I knew Sammy was involved. His living in Scottsdale … too much of a coincidence."

"If you get that meeting set up, we'll find out soon enough. Until then, it's just another tip."

Ron and I finished our beers and shook hands. He agreed to call me the minute he and Sammy were to hook up. I could mobilize ten guys from the task force. No way was Samuel Dieteman getting away from us.

As soon as Ron took off, Detective Udd and I met.

"Well, anything else useful?" he wanted to know.

"Maybe. He's going to try to set up a meet with this Sammy Dieteman. If he does, are you up for a long night of surveillance?"

I thought I would ask instead of just assume.

"Bet your ass. What are we going to do in the meantime?"

"We're going to go look for Sammy ourselves. Just you and me. And I know exactly where to start."

◈

All of the bars that guys like Ron Horton and Samuel Dieteman patronized were in an area on the west side of town that covered about three square miles. There was half a dozen or so of these bars, some within walking distance of each other. Biker bars was a name that locals applied to these places. I thought of them more along the lines of "whiter bars." Occasionally, you could find a minority in one of the establishments, but not very often. I made a list and Detective Udd and I were going to hit them all, hoping to stumble across Samuel Dieteman.

Spending Sundays at biker bars was referred to as "going to church." Instead of praying at the altar of most parishes, synagogues, or chapels, these hellions prayed at the foot of the porcelain altar, the one located in the men's room. Church for these gentlemen and gentle ladies began early in the morning, just as soon as the bars opened. And these soul searchers didn't stop at just one watering hole. They traversed the west side of town stopping at many troughs. It was their form of religion.

If Ron Horton was right and Sammy Dieteman was involved, there would be a good chance of finding his partner. If Sammy had no vehicle, the two would be close. They were a team now, a successful team at that. If he, or they, were out tonight, we'd hoped to run across them.

I pulled the list, and we agreed to conduct outside surveillances first to see if we could spot him coming or going. If not, one of us would do a walk-through to the restroom or go ask the bartender a stupid question like, "Do you serve food, and is your grill still open?" Something to get in and out quickly. Just enough time to case the place and see if we could spot Dieteman.

We were both wearing T-shirts and jeans so at least we weren't dressed like cops. We couldn't hide the fact that we had short hair, though, usually a telltale sign the Po-Po are in the house. Our first two stops that night turned up no sighting of Samuel Dieteman. We'd both burned his photo into our memory before we walked in the bars.

The third stop was a real dive bar. We sat in the parking lot for a few minutes and watched as a few people trickled in and out of the place. It appeared to be fairly quiet. Only one motorcycle parked in front, and most of the patrons we saw looked more "redneck" than biker creed.

It was Darren's turn to go in, so I sat in the truck reading through Sam Dieteman's binder of information. His divorce had been ugly. His wife had accused him of beating her and threatening to kill her. That didn't play out well in domestic relations court. Judges tended to frown on abusers.

My phone rang, and it was Ron Horton. "I've gotten a hold of Sam by text message. What do you want me to say?"

"See if he'll meet you for a drink tonight, but don't push too hard. Try at least to get a location on him, so that maybe we can run him down tonight. My partner and I are out here all night anyway."

"OK, I'll try to get him to meet me. I'll offer to buy his alcohol. That should do it."

"Keep me posted." I hung up.

Detective Udd had been in the bar a few minutes, and I began to watch the front of the place with a sense of urgency. About a minute later, he emerged from the bar. He turned to make sure no one had followed him out.

As he jumped up into the passenger seat he said, "Bro, there's somebody in there that looks a lot like our boy." I could tell he was excited. "Thing is, he's sitting in a back booth, and I can't tell for sure if it's him. Fu$%en place is dark as hell."

"One way to find out."

He knew exactly what I was thinking. It was time for us both to go in and have a seat. Even if we had to sit right next to the guy to make the I.D., so be it. We wouldn't be coming back here to do any further investigations. If it was Dieteman, I had guys with long hair and goatees to hang out in places like this. I didn't care if we got burned as outsiders.

At least we were armed. Detective Udd had his piece in an ankle holster, and I wore a baggy T-shirt, one that was two sizes too big, so I could keep my gun on my side. I needed to know what we were looking at before we walked in.

"Lay it out for me," I said to him.

"There are booths along the south wall. The bar sits on the north side with seating, so you can belly up. I counted about nine people inside, mostly white trash from what I could tell. Only one bartender, and I didn't see any waitresses. Most of the guys are sitting at the bar, except for one booth with two guys in it. Then the one guy by himself."

"What was your intro?" I asked.

"I asked if they served pitchers, and the bartender said they do."

"Let's do it."

We both hopped out of the truck.

Darren entered first. The place was thick with smoke and smelled like stale beer. The horseshoe-shape bar took up most of the north wall. Just off the far end of the horseshoe, I saw a set of swinging doors that must have led to the office. I counted eight total people in the bar, including the bartender. I spotted the guy that he thought might be Dieteman still sitting in a corner booth. The place was dark, and the only way to see him would be from one of the scattered tables that sat between the booths and the bar.

Darren went up and ordered a pitcher of beer, and I made my way to the farthest end of the bar, within about fifteen feet of a white male with long, black hair and a goatee. The man resembled Dieteman's MVD photo, but it was too tough to tell in the lighting. My eyes needed to adjust a little more. I grabbed a seat at a shaky, wooden table for four. Almost everyone at the bar was staring at me. Some of the patrons on bar stools craned their necks to get a look. There was one TV on in a corner behind the bar, and some lame fishing show was on.

Darren joined me at the table with two glasses that looked half-clean and a small pitcher of beer. He poured both of us a glass, and we sat for a second looking at everybody who looked at us. It was obvious we weren't regulars, and that was what drew the most glances.

As my eyes started to adjust, I began to look closely at the individual mired in his cocktail. He hadn't looked up once since we'd come in. He appeared deep in thought. He definitely fit the description of Dieteman—white male, thirties, large build, with brown hair and a goatee. Darren began to watch the other patrons as well. A jukebox in the corner blared out hits from the eighties. My kind of music.

We began to sip our beers. Darren started to mention something about what a dump the place was when one of the drinkers at the bar pushed himself away from the brass rail footrest. I could tell by his swaying body motions once he stood up, the guy was blitzed. He turned and looked at us.

The restrooms were at our end of the place, and he began to stagger toward them. Darren saw the drunk's route, and he, too, began to watch with curiosity. One of the patrons from the bar yelled at the drunk and asked him where he thought he was going.

The guy yelled back, "To the bathroom. Where the hell ya think I'm going?"

The drunk stumbled by us toward the toilets, the whole time staring at me. Darren shook his head slightly. He had seen the drunk eyeballing me.

With our target still focused on his beverage, I actually began to relax for a minute. Loverboy's "Loving Every Minute of It" blasted throughout the bar. It reminded me of my youth. Nothing like a jukebox to kickstart a trip down memory lane.

My cellphone began to vibrate again. It was Ron Horton. I stepped outside the bar to talk to him.

"Hey, Detective, I'm trying to meet up with Sam, but he appears to be preoccupied."

"What do you mean?" I asked.

"Well, it's taking him like ten minutes to text me back after I sent him a message. It shouldn't take that long to reply. He said he was busy, so he couldn't get together. I was trying to make him feel guilty by not getting together, but that ain't working either."

"OK, Ron, thanks for trying. Let me know if he changes his mind."

He agreed to call me. I walked back into the bar and took my seat.

I had almost forgotten about the drunk when he re-emerged from the bathroom. He had been in there about ten minutes trying to find his zipper or peeing all over himself, one of the two. He was in his late thirties, but because of all the alcohol, he looked much older. His black hair, with intermittent gray on the sides, hung to his shoulders. His full beard, with gray starting to creep into it as well, hid a pockmarked face. He was probably about five-feet nine-inches tall and couldn't have weighed over a buck fifty. He looked like Charles Manson.

He'd seen us walk in. We both stand over six feet tall, and Darren comes in at about 220. My weight sits around 195.

Unfortunately, the drunk was going to pick a fight with somebody tonight. Might as well be a stranger, a bigger one at that. Maybe he felt like we were trespassing in his area. Maybe he just wanted to challenge the biggest guys in the bar. Whatever the case, he was walking over toward our table, and he looked none too pleased.

"How you doin?" he slurred.

We both ignored him, hoping he would get the hint. The music blared in the background.

He asked again. "I said, how you doin?"

This time he asked louder, and he leaned in toward our table thinking that maybe we hadn't heard him the first time.

"We're doing all right. How are you?"

Darren was already sick of the guy, and so was I.

He then pointed his finger at me and said, "I know you, dude."

He was swaying, and his finger was moving all over the place. He had trouble just keeping it extended, let alone pointing at me.

"I don't think so, my friend," I answered.

If he was somebody that I'd arrested a long time ago or even recently, I didn't recognize him. I usually do, especially the ones I send to prison.

He began to nod his head up and down and then shouted, "Yes sir, I know you."

He was slurring his speech so badly that even those few words were hard to make out.

I was playing it cool, but Darren had had enough.

"Hey, why don't you just go back to the bar and your drink and leave us alone. We don't want any trouble."

Darren was being more diplomatic than usual. Most of the time, he would have told the guy to go sit down, or we would sit him down ourselves.

The drunk gazed at my partner, but didn't hear a word he was saying. He was fixated on me.

"I know that guy," he insisted, "and he needs to go."

We were both still seated, and I was watching the other patrons now turn their attention toward us and this moron.

The drunk took two more steps toward me. I didn't know if he was going to point again or grab me, and my instincts took over. I pushed out of my chair and knocked his hand away. At the same time, I grabbed the front of his shirt with one hand and his crotch through his pants with the other. I pushed him all the way from our table to the standing bar. His back slammed into the raised oak top.

"Listen," I told him, "I've had enough of you. Get the hell away from me and my friend. I don't know you, and I don't care to know you. Stay the hell away from me."

His eyes were wide open as he winced in pain. He obviously didn't expect what had just happened.

Three of the patrons and the bartender started to yell at us as though we had created the problem. I heard, "Let him go" and "You guys need to get out of here" over and over. Their voices were growing louder. We were outsiders causing a problem in their place. Darren stood between me and the unhappy customers.

Then I felt something hit my right shoulder blade. I would later find out that it was a barstool. One of the patrons had taken a dislike to the way I was handling their buddy.

The rest of the story is hazy because it happened so fast. I heard skin hitting skin. Suffice it to say, there was never a police report filed on the incident. No one that I know of got hurt too bad, so that's a good thing. We didn't have to draw our weapons, and we didn't have to run and escape into the night. We walked out of the bar briskly, got in my truck, and left the establishment. My vehicle didn't get damaged either, though some of the patrons threw things at us as we left.

No injury, no damage to property, mutual combat, no crime.

It was silent in the cab of my truck for at least a minute after we drove away. Neither one of us knew what to say. Then both of us began to laugh our asses off. The last thing that we needed was an internal investigation into what had just occurred. I don't know if it was because I was tired or because of what had just happened, but we couldn't even talk about the melee because we couldn't stop laughing. Maybe it was because we were both punch drunk.

I could see the headlines in the paper the following day: *Serial Shooter investigators involved in bar fight.* We wouldn't be laughing about that, and neither would the bosses. But at that moment, we couldn't help ourselves.

CHAPTER 35

He had chosen the location of his apartment carefully. It was only ten minutes to Sky Harbor Airport where he worked, one minute away from daycare, and twenty minutes away from his daughter's mother's house. Even though it was just a one bedroom, it suited his needs. The rent was reasonable, and out front was a grass play area where his two-and-a-half-year old could romp, though that rarely happened.

Being a criminal mastermind made him paranoid about such things. Even though he had become a renowned shootist, he was extremely nervous about letting his daughter out of his sight. There were perverts that lived in his complex. At least he assumed there were. Plus his daughter had Van Gherkins disease, an extremely rare digestive ailment. Although not a death sentence, it was a good reason to be vigilant with her. He was never going to allow anything to happen to her like what happened to his boys many years earlier.

Keeping an eye on people was important. He'd always been a control freak, ever since he was a kid. It had worked well for him as an adult, too. That was why he insisted on his accomplice moving in with him.

Northwest Phoenix had become too hot for him and his partner. The cops must have been swarming that area. Although the vehicle description that they had publicized could fit half the cars in Maricopa County, it fit his, too. Why take unreasonable risk?

He had decided against trolling around East Phoenix for the time being as well. He hated giving up those hunting grounds. So many idiots just out there walking around, failing to heed any warning about the fear that he and his partner had so carefully orchestrated. What was wrong with these people? But he could always go back there after he sent some shock waves through the east valley. Might as well spread the wealth. There were lots of people to scare in all parts of the Valley.

That was part of the master plan. No community would remain unaffected. They would all shudder with fear, just like all the other American communities that had suffered during the reign of a serial killer. He couldn't wait until the day when everyone was in fear, not just the residents of Phoenix, Tolleson, Glendale, and now Mesa. He and his partner were coming to a community near you.

For the meantime, he needed to concentrate on supplies, especially liquor. He could never keep enough around for his partner, who was surely an alcoholic. But since both were masters at the art of stealing, booze was a mainstay, not just for drinking either. Every time he went to work, which was getting less and less often these days, more and more people asked him for booze. He had become a fence, stealing bottles of Crown Royal, Grey Goose, and only the top-end tequilas. Everybody wanted the good stuff. It had turned into a lucrative side business. He sold it at a scaled-down price.

He spun that off into other areas of demand as well, such as DVDs, electronic games, and music CDs. Selling them at a cut rate of $10 allowed him to feed his rage, his appetite, one that he admitted was growing out of control.

The American system had failed him at every turn. So he decided they would pay. Everyone would pay, with fear. Nobody was going to be immune to what was going on. Everyone would be a target.

Before heading out, he checked his other supply. The small Ziploc bag was sealed tight. It, too, was running low. The little white substance within the bag gave him the invincibility he needed. When they returned from the store, he would smoke the last little bit.

The grocery store was a one-minute drive from the apartment. No thievery would take place here. Walmart and Sam's Club were his hot spots. He and his partner knew the lay-outs of those stores intimately. They also knew where the surveillance cameras were and what they showed. There were always blind spots in those stores. Security tags were no problem. Those were easily removed in areas of the stores where no surveillance cameras recorded.

He had a motto: "Never sh#@ in your own backyard." If you're going to steal or shoot, do it somewhere else. Away from your home. Far away, like east and West Phoenix.

But he had broken that rule with the recent shooting of the bicyclist. There just wasn't any fear in the East Valley. They needed some. They needed to know that their streets weren't safe, either.

As he pushed the shopping cart through the aisles, he thought about just how unfair life had been to him. He had talent, and it wasn't just a talent for shooting people. He had real talent—the kind of talent that at one time had landed him on TV with his own cable boxing show, the kind that made him an extraordinary sports photographer. It should be him shooting magazine covers for *Sports Illustrated* and writing articles for *Ringside Boxing*. Those people just didn't know talent.

He had been studying boxing since he was a child. He loved the brutality of the sport. He knew all the statistics, all the participants, and his show had been formatted around his knowledge. Yet, he could never get a sponsor to buy into that knowledge. So his show had failed. Renting the studio had been too costly, and his audience too small. The show had fed his ego, an ego that called for greatness and success. The success he deserved. Why didn't others see it?

As he pushed the cart through the grocery store with his accomplice trailing him, he couldn't help but be bitter. Look what he had been reduced to, a man employed at the airport, a janitor. A job that, in his mind, was one of the worst professions known to mankind.

He cursed his father and mother. They were the ones who had put him on this path. They had been cleaners all their lives, owning a small business. They had made it seem all right to pick up other people's trash, vacuum their carpets, clean their toilets, and mop their floors.

But he didn't want any part of that anymore. His ambitions were much higher. He deserved more than a City of Phoenix security badge at the airport.

If stardom wouldn't come to him, then reality would come to everyone else. He had the power now. The power to affect millions. Yes, he worked as a janitor by trade, but he was more than that. Much more. He was a thief, an arsonist, a homicidal maniac among mortals. He held the power in his hands, and he would exercise that power at will.

He grabbed three VHS tapes from the aisle marked "Accessories" to record boxing matches. His library of tapes at home contained some of the greatest fights in boxing history, ones he had chatted about on his TV show. Now they were just archives.

The next stop was the generic food area. He needed to fill up on Rice Dream and soy milk for his daughter. She needed these items to survive.

Curse that disease. Why her? Why me?

By the time he got to the register, he was angry. He placed all the items on the belt, and watched as they were slowly rung up. He gave the clerk his phone number, and up popped the frequent shopper card number. He handed the clerk $20, and she handed him his change back.

"Thank you, Mr. Vickers. You saved twenty cents on your purchases tonight. Have a nice night," she said.

"Mr. Vickers," he thought to himself. "You idiot. You don't even know my real name."

All the better, he guessed.

As he pushed the cart toward the exit, he looked around for his partner, but he had already left the store with a bottle of Captain Morgan secured in his shorts. He never listened. He was glad his home was so close. He couldn't wait to light up that glass pipe. The meth would ease his frustration, but fuel his desire. He knew what he needed to do. His partner would soon know as well.

Oh, yeah, Mr. Vickers is going to make somebody pay tonight.

◈

Raising a special-needs child is certainly not an easy task, but the result can be rewarding. That's how Steve and Sandra Blasnek looked at their daughter, Robin. She had certainly challenged them through her first twenty-two years of life.

With a mental age equivalent of about fifteen, she had some difficulties with personal relationships outside of the family, which was troublesome, especially for a family raised in the strictest sense of the Mormon religion. But Robin had turned out to be a success story.

The Blasnek's had raised four daughters, Robin being the youngest. The other three adapted well, and they doted over their youngest sibling. They knew that she struggled mentally and took care to watch over her.

Life, however, is never fair. When Robin was twelve years old, her sister, Rachel, was killed in a car accident. The driver of the other car ran a red light, striking the vehicle in which Rachel was riding. The family's faith had pulled them through that tragedy, so Robin's issues seemed very small in comparison. Nonetheless, they kept a tight rein over her, so other calamities could be avoided.

But Robin was an adult now and would have to learn to stand on her own two feet. She couldn't continue to live at home all her life. There was a great big world out there to discover, and at her age, she needed to learn self-sufficiency.

Her parents decided that she would stay at a halfway house, a house for girls with emotional problems. She could work with counselors and learn from other occupants about how to cope with those problems that affect relationships. The place was a short drive from her home in Mesa. The family agreed that Robin would live there during the week, then come back to the family's house on weekends. The family hoped this would give her the training and guidance she'd need to go live on her own one day.

Robin had landed a job as a secretary doing clerical work. It was good for her, and her family couldn't be happier. She had even met a man. In fact, she had met a few. One of the men in her life was Rudy Reyes, whom she introduced as an acquaintance. But he was more than that to Robin.

They had met two years earlier, and, until very recently, had just been friends. They talked easily with one another. However, there was an attraction there, a physical one. This was where Robin struggled the most. Her friends all told her that she was too nice, that she let guys take advantage of her. Her mental immaturity was evident when it came to men. And now she wanted Rudy. They had hooked up for the first time, and both of them enjoyed the experience.

On Sunday, July 30th, 2006, Robin made plans to see Rudy again. Like a couple of teenagers, they text messaged each other all afternoon. They would arrange to meet and experience intimacy all over again.

It had gotten late on Sunday, and the Blasnek family was huddled around the TV watching a movie. At around 10:00 p.m., they all said good night to each other and headed for their beds. Robin went to hers as well, but not before making plans to go meet Rudy.

She really didn't have to sneak out, but maybe she thought she did. Since she stayed with her parents on the weekends, she was under their roof with their rules.

Besides, she had a job to go to. They would have frowned on her gallivanting around this late.

Rudy lived with his parents also, and at age twenty, he also had to be careful with his trysts. It wasn't easy being in the home you share with your parents, trying to sneak girls in and out. He, too, had to wait until his parents went to sleep. For the next hour, Rudy and Robin texted each other about how to get together, and what they were going to do to each other. There was attraction and there was lust, and this was lust. The two lived only about a half-mile from each other. It would be easiest to cover that distance on foot.

They decided that Robin would sneak out and walk to Rudy's house. Walking time would take her ten minutes, tops. She knew the quickest route.

The temperature was pushing 100 when Robin left her house. She wore a pair of gray sweat bottoms, a pink tank top, and on her feet were the ultimate sign of immaturity: a pair of fuzzy blue slippers. She stayed mostly on the side streets until she reached Gilbert Road, a main thoroughfare that runs north and south through the city of Mesa. As she glided south along Gilbert Road, her watch read 11:15 p.m. She would get to Rudy's in a couple of minutes, have a fling, and be back at her house before 1:00 a.m.

That would be plenty of time to get some sleep, and no one would ever know she'd left the house.

They had left their apartment at 11:00 p.m., after dropping off the groceries they'd just purchased. The large black duffle bag his partner toted carried the only real justice in the world: a 410 shotgun.

Previously, he had carried the sawed-off 410 down a pants leg to and from the car, but that was risky, not to mention uncomfortable. The bag hid their weapon of mass destruction perfectly. It would raise no suspicions with other tenants. The bag looked like any other clothing bag.

It was a tad early to go out shooting, but on a Sunday night, there were fewer cars and fewer witnesses to worry about. On the other hand, there were always plenty of targets out there. Some people never learn.

As they drove east of their apartment complex, they decided that the folks in Mesa would get another dose of reality. Why burn gas driving into Phoenix? They were sure they could find easy prey close to their home. Of course, it would break the rule. Screw it. Besides, he wasn't happy with the result of the last shooting. The victim had survived. The bicyclist had proven to be a worthy foe. The shot he'd fired that night from the driver's seat was tough. He'd had to slow his car and hit a moving rider. No easy task. When he saw him go down in his rearview mirror, he was ecstatic and had congratulated himself on a well put-together hunt.

Then he learned the blast had only hit his legs. There was no chance of getting an obituary with a leg shot. And the victim was probably an illegal alien.

That didn't sit well with him at all. If it hadn't been for his hard work all these months, the press probably wouldn't have even covered it.

So it was time to shoot again. Time to teach another lesson to the pupils of the metro area. He was in charge of the streets at night. He would dictate when it was safe to go out.

They were southbound when they both spotted her.

"Oh, she's dead," he said to his partner as they drove by her. "Look at her, stupid b*#ch."

The partner turned his head to see if the coast was clear.

"You got cars behind us," he said, as headlights appeared behind the car.

"Sh*#, let me get turned around."

He pulled the car off the road and made a quick U-turn. He knew that he had to be swift, for his target could duck into a house or a side street, and he might miss her. "There she is again," he said to his partner, "Is it safe?"

His partner scoped out the back window.

"Nope, you got cars coming up behind us again."

He cursed. "How much longer was she going to be out here on the road?" he wondered. Damn this traffic. He made another pass. She still hadn't noticed them, and this was their third time by her. He tried not to make it obvious, but he couldn't help but stare at his quarry. He decided he would roll up to her slowly, instead of driving by too fast. He wanted his hands to be steady and his shot to be accurate. This may be the only chance they'd get tonight. He needed to make it a good one.

She was about a hundred yards in front of him and on the opposite side of the street. He might not have to pull into the two-way turn lane for this shot.

"It's all clear behind you," his partner said.

He looked up for a brief moment and realized they were alone on the road, except for the target. He pulled the single-shot 410 up from the position he had tucked it, next to his right leg. He took his foot off the accelerator and braked. The vehicle started to slow down to almost a crawl.

The girl began to make a turn onto the side street. If he was going to shoot it had to be now.

The Chase family was used to traffic on the street. After all, Gilbert Road was a main artery, and they had seen, and heard, plenty of accidents. But it wasn't an accident that startled them while watching a movie that night. The explosion rattled the interior. They all looked at each other. There were eight of them, including friends of the children, sitting in their living room that night. What was that noise? Nobody was sure, but it sounded like a gunshot.

The father, Charles, was the first person to his front door. As he looked out, he could see a girl, down on her knees, across the street. She was hunched over, holding her stomach. He sprinted to her, all the while looking around for anyone else in the area. He saw no one.

The girl appeared to be talking on her cellphone. She was mumbling, and he asked her if she was all right. She looked up at him and said, "I've been shot."

Charles's son and wife, Marie, had come outside, and he told his boy to call the police. He told Marie to go get some towels and a blanket. The young girl, whose age he guessed was around eighteen, was now lying on her right side on the hard cement. He didn't want her to be uncomfortable. Her color was gray, and he asked her for her name. She didn't reply.

More neighbors poured out of their houses and approached the young victim lying on the street corner. A man in long-bed white truck stopped and yelled if anyone had called 911. Charles looked up and yelled back that 911 had indeed been called. When Marie returned, Charles grabbed the towel and began to apply pressure to the injuries, which he could now clearly see. The blanket was placed under her head. She had not moved for several minutes.

The first call came into the police at 11:17 p.m. A woman had been shot. Then numerous duplicate calls came pouring in. Some of the callers weren't sure whether she had been stabbed or shot. They just saw the blood. Within three minutes, police were on scene, and paramedics were there within five. They also tried to talk to the victim. She had coded.

Everyone knew what had occurred. The Serial Shooter had struck again. Phoenix Police was advised within ten minutes of the shooting. The victim had no identification on her, just a cellphone.

At 2345 hours, Robin Blasnek—daughter, friend, coworker, sister and twenty-two years young—was pronounced dead at Scottsdale Osborn Hospital. Her wounds hadn't even been addressed. She died as she made her way into the hospital.

I had decided that I should probably make my way home after the little conflict at the bar. Tonight would be just as good a night as any to catch up on some sleep.

My phone rang as I was driving the newly constructed 202 freeway that stretched from downtown Phoenix to Chandler. It was Lieutenant Brent Vermeer.

"Hey, Clark, it's Brent. We just got a call through our dispatch that there's been a shooting in Mesa."

I'm sure there was at least a moment of silence from me, but I wasn't shocked at all.

"I'm listening."

I already knew it was our boys.

"Looks like a white female was shot on the corner of Grandview and Gilbert. I don't know where the hell that is, but they said it's just north of Brown. Are you familiar with that area?"

"Yeah, that's about a mile away from the last one."

"They would like you to respond, if you don't mind," he said.

"I'll start that way. Do you want me to call you when I get out there?"

"Please, and keep me posted. And Clark, I don't know her condition at present. I was told that she was critical as she left the scene."

He hung up the phone.

Mesa Police had the outer perimeter secured and an inner perimeter two blocks north and south of the crime scene. The first perimeter officer stopped me because I looked like Joe the ordinary citizen in my raised black truck trying to circumvent the road blocks. As he was getting ready to chew my butt out for not paying attention to his hand signals, I flashed my credentials.

"Sorry, sir, I didn't know you were police. You can park anywhere on Gilbert Road. The crime scene is about half a mile up the road."

"You don't have to call me sir, and thanks for paying attention. Can I get you anything while I'm up there?"

It was a hundred degrees out, and I was sweating inside my truck. He was standing outside with the smell of road flares searing his nostrils.

"I'm fine. I got my drink, and I'm good. Thanks."

He lifted the crime scene tape up and over the top of my truck, and I pulled into the outer perimeter of the crime scene. As I walked up, I noticed a TV camera was already filming what was happening.

I could see Lieutenant Wade Pew standing across the street from the crime scene. I looked to my left and saw the usual aftermath of a shooting. The victim's clothing and what looked like a pair of slippers were lying on the sidewalk. There was also a blanket and towel. There were the usual remnants of paramedic trash: the gauze bandage packaging, needle protectors, and IV casing. And sitting in the street was a white object, which even from across the street I could tell was a shot cup. A bright orange cone sat next to it.

South of where Lieutenant Pew was standing, several ATF agents and their ASAC, stood by Mesa's activity vehicle. The large RV had been rolled out to house and refresh the investigators and the brass, too.

Lieutenant Pew and I shook hands, and he thanked me for coming.

"We're waiting on our case agent and our crime scene investigators to arrive," he told me. "As soon as they get here, we'll start the briefing. Our main case agent just got back from vacation, so he may be a little slow. You know how that goes."

You bet I did. There's nothing like spending a relaxing vacation away from the job, trying to forget all the bad things that happen in your city. Then the day you return, you get slammed. Welcome back to the real world.

"Chief Fowler is in the van. He would like to see you," Lieutenant Pew added.

"OK." I couldn't help myself but I had to ask. "What is ATF doing here?"

Lieutenant Pew just shook his head. "I don't know. The Chief is friends with the ASAC, and he called him. What they're going to do out here is anyone's guess. We clearly don't need them."

Then he added. "The victim died a few minutes ago. We still don't have her ID'd. She was dressed in what looks like pajamas with slippers when she was gunned down. As soon as we're briefed, we'll start to canvass the neighborhood. Hopefully, she was just walking to get a cup of sugar from some neighbor."

Pajamas and slippers? I phoned Lieutenant Vermeer and updated him with what little I knew. I would call him back after the briefing.

Mesa's activity van was similar to the ones Phoenix police operated. There were seats with counters so multiple people could write, phones and radios with which to monitor other police activity, and a large dry board to write down assignments and follow-up duties. There was also a room in the back with a partition for those interviews that needed to be private. It was its own police command center, but mobile so that it could be anywhere in the city it needed to be.

As I climbed up into the RV, I saw Chief Fowler sitting in the captain's chair. He was talking to Commander Tolan, who was seated in the front passenger seat. Chief Fowler swiveled around in the big chair.

"Hello, Detective. No offense, but I hoped I wouldn't have to see you again after your briefing last week."

No punches pulled there. I wasn't sure whether to apologize or just turn around and leave.

Commander Tolan then looked my direction.

"Well, Clark, it looks like you were right. I'm guessing it's the Serial Shooters. We're going over our plans for increased undercover coverage. Before we know it, we're going to have as many cars on the street as you guys do, maybe more. We gotta catch these guys. Did Wade fill you in on the facts?"

"Just briefly. The victim is dead, and we don't know who she is or from where she came." I paused briefly. "I'm going to assume that the little white object out there is a shot cup. Is it a 410?"

"Looks to be. She was hit all along the left side of her body," the commander replied. "We're checking her cellphone for calls. Hopefully we get her ID'd soon. She looks fairly young."

Lieutenant Pew came into the RV and stated the briefing would be starting. We all gathered our notebooks and headed out into the sweltering summer night.

In Phoenix, briefings, for the most part, are given by a sergeant, either a patrol supervisor or a detective supervisor. In Mesa, patrol officers were paraded up one at a time to tell the response team what it was they found and did upon arrival. They had asked witnesses to write out their statements. Most of those pertained to hearing a shot, then coming outside. No actual eyewitnesses, again.

Lieutenant Pew introduced the case agent and lead investigator. His name was Donald Byers, but everybody called him Donnie. I had never met him before. The man, who I would also come to call Donnie, turned out to be one of the best investigators I have ever known. On top of that, he's funny as hell and a dedicated hero.

Donnie Byers was a twenty-seven-year veteran of the Mesa Police Department. He had spent twenty of those years working homicides. He had more tenure in the Homicide Detail than most officers have in their entire career. Donnie and I were introduced this night, but we would spend many days together. I could tell that he was busy trying to ascertain the facts of the case from all the reporting officers and detectives. I left him alone so he could do his job. There would be plenty of time in the future for us to sit and talk about all the cases and the task force.

In the meantime, I approached Lieutenant Pew.

"Lieutenant, I can have every available asset of the task force here within two hours if you need any help with anything. They're all just a phone call away. You just give me the word, and I'll start waking up my chain of command to get the resources here."

He reflected for a minute and then answered. "I think we're OK for now, but I appreciate the gesture. I've got eight investigators coming, so we should be good."

He didn't want any more brass out there than he had already.

Mesa was a part of the task force now and had been since the bicyclist shooting. All Lieutenant Pew had to do was ask, and the dollars being on spent in overtime would be acceptable. There was nothing we wouldn't do and no expense spared to nab the Random/Serial Shooters.

I phoned Lieutenant Vermeer and told him that they didn't need any additional manpower at this time. Neither of us discussed waking up our chain of command. There was no reason to. Why wake everyone up just to tell them that they're not needed?

Detective Steve Purington arrived on scene. I had never met Steve either, and Lieutenant Pew introduced us. Steve would be conducting the crime scene investigation. "I heard Phoenix was out here. It's nice to meet ya. I wish it was under different circumstances."

"Yeah, me too."

We all wished that. I told Detective Purington I would help him with the crime scene investigation, if he wished.

"That would be great," he said.

Detective Purington turned to Lieutenant Pew and asked, "Who are those guys standing there, and why are they in my scene?"

Lieutenant Pew just shook his head and again said it was ATF. Steve looked at me, and I just shrugged my shoulders. What was there to say? The ASAC from ATF had meandered into the inner crime scene and was holding a flashlight and pointing it at the asphalt in the street. He seemed fascinated with something sitting there.

Detective Purington, I, and a host of others who were standing together, including lead Detective Byers, all stared at him, wondering what he was looking at. He stood over it for a minute or so, his flashlight burning a hole in the object. Obviously, a patrol officer had marked it because he recognized it to be possible evidence, the value of which would be later determined by the scene investigator. But he was enamored with the object.

Detective Purington cupped his hands over his mouth and yelled, "All right! Everyone over there needs to move out of the inner crime scene so the photographer can start the overall pictures."

The photographer hadn't even arrived yet, but it was a good ploy. They scurried like rats.

"There's a cigarette butt in the roadway there. Think we might collect that and possibly get some DNA off it?"

Before any of the detectives had a chance to pop off, Lieutenant Pew jumped ahead of everyone by saying, "Oh, yeah. If there's evidence there, it will be collected and analyzed."

Detective Purington looked at me and tilted his head toward the crime scene, implying that we should walk over there together.

"How many of these cases have you investigated now?" he asked.

"Fourteen, personally, including your one in Mesa. Two dozen or so others, researched and reviewed. That's why they called me out here, and how your department became involved in the task force."

"That's unbelievable! Three dozen shootings and no idea who the hell is doing it. That's scary, man."

I just nodded in agreement.

As we both stood there looking up close at the aftermath of the shooting, Detective Purington moved the orange cone in the street. I could clearly see the shot cup, and it definitely was from a 410 cartridge. There was very little blood, typical of the other crime scenes I had investigated. A small cultured stone wall curved around the property on the corner. It was marked with the birdshot that had missed the young girl. The corner of Gilbert Road was well lit, but Grandview was pitch black. Bad luck for the victim. A minute later, and she would have disappeared into the darkness, never to be seen from the road.

As we inspected the wall, Detective Byers joined us and began to brief us on what he had learned so far.

"I just got off the phone with the detective at the hospital with the victim. He says she is a real small gal, maybe five feet tall. She got hit from thigh to chest with the blast, all on her left side. At least twenty in her."

I walked out to the middle of Gilbert Road and aligned myself with the wall. If a passenger had shot, he would have had to travel past the target and shoot backwards—no easy task, but still a possibility. It would have been a much easier shot for the driver to pull off. He could slow and fire, maybe from the two-way left turn lane, just as he had when shooting Garry Begay.

We decided to check the residence that sat just behind the shooting location for any additional strikes. No strikes were found on the house itself.

Looking at my cellphone, I noticed it was pushing 4:00 a.m. The bar incident was a distant memory.

Detective Byers was getting ready to leave the scene. A group had gathered around him, so I joined them to say good night. There was nothing more I could do here. "We have the victim identified. Her name is Robin Blasnek. Detectives located her through the cellphone that was found at the scene," Detective Byers said.

I opened my notepad and began to write.

"She's twenty-two years old and lives a few blocks north of here. We're out with her parents now. It looks like they thought she was in bed and had last seen her around 10:00 p.m. They had no idea she had left the residence. According to them, she is slightly handicapped, so that may explain why she was in her nightwear walking down the street."

I scribbled as Donnie continued.

"They don't know where she'd be going, and there's no reason to believe that anyone would want her dead. We're looking through the address book in her phone to see if we can figure out where she was heading, but we're gonna wait and start contacting people in a few hours. It's almost 4:00, and I don't think anyone is going to answer their phones anyway."

After the identification news, everyone broke up to continue on with the tasks at hand. I approached Donnie and told him I was heading out. He thanked me for coming. "Let's get together later today, after we get some sleep.

We'll sit down and talk some strategy. I can't wait to hear what you've got to say about this whole mess," he said.

"That'd be good. I don't know how much sleep I'm going to get, but this afternoon would be a good time for you to brief the task force chain of command. I'm sure they'll want to hear what you've learned by then." I closed with a smart aleck comment. "Oh, and by the way, welcome to the party."

Detective Donnie Byers smirked and shot back, "Yeah, thanks. It's good to come back to a Phoenix sh*# sandwich."

Amen to that.

While driving to my home, I couldn't help but wonder if there might have been some way to prevent this shooting. I ran it through my head over and over again. Did I miss something, anything? Did the task force fail this young, female victim? Did I fail her? In a few hours, the whole world would know about the murder of Robin Blasnek, and they would assume that it was the work of the Serial Shooters.

Today was Monday, July 31st, and a large number of people would be doing a lot of armchair quarterbacking.

CHAPTER 36

As my phone started to ring, I realized that my radio alarm was playing from its usual 6:30 a.m. setting. The clock now read 7:02, and I had slept right through the music. I answered the phone as quickly as I could.

It was Sergeant Clarke. "Clark, its Stu. Are you awake?"

"I am now. I must have slept through my alarm."

"I heard there was another shooting last night."

"Yeah, Mesa had another one. Occurred around 11:30 last night, and the victim is dead."

"Yeah, we heard. You need to get in here right now."

He didn't seem too happy.

As I sat up in bed, my head throbbed from exhaustion. I was too tired to care about supervisory moods. I wasn't too happy, either. At least they weren't up all night.

When I arrived at police headquarters, my partner, Detective Udd, pulled me aside. "Hey, I need to talk to you."

Oh crap! They found out about the bar fight, and that's why they're angry. There was no coming up with an excuse for that. We were just in the wrong place at the wrong time. At least we hadn't picked the fight.

"Stu and the Lieutenant are pissed about last night. I guess they're upset that you didn't notify them about the shooting, and now they think they've got egg on their face."

I was relieved that was all it was.

"Thanks for the heads up," I said. "I already fielded a call from Stu this morning. They're going to have to get over it because we've got a lot of work to do."

"They're a bunch of crybabies when it comes to this. Just watch yourself. I think they think you're holding back information from them on purpose."

"Whatever. I've got too much to do to play games."

I made my way to Sergeant Clarke's office, and Lieutenant Vermeer was in there. He had obviously caught some wrath well because as he gave me a head nod when I walked in. I wasn't going to make any excuses. "OK, what do you want to know?" I asked, of course referring to the case.

"Everything! Since you didn't inform the chain of command about this shooting," Sergeant Clarke said. So much for being thoughtful and not waking everyone.

"Mesa Police said they could handle the case. They didn't need any help from the task force. I asked them three times, and they said they had plenty of people to handle what was going on. I was trying to be thoughtful and not wake everyone up and lose sleep over it, especially since there was nothing we could do."

"All right, well, you still should've called." He wasn't getting over it, and if he wasn't getting over it, then I could only imagine the butt chewing the lieutenant had received. "So, what happened last night?"

"Are we talking about the shooting, the important issue, or are we still talking about the notification protocol?"

I wasn't trying to be a smart a@$, I honestly didn't know.

"The shooting," Sergeant Clarke said. Good, at least we were all on the same page now.

I explained the shooting, that it fit our boys' M.O., and that a 410 shot cup had been found at the scene. Using my notes, I started to talk about the victim.

"You should also know that I talked with Ron Horton last night, and he is willing to come in as a witness and submit to a video-recorded interview. He is more than happy to go on the record as a witness for the State about everything he knows."

"That's good for us then, right?" Lieutenant Vermeer asked.

"Yes, it means he can come out of the shadows and testify in court if his information leads us to the killers."

That was yet to be proved, but it was still our best lead. Only a few of us knew about the ex-employee.

"Sounds to me as if this guy that ATF has been looking for is the same guy that Horton fingered, right?" Sergeant Clarke asked. "Why haven't they found him?"

"He's still just a lead in their arson cases, and they have no idea where he's at. Until I can get some corroboration on what Horton said, it's all moot," I said.

We decided that we needed to get all of the intel that ATF had on this Samuel Dieteman guy. The only way to do that was to meet with ATF and tell them it was time to show all their cards. We agreed that if they refused, our chain of command would be notified, as would all the other task force players, including Mesa and Scottsdale. Political pressure can go both ways.

Just as the meeting broke up, I received a call on my cellphone. It was Ron Horton. "

"Detective, I'm sorry. I don't know what to say. I never meant for anyone else to get hurt."

He had heard about Robin Blasnek and was blaming himself.

"Ron, it's not your fault. There's nothing you or I could've done to stop this."

"I should've given you the cell number quicker. Maybe you guys could have found him and stopped this."

"Ron, if he was responsible, we wouldn't be able to locate him by his phone for days. It requires a lot of background investigation to find someone through phone records."

I was of course simplifying the facts. He didn't need to know anything else at this point.

"All right, Detective. I'm going to find out where he is, and I'm going to get a meeting with him for you guys."

Ron Horton was now on a mission, and I couldn't be happier. He could move in those circles very easily, unlike me, as proven by the previous night's bar incident.

"Thanks, Ron. Let me know the minute you contact him." I closed the phone.

It was time to find Samuel Dieteman.

As I made my way to the command center, Police Spokesman Sergeant Andy Hill was just coming around the corner.

"I just got off the phone with Chuck Trapani of Mesa, he said. "He told me what happened. Is it our guys?"

"I'm positive it is. What's Mesa's response to who's responsible going to be?"

"Right now, they're going to hold off on tying it to the series officially. The press has already made the jump, and my phone and his have been ringing off the hook for comments. Their official response is going to be they're looking into the similarities with the task force. They're also going to release the victim's name soon."

That wasn't going to hold water very long. I was sure the media would be all over Robin Blasnek's friends and relatives, trying to get some insight into why she was out there. I hoped Mesa Police had contacted everyone that needed to be interviewed before the hordes of press got to them.

As soon as I walked into the command center, I saw that Marjorie was already hard at work putting the leads into the computer. She turned to look at me.

"You doing alright?" she asked.

She really had become my mother.

"I don't know yet. I'll tell you when I wake up."

I felt worse than I looked, I'm sure. All the other analysts were looking at me, and I was certain that Marjorie had shared my intuition about the timing of the previous night's shooting.

"Where are we now?" she asked.

"I'm bringing your cronies from ATF over to see if we can't locate this Dieteman guy. I don't know what they know or how hard they've pressed. Have you heard anything that I should know about through unofficial lines of communication?"

"Nope, just that they're coming over here, and they asked if we had any additional information on Dieteman as well. That was from their immediate supervisor."

As I sat, my mind began wandering, and the conversation I'd had with Ron Horton the night before started bothering me. I checked my phone and looked at the times that Ron and I had talked—a little after 5:00 p.m. and a little before 9:00 p.m. Ron had said that Dieteman appeared "preoccupied" and was taking forever to text him back. Those were his words, not mine. Dieteman appeared busy last night. If Dieteman was out hunting, that could have been why he was tied up and not able to meet Horton. It could also be why it was taking him so long to text Ron back.

It was a long-shot guess at best. I grabbed my journal of notes and scribbled down the times of Ron's calls.

I really didn't have time to meet with the ATF/gun squad agents and/or detectives, but I didn't want any more grief from my chain of command. I wasn't going to learn anything more about Samuel Dieteman's whereabouts. It was obvious they had no idea where he was, but seeing what they had done to find him could be interesting.

Detective Smith and the other agents funneled into the hallway that leads to the interview rooms at the Violent Crimes Bureau. The command post was tied up with an executive meeting, whatever that meant, and there was no other place to meet. We pulled chairs out of the interview rooms and gathered in a circle.

The object of the meeting was to find out what ATF had done to locate Sam Dieteman and what more we could do. The case agent was not present, which I thought was a little odd.

Surveillances had been conducted on Dieteman's supposed address on West Elm Street. He was staying with a Jeff, now last name identified as Hausner. They had never seen Dieteman at the apartment/condo complex during any of these surveillances.

They had placed a GPS device on a car driven by Jeff Hausner to see where it would lead them. At this point, besides going to the bar every day after work, Jeff Hausner had never met up with Dieteman. They had conducted stakeouts of the bars that Dieteman was suppose to frequent, all with negative results.

I asked if they had done any follow-ups with friends, drinking buddies, or acquaintances of Dieteman, besides their snitch, and they said not really. They had talked to a couple of people who knew him, but that was it. They didn't want to alert Dieteman that he was a strong lead in the arsons. They had no idea where Dieteman was and no one who could lead them to him, except maybe Ron Horton. And they had a plan for Horton.

They wanted to bring Horton in and pay him as a confidential informant. They laid out how they would handle his C.I. file. They could get him a good chunk of money right away, and that would entice Ron to go to work for them. A guy like Ron could surely use a wad of cash, and nobody would have to know that he was involved. Why, he could even testify federally as a protected witness and never have to show his face in a court of law because they know what can happen to a snitch on the street.

I looked around the group and tried to keep my composure. I knew immediately where this plan had been cooked up, and I knew why. There was no way around this, but I was going to have to burst their bubble and probably the bubble of their supervisors. I was not going to sugarcoat it.

"Well, that sounds like a real, well thought-out plan. What you're talking about doing in any other case is legal and happens quite frequently in federal law enforcement. There's only one problem. I'm not going to let a witness who is willing to testify in court out of his own good conscience be given what could later be construed as a pay-off. It doesn't look good in court, and it looks like money is the motivating factor for the witness to come forward."

They were out of their fu@*en minds!

I let that sink in, and then I continued. "Last night, I met with Ron Horton, and he told me that he's more than willing to come forward and testify, in open court, about what this Dieteman guy told him. There's no reason to muddy a perfectly good, willing witness. He has no problem facing the guy in court, if in fact, Dieteman turns out to be involved. Besides, if Dieteman is involved, there's a huge Silent Witness reward out there that Ron Horton will have for coming forward. So the answer is no! I don't want him to be on anyone's payroll."

Looking at the shocked faces of the agents, I could tell this was not sitting well with them. Ron Horton was their golden goose, their shot at glory and prestige. If his information was good, it was a huge feather in their cap and maybe a stepping stone for some of the agents, not to mention their bosses, to a better pay grade. This didn't go over well at all.

There was nothing else to discuss about Ron Horton. As far as I was concerned, the topic was closed. But in their minds, it wasn't. They were going to have to report back to their bosses that the supposed meal ticket was the property of Phoenix Police and the Random/Serial Shooter Task Force, not ATF. I knew my bosses would back me on this, or at least I thought they would.

I changed subjects and pushed on. It was time to find Dieteman and the discussion turned to his cellphone. A subpoena for his records and a court order for a trap-and-trace device to be placed on Dieteman's phone. It would be up and running by the following day, and then we would have a chance at narrowing down his location.

The meeting was then adjourned. Not one of the agents was even cordial when they left. They were upset, but I didn't care. I wasn't running this task force to nurse their egos or those of their bosses. Get over it, and let's get back to work.

Problem was, they weren't going to get over it. Not yet, and maybe never.

By the time I worked my way back to the CP, the executives had adjourned their top-secret meeting. They were, I assume, talking about the latest Mesa murder. and would probably start to banter about how they could get in the way of the investigators. Marjorie was going over data on the ex-employee, trying to see if there were any possibly related leads.

Detective Donnie Byers made his way in after at least getting a couple of more hours' sleep than I'd gotten. "You look well rested," I cracked.

"Yeah, right. I had to sit outside in the lobby for about twenty minutes while the bigwigs met in here." He looked around. "Geez, Clark, could you guys pick a smaller place for your command center?"

"Yeah, we could have, but a storage closet downstairs was full. At least there aren't any roaches crawling around on the floor here."

"That's true."

Donnie then began to lay out what it was the Mesa Homicide Bureau was doing in reference to the murder of Robin Blasnek. They had dispatched numerous detectives to canvass the surrounding neighborhoods. They were sending investigators to every local business within a six-mile radius looking for any surveillance video that might show the killers. There must have been dozens of businesses in that area. It would be a monumental task.

Since Detective Byers had never been to the command center and had no idea what we as a task force were doing to try to catch these guys, I gave him a crash course. I introduced him to Marjorie, the ATF analyst. He promised he wouldn't hold it against her that she worked for ATF. She then began to explain to him the tip sheets and the database where all the leads were stored. Dozens of notebooks on the shootings sat on the only meeting table.

His boss had been calling him, so after the indoctrination, he called him back. He was wanted back at Mesa to brief some other managers on the status of his investigation. We bid farewell, knowing we'd be getting together soon if anything surfaced.

Just as I sat down and tried to rest my eyes for a minute, Lieutenant Benson walked in. He beelined to Marjorie with a couple of questions. I had been able to avoid him all day in the hope that he would get over my protocol oversight from the night before.

After a few minutes, he walked up to me and said, "I need to see you in my office."

I slowly followed him to his office, and he let me sit down first. He then closed the door.

"I just got off the phone with ATF, and they are very pissed off," he told me. "They think you're keeping things from them. They are threatening to pull their people out of here unless you start to play ball."

I almost started laughing. I should have seen this coming after our meeting. At this point, if they left, the only thing we would lose was their database. They hadn't done anything to help find the shooters. I would miss Marjorie because she kept the command center, what little of it there was, up, running and organized.

Before I had a chance to comment, he laid into me with some theories that had obviously been passed onto him.

"Their ASAC thinks that you are suffering from sleep deprivation. He thinks that you don't know what you're doing. Now, I hear that you're meeting with a C.I. by yourself. Do you know that is a violation of policy?"

I now knew for sure what was going on. ATF didn't like my answer on Ron Horton. They were upset that I didn't let them sign him up. They were going behind my back, and I felt like I was dealing with children. It was time to enlighten the LT a little. I wasn't going to stand by and let ATF sabotage the case for career-climbing enthusiasts.

"LT, I wasn't trying to ignore protocol, or policy, and I'm not hiding anything. Mesa didn't need any help, so I decided to let everyone sleep. There was nothing any of you could've done out there besides stand around. ATF is pissed off about me not letting them sign up Ron Horton and pay him, like they do other snitches. That's what this is all about."

"I understand that, and don't think I don't know what ATF is trying to do. They need a win, and this is the perfect case for them to get one. But you can't do all this by yourself. You've got to share what's going on. I talked to Marjorie, and she tells me that you predicted that the shooters would hit again last night. Is that true?"

"Kinda sorta, I guess. It was just intuition more than anything else."

"See, that's the kind of thing that gets circulated, and it gets turned around and shoved up our asses for not sharing. Damn it, Clark, you have to talk to people. That intuition you have and all your background was the reason I asked you to lead this investigation in the first place."

I thought about that for a moment. I thought about the fact that I could've been wrong. If I had been, would people be calling me an idiot and saying I was careless and clueless? I could see them shoving that up our asses further.

The LT wasn't finished yet.

"You need to watch it, and I want your partner caught up on everything that's going on. God forbid something happens to you, like falling asleep driving home. Where would we be then? At least that way he can step in and take over."

It was ironic that he wouldn't have Detective Jewell come in and run the investigation.

We were finished, but I had learned something valuable, and it had nothing to do with protocol or policy. Everybody who came on board was checking their egos at the door and were willing to work together for the common good of the case, with one exception. I now knew who that was. Lieutenant Benson wasn't fooled by the rhetoric, either.

CHAPTER 37

Technology is a wonderful thing, when used correctly, but it can also be misused.

The Internet has led to unbelievable personal destruction. Numerous perverts surf the Net for children to take advantage of and harm. Because government is sloppy, public records can be scoured for personal information to steal causing a huge jump in identity theft. Search yourself over the computer sometime, and you'll see what I mean. Someone, somewhere, has sold your information to somebody. It's out there, with no control over who uses it, or how they use it. Pornography is everywhere for children to see. And it doesn't matter what filters you place on your PC. Someone else is never as careful.

In police work, however, the Internet has also provided a valuable link to find individuals you could never locate through old policing networks. I now regularly search Facebook and other social networks to try and locate people by their names or nicknames. I find information that never would've been available twenty years ago.

The hunt for Samuel Dieteman had proven to be a little trickier. He didn't have a website or a domain name. He didn't have a personalized profile on any network. Samuel Dieteman was a man who existed by name only—with no current employer, no social services background, no current address, no registered vehicle, just a cellphone. So we would use that.

On the afternoon of August 1st, I was introduced to Agent Mike Westcott of the Immigration and Customs Enforcement, a man dedicated to tracking people through our best friend, technology. Our adventures took us to Mesa, the site of the last two shootings by the Random/Serial Shooters.

Around 6:00 p.m., I received a welcome call. Ron Horton had gotten a hold of Samuel Dieteman. At 7:00 p.m., they would be meeting to have some drinks at a place called the Stardust Lounge, located at 43rd Avenue and Dunlap. No more guessing; the game was afoot.

As over controlling as he was, there were certain things he didn't have control over at all—his ex-girlfriend's manipulation of his daughter's visitation, his airport supervisor actually following up on his unexcused absences, and his partner's previous life and contacts.

Being in control of his accomplice is what made their partnership so unique. He could tell him and show him how to do things, like how to lead a target when shooting so as not to miss, how to deceive clerks and store personnel so as not to get busted for theft, and how to pack a meth pipe to get every last crystal smoked.

But his partner did have a life before he met him, and that life had other people in it, like family and friends. He had met his partner's two daughters a few weeks back when they came to visit from Minnesota. He even took photos of the girls with his partner, standing proud like a dad ought to be. The girls had wanted to spend more time with their dad, but he wouldn't allow that. It was too risky, especially since the girls were staying on the west side of town, where all those shootings had occurred months before.

He didn't entirely trust him, either. Though their killing bonds had tied them to each other, his partner drank too much. He talked constantly when he drank about how worthless he was, how he had no job, no life, and his kids lived out of state. He acted depressed.

He trusted his partner to watch his back for witnesses when they went hunting, but truth be told, he didn't trust him to keep his mouth shut. Drinking and depression make for a very unstable person. He knew that, and that was in essence the reason he moved him into his small one-bedroom apartment. He needed to keep a close eye on him. It was easy to watch his partner with no car and no way to get around but on foot. The few days that he went into work, he made sure that his partner was so liquored or methed up that he would sleep until he got home. He spent so little time at work that those times away from his partner were almost nonexistent, anyway.

Tonight, he had agreed to let the other half of his killing team out for a little R and R, a trip to one of the many dives his accomplice used to frequent. He even agreed to transport him and although he wouldn't accompany him, he would be close by. But that didn't mean he was happy about it. In fact, he was jealous. He was jealous that his partner's old friends would want to get together, have some drinks, and enjoy some laughs. He didn't have friends like that. He had his daughter and his mission: to kill and terrify. That was all he needed. He was pissed that his partner had other needs.

He just didn't understand human nature. This bonding thing with friends and family was completely overrated. He had never felt that way. He didn't care if he ever saw anyone he'd grown up with, and he could take or leave family. In fact, it was his family that had made him the monster he'd become—all the abuse, the neglect, the fighting with siblings. It was little wonder that killing came so easy to him.

He also took women with a grain of salt. They were good for only one thing, sex. Sure, he'd loved women in his life, but when it came right down to it, they had been put on Earth to please him. That's what the Bible had taught him, the Satanic Bible, that is.

He realized that his jealousy of his partner was much deeper than just the fact that he had friends. He was attached to his partner by their crimes, but he wanted him for more than that. He wanted him emotionally and physically. He had been fighting the so-called demons of homosexuality all his life. The truth was that he liked men better, and he liked his partner a lot. He craved sex and had been looking forward to taking advantage of him once he got him moved in.

So this trip to the bar to meet one of his oldest buddies had better just be a get-together of old acquaintances. There better not be any bitches that he tries to take home. In fact, there wouldn't be. He would make sure of that.

He was getting the urge to do something out of frustration. This would be as good a night as any. It had been a couple of days. His partner would be drunk. He had money for meth. Another message would be sent.

His partner wouldn't dare turn him down. Oh, yes, this trip up north might turn out to be all right after all.

<hr/>

The Drug Enforcement Bureau of the Phoenix Police Department is split into several distinct functions. They have street-level enforcement, to go after users and small-time sellers. They have a conspiracy squad to go after mid-level and major traffickers, and they have a clandestine drug lab squad that responds to labs that are discovered in the city or county and in need of specialized cleanup.

The task force had been given the use of the drug lab squad, supervised by an old buddy of mine by the name of Don Sherrard. Don and I actually both had roots back in Wyoming. Don had worked in the small town of Sundance as a cop and coroner, an unusual combination. We used to laugh about how he would patrol by night and then conduct some form of an autopsy by day— not the full-blown kind, of course. Those were shipped to other facilities when violence was involved. But Don handled a drunk found dead or an overdose. He used to say that anyone who was killed by discreet foul play and given to him probably got screwed out of justice.

I arranged to meet and brief Don's unit that would be arriving later. They had been a part of so many surveillances in the Baseline Killer case that they needed to know what and who they were working. Plus, this was surveillance only. No probable cause existed for Dieteman's arrest. We met up a mile away from the bar. Sergeant Sherrard and four of his team were waiting. I looked at my phone, and it read 7:00 p.m.

Just as I was briefing them, word came from one of the surveillance units at the Stardust Lounge that they believed Dieteman had just arrived at the bar. He had been dropped off by a white male who was driving a silver/purple Toyota Camry. They wanted to know what should they to do? Stay with Dieteman, or follow the car?

The teams were split up immediately, and with unbelievable precision, did not lose the car or Dieteman. All radio communication inside the bar would cease, but the car would be tailed, and any real time information passed on to the task force. Detective Udd was standing by at police headquarters to run any and all information through data banks, and he'd then relay it back to the surveillance officers.

Mike and I headed to the Stardust Lounge to help with surveillance. This was going to be complicated. We now had a mobile target with an unknown occupant and Samuel Dieteman in the bar with one of the good guys, Ron Horton. We could not risk losing either of the leads or risk Ron Horton's life if things went bad. We had already decided if we found Dieteman and any vehicle associated with him, we'd place a GPS tracker on the vehicle. That is no easy job in itself. You need a little time and some care so the device isn't located and is stable enough to stay on the vehicle no matter where it goes. Timing was everything. Where was the driver of the car that had dropped off Samuel Dieteman heading, and would there be time to place the GPS?

As he left the parking lot and pulled onto the road, he decided that he could get a little shopping in while his partner played pool and drank. MetroCenter Mall was just a two-mile drive away. That was OK with him, just as long as it didn't turn out to be all night.

As he drove, he dug through some of the papers that he kept stashed in the middle seat compartment. There was a movie he had wanted to see— maybe the DVD store at the mall had a copy of it. He drove with one hand while the other searched the compartment. He had written the correct title down somewhere. He found the small spiral notebook paper with the title: *The Las Vegas Serial Killer*. That's the one! He hoped they still had it in stock, or he could order it.

He had read about the movie in one of the magazines lying around the lunch room at work. It sounded right up his alley. In fact, he could have starred in it. It was about a photographer who killed women in Las Vegas in the 1970s. Heck, he was a photographer, a damn good one. He was killing people too, and damn good at it. He'd been dubbed the Serial Shooter of Phoenix. That was something no one else could claim. Of course, his story was real, and he knew that if he ever got caught, which he figured might happen one day, there would be books and movies about him, too—just like his childhood idol, Charles Starkweather.

He had spent his youth studying Charles. He believed Charles was a man with talent, a man wronged by the system, just like him. Both of them operated out of a hatred for what society had done to them. And just like Charles, he had an accomplice willing to kill. The only difference between him and Charles was that Starkweather was more of a spree killer than a serial killer. But the two came from alarmingly similar backgrounds, their crimes separated by almost forty years.

He had grown up in Omaha, Nebraska, Charles in Lincoln. He had learned that Charles had a speech impediment as a child, and so did he. They both came from large families, although supposedly Charles had never been abused. He didn't buy that one. They both sucked at school and hated it. They were both jokesters, labeled class clowns. He and Charles enjoyed athletics—he loved boxing, and Charles gymnastics. They even shared the same physical build. Charles collected garbage as a sanitation worker. He collected garbage as a janitor. It was as if he had been reincarnated as Starkweather himself.

Most importantly, they both shared a deep hate for those who were born with silver spoons in their mouths. Who were they to get what they wanted just because they were rich? That honor shouldn't be bestowed on people with money, but rather on people with superior willpower. Those who could look someone in the eye and beat their ass down or intimidate a man into peeing his pants in front of a loved one, or hold an entire metro area in fear. That's power. None of the rich could do that.

He'd known, just like Starkweather, he needed an accomplice. Someone to watch his back, maybe even drop a few useless humans along the way. Charles had Caril Ann Fugate, a girlfriend he'd met when she was fourteen years old. His partner was older and wiser. Starkweather killed her parents, and together they'd murdered and robbed their way across Nebraska, finally getting caught just outside Douglas, Wyoming, but not before they had killed eleven people. He was adding to Charlie's total.

He found a spot close to the mall entrance and jumped out of his car. He couldn't remember where the DVD store was, but he had some time. He might even pick up a candle for his apartment. The smell of two grown men living in a one-bedroom apartment was overbearing at times.

As he walked to the front entrance, he never noticed the black Suburban that drove by him or the white van that parked two spots away from his Toyota Camry. Why would he? He was in control, and there was nothing anyone could do about it.

◈

The sliding door on the van opened just as the driver entered the mall. It would take half an hour, tops, to place the GPS device on the car. The detective walked around for a few minutes, making sure no other mall patrons were watching, and then ducked under the car. It was a tight squeeze. He had ruined so many pairs of pants and T-shirts scraping across asphalt and cement over the years that he had lost count—not to mention the grease and oil of leaky vehicles that he had to roll through. But the job had become routine for him. His main concern was always the owner or driver of the car returning abruptly. It would be tough explaining to him why he was under his car with tools and holding a small electronic device. He turned up his portable radio with an earpiece. There were two undercover units with the car's driver. He would hear quickly if the man was coming back to the car.

Sergeant Don Sherrard drove by the Toyota Camry and radioed back the license plate number. Detective Udd was already pulling up the registered owner, Dale Shaun Hausner. It was a 1998 four-door sedan. There was no lien on the vehicle. It came back to an address on East McKellips Road in Mesa.

Just then, one of the undercover units radioed that the driver had left the DVD store in a hurry and was headed toward the mall exit. The GPS wasn't quite in place. Then came a flurry of panicked voices.

"He's heading out. You need to move."

One of the units radioed that he could stall the man for directions once he exited the mall. There was a mad scramble to avoid detection.

"I need another minute, dammit," the detective whispered into his mike.

The GPS device was delicate, but stubborn.

"Somebody pull up to the exit and block his view," a voice yelled.

"He's about thirty seconds from the doors," the unit squawked.

A car squealed toward the entrance. The driver burst from inside the mall.

The detective rolled out from under the Camry and stayed bent down between cars. He darted to his left and took cover behind a pickup. The driver triggered the alarm to the Camry. Everyone stood by in silence, waiting for the confrontation, the detective only one vehicle away, crouched down.

The driver entered the Toyota without looking around or under the carriage. He started the car and slowly pulled away.

Sergeant Sherrard was back on the air.

"Unit is in place and undetected. The car is exiting the mall parking lot."

ICE agent Westcott and I looked at each other, shook our heads, and let out the breath we'd been holding for the last minute. Unbelievable.

The calls of the roving undercover units following the Camry took over the radio. It would be a combination of units circling, doubling back, driving by, and stopping in and around the Hausner Camry. That was, if the car actually belonged to Dale Hausner, and he hadn't lent it to someone, like Jeff Hausner. It was obvious they were related. We just had to identify the driver.

The driver of the Camry pulled into the parking lot of the Stardust Lounge. We were parked right off the main entrance to the bar. It was dusk, but I could clearly see the vehicle as it slowly pulled into the lot. The car was maybe fifty feet from me. Our windows were pitch black with tinting. A chill went up my back.

The car that Joseph Roberts had seen seconds before he was shot, the car seen on the ADEQ video surveillance camera downtown, and the car that victim Ashley Armenta had described almost to a T motored slowly past me. It looked silver in the dusk light, but as it moved under the parking lot lights, it appeared to change colors to a light blue or even a purple color.

I laid my head back against the headrest. All the cases came rushing back to me. There were too many coincidences. Dieteman's admissions to Ron Horton, the described car, and two guys together at the same time. What were the chances of that?

Horton was in the bar with Samuel Dieteman, and the driver now sat in the parking lot, the car turned off. Then, the eye closest to the bar said that Dieteman had left. I could see him walking toward the Camry. He was a big guy, and he ambled as he walked, slightly side to side, not like a person with nothing but time on his hands.

He approached the Camry smoking a cigarette and then bent over and into the open front passenger window. He was engaged in a conversation with the driver. He leaned in for a minute or two, then opened the door, and sat down. He dumped the cigarette. There was obviously no smoking in the car. I could see his feet still sitting on the asphalt of the parking lot.

Twenty minutes later, Samuel Dieteman stood up, closed the passenger door, and stretched his arms above his head. He bent down and peered again into the interior of the car. A few more words were spoken, and then he began to walk back towards the bar.

The driver of the car started the engine, and I saw the rear taillights activated. The backing lights came on, and he began to pull out from the parking space. I notified everyone that the car was exiting. By this time, there were four other units outside the bar in undercover cars. Three detectives would stay inside the bar to keep an eye on Sammy.

All the UC units began to make their way out of the parking lot using different exits. A detective back at headquarters would give real-time GPS tracking directions. If, for some reason, the driver was alerted to our presence, the GPS device would track him.

The Stardust bar was only a few miles from the freeway. The Camry motored toward it. But as the car rumbled south on I-17 and then west onto the I-10 inter-loop, a strange thing occurred. It exited the freeway at 7th Avenue. We, of course, followed. The car had gotten off a freeway that could have taken it all the way to Mesa and instead had taken a path to downtown Phoenix.

There was no reason to believe the roving surveillance had been burned. So, we moved right behind the Camry. "What the hell is he doing or where the hell is he going?" The Camry turned left onto Adams Street. *He was driving right behind Phoenix Police Headquarters.* What the hell is he going to do, turn himself in? There was hushed silence over the radio as the GPS monitor voiced the route.

He made his way to Van Buren Street and stopped at the light. The driver, ever conscious, turned on his right turn signal to make the turn to go east on Van Buren.

I sat back and realized what was happening. Van Buren had been the scene of at least five shootings, and the driver was scouting humans. I checked my cellphone. The time was approximately 8:40 p.m., too early for any shooting. The GPS monitor continued to voice speed and direction.

When the Camry got to 52nd Street and Van Buren, it jumped onto the Loop 202 freeway heading east, a direct route into the East Valley containing the cities of Scottsdale, Mesa, Chandler, and Gilbert. We headed back to Phoenix headquarters.

I thanked Mike for his help, and as fast as I could, scurried up the back stairs to the Violent Crime Bureau in search of Detective Udd. I found him at his desk monitoring the radio.

"Here's your packet on Dale Hausner. We've still got two units inside the bar with Dieteman and Horton. There are two more units outside in case they leave. One of the unit's text messaged that Horton and Dieteman are playing pool. ATF is apparently out at the saloon, also."

Sergeant Clarke came up to the desk and chimed in. "I guess they have three units out there. Nobody knew that until a few minutes ago."

"Well, it would be nice if they let someone know," Detective Udd snapped.

I began to look through the folder marked *Dale Hausner*. There was an MVD photo from 2004, and an insignificant rap sheet—mostly reports from him as a victim of property crimes and as a suspect in some petty fights and disorderly conducts. There was an arrest for a robbery back in 1991, but it obviously had never been filed.

His driver's license and car registration showed the same East McKellips Road address in Mesa, an apartment. Without Lisa Ruggeri, my background analyst, any further information on Mr. Dale Hausner would have to wait. Besides, the night was just getting started.

The laughs and Captain Morgan flowed easily between the two friends inside the Stardust Lounge. As in any bar, you can find yourself a money game around the pool table, if you look hard enough. Ron and Sammy would take on all bets, as long as the game involved no more than a $20.00 wager. No high-stakes pool here, just enough to pay for all the rounds, with tips to the waitresses. Maybe they'd pocket a few dollars when all was said and done. Sammy missed the west side with its seedy bars, biker mentality, and trampy women. He felt at ease for the first time in a long time.

The thirty-inch television sat just above their heads, mounted to the wall behind the bar. There was little in sports on at 10:00 p.m., so a local channel aired the news. The lead story was, of course, none other than the Serial Shooter. Under the watchful eyes of Detectives Travis Bird and Johnny Chavez, Sammy Dieteman stood still and began to carefully watch and listen to the newscast. He placed his arms behind his back and interlaced his fingers as if to study the broadcast, as if he were admiring a fine piece of art. Horton also took note. He, too, watched the newscast.

"Somebody better catch those guys," Sammy said pointing toward the screen. "It's getting dangerous out there." Ron Horton knew exactly what Sammy meant. Not just a guy, but guys. He wondered if anyone else in the bar had overheard the comment.

After the pigeons at the pool table had run out, Ron and Sammy decided to go kick up their heels at one of the other saloons on the west side. The next stop would be Stingers, just a few minutes ride from the Stardust.

Sammy had arranged with Ron to get a ride home that night. It was during this conversation that Ron learned Sammy wasn't living in Scottsdale, but in Mesa. What he didn't know was that he had a roommate, the one that Ron hadn't seen tonight, the one that had dropped him off at the bar, the one that he constantly texted all night.

Ron couldn't stand it any longer. "Who the fu*# are you texting so much? Some chick, I hope."

"Nah, I wish," Sammy replied.

Stingers was dead, as was customary during the week, so it would be just a one-drink stop. After talking briefly and determining that they had some money in their pockets, they decided that their night shouldn't end there. A trip to the Indian casino was just what the doctor ordered.

As Ron and Sammy headed south toward the Gila River Indian Community, it was confirmed that the driver of the car was Dale Hausner. He had stopped at the apartment complex located at East McKellips Road, and a physical description was broadcast about the lone white male driver. The following day, we would verify this information through the apartment leasing office to see, if in fact, Dale Hausner lived in the apartment. We already knew what the answer would be.

It took about twenty minutes for Ron to navigate the thirty miles to the Gila River Casino. He drove like a bat out of hell. After all, how often do you get to drive as fast as you want without fear of being ticketed when the cops are following you? He smiled to himself as he pushed the truck's speedometer close to ninety miles per hour.

Ron knew that Sammy was involved, but for the life of him could not figure out who he was texting all night.

"I'm going to take that phone and throw it out the fu#&en window if you don't get your head out of that som' bitch."

Ron was trying to make light of what seemed like obsessive behavior.

Sammy just smiled and stated, "I have to check in with my mom a lot, you know."

That was it in a nutshell. Although it wasn't his biological mother he was checking in with, that's what it felt like. His partner was paranoid … and for good reason.

◈

With Ron Horton, Sammy Dieteman and seven undercover units circling about the casino, we at the command center could sit back and take a break … or so we thought.

A little after 1:00 a.m., the driver of the Toyota Camry, a person believed to be Dale Hausner, exited his apartment. He walked to the car, hit the alarm button, climbed in, and started the car up. At the time, there was only one unit at the apartment complex, Detective Brian Benson. He radioed the other units that the Camry was leaving the McKellips address. Detective Udd and I looked at each other.

"Where the hell is he going at this hour?" I asked. I began to get a sick feeling in my gut.

The monitor of the GPS again began to call out speed and direction. Dale Hausner was heading onto the Indian reservation and moving toward the casino. He parked his car a good quarter mile away from the front doors.

Inside the casino, Ron had lost track of Sammy. He received a text message and was told not to worry. He could leave, if he wanted.

Ron called and said, "You better not lose him."

That was the least of my concerns.

UC radio broadcasts of the surveillance of Dieteman and now Dale Hausner showed them hooking up. At the Camry, one of the UC units saw the trunk open. Both men were staring into the trunk. Although no one could say for sure what was removed, Sammy took what appeared to be an item out of the trunk and placed it in the backseat.

At this point, it could be something, or it could be nothing. If they headed home and went to bed, it was nothing. But if they didn't, this would be the longest night in my police career.

With GPS tracking, numerous undercover units in UC vehicles, and all the important agents of the task force listening, the rolling surveillance of Sammy Dieteman and Dale Hausner commenced.

The undercover units were the best that the task force could offer up— drug enforcement investigators who conducted these types of surveillances for a living. That was the crux of their job. There had been some discussion that, if and when we found the killers, that might be a time to call in SWAT officers. But the drug guys were better suited for the job at hand.

"The vehicle is eastbound on Wild Horse Pass Boulevard," the GPS monitor called out.

The other UC units verified that the two were leaving the grounds of the Indian Casino.

"Westbound on the I-10 Freeway," the monitor said.

That would be the quickest way back to Hausner's apartment, I thought to myself.

"They are now eastbound on the US 60 approaching Rural Road. Speed is sixty miles per hour."

Four roving units in and around the car at all times, switching leads and followers. The other units were on side streets just off the freeway, but traveling in the same direction.

"OK, he exited the 60 and appears to have stopped," confirmed the closest unit. "He is now heading south on Country Club Road."

That was going the opposite way of his apartment. They weren't going home. A light rain began to fall.

My phone rang, and it was Lieutenant Brent Vermeer. "Clark, what the hell are these guys doing?"

At that point it had only been about forty minutes into the rolling surveillance.

"I don't know. They could be cruising around to try and score dope. I don't think they're lost. Sh@# Brent, I just don't know."

I looked at my partner who shrugged his shoulders.

An hour into the surveillance and these guys were driving in circles around the city of Gilbert. I cussed to myself and prayed, "Don't let them gun anyone down while we're watching them."

I radioed, "Keep someone on their ass at all times!"

The Toyota Camry moved out of Gilbert and into Chandler, my hometown. I looked at my partner, and he read my mind. Within seconds, I ran from police headquarters, and drove like a madman from downtown Phoenix.

The UC units, after about the first hour, also realized the dangerousness of the situation. They had been following targets in both of the serial killer investigations. I could hear the tension in the voices over the air.

"Back off. Whoever is in the Suburban, you're too close!"

"Watch out! It looks like they're stopping," another unit yelled into the mike.

Detective Bryan Benson was one of the units following the car. He thought he was going to puke on his dashboard. He realized that these could be the

Serial Shooters, based solely on their driving behaviors. He and one of the other UC units pulled up to each other and began to speak.

"I'm not going to let anyone get shot, fu*# that," Benson yelled. "What the hell are we going to do?"

The seriousness of the situation weighed in on them.

It was a daunting task. No one had ever been prepared for this type of scenario. Stay close enough so they don't shoot anyone, but don't give yourself away.

"If a gun comes out, ram em," one of the supervisors voiced.

I listened intently as I flew down the highway en route to Chandler. One of the scariest thoughts crossed my mind as my speed gauge pushed a hundred MPH. What if one of my neighbors couldn't sleep and was out walking? What if one of the people whose kids go to the same school mine do decided to exercise early this morning? Every horrible scenario came rushing to me, and I knew who would be blamed if anything went wrong. It was 2:40 a.m. They had been at it for well over an hour and a half.

Detective Bryan Benson and his partners geared up for a shootout. Sergeant Sherrard and his team donned their bulletproof vests, something that rarely occurred for these guys.

"They're slowing down," one of the units yelled.

They could see a pedestrian walking on the side of the street. The closest unit bolted up right on the bumper of the Camry. He saw no gun coming out of the window as it passed the pedestrian, who walked without a care in the world.

Detective Benson snapped. Two surveillance cars back from the target car he pulled to the side of the road and began to yell at the pedestrian, "Get the fu#@ out of here. Get to your home! There's a sniper out here!"

The pedestrian looked at him like he was crazy. From a distance, with his full beard and undercover look, he could easily be mistaken for one of the band members of ZZ Top. Who the hell was going to take him seriously? He looked like a nut.

The high intensity surveillance continued. The GPS monitor called out directions. The UC units barreled down on the car as it slowed in the roadway. All of us chewed the hell out of our fingernails, trying to figure out a way to stop whatever was going to happen. The Camry moved into Mesa, Tempe, back to Gilbert, and then Chandler.

At around 3:45 a.m., the Toyota Camry took a left turn from Gilbert Road onto McKellips Drive. After a stop at a McDonald's drive-thru, the car eased back into the apartment complex from whence it came.

Detective Travis Bird had already beaten them to the parking lot, however. He had been able to position himself behind some shrubbery and hunkered down. He had ascertained the car's assigned parking location and sat a mere forty feet from the car as it pulled to a stop.

The occupants remained in the car for a brief moment as the engine was turned off.

The night had started out to be rather promising. He had hoped to put another notch on his belt, but it just wasn't in the cards. Tuesdays had been very good for him over the last sixteen months. Even with all the media attention, there were still those fools out there that just wouldn't obey the warnings.

As he parked, he looked over at his partner. He was disgusted with him. There had been a couple of opportunities for his partner to get off a shot, but he was too slow. They could have really sent a message if Sam would have shot the two kids riding on the bike. Could you imagine those headlines? "Two youths gunned down as they pedaled home; Serial Shooter doubles up."

"They did it again," he thought to himself.

But it was not to be. He began to worry about his partner. His accuracy had sucked lately, missing the chick on 44th Street from just a few feet. How he didn't cut her in half was beyond him. He wondered if his partner had lost the stomach to do what was right, what was necessary, for the good of mankind. It was too bad those kids weren't on his side of the car.

As he turned off the engine, Dale Hausner sat and pouted for a few seconds about what might have been. Samuel Dieteman sat in the front passenger seat, looking pathetic.

"You know, you got to be quicker," Dale said.

He wanted to chew his ass, but what good would that do? He had enough self-esteem problems as it was.

Before Sam had a chance to answer, Dale exited the Camry. He stood outside the driver's door for a brief moment. Sam then slowly got out, but not before he removed the black duffle bag with their prized possession. Dale waited for him to remove the item, then hit the door locks and set the car's alarm.

Samuel Dieteman knew that he had missed an opportunity, and he knew that Dale wasn't too happy about it. But it wasn't his entire fault. The weather sucked, too. It was hard to do anything in this rain.

Sam placed the bag on the top of the car and gently stroked it, like a beloved owner would stroke his pet. As Dale watched him, he decided to give some words of encouragement.

"There just wasn't a whole lot of losers out tonight, was there?" Dale asked.

"Nope. Probably had something to do with the rain," Sammy replied. Both of them looked up to the sky. There was nothing else to say. If they had, Detective Bird would have heard them as he squatted just a few feet away.

CHAPTER 38

The meetings would begin as early as 8:00 a.m. Lieutenant Benson had been summoned upstairs to meet with the chiefs and brief them on what happened last night and early this morning.

It would not be pleasant. The phone had been ringing that morning, and there was dissension in the task force. A certain agency did not like the way the surveillance had gone. This same agency did not like the way the investigation was being handled and certainly did not like the way Detective Clark Schwartzkopf was leading the investigation.

In an attempted coup, The Bureau of Alcohol, Tobacco, Firearms, and Explosives dropped a bomb on the task force. They were going to file a complaint of misconduct against me. Although I would not find out until later about the misconduct complaint, they once again threatened to pull their teams out of both serial investigations unless I was removed as case agent and lead investigator. They had somebody else in mind to lead.

The move came out of desperation and lack of professionalism. One boss believed they were being left out of the investigation, cast aside as meaningless analysts. Unfortunately, that was the reality of the situation. Extremely upset, ATF felt they had the power to threaten both investigations and decided to vent their anger at me. I was the most vulnerable person since I sat lowest on the chain. Even though I knew the case backwards and forwards, had personally investigated two-thirds of the cases, and had assembled the backbone of the investigation, ATF wanted me removed.

The complaint caught everyone off guard. Lieutenant Benson didn't buy it, and he told them so. If what they claimed was true, there had clearly been no malice on my part to carry out misconduct. But the ASAC was insistent, and he had the backing of his entire office, he claimed. Everyone in my immediate chain of command knew what the motives were for the removal of me as case agent. It was a typical federal law enforcement power play.

When I arrived at work, I was summoned to a meeting. The bosses had decided to brief the local prosecuting agency on what had transpired so far and to get any other ideas as to what may be needed once the suspects were arrested for a successful prosecution. The local prosecuting agency was the Maricopa County Attorney's Office.

The MCAO, as it was commonly called, handles all felony cases in Maricopa County. They have criminal divisions to prosecute all types of crime from homicides to property crimes. Anything that could result in a defendant being sentenced to prison was sent to the MCAO.

At this meeting, I was introduced to Deputy County Attorney Vince Imbordino. I had never had a case prosecuted by Mr. Imbordino, but his reputation had preceded him.

Vince had been with the county as a prosecutor for over thirty years. He spent most of his time working in child crimes and homicide. He had tried numerous homicide cases and was considered one of the best legal minds in the state. Although no one had ever prosecuted a case of this magnitude, I was confident that Vince Imbordino would be just the experienced counselor this case would need.

When we met, I briefed Vince about what had been gathered thus far. I told him how we got onto Samuel Dieteman through Ron Horton. Samuel Dieteman had now led us to a Dale Hausner, and I proceeded to tell him about the events of last night and the early hours of this morning.

We discussed in-depth the lack of witnesses in all the cases, and that not one victim could identify the shooters. Ron Horton was a first person hearsay witness to Samuel Dieteman admitting his involvement, and that was it. I told him how ATF wanted to pay Ron as an informant, and he agreed that would be hugely detrimental to the case. At least we agreed on that.

Vince was befuddled with the lack of any proof in the case. After an hour, Vince looked at me, and I will never forget what he said. "You don't have a case, do you?" It was more of a statement than a question.

He was, of course, right. As I had said all along, Ron Horton wasn't enough nor was the surveillance last night. It was a start, but clearly well below the threshold of probable cause to effect an arrest. We would need more, a lot more, to be able to convict the two shooters of multiple murders and attempted murders. Right now we only had statements by Samuel Dieteman. We had nothing on Dale Hausner.

As the meeting ended, Lieutenant Benson came up to me and told me he needed to speak to me. We went to the commander's office, and he closed the door.

"What did the county attorney have to say?" he asked.

"Same thing I've been saying all along. We don't have a case yet. We need a lot more intelligence and evidence if we plan to move on the two guys we followed last night. This is just the beginning," I said.

Lieutenant Benson then laid out ATF's threats. I knew that me shutting down their use of Ron Horton as a paid informant had pissed them off, but more than that, they were used to people kissing their ass. I didn't do that, and neither had any of the other local cops involved.

But there was more. By me briefing them about what could occur if the suspects were located, a dangerous high stakes surveillance, it had come home to roost last night. Nobody got killed, but that didn't sit well with them because they didn't understand the nature of this case, its lack of evidence, or identification problems. To them, it was black and white. Ron Horton was the key, not the process.

After listening, I simply asked, "What's their complaint? I'm a little confused."

"I don't know exactly. It has yet to be written up and submitted. It was just voiced to our chief's office."

I wanted to laugh, but thought better of it. It was no laughing matter.

"I see. So there's a complaint about something I've done, we don't know what it is yet, but they want me removed. Just me, nobody else?" Lieutenant Benson knew where I was going.

"The decision sits with the chief, I've been told," he said. "We should hear something soon. In the meantime, I am not removing you. I just want you to fall back and observe what's going on. Don't say anything to anyone. Keep a low profile, and I will battle to keep this going in the right direction, your direction."

I was being neutered. I understood him loud and clear. But it would be a little tough to sit on the bench with my hands under my butt while the investigation was hijacked. In fact, I wasn't going to allow that to happen. I just had to be coy. Two could play at this game.

Turns out, nobody figured I would go quietly.

"I need to talk to you for a minute, Marjorie," I said.

Together we walked back to the command center.

"A boss over at ATF has threatened to file a misconduct complaint against me," I told her. "I have a pretty good idea what it's about, but there is nothing in writing as of yet." I paused for a moment. "I'm not sure how long I'm going to be in charge of this investigation, and they haven't named a replacement yet."

Marjorie looked like she had been punched in the gut. Her mouth dropped open, and she was visibly upset.

"What? I don't understand."

"Nobody does yet, but you need to work hand in hand if there is a replacement. They're going to need to get up to speed quickly on all the major targets out there currently under investigation because I'm not sure anyone does. Plus, you're going to have to show them the database, how and where the leads are kept. You'll also need to keep them abreast of what the analysts are running, all the books and what they contain."

We now knew from the murder of Robin Blasnek that the ex-cop wasn't involved. In that night's surveillance, he had stayed home, never leaving his residence. At least she didn't have to deal with that hot potato any longer. It also freed up some bodies.

She was shell-shocked. She knew that bringing on someone would be difficult this late in the game. I reassured her that she could pull it off, even if it turned out that our two main leads are involved. She would have to act quickly. I was also sure that this nugget would quickly get back to her chain.

As I left the command center, I was asked to attend a briefing of an SAU/SWAT intelligence team. They, too, had heard what happened last night, and they needed a threat assessment on the two guys who had been cruising around the southeast valley. They would, of course, want to know everything about them, but I was told to lay low. How I was supposed to do that and keep everybody well informed was beyond me. So I looked at it this way. Until I was officially removed as case agent, I was still the lead investigator, and the lead investigator controls the information and the direction of the investigation.

The meeting was held in the chief's conference room. I didn't recognize any of the SWAT guys, but I did recognize Lieutenant Vince Piano of our Drug

Enforcement Bureau. His guys had done an excellent job of tailing Dieteman and Hausner last night, and he wanted to put in his two cents worth.

The meeting started with a briefing of the cops on the facts of the case. I noticed an ATF supervisor was present. I made sure to emphasize the fact that no probable cause existed, yet. The focus was on how to stop an attack. Different sceneries were brought up about how to deploy a team in a dignitary type move that could actually prevent the loss of innocent human life. Ideas were bantered around about how the Secret Service uses cars and human shields to protect VIPs and politicians. None of them sounded remotely possible, especially since these shootings can occur in a matter of seconds.

The angst that last night's surveillance caused was evident. We, being the police, would not sit idly by and let these two gun down someone in front of our very eyes. He emphasized this because ATF was present, I'm sure of it. That also confirmed to me at least one part of their complaint against me.

As I sat and listened to the talk, an idea popped into my head. In order to make this case, besides witnessing them shoot or kill someone, we were going to need more of what we had last night from Detective Bird—conversation. Ron Horton was just the start. We needed to get more human intel from these two.

Numerous things began to run through my mind. Could we introduce someone into the mix, maybe even Horton, someone they could trust? Could we plant a bug or some type of listening device to monitor their conversations with Ron? Ron had already said that he would do what needed to be done. I'm sure he would wear a wire.

The only trouble was, we didn't have a lot of time. They had gone out last night just two days after the murder of Robin Blasnek. They were stepping up their time table. We might not have days to put something together, and re-introducing Horton right away could seem fishy. I mean, he might get Samuel Dieteman to say something again, but we needed his partner as well. As the meeting ended, I grabbed Lieutenant Piano for a brief moment.

"You got a second, Lieutenant?" I asked.

"You bet, Clark. What's up?"

"I'm just thinking outside the box. Is there any way to get some listening devices used on these guys? I know that a full-blown wiretap is out of the question, but is there something that your guys have used in the past that we might be able to deploy to get some intel here?"

I know it sounded like a stupid question, but it wasn't my area of expertise. Lieutenant Piano thought for a moment, then responded.

"I don't know Clark, but we've got a conspiracy squad that dedicates themselves to doing those types of investigations. Let me check with them, and I'll have them contact you. Maybe they can come up with something."

"Thanks, Lieutenant, I appreciate the help. Oh, and by the way, your guys did a fantastic job last night under extreme duress."

"I'll let them know, thanks."

He headed out of the conference room.

And so the seed was planted. It was a long shot, but what the hell could it hurt? Maybe the guys in drug enforcement had some other ideas.

Besides, laying low wasn't my style.

<hr/>

As afternoon rolled around and I looked at the news headlines on my computer at my desk, I felt a gentle tap on my shoulder. Detective Rich Label was now standing in my cubicle space.

Rich and I had met years ago, but I hadn't seen him in a stretch. I wasn't even sure why he was bothering me. I offered him a chair from one of the other cubicles, and he sat down and pulled it up close.

"Hey, Lieutenant Piano came to me and asked me to talk to you. I hear you're knee-deep in it. Sorry to bother you. He thought we might be able to help."

"Bother me, hell, I asked for assistance. Rich, I don't know if you can help me or not. Let me tell you what I've got, and you tell me."

I laid out the case of the task force, and what information we had gathered on the two top leads. I told him everything.

After I finished explaining the case for the two hundredth time, Rich just looked at me and kind of shook his head.

"Clark, you just don't have enough PC for a wiretap. I mean, we follow and gather intel for months on our wires. We do everything we can investigatively, which is required by law, before we can even put together a court order to ask for a wire. We check and crosscheck sources, follow-ups, and monitor to make one of these cases. You guys have one night, and some conversations of a third party. Sorry dude, I just don't see it."

It was worth a shot. But before I got to delve into Ron Horton wearing a wire, Detective Rich Label stopped our conversation. It looked as though he was deep in thought, and a light bulb had just exploded in his mind.

"Clark, let me check on something. I just thought of something, but I'm going to have to contact the county attorney's office. I assume you're going to be here today?" he asked.

"Of course, all day, every day," I responded.

"Let me get back to you," Rich said.

He then walked away.

As Rich left, I found Detective Udd in the hallway, and before I had a chance to say anything, he let go with some choice words.

"I just came from Stu's office. What the fu#@ is going on? He said some bullshit about ATF filing a complaint, and that they may have to remove you. What the fu*# is that all about?"

I could tell he was pissed enough for both of us.

I tried to calm him down.

"Don't worry about it. One way or the other, it'll work."

As I was just getting Darren calmed down, my cellphone went off. It was Detective Pete Salazar from Scottsdale.

"Hey, Clark, I just got a phone call, and Sergeant Clarke asked me if I could conduct interviews on all your cases, if I had to. What the hell is going on over there?"

Now I had two people to calm down.

"Pete, I don't know yet. Where are you at?"

"I'm over at my office. I told Sergeant Clarke that there was no fu@#ing way I could take over all your cases. There were too many. What the hell are they thinking?"

"Doesn't matter, Pete, just get over here. Nothing is in stone yet. But you and Darren need to be prepared because this is a political hot potato."

I turned my attention back to my partner.

"I need you to start an affidavit for a search warrant on the Hausner apartment, car, and anything else we find. Fill in as much information as you can, and hopefully we can come up with some idea of how to get enough PC on these guys to hit them and their apartment."

"You got it."

Detective Udd was one of the best writers of paper I knew. He had a knack for being able to spell things out clearly and concisely, even a big a mess as this case.

I was told there was another meeting scheduled in two hours. That was the fourth one today. No wonder managers never get anything done. They're always in meetings.

As full as my plate was, I had an ace in my pocket that I didn't even know anything about. Detective Rich Label was inquiring into my predicament. He was asking questions of the one person who might just be able to save the day—a person with so much knowledge on wiretaps that she was considered the top person in the state.

Her name was Laura Reckart, and she was an attorney at MCAO. Together, she and Detective Label would come up with something extraordinary. Something I had never even heard of. A little known statute that up until this time had been used so rarely that most legal scholars didn't even know it existed.

But Deputy County Attorney Laura Reckart did. And it might just work.

◈

Buried in the *Arizona Criminal Manual* is an obscure statute dealing with eavesdropping and communications. This particular chapter of criminal law deals with the most common type of eavesdropping: pen registers, trap and traces, and a wiretap. Yet, one of the statutes explicitly lays out the means to eavesdrop on suspects without the cumbersome gathering of months of intelligence. It is simply called an Emergency Interception.

The statute states that *not withstanding any other provision of this chapter, if the Attorney General or a County Attorney reasonably determines that an emergency situation exists involving immediate danger of death or serious physical injury to any person, and that such death or serious injury may be averted by interception of wire, electronic, or oral communication before an order authorizing such interception can be obtained, said authority may authorize a peace officer or law enforcement agency to intercept such wire, electronic, or oral communication.*

But there was a catch. The emergency order can only be in place, if granted, for forty-eight hours. Before that forty-eight hour period is over, the law enforcement agency must obtain an Ex Parte order for the interception. That would be the grueling, detailed order that all wiretaps fall under.

There were two problems. One, we had to convince the County Attorney that the guys targeted for this emergency wire were our killers, and secondly, we had to get listening devices in place quickly in Hausner's car and in the apartment.

It was a daunting task. Detective Rich Label and Deputy County Attorney Laura Reckart would brainstorm the information and put it suitably into an affidavit that a Superior Court Judge would read and have to sign. Detective Udd was sent to the County Attorney's Office to brief Andrew Thomas, the elected Maricopa County Attorney. I had given him all my notes, papers, everything that he would need to convince Mr. Thomas that an emergency truly existed. That was the easy part.

Everyone knew that trying to prevent the killing of any other citizens was truly an emergency situation. An emergency interception was clearly the route to go. But it was convincing a judge that Samuel Dieteman and Dale Hausner were the two responsible for all the shootings that would be difficult.

Another meeting with all the major players was set for 5:00 p.m. ATF brought their whole contingency of supervisors, including the ASAC that wanted me removed as case agent. I just quietly sat and listened as the people who knew the least about the case bantered back and forth about what to do. Three of the detectives assigned to the task force were in attendance. It was clear that ATF would not stand for any more surveillances of the two suspects. Ron Horton was all we needed. Even though he had never seen Samuel Dieteman with a shotgun, never witnessed him shooting anyone, never caught him with as much as a water pistol, his words alone, along with the driving around last night, would carry this case through a successful prosecution.

Since my position was tenuous because of ATF's supposed misconduct complaint, I was not asked my opinion on whether or not sufficient probable cause existed to arrest Dieteman and Hausner. It was ATF's job to make their case, and they thought they had done so. With just two simple pieces of a pie so large that no one in the room actually knew the size of it, arrests should be imminent, according to them.

As everyone sat quietly for a moment, one of Phoenix's chiefs spoke up and asked if the investigators had anything to add. He looked straight at me. I looked straight at Lieutenant Benson, who had been sitting idly by and had not commented on the proceedings either. He gave me a look like *watch what you say*.

"We don't have enough to pick these guys up. The case is too large to risk losing because we hit the panic button over their traversing the city last night. Ron Horton's information is good only if we can prove it through direct evidence, not hearsay."

Chief Kevin Robinson spoke first.

"We can't let these guys kill anyone else. We can't let them go out again like that and cruise around targeting innocent citizens. We just can't do that."

"I understand, but that doesn't make the case stronger. Right now, we're trying to get some court orders. I suggest we let that play out and see where it leads us."

You could have heard a pin drop. I could see the disgust in the face of the ASAC. I said what needed to be said. It would be the last time I would address this crowd. One of the ATF supervisors then came up with the idea of arresting Dieteman on his outstanding misdemeanor warrant. That would take him off the street, and he could be questioned about the shootings.

Detective Donnie Byers of Mesa Police, the lead investigator of the Robin Blasnek shooting, chimed in. "What if he doesn't confess? What if he says he doesn't know what you're talking about? What if he doesn't know what you're talking about? As I see it, he has only talked about one murder, a possible murder in Scottsdale. And we don't even know if that is the one he was bragging about." He paused for a second, and then continued. "I'm with Clark. We're way short of where we need to be from my chair. I don't have anything to connect these guys to the murder of Robin Blasnek, and it sounds like Clark doesn't have these guys for all the dozens of cases he has either. We should sit and reassess before moving on these guys."

As the meeting wore on, I received a phone call from Detective Travis Bird. He was sitting on Hausner's apartment. Samuel Dieteman had carried a black plastic trash bag to the closest dumpster and thrown it away. Both Dieteman and Hausner then left in Dale's car. Surveillance units were following their every move. Detective Bird had retrieved the now common garbage.

"Get your ass down here right now," I said.

"Already on my way."

Someone else in the meeting got the heads up on the newly discovered evidence. Although no one was sure what it was, the arguing again centered on making the arrests of these two. That was before I even had a chance to examine the garbage. I guess the case agents, the only ones with homicide experience, weren't enough to placate some. It was evident that pressure was mounting to make arrests.

The black trash bag was a standard lawn garbage bag with no tie. Detective Bird said that it was the only black trash bag in the dumpster.

As I opened the bag, the first thing I saw was the Valley section from the *Arizona Republic*, dated June 21st, 2006. That would be the next-day edition, printed right after the shootings of Fredric Sena and Tony Long. There was nothing cut out from the paper, and I didn't recall any articles about the shootings being printed.

The rest of the contents were carefully removed and placed on a table covered with butcher paper. Most of it was household trash. A sealed, red Marlboro Cigarette envelope showed the name "Dale Hausner" in the address box.

Also, neatly folded in four squares was what appeared to be a white sheet of paper. I carefully unfolded it. The map was a Metropolitan Phoenix Area map, twenty-four by thirty inches in size. On it, I counted twelve markings in both blue and red felt markers: eight and four respectively. One spot was very close to where the murder of Claudia Gutierrez-Cruz took place. The spot where James Hodge was shot was marked dead on, as was Fredric Sena's location at the liquor store.

What I found most significant was a blue line that had been drawn on the map. This line extended from about 20th Street to the 202 Freeway, right along Van Buren. It was obvious that the only spots marked were recent shootings, i.e., 2006. There was nothing marked on the downtown area where Jose Ortiz and Marco Carrillo had been murdered, along with Timothy Tordai's shooting. There were a few marks on the west side of town, but none marking the location of David Estrada's murder in Tolleson.

Then there was a mark located just off the I-17 Freeway and Bethany Home Road. I knew of no shootings in that area. Was that a mistake? Did they mark a wrong spot, or did we miss one of the shootings? This map and its contents clearly showed that someone had been following the Serial Shooter series. It was a huge piece of evidence. But evidence of what?

As I continued through the trash, I noticed a can of Cherry Vanilla Dr. Pepper. A rattle from inside caught my attention. I could see a shiny object which appeared to be metallic. I turned the can upside down, and the object fell toward the mouth of the can.

With gloved hands, I pulled the plastic object out of the can. It was a shotgun shell casing, 410 to be exact. The markings on the shell read *Winchester Super Max, 410, 3 inch, 4 shot.* The same type of ammunition used in the last two Mesa shootings.

It was a good thing most of the trash bag was empty because it made it easier to find several torn pieces of paper, all from the same source. They were ripped into five pieces. When placed together they read; *Robin Blasnek, 7-30-06, 1120 pm*, written in red ink. The last murder victim's name, date, and time of her shooting.

This was unusual, and clearly could be considered circumstantial evidence, just like the map and the shotgun shell. But again I asked myself, evidence of what?

Numerous people were following this and the BLK case. They watched and read everything they could get their hands on about these cases, much like experts followed and studied serial killers. If asked, they could recite specific facts to friends or colleagues. It may border on obsessive/compulsive behavior, but it is innocent.

Although I knew better, I had to keep in mind that Dale Hausner and maybe even Sam Dieteman could fall under this heading of *too curious for their own good.* Everything found and said so far could be easily explained away. I didn't have the luxury at this point of assuming, even with the map, that they were involved.

Detective Udd and Label came back from their briefing with the County Attorney. The finding of the map and shotgun casing had been passed onto them. It made the decision to authorize the emergency interception a little easier.

The only question that remained was, with this new evidence, were we going to get the emergency wire up and running before the bosses decided to move in.

As nightfall approached, I received a call from one of my buddies that worked in SAU/SWAT. He had been at the earlier briefing where I had explained that there wasn't enough probable cause to affect an arrest. Now he was being told differently. The chief of police of Mesa and Phoenix told them to be ready to make an arrest, that an arrest was imminent. He was none too happy. They didn't want to jeopardize the case. I took the call as I sat next to my partner and Detective Pete Salazar. Detective Udd was feverishly writing the search warrant for Hausner's car and apartment. Apparently the brass wanted it done right away, which worried us.

As I listened to the play-by-play of what was said at this meeting, I became thoroughly disgusted. It was obvious panic was setting in. Nobody was listening to me or to any of the other case agents.

Detective Udd and Salazar heard most of my conversation.

Darren asked first. "What the fu#* is going on?"

I looked at both of them and shook my head.

"SAU has been given the green light to arrest Dieteman and Hausner. It came directly from our chief's office and from Mesa. I'm sure that ATF had some input, too."

Detective Salazar blurted out sarcastically, "Did they check with Scottsdale before they made this decision?"

"I don't know, Pete. In fact, I don't know what's going on anymore. This case is now out of our hands."

"I'm going to call my bosses. This is bullshit. How many times do we have to tell them that we don't have a case yet?"

Pete stormed off to make the call. Hell, we were all pissed.

My partner became hostile.

"What the hell did I go over to the County Attorney's Office for and present all this shit for a wiretap if they're going to move on these guys tonight?"

He stopped typing the search warrant affidavit for a moment and turned and looked at me.

"I don't know, brother."

I didn't have any more answers. The decisions now rested with higher authority.

Detective Salazar rejoined us.

"I talked to Don (Sergeant Bellander)," he told us. "He's pissed. He's trying to reach up our chain of command and see if we can stop this thing."

Detective Udd then stopped typing. My mind ran through the recent evidence discovery: the map with locations marked, the 410 shotgun shell, the GPS monitor of Dieteman and Hausner trolling for victims the night before, and the silver/blue 1998 Toyota Camry. Was it enough? If the bosses moved, it better be, or they'd blow the entire investigation.

Then my partner of the last five years spoke. He said something that was either utterly brilliant or completely mutinous.

"You know, besides this warrant, I haven't put pen to paper on any of this case. I haven't typed one word about anything that I've done so far. They're threatening to remove you as case agent. I say we walk away from this mess and leave the brass to make this case."

As tired as I was, I comprehended everything he said. I, too, had put few words on paper. Most of my investigation was in my head, notes, or in my journals. I had not typed one word about this large Conspiracy to Commit Murder report, the report documenting this entire investigation. None of the investigation was there for anyone to pick up or read. I hadn't done it on purpose; I was just too busy to type it.

I looked at him and suddenly realized he was right. We were both exhausted. I started counting the hours of sleep on both hands since the murder of Robin Blasnek. Hell, since more than a week ago. ATF's ASAC said I suffered from sleep deprivation. Maybe he was right. At least we could claim that.

The idea that my partner came up with was the best idea I had heard today. There was no reason to push on. The investigation was out of our hands. Other people were pulling the strings. It was time to get some rest and let others stress what was about to happen.

Detective Pete Salazar agreed. "Fu@% 'em."

"I agree. Let's go tell Stu that we're done. And damn sure tell him why."

Both my partner and I jumped up from his desk and headed to Sergeant Stu Clarke's office. He was feverishly working on some logistics of some kind. He looked up at us as I walked in first, then Darren who shut the door behind him. I sat down in what had become my customary chair, as my partner stood by the door with his arms crossed, his body language showing complete disgust.

"What's up, guys?" Sergeant Clarke's question came from someone concerned about what he was tasked with, not about what we were going to lay on him. He had no idea what I was about to say.

"Stu, both Darren and I are done. We're spent. It looks as though this investigation is being handled by the brass now, and we're going to walk. Besides, we can't function anymore. There is no sense in us being here. We need to get some rest, at least a couple of days."

The curious look on Sergeant Clarke's face turned upside down. He took a deep breath as we both stared at him. Before he had a chance to say anything, we unloaded on him.

To say that it was insubordinate would be an understatement. But the rant that my partner and I went on would never have come about if we weren't dead tired and dead sick of people making decisions on the direction this case was moving. We had put too much time in, as had all those other members of the task force, to see it swept away because of politics.

Much to his credit, Sergeant Clarke listened and took it. Our vents were clear and concise. There would be no mistaking why we walked away. If anyone said otherwise, we were prepared to fight for our reputations and integrity.

Sergeant Clarke tried to convince us that both he and Lieutenant Benson had said and done whatever they could to wrangle back control of this investigation. They may very well have, but we didn't care. The only way to get this investigation back in the hands of the case agents who built it was to walk away, to make a statement.

So we did. Both Detective Udd and I walked out of Sergeant Clarke's office. Detective Udd went back to his desk to gather a few things. I needed to go talk to Marjorie in the command center before I left. She deserved to hear it from me that I was going home for a few days of rest.

I learned that Marjorie had stepped out. She was going to go get herself some coffee. I put some of the books together and placed them in chronological order. The next investigator would need to reference the cases efficiently. It was the least that I could do. I sat down and gazed at the poster-size map of the Phoenix Metropolitan with all the shootings marked. I started to feel sorry for whoever took over the case.

I walked out of the command center and back to Detective Udd's desk. As I stood behind him, a thought occurred to me.

"Let's go get a drink. I'm buying."

A smile came to my partner's face.

"You're on, only if I get to buy the second round."

"Deal," I said as he closed down the Word document where he had been typing the search warrant.

As we were about to get up and walk out, Lieutenant Rich Benson walked in the main door of the Violent Crime Bureau. Detective Udd's desk sat right next to this door.

"Clark, I need to see you."

Sergeant Stu Clarke was right on his heels.

I looked down at Darren, and he smiled wryly at me. We started toward the commander's office. I figured that they were going to threaten me with insubordination or some other policy violation. Either way I was ready, if only my mouth could catch up with my mind. I was exhausted, and I hoped I could make some semblance of sense.

As we walked in, Commander Joe Klima was seated behind his desk. Joe was always friendly, whether it was good or bad news he was about to deliver.

"Come in, guys, and have a seat."

He was on the phone and then hung up.

Commander Klima looked at me and asked a very forward question. "I need to know how pissed off you are right now. About the complaint that is."

It was an odd question.

"I'm not really pissed off; I'm more confused."

I decided not to elaborate. I was confused about the complaint, but I was more pissed off about the direction the investigation was going. He asked about the complaint.

"Confused is good. I can deal with confused, but I can't deal with somebody who's pissed off. That leads to bad decisions and hard feelings. I need to know that you're not too upset to lead this investigation," the commander said.

"Well, I would like to know what the complaint is in reference to. I'm not exactly sure what I did that was wrong," I said.

"Forget about the complaint! Can you put that aside and lead this task force? I need to know because these two guys sitting next to you tell me that you're the man to bring this baby to a conclusion."

I wasn't going to pull any punches.

"That's what I've been doing for months. The task force has been on the right path all along. I'm right about the direction of this investigation, and it has been heading toward a successful conclusion until this distraction."

I realized that right then and there both Sergeant Stu Clarke and Lieutenant Rich Benson had stuck up and fought to keep me as lead investigator.

"The chief has told me to make the decision as to whether to keep things the same or go in a different direction. I'm going to keep you in charge of the investigation."

I looked at my supervisors. They were satisfied, and so was I.

I looked at the commander and said, "Thank you. You won't regret the decision."

"I know I won't. By the way, there will be no arrest of these two guys tonight. We've all decided to let the drug boys play with their listening devices."

This was turning out to be a good night. I had been given a reprieve, another chance to bang away at PC to make a case on Samuel Dieteman and Dale Hausner.

As I left the commander's office, I returned to my partner's desk. Darren had been sitting there waiting for his turn in the hot seat. "We're back in business. No arrest, and no change of direction. Best of all, the wire goes up."

"Thank Christ. Somebody finally made a good decision around here. Now what?"

Now the fun begins.

I had received surveillance notes from the activities of our two boys from last night through today. They had stayed put until about 3:00 p.m., when they left the apartment complex and drove to a restaurant. From there, they drove directly to a day care center, where Dale Hausner picked up a young child, a female, estimated to be around two years old.

At around 8:15 p.m., Samuel Dieteman was seen leaving the apartment. He walked to a Walmart about a mile away. He was seen grabbing an unknown item off the shelf and entering the men's bathroom.

When he left, he walked right past all the check-out counters. He then took a used hair dye kit, with black dye stuck to the white gloves used for application in the bathroom. Dieteman intended to change his appearance! The only explanation for that, and the way he did it, was to mask himself from identification.

I began checking DES state records and found that Dale Hausner did have a daughter, Rebecca. She was born on January 4th, 2004 to a Dale Hausner and a Linda Swaney. That apparently was the young child seen with Hausner last night.

Who the hell is Linda Swaney? That questioned would have to be answered.

As I scoured the contacts of Samuel Dieteman and Dale Hausner looking for anyone to gather more insight on these two, Sergeant Stu Clarke burst into the monitor room.

"You're not going to believe this sh@#!"

"What sh*# am I not going to believe?" I said, matter of fact.

"Look at this." Sergeant Stu Clarke handed me a supplement to the shooting of James Hodge that occurred back on May 31, 2006. It was a supplement that had been called in and recorded on a voice writer to be typed up later. Hodge was the first of three shot that night. Patrol officers had investigated all the crime scenes.

Dale Hausner and Samuel Dieteman were listed as Witnesses 1 and 2. Sam's last name was spelled incorrectly. That was why the report had never been triggered. I began to read the supplement.

Both Hausner and Dieteman gave statements to police. They alleged they were out looking for a cat and happened upon poor Mr. Hodge, who had been shot in the back. They flagged down police and directed them to Mr. Hodge. They didn't run from the scene. They stayed around and gave interviews! Both of them claimed to know nothing of who shot James Hodge.

I turned to Stu, "These bastards were identified at one of the scenes! This is huge."

"I know," he said laughingly.

Still circumstantial, it put Dieteman and Hausner at the scene of a crime. No way could this be considered coincidence or curiosity. Their car hadn't been recorded as being out there. That was OK by me.

This fit perfectly into the notoriety theory—returning to a scene to inspect what carnage they had inflicted, contacting police, and then laughing at us as they walked away, free to continue on their rampage. No wonder they felt so emboldened.

I ran to Marjorie in the command center. I looked crazed, and she knew why already.

"Crack the crime books and start looking for any unknown witnesses that fit Hausner's and Dietman's description. If they've been at one scene, they've probably been at others." Then I added, "Keep this under your hat."

CHAPTER 39

As he propped himself up off the air mattress that he called a bed, Samuel John Dieteman took a minute to reflect on his situation.

Two years ago, he had been a successful electrician working for Honeywell. Even though he'd lost that job due to his temper, he had all the skills necessary to be gainfully employed. He was semi-intelligent, a skilled handyman, and excellent with electronics.

Yet here he was sleeping on the floor of the living room of a guy he had met just a few months earlier. A guy who once again had gotten him hooked on meth. A guy so rotten to the core that nobody could save him. He could not believe how out of control everything had become.

He needed money to get out of here. He needed to find himself a place of his own and distance himself from his current situation. So Sam had come up with a way to get some. It would be tricky, but others had done it. They'd been able to pull it off with a simple phone call.

He picked up his mattress and placed it behind the front door as mandated, flipped on the TV, and settled on the couch with the realization that things could be a lot worse. He adjusted the volume in case Rebecca was sleeping. At least he had a roof over his head and something to look forward to, even if it caused him great internal turmoil.

As he looked at the clock, he realized it was almost four. The news would be coming on in a minute. It was time to wake up and pay attention, for his partner would be up and quizzing him shortly.

◈

The headsets were on, and the recorder running. The boys back in the monitoring room were cussing their unfortunate predicament. The TV volume was loud. The programming broadcasts would be recorded very well, but any conversations may be another story. The microphone placed underneath a standing TV cabinet through a neighboring wall. A lousy break in a case full of them.

◉

The toilet flush clued him into his partner's awakening. It was almost 6:00 p.m. No tiny footsteps or dainty voice, so he assumed that Rebecca had been taken to day care or to her mom's some time while he was sleeping. He needed to quit drinking so much and do a better job of paying attention. Even though his partner liked him, the guy was whacked. All those stories of past horrid deeds should make him realize that nobody is safe around this guy. One wrong move, and he could wake up with his throat cut.

As he switched the TV from channel three to channel fifteen, he heard his voice and looked at his sleepy-eyed roommate. He'd watched all the four, four-thirty, and five o'clock newscasts. "There's been stories all over the news about you know who and even an interview," Sam said with a hint of satisfaction in his voice. The TV continued to blare other news stories as they talked.

"Who's that?" he inquired. But before letting Sam answer, he cut him off. "I've got a lot of catching up to do."

He was still trying to wake up.

"Yeah, you do," Sam said. "The interview was of the guys from the ATF office. Some local guy, plus the agents that worked in Washington, D.C. on those two snipers. They're a lot more experienced than us, and have more technology and friggin' know-how ever since they worked on the case of the friggin D.C. snipers." Sam paused for a second before continuing. "Here is the other one hot off the press. Police just released this new bit of information that the sniper or serial shooter may circle around the area a couple of times to make sure there's no witnesses. Jesus, yah think?"

"Yah think? Yah dumb mother fu@#ers! It took them a year and a half to come up with that? Wow."

It was just like he thought. The police were too stupid to catch him or Sam. He laughed to himself. These cops were bungling and walking around in the dark. It was the first time he'd ever heard that the cops believed they were conducting surveillances of areas where they targeted pedestrians. And he would know.

"Hey Sam," came the voice from the back bedroom. Sam decided not to answer.

"Hey Sam." He still ignored him. He wasn't his dog.

Again from the back bedroom, this time with frustration, "Sam!"

"He's no longer here. It's Grandmaster D."

He could hear the chuckles from the back bedroom. Sam "Grandmaster" Dieteman. That had a pretty good ring to it. If he was ever cornered or cut down in a shooting with police, that would be his battle cry.

The six o'clock news lead story official linked the murder of Robin Blasnek to the Serial Shooter. In fact, the first six minutes of the news cast was dedicated to Robin, her murder, and the hunt for justice. Dale was already moving to the living room. There were live shots of the crime scene and the investigators that had responded. A picture of Robin flashed onto the screen. Another town hall meeting was about to get underway in Mesa, and a live feed to a remote reporter chirped about the meeting being for the Spanish-speaking community.

A commercial break made way for the two to catch up some more. Sam had picked up a newspaper and realized that it was today's *Mesa Tribune*. His partner must have brought it home this morning. The front page of the paper read, "High Anxiety." He flipped off the picture of the Mesa Public Information Officer. "In your face."

The sound of ice being pulled from the freezer was music to Sam's ears. He needed a good drink to start the evening off right. A nice smooth drink would be fine for now.

As the blender started and the TV roared, the voice from the kitchen was muffled. "I wonder if the media cares about the illega ... you know, that guy that got hit." He paused for a moment to collect his thoughts. He was pissed at himself for not waking up to see the five o'clock news. He hated needing to rely on Sam for his up-to-date info.

"So when did you hear this stuff about the, about the DC sniper stuff ... Today?"

He needed to know if there was a new sheriff in town.

"Yeah, it was uh ... five o'clock, four thirty, one of those two," Sam answered.

He handed Sam a drink, and together they banged glasses. It was a toast.

"Told you we'd love it."

The two started to laugh, and he grunted like one of his favorite characters from the Three Stooges, Mo. In fact, he could impersonate all the Stooges' voices.

Sam's attention was diverted to one of the many newspapers sitting on the dining room table. He decided to fill in his partner on more details from the earlier broadcasts. "On the five a.m. news was when they first said that the last shooting was related. Phoenix and Mesa police have now officially linked the shooting death of a young Mesa woman to the serial killer, which now brings their total to six."

That pissed him off.

"Six! It's higher than that. What about the guy I fu#*ing shot on 27th Avenue in the yard?"

They both agreed that one had been completely overlooked.

Sam continued. "Yeah, they're working with feds and other states because they believe that these people may have begun in another state . . . are looking for similar crimes in other states."

He wasn't sure if that even made any sense.

His partner thought about that for a moment. "Really." That was interesting. If only they knew what he and his brother had done in Nebraska. Then, in his best Curly imitation, he blurted, "Hmm. We're being copycatted, Sam? We're pioneers, Sam? We're leading the way to a better life for everybody, Sam."

Sam ignored the impersonation, and in fact, hated it. It grated on him. That squeaky voice was enough for him to want to gun down his roommate, his co-conspirator, his partner. It was enough to make anyone want to kill him.

Then Sam replied, "I guess it started in another state . . . and we're here to finish it."

There was a good chance one day he and Dale would get caught. He'd have to decide at that point whether to be taken alive or fight and risk dying. He'd never been fond of police. His dad had taught him that early on. But he really didn't have the stomach to shoot it out with cops. They have families, too.

"Don't trust the police to help you if you get in a jam and don't trust them to do yah right either. Take care of yourself, and keep the cops out of it," his dad would tell him.

Don't trust the police? He was having a hard time trusting his own decision making. How the hell had he gotten involved in this? What was he thinking? Beating guys up in bars was one thing, but murdering people? Where did it all go wrong?

Then his partner's familiar voice beckoned from the kitchen. "You know how they got the uh . . . they think that they circle around. They probably saw my car in that fu@%ing . . . fu@*en surveillance camera about three times."

"What surveillance camera?" Sam thought to himself. He must be referring to the cameras on the traffic lights that can be seen at almost every intersection in the East Valley. What does he mean by "they circle around"?

Before he could answer, the phone rang, and Dale began to field questions from someone on the other end. He was late and supposed to be somewhere. Sam wondered to himself if his partner in crime had a dual personality, one that could separate himself from the awful things they'd done. It was not the first time Dale had referred to others as being responsible. Maybe that made what he had done more internally acceptable.

But, for Sam, what he had done was anything but acceptable.

Frustration mounted back at the wire room as the investigators scrambled to hear and understand what was said. It wasn't just the TV that interfered. It was all the other noises that the mike would pick up. Noises that you don't actually pay attention to—the running of water in between the walls from the apartments upstairs, the air-conditioning unit kicking on and off in the midsummer heat, the ruffling of papers, and the fact that two people talked at the same time.

Then all of sudden there was dead quiet. The TV was turned off, and there were no voices. The only sound was the closing of a door. Samuel Dieteman and Dale Hausner had left their apartment and were walking towards Dale's car. The vehicle was seen leaving the complex with Dale driving.

One monitor turned to the other and asked, "What did they say about the DC snipers?"

I grabbed Hausner's notebook and started turning the pages. Just as I discovered the reason for his stop, one of the UC units corroborated what I already knew.

"Looks like he's picking up his daughter. He's loading her in the backseat."

The address came back to the mother of Dale's daughter, Linda Swaney.

According to UC units, the three arrived back at the apartment at

7:40 p.m. The monitoring boys had already received word that the occupants of the apartment would be back inside momentarily. They cracked their knuckles and put down their sodas. It was back to the headsets and computer terminals. The voices of the three occupants could be heard with better clarity. It was a good sign. They checked the recorder, and it was operating. It would record everything.

The cluttering sounds of dishes could be heard in preparation of dinner. The child asked a question, but her petite voice was drowned out by the banging of porcelain. Then some more banging, and the TV came back on, louder this time. Damn it!

The voice of the child could no longer be heard as she was engrossed by the now playing movie. And for that matter, the two male voices dropped as well. TV was the great escape for parents of small children. Even if it was on for just a few minutes a day, it provided a little downtime to keep their children occupied.

I received the call a little after eight o'clock. Nothing to report from the wire room unless it had been awhile since I had seen *The Jungle Book*.

Sam stood in the bathroom and took a hard look at his new appearance in the mirror. The hair dye wasn't as dark as he thought it would be. His hair, which had been medium brown, now looked just slightly darker. He had only colored the bottom of his goatee, which was also a semi-black. He wondered if there was any other way he could change his appearance. His eyes were sunken and withdrawn from too much alcohol and meth.

Dale was preparing Rebecca's night-time formulas—soy milk and water. Sam felt bad for the little girl. She was surely a sweetheart. It was unfair that she had so many health problems at such an early age. Sam thought about his two girls when they were that young. He was fortunate. They had not had any significant health problems. Now he missed them greatly, but he was in no condition to care for them or even see them. Their recent visit was so unnerving that he could only keep the girls three days of what was meant to be a weeklong visit. Of course, it didn't help that Dale kept texting all hours of the day and night. Plus, once again, Sam was hooked on meth.

"I'm going to get some of that tanning stuff. I figure with black hair, if I can dye the rest of my facial hair black and then tan real well . . . they'll think I'm a Hispanic guy."

"I got shot by a Hispanic guy," Dale roared.

They couldn't wait to see that reported in the media.

Then Dieteman thought about the *America's Most Wanted* program, the one with the crime re-enactment of Joseph Robert's shooting.

"I'll put on a yellow hat."

They both howled about that. Where did that come from, anyway? What idiot told police the guy that shot Roberts was wearing a hat, let alone a yellow one? Once again, it just showed what they had thought all along. Police were incompetent, and their victims and witnesses lame.

Sam looked down at his hands and realized that the black hair dye had stained them. His hands looked darker than his hair. He held his hands up for his partner to see.

"At least I got some of it on my head though." Damn, messy stuff. "It kept soaking right down to my skin."

The instructions had said to leave the dye on for no more than five minutes. He hadn't been patient enough to let the color darken.

It was time for Rebecca to head to bed, and Sam had already told Dale that he needed a hit. A little pick-me-up. Hopefully, Rebecca would stay in the room and go right to sleep. That wasn't always the case.

Dale Hausner loved to play parent, even though he had been a terrible one. He had shucked his duties at parenting, all for the cause of notoriety and his blood thirst. He had other things more important than being a father.

"Rebecca . . . it's time to go night-night," Dale yelled from the bedroom.

He'd been setting up her feeding pump, making sure the tubes were clean.

Sam saw the little girl get up from her spot on the floor and dejectedly walk away from the movie before it was finished.

"It's time to give Sam a hug night-night."

The little girl had been around Sam long enough to feel comfortable, but not loving.

"I want to give Becky a hug," Sam said.

"Becky, give him a hug night-night."

The child was still unsure and looked at her father for some sort of reassurance.

"Nah . . . she ain't going to give me a hug."

Maybe if he played coy, he could sneak one from the child, Sam thought. Even he knew there was nothing like the warm hug of a child.

Rebecca had already made up her mind.

"Give Sam a hug. Awww isn't that nice."

The toddler wrapped her arms around the big roommate. Even Sam, the cold-blooded murderer, was moved by her touch.

"Say good night Sam."

"Good night Sam," Rebecca repeated.

"Night-night, Becky," said Sam.

"See you in the morning," Dale said.

"See you morning," she stuttered.

"Say: Don't kill anybody."

The despicable father had committed the unthinkable act. He wanted his daughter to revel like he did. It was uncalled for, and even Dieteman felt uncomfortable with that statement.

"In the morning, that's too early."

Sam wanted the conversation over. He now wanted the child out of the living room and in bed. This joking around had gone too far. There was no need to bring the two year old into this.

Dale couldn't leave it alone. He was obsessed.

"Say: don't kill anybody."

Finally the child succumbed. "Don't kill anybody."

There. She'd said it. Now the idiot ought to be happy.

"Oh, alright. Since you asked."

Sam saw the child disappear into the back bedroom. Thankfully, no more sick child games and word plays. He could get high and drink.

Samuel realized that he was out of mixture. He needed more Coke if he was going to drink himself into oblivion. It was time for a run to Walmart. By the time he got back, Becky would be asleep, and he could start to numb himself with a little help from his partner.

As he slammed the front door, he grabbed the black garbage bag that sat on the front porch. He had become the wasteful garbage disposer, whereas his roommate had become the human garbage disposer. At least that it was his partner called himself. He claimed he was doing a service. Cleaning up the streets of all the human garbage that live there, walk there, thrive there.

The dumpster was on his way out of the parking lot. As he walked up to the large metal container, he realized how quiet it was outside. It was a peaceful night. He lobbed the bag over the top of the rectangular bin. It landed with a clang.

Deputy County Attorney Laura Reckart had joined the boys in the wire room. She was down there to monitor the activities and conversations of our shooters. She was there to pull the trigger if the talk went personal and make sure the boys minimized those conversations so that the wire evidence would be void of any private intrusions.

All the chiefs and managers of the task force had moved to a command center set up in Mesa. Representatives from her office were there as well. Her allies had relayed that SWAT was moving in on Dieteman. A decision had been made to take them down if they leave, even though Sam was alone.

"Tell them to back off. We're just now getting started. We think that they may say something incriminating. Tell them to relax!"

She, too, could not understand moving on these guys since the wire was so fresh.

Just as SWAT got loaded up and began to move on Dieteman, the word came to stand down. The boys in the wire room and the investigators had won a reprieve.

As they listened, the channel surfing inside the apartment continued. There are five local TV stations in the Phoenix metro area, and Dale Hausner was watching them all for brief periods of time. The boys in the wire room started to watch and follow along on their own TV. When Hausner switched channels, so did they.

Even though it was after 9:00 p.m., the channels banged back and forth between newscasts. The main topic of conversation: The Serial Shooter investigation. "Police have confirmed that the death of the young Mesa woman has been linked to the Serial Shooter," the newscaster stated. They would then show a picture of Robin Blasnek and the live footage from the night of the investigation.

"No leads yet in who is committing the crimes."

He couldn't ask for anything better. News coverage on every station about his crimes. He had truly become a folk hero, a legend. People would write books about him someday. But for now, he wasn't even close to being finished.

As he sat and watched the newscasts, hoping to catch something about the D.C. Sniper case, he listened to an account of one of the witnesses who came upon Robin Blasnek. Her name was Marie. She was interviewed by one of the local field reporters. Marie had tried to comfort the victim, but it was too late. Robin's wounds were too severe.

He chuckled to himself about the anxiety brought upon this witness. She was nervous during her interview, but he could tell she was more upset about what she had witnessed—a young female lying on the sidewalk, gunned down in the early stages of her life.

He could only imagine what the press coverage would've been had his partner pulled the trigger a few nights ago. Two young boys gunned down on their bicycle would have been front page national news, hell, international news. His partner had let him down again.

Dale grabbed his phone and typed in "Got News." He would wait for the response. If that didn't get his partner excited, nothing would. Speaking of news, he just wasn't getting his feel of it through the old tube. He texted Sam again and asked him to pick up a newspaper. He kept forgetting to record the news broadcasts. The local newspapers had more in-depth coverage of the shootings.

Besides, he needed more material for his scrapbook.

I received the phone call as soon as it was retrieved. Another bag of trash had been thrown away. There was still no word from the boys in the wire room, and Detective Hugh Lockerby from Scottsdale had joined the bosses down in Mesa. He was there along with several others, ready to execute the search warrant on the apartment if and when Dieteman and Hausner were arrested.

The main concern now was Hausner's daughter. How would they take them down? Would they shoot it out with police with his daughter there? She could be struck by return police fire, or worse, used as a hostage.

There were numerous problems with the young child being present. All signs led back to leaving them be for tonight and letting the wire work. There was no reason to believe they were going anywhere. Dieteman had walked away from the apartment, not driven. The car was still there, and it could be disabled if for some reason they looked as if they were gearing up.

I hadn't slept in over forty hours, and everyone was exhausted. My mouth tasted like the hoof of a mule. My head bobbed forward as I started to doze, then violently backward upon snapping awake. I prayed that no arrest would commence tonight. An arrest meant interviews. I was too tired to think, and I was starting to blur the facts of all the cases.

My phone rang. It was one of the surveillance units.

"Just wanted to update you. Sam's back in the apartment, and we can see him walking in and out from the porch. My guess is he's smoking. I just can't tell what," The detective said.

"Thanks. Keep me posted, would you?"

I hung up as quick as I could.

"So what did I miss that was so important that you would bother my trek to the store?" Sam asked as he re-entered the apartment.

Dale turned the TV down to make sure his partner could hear him.

"Good stuff, man."

He grabbed the grocery bag from Sam and pulled out the newspaper. He opened the paper, mumbling to himself, seeing the composite photo of the Baseline Killer front and just below the fold. He read the caption.

"This fu#@in guy," as he pointed to the composite. "No it's not … two guys are better than the Baseline Rapist."

"Fu*&ing loser homo. He probably uses his cock instead of a gun," Samuel replied.

"One's got a gun, and one's got a condom." Both burst out in laughter.

"One prophylactic, semi-used," Sam said. He grabbed the last half of the newspaper and was now thumbing through the obituaries. "Damn it!"

"What?" Dale looked up from his news article to see what had intrigued his partner.

"Here's what I have to do. I'm getting me another obituary."

His partner was puzzled. Was he going to cash out on him in the middle of all the fun? He had talked about killing himself before because he was so useless, but maybe he was really contemplating it. He decided to make light of it.

"It'll be in both the Mesa and the *Arizona Republic* newspapers. You might even get your picture in there."

Sam looked up at him like he was an idiot.

"No . . . I mean not worried about getting my own. I'm getting another one to put in there."

Dale understood. You had a chance two days ago and didn't do it. Now all of a sudden you want to kill somebody. It sounded like the meth talking.

"Got to be quicker."

Then Dale remembered what was so important that he texted his partner in crime. "Hey dude, you know the one where she was shot? Where we shot that bitch? Fu@#in cu*@! They shot her, and when people looked that way, ughhhh! They ran out. She was on her knees, 'Oh, I've been shot.' Blood pouring out, right? Oh my god! A rag or a towel is not gonna cut it, and they got a blanket, you know. She goes, 'She's been shot' . . . "

He covered his eyes pretending to cry and acting out how the witness described the event to the reporter. They both started to laugh. It really was comical to them how people could get so emotional.

As Sam flipped the pages of the paper, he came upon someone he recognized. "Oh, my God! She looks familiar from somewhere!" He paused momentarily, "You know a Blasnek?"

"Ummmm . . . no, don't think so."

"Hmmm . . . for some reason she kinda looks familiar."

Dale put down his section and looked at the obituary page briefly. "I know a *Blast-nek*."

As in shotgun *blast*. He was quick with that one.

Dieteman continued reading. "Here's a Samuel Farber. Same name as mine."

He was amused by the obituaries. He thought about how his own would read. There wouldn't be a whole lot to put in there, unless of course he got caught for being one of the two infamous Serial Shooters. Then they would have to use a half a page, whether he was taken alive or not.

Dale just shook his head as he read the idiot tripe that some of these so-called newspaper people actually wrote. The title to the article was ridiculous.

"Are you ready? These angels don't fear the path they tread."

It was an article written by a writer who spent a day walking up and down the streets of Mesa with the Guardian Angels. As he read on, he got disgusted. "We gotta do them next, man." He meant the Angels. He threw the paper down. These people getting ink . . . and for what? Walking around like idiots with red berets on their heads.

Sam skipped to another article describing the two sets of serial killers, them and the BLK. "This is just speculation, but the two may be competing with each other."

That's exactly how Dale perceived it—a competition. It was the Serial Shooters versus the Baseline Killer. It was a battle for bragging rights, a game that he and Sam had to win. Why were they still even putting this guy's crimes in the paper? He hadn't struck in weeks. Here they were active, pursuing, causing panic and fear throughout the valley. The Baseline Killer had probably gotten high and cut his penis off or something.

They both looked at the time and realized it was almost ten o'clock. It was time for their hourly dose of egocentrism.

The TV surfed from channel to channel, but there would be nothing new reported on the Serial Shooters. The only breaking news was a Baseline Killer update. It was about the death of one of the earliest victims. Tempe police had arrested a man and charged him in the death of the female, only to later realize the man had actually confessed to the killing to get out of a Kentucky jail to do time here in Arizona. His story had been blown when Phoenix Police looked into the case and realized that the BLK was actually responsible for the murder. The alleged suspect, James Mullins, had his case and charges dropped by the County Attorney.

The newscaster said, "Mullins will now be sent to Kentucky to face charges in an unrelated case. The Baseline predator is suspected of twenty-three violent crimes over the last year. That included eight murders, eleven rapes, and eight robberies. Many of those had been linked forensically before this murder."

It was Sam who spoke up first. "Twenty-three violent crimes? I thought there was twenty-seven altogether."

"Yeah what the fu*^. It's not twenty-three, add it up, add it up,"

Dale sounded off as well. It was obvious that this news station script writer couldn't add, or the newscaster had read the wrong line. Leave it to Dale and Sam to have the facts correct.

"Twenty-seven . . . it's still thirty-five. Actually thirty-six," Sam added.

They were way ahead on the body count, but they were behind in the murders. Or at least Sam thought so. He knew he missed a chance the other night, and Dale wouldn't let him forget it. There had been at least one other chance to take down a male walking. "I had a feeling I was gonna miss. I'm looking up, once you pointed him out, I came in and then I looked up and that freakin helicopter. I don't know why I'm so paranoid about that, and I'm looking back, and lookin this way, and by the time we're up there, and I cock it and started bringing it up, that fu@#er was almost on top of me."

Dale looked at Sam with some sympathy, but not much. It was obvious he didn't have the nerves of steel that he possessed. He had blown too many opportunities to be considered a true assassin.

"You see how I do it."

Sam understood perfectly. It was a job to Dale. A skill set and a guilt-free personality to go with it. No sorrow, no remorse. He remembered the first time he shot someone with Dale, the black male on 44th Street. After Dale fired, the victim screamed and hollered at them. Sam thought that was funny as hell. The guy was dancing around like he had napalm in his underwear. They laughed all the way up till when Sam pulled the trigger and killed Claudia Gutierrez-Cruz. Then it wasn't funny anymore for him. Dale was still jealous of that shooting. He learned that was Scottsdale's first homicide of 2006. He just wished it was him instead of Sam.

Sam was impressed by his partner's skills. It was obvious that he had been doing it for quite a while.

"You're fu#*ing quick with it! You just frickin' get up there and get your bead right on them and . . . *Bam!*"

Hausner simulated holding a shotgun and yelled, "Bam. Quick, and it's not even a handgun. Twelve gauge, too."

That was something they reveled in, watching their prey go down. He was an artist at back shooting. He even coined his own Latin term, "Shootius in the backius."

As the meth started to kick in, Dale fixed him another drink, and the talk turned to their next run. The city was lucky that he had his daughter tonight.

"I'm fu#*ing high. Remember that interrogation room at the casino," Dale spouted. Those pricks. Thought they had us."

"You're an angry fu*%, aren't you?" Sam said.

"Yeah, well, you're a crummy shot. Did you get hit in the head?"

Maybe that was why he couldn't shoot straight.

Sam decided it was time to have a cigarette and step out. He didn't need to hear anymore about his lack of ability. Dale turned the TV back on and decided to give it a rest. But from now on, there would be no more excuses.

The boys in the wire room were frantically exchanging notes. The taped sessions had been cut short to allow some of them to review the conversations while others listened live.

"I can't understand a damn thing. If it's not the TV blasting, it's the air conditioner. If it's not the air conditioner, it's the god damn blender."

"OK, I got them talking about some shootings, and it sounds like they were reading something. I don't know if they were reading or speaking from their own experiences."

Laura Reckart was listening as well. She was aware of how important these conversations were, even though she knew nothing of the particulars.

"They just said something about being shot in the back, or someone shooting someone in the back. What the hell was that?"

She was right on the front lines hoping to hear something incriminating as well.

"What was that about something being blasted or blasting someone?" asked another monitor.

They all listened again. Who are they talking about? They had no idea who the victims were. They had only been briefed on limited information.

"Find the part about Sam not killing someone," Lieutenant Piano asked. "It was in session forty-nine."

They all listened again to what one of the men, possibly Hausner, said to Dieteman.

"He said, 'Don't kill anybody," right?"

They all looked at each other. Was there consensus on that point at least? They kept listening.

"I'm getting word they're moving on the two and soon," one of the undercover units stated.

Laura dialed up her bosses in the command center.

"You have to stop them from arresting these guys. We haven't had the time to listen to these conversations, and they're talking. We need more time!"

Her boss relayed to her that they would try, "But it's not our show."

"We have to work fast and furious 'cause this wire is going to go down quickly. Put everything you can into note form, and start dissecting it. Move and move fast," Laura said.

Nobody in the wire room could see the hurry. Why not take some time and listen? What are these people thinking? Dieteman and Hausner weren't going anywhere.

So they thought.

◈

My phone rang, and it was Sergeant Clarke.

"Hey, I've got some good news. The chiefs have decided to hold off on the arrest of these two clowns until tomorrow. Go get some sleep and be ready to interview them after you're rested."

Thank God. There had been no useful information coming out of the wire room, and there had been no movement reported by the UC units outside the apartment. Even if I just got four or five hours of sleep, it would seem like a week's worth. I was elated. I passed the good news on to my partners.

"OK. Are they going to take them off as soon as they wake up or what?" I asked.

"They're concerned about the little girl. They don't want to see anything happen to her," Sergeant Clarke related.

"Yeah, and besides, once tonight is history, they're going to have to drop her off at Mom's or day care or something before tomorrow night. That gives our boys in the wire room time to get what they need," I added.

"Go get some sleep, and I'll see you bright and early." Sergeant Clarke hung up.

Detective Udd high-fived me, and together we walked out of police headquarters. I told him to be careful driving home, and he said the same. I had rented a hotel room a mile away. I couldn't wait to crawl into that bed.

As I was driving, I got a phone call from Lieutenant Piano. "Clark, we think we might have some good stuff, but we're having problems with the listening device. We're working on it, so hopefully we can get you something soon."

"Thanks, Lieutenant. You may have some more time. I just got word we're standing down on the arrest and going to wait until tomorrow."

He hadn't heard that. He was shocked.

"The boys will love that."

My room at the Best Western was standard and acceptable. A pile of hay in a rain forest would have looked good to me. I quickly showered and looked at my watch. It was almost midnight. With any luck, I could fall asleep in one minute and put the last forty- eight hours behind me. Tomorrow would be just as rough.

"Did you just hear what I heard?"

"I heard something about getting rid of something or finding a place to hide something," replied the other monitor. "They got to be talking about evidence."

The phone call went out from the wire room to the boys outside the apartment. They might be trying to destroy or get rid of evidence. Be on the lookout.

"OK, I got Dieteman leaving the apartment. Looks like he's heading to the laundry room. I don't see that he's carrying anything," the surveillance officer reported.

The argument over search and seizure and destruction of evidence started immediately. A laundry room is considered public, and there is no right to privacy if someone were to abandon something in there. If the property were clothing, it might be different. But Dieteman wasn't carrying any clothes.

The city legal eagles left nothing to chance. They looked at the search warrant that Detective Udd had written and realized that the area of the laundry room wasn't covered. Why would it be?

"This needs to be rewritten to include the laundry room," the lawyer yelled.

"Dieteman is now exiting the laundry room. His hands are empty, and it looks like . . . yep he went back inside the apartment." There were three sets of eyes on the apartment.

With this news, a decision was made. The search warrant that had taken Detective Udd two days to meticulously compile needed to be rewritten to include the laundry room and a no-knock provision for going in after the two added. People were panicking. There was too much movement of the suspects.

None of the investigators understood the urgency. Sergeant Stu Clarke had floated the idea, again, that we disable the car. A flat tire would do the trick. They also had a young child to care for. Nobody really believed that they would take her along or leave her there alone.

It didn't make sense to move now. The wire was up, and the boys were comfortably inside, hopefully discussing past trophies. The recorder was rolling, and all we needed was them to admit to one shooting.

Time was on our side.

CHAPTER 40

When I heard my phone ringing, I wasn't sure where I was or even what day it was. My room was still dark, and for some reason I felt as though I hadn't slept at all. I'm not sure whether I heard my phone ring on the first cycle or not.

When I answered it, I only remember a couple of words.

"They got 'em, Clark. Good luck, buddy," the voice said.

I could barely open my eyes, and I could not read the time on my cellphone. I switched on the light and tried to focus. My eyes felt melted together. I couldn't open them, no matter how hard I tried. It took me at least three minutes to get my eyes adjusted.

The date and time on my cellphone shown August 4th, 2006 12:04 a.m. I shook my head in disbelief. I must still be asleep or dreaming. That would mean that I had only been asleep for five minutes. I lay back for a moment on the bed, my mind half conscious and half unconscious. I needed to remain calm and think through what had just happened.

It was a prank, a sick joke. Somebody was messing with me. One hour ago, I was told to go home and get some sleep because the arrests were being put off due to safety concerns over the child. I agreed with that assessment, plus the wire was running.

I sat up and grabbed my phone. I called Sergeant Clarke who answered with a very shallow "Hello." I knew then it was no joke.

I tried to stay calm.

"Stu, what the hell is going on? Somebody just called me and told me Dieteman and Hausner were just arrested. Please tell me it's a joke, and somebody's just fu#*in with me."

"I'm sorry, Clark, we tried. Dieteman walked to the trash dumpster, and they took him. After they took him, they entered the apartment and arrested Hausner." He paused. "Both are in custody, and no shots were fired. Dieteman should be on his way downtown now. Hausner is being kept here until the kid's mother shows up to take her. Apparently, the kid is sick and needs constant supervision." He paused again. "I don't know what to tell you."

I sat and listened. There was no reason to go off on Stu because the decision was made above his head. But that didn't mean I couldn't voice some displeasure.

"I guess so much for 'go get some sleep and be ready for the interviews tomorrow,' huh?"

I was pissed now. No, I was ultra pissed.

I think he thought I would go off worse so he took this opportunity to drop some more bad news.

"Clark, you need to know the media is all over this place. I just got the word that camera crews are popping up all over the apartment complex."

I looked at my cellphone. It was now 12:10 a.m. Someone had tipped off the media. The arrest of two guys in an apartment complex wasn't that big of a deal, unless of course it was the arrest of the Serial Shooters. This was someone's political agenda, an exclusive traded for political gain.

"This fu#*in stinks, Stu. I can't wait to see what other surprises are in store."

I was beyond mad now. I had been screwed on sleep and lied to, plus the element of surprise was gone. Screw the wire, I guess. I hung up the phone.

For the next minute or so, I think I used every foul word I have ever heard in my entire life. I even made up new ones that didn't make any sense. As I stormed around my hotel room, I grabbed clothes from my bag and fired them around the room. I yelled like some actor preparing for a cold script reading. Every other word had an f-bomb in it.

I tried to become rational, but couldn't. We had unzipped our fly. No more waiting, no more secret recorded conversations, if we even had understandable ones. The search warrant was the last chance.

I could only hope.

Police headquarters was nearly empty inside. Word had traveled fast in the media about the arrests. The TV trucks parked outside were all running, getting ready to transmit the news.

Samuel Dieteman had just arrived and had been taken down a back ramp to a secured underground entrance. The large aluminum door opened for the transport vehicle and then promptly closed after entering. No media had rushed the police car. He had been safely hidden without them knowing who he was or from where he came.

Sam was brought to the second floor and placed in an interview room. He was dressed in a brown T-shirt, jean shorts, and shoes. I watched him through the camera as he was handcuffed to the table. I wondered to myself how this guy was a mastermind behind this whole string of chaos. He looked simple, like a blue-collar worker. He was kind of dopey looking, his hair an uncombed mess. His body was dumpy looking and his whole appearance disheveled. Dieteman put his head down on the table and tried to make himself comfortable.

Detective Jewell looked at Dieteman and seemed irritated. "Well, at least you'll be able to clear your cases," he said.

I looked at him and tried to make light of the comment. "You never know, Cliff, what's going to happen tonight or what will be found during our search warrant. It's too early to kiss your .22 cases goodbye."

I had determined that I would interview Dale Hausner first. He was the smaller of the two in stature, the one who had the least reported violent criminal history. Sam Dieteman was going to have a long time to wait before he talked to investigators.

Detective Udd showed up, and he was pissed. I had gotten over my anger of no sleep and being lied to. He, however, had another reason to rant.

"Did you hear what they're doing?"

I assumed he meant the arrest of the two against our wishes for more time and sleep, so we could be more prepared.

"Yeah, Dieteman is here now, and Hausner is a few minutes out," I said.

"No, damnit, they're changing the whole search warrant and rewriting it. Can you believe this sh#*?" he spewed.

"What!"

I couldn't believe my ears. If that were true, it would delay the search warrant for hours. These guys would sit in the interview rooms, twiddling their thumbs. I needed whatever was found now before I confronted these guys.

I phoned Stu Clarke and asked him what the hell was going on.

"We had to rewrite a small portion of Darren's search warrant. Hopefully it won't take much longer."

As I sat looking at Dieteman, Dale Hausner was being placed in Interview Room 1. He wore a pair of blue shorts that almost looked like swimming trunks. He had no shirt on. I was told he was cold, so we provided a blanket for him.

When Dale Hausner was brought in, it was as covert as Dieteman. As I looked at the dual monitors, I watched both of the men for any clue—restlessness, nervousness, or uncooperative gestures or statements. Dale Hausner was talkative as the police officer sat just outside outside his interview room. Samuel Dieteman kept his head down on the table, trying to get some shut eye.

The rooms themselves are about eight by twelve feet. There are a couple of chairs, one on each end of a small table. The table is just about big enough to write on and provides a slight separation from interrogator to suspect.

As I waited for any news or evidence from the search warrant to come, I received a call from Lieutenant Piano. He and his cohorts were still in the wire room trying to decipher the conversations.

"Clark, we're having a hell of a time hearing these conversations. We have a couple of things, but I lost some of my guys when the arrest went down. I hope to get you something tangible soon."

There was still no word from the search warrant teams. They had to be in there by now!

I was wrong. I soon learned that they were still rewriting the search warrant. Hausner and Dieteman had been in custody for more than three hours, and we still hadn't entered the apartment or his car. The whole idea of having the search warrant ready was to move in upon their arrest. I wanted the place at the very least to be given a good once-over by the time I started my interviews. Hopefully, if there were guns or ammunition in there, it would have been found and identified as .22 caliber, 410, or 12 gauge. Hopefully, the shotgun ammunition would have at least been identified as the same shot used in some of the murders or attempt murders.

I couldn't wait any longer. I decided to start the most important interview in the history of the Phoenix Police Department with little more than some circumstantial evidence and a tip from one drinking buddy. The only thing I could hope for was for them to talk, to give me something to tie all this together.

Dale Hausner would be the first to be interviewed.

CHAPTER 41

"Morning," I said.

It was a friendly greeting to gauge his temperament.

"Morning, how are you?" Dale replied.

That was a good sign. He was cordial and inquisitive.

"Good. How are you?"

Like I truly cared about how he was doing.

"Pretty good."

"Dale, I'm Detective Schwartzkopf with the Phoenix Police Department. I asked that you be brought down today. I have some questions I have to ask you about some stuff."

That left open an array of possibilities as to why he was down here. I hoped he hadn't figured it out, but assumed he had.

"OK," Dale said.

I then advised him of his Miranda rights and told him the reason I was doing that was because he was in our custody, and it's not because we thought he was going to be charged with anything . . . necessarily. That was bull@#it, but he didn't know it. The statement left the possibility of him walking out of there after we were done with him. He understood his rights.

Dale Shawn Hausner was kind enough to spell out his name for me, give me his address, spelling the street Mckellips out for me, and give his Social Security number and date of birth. He worked at the airport in the custodial department at Terminal 2. He referred to his job status as a "high paid janitor." That was interesting. He was forthcoming with all his personal information.

"I'm not going to hide anything or give you a hard time," Dale said.

"I appreciate that."

He was making nice, and so would I.

He gave me the background on his daughter and her disease, custody arrangements, and that he had a *roommate*.

"OK, and who is that?"

"Sam Dieteman. He's thirty years old. He was born a day before my brother which would be October 17th, let's see what's the year . . . '66, so maybe he was born in um . . . '76. I know he's thirty years old. He has been there a little over a month."

At least he was truthful, but what kind of man knows that type of information off the top of their head about a roommate? He obviously studied Dieteman or knew him much longer than a month.

"How long have you known Sam?"

"Probably about six months . . . a year . . . Ah, let me think. Probably the better part of a year. Maybe nine months to a year. We met through my brother Jeff."

Which is it, idiot? If it was six months, Dieteman wasn't involved in the .22 caliber cases. If it was a year, then he probably was involved. I pushed on.

"Do you own a vehicle?"

Of course, he does, but he didn't know I knew. These were all test questions about his truthfulness. So far he had passed.

"Yes I do. It's a 1998 Toyota Camry, and it's ah license plate is RHZ-537. Unless it's the other way . . . and uhm it's blue. I bought it February 3rd of 2005, the day before my birthday."

So far so good.

It was time to ask about his current mental faculties.

"Have you had anything to drink tonight or smoke anything tonight?"

The surveillance guys weren't close enough to see what Dieteman was blowing outside.

"I'm gonna be honest with you, I've been drinking a little bit, and I've smoked a little bit." Here we go. "I was making some mixed drinks, like Amaretto. I had some vanilla schnapps, maybe a little vodka." I didn't smell anything on his breath, and the room is small. He obviously wasn't impaired. "A little methamphetamine, but it wasn't tonight."

I delved into the background on his daughter and the mother of his child.

"No what it is . . . she's a typical woman. She gets mad at me because I didn't want a committed relationship even though we have a baby together. Two weeks ago, we got into a big fight, and I told her I would never be with her, I'm tired of listening to you, I'm not going to be with you. Two or three days later, somebody knocked on my door and said 'Court order papers,' and what it was is she wanted to change Rebecca's last name to Swaney. She knows I fu#*in hate that. She wants me to go to some parenting classes. She also wants me to pay child support even though, this pisses me off, and I pay more than I should. She also wants me to be tested constantly for methamphetamine."

I had hit a nerve. Hausner's demeanor changed. The water bottle he was holding became a wringing towel. He fidgeted with the cap, twisting it on and off. Could this be the motive for his shootings?

"We just go back and forth. She gets pissed off at me because I didn't want to marry her. I didn't want marriage. I just wanted to have a baby, because I had two kids before that passed away in a car wreck in 1994."

Again, Hausner had shared something personal, something he didn't have to. I wasn't sure why. Could this be the cause at the root of his violence? His posture changed after the story of his kids perishing in a wreck. His hand was pressed on his head as if he were trying to push the memories out of his mouth.

It was time to get down to it. I had created the rapport I wanted, and he had told me, a complete stranger, some of his emotional secrets. It was time to find out if he would incriminate Dieteman and maybe implicate himself.

"Do you have any idea why you're down here?"

"I think so. Sam and I were at the Casino about a week and a half ago, and they pulled us in there and read us the riot act. They said we were slashing a bunch of tires out in the parking lot, which is a filthy lie. They grilled us, took our pictures, they looked through my car. Found my ice pick, cause I'm also a bartender, and they gave us a bunch of sh#* about that, and said you're never allowed back on the casino property. We have you on tape slashing tires. I'm like, look, I'll answer all your questions. You don't need a search warrant. Check in my car for anything."

"Did they say anything about this incident being captured on video?"

I wanted to put them together on the night of a shooting, on video hopefully.

"Yes, they did. They said, 'We have it; we know it was you. But we're not going to prosecute you.' I'm like; 'If you have it on video and you knew it was us, don't think I wouldn't know you'd prosecute me. You're doing what you can which is fine.' I never came back, and I have a feeling that they decided to bluff our ass on it so I'm pretty sure that's what this is about."

Hausner had played them. He called the Casino's bluff and they folded, thus empowering him. He must have walked away laughing.

Hausner was anticipating a response as to why he was there, so I gave him one. "It's a little more complicated than that. Unfortunately, the person that you've allowed to come into your home, Mr. Dieteman, has made some very curious remarks to some different individuals about a series of crimes I'm currently investigating across the city . . . "

Dale interrupted, "That figures."

He figured Dieteman couldn't keep his mouth shut.

"Does this have anything to do with my daughter?"

"No, not at all. This concerns Mr. Dieteman. I want you . . . you need to be honest with me."

"I will, I will tell you everything you wanna know."

Once again, a promise I hoped he would keep.

"Does Mr. Dieteman own any weapons?"

"Not that I know of . . . He might have a . . . He's got a lot of knives, and stabbing weapons and like I said tools, but I'm not his mom so . . . " Stabbing weapons? What does that mean?

"OK, so no guns as far as you know?"

"As far as I know," he said hesitantly. "I have a lot of guns!"

Dale said that without being asked. He just blurted it out. It was time to explore this for the sake of curiosity, and also the sake of the searchers.

"Can you tell me what kind of guns you have?"

"I will tell you every gun I have."

And so he did. A twelve gauge shotgun that his Dad gave him to which he had ammunition for; a 303, with no ammunition; a 28 gauge, single shot with ammunition; a 20 gauge single shot with ammo; and the piece de résistance . . . two 410 shotguns, one pump action, and one a single shot with lots of ammunition.

"Are you a hunter?"

That would explain his guns and ammunition. If he was, things could be difficult to prove.

"Yes . . . I . . . not technically a hunter. I like to go out shooting in the desert and stuff." Sorry that doesn't qualify as hunting.

"So you're, or do you consider yourself, a weapons person?"

"Yeah, I love weapons. Yes I do!"

He was more than eager to tell me about his passion, and I wanted him to expound on his 410 shotguns. I wanted size, style, length of barrel, grip, everything.

"Is that a pistol grip or . . . "

Hausner cut me off.

"One of 'em had been sawed off to make into a pistol grip . . . not the pump. That one is just regular. I haven't modified it at all. The only gun I modified was my 410 single shot, break open, because I didn't like the way the thing felt on my shoulder. The modified part, which doesn't make it illegal, had the handle sawed off."

I was stumped. Most people saw off the barrel to conceal a weapon, making it shorter and easier to carry undetected. He sawed off the butt or stock of the gun. This was interesting, but I tried not to make a big deal about it. The more important fact was that it was a single shot 410, meaning you can only fire one round without reloading. Just like in all the shotgun shootings.

As I watched Hausner discuss his guns, he became very animated, almost excited. His hands started to move in and around, and he sat up straight. He truly was a gun enthusiast with the exception of handguns.

"Any handguns?" I asked. He had already told me Dieteman had none.

"No, sir."

"So you're a shotgun type person."

I was pushing it here, but I figured the more he talked about shotguns, the more he could incriminate himself.

"Uhm . . . yeah. I don't . . . I'm not accurate. I can't hit sh#* with a handgun. I've tried. I can't hit anything. In my hand, I have a bad hand, so it's hard for me to shoot anything. I got stabbed right here."

He showed me a scar in the middle of his right hand.

Although, I didn't catch this right away, it dawned on me later that sawing the butt off the shotgun made no sense now. He makes a pistol grip out of the stock, yet he says that he can't shoot because of a bad hand. Then why manipulate the stock? There were only one or two logical explanations—to conceal the weapon from sight and/or to make it easier to maneuver inside a car.

As I took notes, it finally dawned on Hausner that he should shut up and figure out what it was that Sam had been saying.

"Now, real quick, you said Sam was . . . he was yapping about doing some crimes or something like that you said."

He was trying to play clueless, but it was too late.

"Yes, that's why you're here. That's why I asked about your guns. Do you keep your guns locked up?"

"No, unfortunately, I don't even have a gunlock. That's not illegal though. I'm careful. I have a thirty-one month old daughter who is inquisitive. I don't have a gun safe."

"The reason I'm asking is that Mr. Dieteman lives with you, correct? So, in that period of time, could you say where he was at any particular time?"

The whole idea was to paint a picture of Dieteman as the sole bad guy. With that, Hausner might just incriminate himself while talking about Sam Dieteman.

"Tonight I can; he was with me. I go to bed between nine and eleven. Depending on what night it is. When I'm home, I can never leave my daughter. I have to be there all the time. But as far as he is all the time, I have no idea. He could be anywhere."

"Has he ever talked about, made mention of the fact that he actually used any of your weapons in any crimes?"

"No, absolutely not! If he's ever robbed anybody with my guns, he never told me about it. I would throw him the hell out of there. I'm a very law-abiding citizen. That's why I was very offended at the Indian people when they said that I was slashing tires. If you check my criminal record, I have not been in any trouble." Aside from shooting people.

"I don't see a violent history here in your past."

"No, I'm not violent."

He was deflecting, which was good.

"Alright, here are the nuts and bolts of this. Mr. Dieteman has decided to flap his gums, and because he's flapped his gums, he brought his world into your world."

Hausner began to lick his lips, and nervousness started to spread through his body. I continued.

"I'm going to ask you some very specific things about what you do or don't know. Don't B.S. me. Just be honest with me."

I figured he wouldn't if it just implicated Sam, and not him.

"I will be very happy to answer all those. I'm gonna tell you anything you wanna know. If he's robbed anybody with my guns, you can confiscate them and do whatever you need to do with them."

Once again, he came back to robbery, not gunning down people. In the short time I had spent with him, I could see that Hausner was a cunning manipulator. He chose his words and phrases well. Getting him to spill the beans on Sam and implicate himself was going to be tricky.

"Has he ever mentioned anything about shooting anybody?"

"No, absolutely not. If he did I'd . . . with my guns? No, absolutely not. What he does on his own time is his stuff."

He would surely report it if Sam admitted to it. But he hadn't, according to Dale.

He wasn't budging off his position, so it was time to talk some more and see just how much he knew or was willing to divulge.

"Have you been following at all what's going on in the city of Phoenix lately?"

"Absolutely, I've been following the Baseline Rapist, and I've been following the serial killer."

"What do you know?"

"I know everything that's in the newspapers because I even clipped them out and saved them. I have all the clippings at the house, that's the reason . . . I even have some backdated stuff. I keep track . . . I know they're looking for a black guy with a wig . . . he's twenty-five to thirty, he's five feet ten to six foot, he's a hundred seventy pounds, and I keep track of the serial killer; the other guy that's going around shooting people."

"What do you know about that particular case?"

I was implying about the Serial Shooter.

"Uhm . . . thirty-five people shot . . . animals, horses, dogs, uh five to six people dead . . . several cities, counties, shot up. Let me think . . . that's about it."

The only thing I could think was Wow! Did I really just hear what I thought I heard? He follows both of them. He knows the body counts and types. It was time to clarify if this was fascination, compulsion, or reality.

"Is there any particular reason why you've taken such an interest in these? It's just . . . "

"I find it interesting. I have a movie called the *History of Violence*. I also have the movie *Starkweather*, which was the first time . . . I don't know if you know anything about this stuff . . . Charles Starkweather was the first person to ever go on a serial killing spree in America. He was from Nebraska, which is, you know, my hometown."

Playing Columbo seemed to be the right maneuver. "Well, enlighten me, cause I don't know . . . I've never followed serial killers."

"It's fascinating. I don't know why it is, in fact it'd be on . . . you can't turn the radio on or anything without them talking about it. It kinda deals with the morbid side of people, like the boogeyman or something like that."

He was getting excited again. He was reveling in his knowledge and glad to share it.

"You can't go anywhere without hearing about it. I'm sure you get sick of hearing about it being a police officer, but you can't go to a bar, you can't go anywhere . . . my work. It's everywhere. I find it very interesting . . . "

I cut him off.

"This series?"

I wanted to make sure we were talking about the Serial Shooter.

"Yeah, this series, but it's all of it. Starkweather I know because I'm from Nebraska. I don't know much about the Son of Sam or the Zodiac Killer. I know a little about the BLK because that just happened. But historically I don't study them with a passion. I would love to sit down with some fool like Jeffrey Dahmer and ask him why in the hell would you wanna eat all those people . . . The BLK, he's killed eleven people for absolutely no reason. What the hell were you thinking? Why are you normal one second . . . What makes you click over. And to me it's just fascinating; nothing really wrong with it, but . . . I've saved all the clippings from the BLK, excuse me, the serial killer and from the serial sniper. I have them at home in a scrapbook."

Hausner was naming others, but talking about himself. Asking why they were normal one second and killers the next? I wanted to see if he saw what I saw in him, a savage killer. Or did he see someone else doing all this? I wanted his insight, his perspective.

"OK, give me a feel for . . . what is it . . . what is it you think that's going on? Give me an idea . . . " I was having trouble spitting out my question. He understood perfectly.

"I have these two things, OK? I think the Baseline Rapist could very well be also doing the shootings, cause there's reason to cover up . . . reason to kill people, OK. Greed, jealousy, covering up another crime, homicidal maniac, I can't think of the other one . . . But I think he's just a fu@*in nut . . . the Baseline Rapist. He's saying if they're looking for me, let's look for somebody else too, and he drives around and shoots people. Or it could be gang related, too."

I explained my extensive knowledge of gangs to him and told him these crimes did not fit in the category of gang initiations, retaliations, or any such matter. We needed to keep focused on individuals, like him and his partner. I decided to give credit where credit was due.

"You're pretty up-to-date on this stuff," I said.

"Oh, listen, I love this stuff! I wish they would catch the guy, but I mean ... I love this stuff."

Really! "Which guy would you like us to catch?"

"Both ... *especially the rapist*. I mean that guy is worse than the Serial Shooter cause he's killed more people, and rape is a very personal thing. I mean, they don't know who's doing it. If they do, they're not telling us. They're not telling us the caliber of the weapon, although we know it's a shotgun because they showed him on TV, the guy lifted up his shirt . . . some old fart on TV showed us his back. I know what a shotgun blast looks like. I own what . . . five or six shotguns. I know what they look like. It could be a gang; 'use my brother's 410, we want to hear it on the news.' Or it could be the Guardian Angels."

A 410! His mouth was now starting to pay dividends. Not only did he admit to clipping articles and watching TV coverage, he had brought in the use of the 410 to shoot someone, not me.

It was now 4:05 a.m., and I needed a break. The search of the Hausner apartment hadn't even begun yet. Samuel Dieteman was asleep in his interview room, and the microphones were picking up snoring. That was OK by me.

My plan was still to get Hausner to implicate Dieteman, and, by doing so, implicate himself. The Toyota Camry was the key to at least tie Hausner to its use in the shootings.

"OK, in talking about Sam, I may have asked you this and forgot. You've known him how long?"

"About nine months," Dale said.

"Has he ever had access to your vehicle where he drove . . . where he had the keys and he took off . . . ?"

"Uhm, no, I have a spare set hanging up by my front door. I've got several sets, but I keep my set with me. Nobody drives it; nobody can get in it."

"So he wouldn't have access to the car without you being there, nor would he take the car without your knowledge?" I asked.

"No, driving without my knowledge, no. *He doesn't drive my car.* I guess he could . . . he doesn't drive my car. I've never come out and went to use the bathroom and Sam not been on the couch and walked out and seen my car missing. The answer is no, definitely not."

That cleared it up. Hausner and Dieteman were together when they shot people. He just confirmed that. On to another subject.

"Let's, let's, let's . . . " once again Hausner cut me off.

"I'm sorry, so he's been running around telling everybody he's been shootin' people with my gun and in my car or . . . ?"

I had to tell him more or risk the conversation stopping.

"A person came forward and gave information that Mr. Dieteman has been bragging about being the shooter in this particular series of crimes." I paused for a moment to see his reaction. He looked down, hoping it didn't implicate him. He was concerned as I could see the cockiness exiting his body. "Does that shock you?"

"Yes that does! I can't believe that! I don't really think that he's been in trouble with the law a lot, I'm sure you have his rap sheet for violence and stuff . . . "

He was a skilled actor.

"Do you think it's possible . . . that he could do something like that? You know him. I don't."

Hausner was perplexed. I could see it running through his mind . . . how was he going to lie about his roommate's involvement if he'd been bragging about shooting people?

I continued. "The ammunition that you and I are talking about here is the same that we believe has been used in some of the shootings. What I need from you is why do you think he would even mention the fact that he was involved?"

Dale perked up to protect his partner. "OK, let's say I'm Sam in the bar. I'm talking sh*# and he says to his buddy, 'Hey, I'm out shooting people.' Why would he do that? Uhm . . . self-esteem problems . . . "

"Does he have self-esteem problems?" I asked.

"Yeah, he doesn't have any self-esteem. He tells me he's worthless. He said he can't wait to die. He says he wishes he could be like me. 'You got a job, a car, a house, a kid you get to see all the time. My kids are in Minnesota. I'm just fu#*in worthless, a drain on society.' But if you ask me why would somebody do that? Why would someone say something . . . maybe to make people afraid of you or to, in a sick way, boost yourself up."

"Notoriety?" I asked.

"Yeah, you know, got nothing else goin' on. Just wandering the streets drinking and smoking and you know, maybe notoriety. I can't believe he would say something."

Dale Hausner was coming to the realization that his partner was a complete fool. He had talked, and somebody had come forward. He just couldn't understand why.

"Has he taken the same interest in the series of shootings that you have? Does he follow it?" I asked.

"Yes, we both do. We'd watch the news at night and stuff; that's what we would do."

Numerous connections could be reached thus far, so I decided to throw out a line and see if he would bite.

"You don't have any small caliber rifles do you?"

"What's a small caliber rifle?"

Good answer. I needed to be specific.

"Like a .22, or anything like that?"

"No. I did a long time ago and, I believe I left it in Texas with my wife . . . seven to ten years ago."

It was worth a try. The fact that he owned one at anytime was enough to pursue. I just needed to run down where in Texas. Back to Sam.

"Has Sam ever made . . . when you guys are watching all this stuff . . . has he ever come out and said, 'that's cool'?"

"We joke around sometimes, you know. I'll say 'That's what you fu@*ing get when you walk down the street at 3:00 am, man. Someone's gonna drive and shoot you in the ass . . . people just don't listen, you know. People take this sh*# as a joke.' That's the kind of stuff we talk about. It was back and forth, you know, how can you have a hundred and fifty fu*#ing cops on this and not have any kind of clues themselves? How hard can it be to catch somebody doing this?"

In his own way he was bragging and calling me an idiot. I decided to play-off of that.

"How stupid are we . . . ?" I said.

"Yeah, why don't they put . . . I don't want you to be insulted, parked car for sale and sit in it. Use night vision binoculars and write down people's license plates. Track the thirty five hundred or so plates and look for histories of violence."

It was a great idea, in his mind: to track the cars and the people with violent records. But then he would never come up, nor Sam for that matter. Dale had just let me know what he thought and what he would look for when he was out trolling. He didn't stop there.

"This could be a law enforcement officer. It could be Sam; it could be anybody. But a person's got to be smart, 'cause they've been getting away with this for a long time. There's never a witness of course. Nobody ever sees anything. It's amazing."

He liked the idea that the person was smart. He was, of course, referring to himself, indirectly. Now it was time to hit Dale Hausner with more intelligence that had been gathered.

"Have you ever heard the term RVing?"

"RVing? There's a . . . ah movie with Robin Williams . . . "Recreational Vehicle . . . No I don't own one. Never rented one. No, I'm sorry I don't know. What is that?"

He was testing me. "Well, I was hoping you could tell me. That's why I'm asking you. That's what he (Sam) mentioned to this particular source. That's what he called this crime spree . . . RVing." I looked at Hausner, and again his eyes shifted down. He knew what the term meant. He may not have used it, but he knew.

I asked Dale about barhopping and drinking with Sam. I wanted to see if I could catch him in a lie.

"I've been to the bar, I think maybe twice. I'm always the DD, and I never like to drink there. I never drink."

That was a lie; he just told me earlier that he'd been drinking this evening. He was starting to waver.

"We've been to the tavern on 43rd Avenue a couple of times. Sometimes I'll drop him off there. In fact, the other night . . . like Tuesday, I dropped him off at 43rd Avenue and Peoria and then . . . "

It was time to play stupid.

"What's at 43rd Avenue and Peoria?"

"It's a place called the Stardust. "

"I know where that's at," I said to reconfirm my knowledge of the area.

"And uhm, I went home and cleaned my house up; texted him periodically to see if he needed a ride. He went to the casinos and then I texted him about one or two in the morning and asked him if I should pick him up. He said 'yeah,' but he was on the I-10 . . . Wild Horse Pass, cause we're not allowed at the one anymore because of some asshole slashing those tires. So I picked him up there took him back home and that was that."

He had done so well until the last part. The part where he picked him up at the casino and went home. He failed to mention the cruising around for hours looking for victims to shoot.

Then Hausner shifted gears. He again threw out a personal story that I had neither asked about nor reflected on. It was coming from deep within him.

"I'd tell him, if he wants to go out with his friends, I'm not . . . I'm . . . it's not like we're boyfriend/girlfriends . . . I'm not gonna be a jealous little bitch and say he can't go out! He wants to go out and have fun, you know, just don't ever bring any of your fu*#er friends to my house."

Whether it was the emotion of Sam bragging about the killings or the ease at which we were speaking, Dale Hausner just referred to Sam Dieteman as if he were a lover. He would never have mentioned the boyfriend/girlfriend or the jealous bitch comment if they weren't in some type of relationship or Dale hadn't sought one. I've worked violence between gays. The term *bitch* is used for the feminine part of the duo. He was referring to himself as the *bitch*. But, make no mistake, if Sam was stepping out on him, Dale wasn't happy about it. I made a notation to myself to check on Dale's sexual preferences.

"One of the issues that's come up, at least as far as the shotgun cases go, is the car. I'm sure you've seen the vehicle description of the car in the paper?"

Dale answered quickly. "Yeah, it's a midsize four-door car."

"Right! Do you know the color by any chance?"

"It just says light colored, doesn't it? It's funny 'cause every time I'm in a group of like eight or nine cars at a stoplight, I'll look around and like there's four midsize cars. With that kind of description no wonder they can't, you know . . . "

"I'm going to be honest with you. There was . . . and I only know this because it's never been released, but there was an actual detailed description of this particular vehicle given by one of the witnesses."

Hausner's reaction was one of surprise. He had no idea we had the very detailed description that Ashley Armenta had given us.

"Wow!" He said.

Here comes more bad news Dale.

"She describes your vehicle to a T. Matter of fact, she only missed the model year by two years. She knew that because she dates, or at one time, was involved with a car nut."

"Wow!"

Again this was his reaction. He was reeling with the new information. It was time to pile it on. If he wasn't going to give Sam up, it was time to bring him into the equation.

"So you see where I'm going with this. I know you guys are friends."

"No! We're buds, but, man, if he killed 85 people . . . if he killed however many people, that's on him. That's not on me. I'm not protecting anybody, so . . . "

"So as far as you know, you guys have never been together doing anything violent?"

This struck a nerve.

"Oh no!! Hell no!! No way!!"

Time to keep at him.

"Some of the shootings, one in particular, had a 12 gauge that was involved. You own a 12 gauge."

It was time to deflect.

"OK, now hold on. I've only had that 12 gauge in my custody for only about a month now." How convenient. "My father gave it to me maybe a month, month and half ago. so . . . "

"OK the 12 gauge you've had only . . . what . . . and you've owned the 410s for how long, and the 20?"

He was becoming concerned. I could see the tension rising in his facial features.

He looked down and answered, "Long time."

I explained to him the retrieval of evidence at numerous shooting scenes. "OK, now here we have Sam bragging about this . . . we have your car perfectly described at one of these shootings . . . we have 410 ammunition. You see where I'm going with this?"

Hausner looked right at me and said, "I understand."

One last chance to spill your guts, Dale.

"Now is there anything else that you'd like to tell me about Sam that you haven't already told me that you think you might need to tell me before this comes crashing down on you?"

Without missing a beat, Hausner answered. "No, he doesn't get along with his parents . . . "

That wasn't the answer I was looking for, not even close. He was good at playing stupid, but he was back on his heels. It was time to pull out a piece of the evidence and watch his reaction.

"OK, I'm going to show you something that's in here . . . This is very curious."

I pulled out a copy of the map that was found in his garbage bag. The one dumped by Dieteman and recovered by Detective Bird. I unfolded the copy and laid it out on the table.

"Have you ever seen this before? Does that look familiar at all?"

Hausner stared at the map for a few seconds. I could see the wheels turning in his mind. He wanted to know how we found this, and what the hell was his excuse going to be. For seconds, he inspected the map, moving his head up and down the grids, trying to act like he'd never seen it before.

He shook his head and answered, "hu-uh. Sorry, no."

His face said otherwise.

"This was taken a couple of days ago from your garbage, and on it you can see different spots that had been marked in red and you've got some in blue. You see that?"

"Uh-hum." He answered, nodding his head.

He didn't deny the you've part. He wasn't thinking quickly enough now.

"You see this line right along here? You know what street that runs on?"

"Washington." Another good answer, but we both knew better.

"No, it's actually Van Buren."

"Oh, I'm sorry, is it?"

Now he was being smug, playing dumb.

"This specifically corresponds to different spots that are very close to the spots that I'm currently investigating for this series of shootings. Can you explain to me how this ended up in your trash?"

Hausner shook his head no, all the while looking at the map and trying to figure a way out of this trap.

"Sir, I'm sorry. I apologize, no I do not. I . . . I have a map of the United States in my closet, but I don't . . . I don't know . . . "

He was stumbling badly, and he knew it. It was time to keep hammering him.

"It's good size, I mean, you'd think you'd see something like this, if you had it?"

His next words were typical of a man desperate to explain away the unexplainable.

"Well, why would I throw it away? I mean that doesn't . . . you know what I mean . . . I . . . If I'm . . . keep it, I'm gonna keep a map." He gathered himself because he knew he was stumbling badly. "No. I haven't seen this. Sam is pretty good about taking trash out. I throw it out on the porch, and he throws it out for me. In fact, tonight, he went to take the trash out and never came back. About five minutes later, the SWAT team came in so . . . "

Hausner admitted that we would find a map from the paper that he cut out. He'd circled areas of interest. "The only other thing you're going to find is like in my scrapbook. I have all this stuff. I circled areas in the pink where people have never been hit before, as far as the shootings that were in the newspaper."

Hausner explained he was trying to think like police by theorizing where we should deploy our units. The only problem was, he wasn't trying to help us, just help himself and Sammy. He was looking at areas where no crimes had been committed because he had either made our surveillances or heard about the surveillances.

Time for another slap to the face.

"In your conversations with Sam, did he ever mention or talk about the fact that he may have been in or around one of these shootings at one time or another?"

I was referring to the James Hodge shooting, where both of them were listed as witnesses.

He shook his head. "No, no, he's said nothing like that."

"OK, and as far as you're telling me, have you ever been in or around any of these areas where one of these shootings has occurred?"

I could see the panicked look on his face. It was time for damage control. "Oh, yes, actually we were. We were at my brother's house, and an old man got shot. I came up on him, the cops showed up, I flagged them down. Sam and I were there at one of the shootings. I gave my I.D. and everything to the police officer . . . Gave a full statement . . . Stayed around as long as I could."

How chivalrous.

Before beating him up further, it was time for another break. He could ponder his next batch of denials over the urinal. Besides, I needed to touch base with the wire guys. After the Hodge shooting, I was hoping to hit him with some incriminating statements off the wire.

I could only hope.

Everyone jumped on me the minute I left the interview room. Each investigator had about a dozen questions. I asked them to write them all down. I would get to them in a minute. Right now, I had to make a phone call to Lieutenant Piano. He answered immediately.

"Clark, we got a couple of things that I'm going to pass on to you. There were a couple of conversations that seem somewhat unusual and possibly incriminating, but you'll have to decide for yourself."

That was at least encouraging.

"Alright, let me have it."

These would only be useful if Dale or Sam didn't invoke their rights or decide to stop talking in Dale's case.

"OK, there's talk about altering their appearance, going into hiding, and something about a yellow hat?"

Yellow hat? I had no idea what that was in reference to.

The lieutenant continued. "Dieteman calls Hausner a chicken, and then Dieteman starts reading the obituaries. They were commenting about the news and them being copycatted by someone in another state or something close to that."

That last part was somewhat incriminating.

"OK, keep 'em coming."

"He referred to themselves as 'pioneers.'"

I almost had to slap myself. That was huge. Pioneers go where no one else has gone. They break ground, explore new frontiers, and set the standards for others to follow. If they were referring to themselves as pioneers, there could be no mistaking that for anything more than this series of shootings.

"What else?"

"We believe that Dale said something to the effect of 'What about the guy I shot at 27th Avenue and Northern?' Does that sound familiar?"

27th Avenue and Northern? There was no shooting at that location reported as being part of this series. Maybe it was one we missed, or it was never reported. That was news to me.

"Here's the best one. Looks like Hausner says to the kid 'Tell Sam goodnight. Tell Sam not to kill anybody tonight.' He also said that the shooting on Sunday was his favorite shooting."

Both those comments were telling. Robin Blasnek was shot on Sunday, July 30th and the killing comment spoke for itself. I wasn't sure whether to hit Hausner with that one, or wait until I talked to Dieteman.

Lieutenant Piano agreed to fax over the comments and what little else they had on nonincriminating statements.

Lieutenant Benson had joined us from Mesa and stopped me. He had been in contact with the investigators at the apartment. They had finally gotten in and started the search. They had seen numerous rounds of 410 ammunition, particularly four shot. Hausner had already admitted to that.

As I re-entered and sat down, Hausner was bent over complaining about the cold room. He was given a shirt. I wanted more information about the Hodge shooting.

"OK, we were talking about . . . " He never let me finish again.

"We see some guy sitting on his porch. He walks up and he goes . . . Whoa . . . I'm like what the hell man? He's got blood pouring out of his pockets. I'm like, 'What happened?' He said they shot me . . . and I said, 'Who shot you?' Round and round like that for a little bit. I said 'Don't touch me,' cause he wanted to touch me. I said you stay here I'm gonna get my cellphone . . . The cops pulled up . . . flagged em over there. I gave a full statement."

I took out the supplemental report of their interview that night. Maybe Dale had told Sam not to talk to police or act like he was drunk, but, whatever the case, Sam gave a statement. I wanted Dale to know that.

"It does appear that they talked to Samuel that night. He gave kind of the same statement you did, you guys were both looking for your cat . . . and you heard screaming and observed my victim walking down the sidewalk covered in blood."

"God it was terrible!" Dale said.

From this topic, I learned that Sam actually lived with Jeff Hausner for about a year. That placed Sam and Jeff together in 2005. If Sam and Dale were shooting people in 2005 and 2006, one could only assume that Jeff was a part of this or at least knew something about it.

Hausner saw where I was going with this questioning. So I changed course. He hadn't admitted his or Sam's involvement. There was no reason to believe he would give up Jeff.

It was time for another punch to the gut.

"OK, up to this point you've been completely honest with me about everything we've talked about?"

"Yes, I have."

"Well, I'm going to ask you some specific things right now. Mr. Dieteman came under our radar screen last week, and at that point we did what we believe to be specific targeting . . . meaning that we had surveillance on him . . . meaning electronic surveillance on him over a short period of time. We also had electronic surveillance in your apartment."

Hausner stared at me to see if I would blink or flinch or give any sign of untruthfulness. He didn't want to believe that we bugged him. He was hoping I was lying.

"We've picked up some very interesting conversations with Sam . . . and you."

"Kay."

That was all he could say. His mind was scrambling, trying to remember if we did bug him, what it was he said. He was listening to me, but he was hearing his own mind scrambling. His face had been white, but now it turned ghostly white.

I figured I would ask this, but I knew the answer already.

"Do you know what you and Sam talked about in your apartment?"

He shook his head no and answered, "Huh-uh."

There was no way he was going to give it up since there was the possibility that I was bluffing.

"Sam had made some specific remarks about these shooting, and I know that because I have the transcripts from those remarks."

I pulled out the fax and laid it on top of my notes.

Hausner needed to counter, so he did.

"Oh yeah, we'd been, you know, flapping our gums . . . He'll get drunk and talk stupid and stuff . . . "

He was losing it. Up until this time, he had a somewhat logical answer to everything. Now he had none. I jumped all over him. He wasn't going to minimize this. He had his chance to come clean and didn't. Now I'm going to square him up.

I began to read the fax with both the casual conversations and the incriminating ones.

"Were you watching any show about the DC Sniper?"

"No! If you tell me what time it is, I can tell you whether I saw it or not."

It wasn't that important. Just giving him a little taste.

"Did you make any particular comments, you specifically, about being involved in these shootings?"

His eyes went down as if he was thinking, and I stared right at him. He was still trying to figure out what he had talked about with Sam.

"If I did, it would be silly stuff, you know. Nothing special . . . and as far as saying 'It was me, it was me' I don't . . . I wouldn't do something like that. If I did, it would be something silly. I don't go around killing people for no reason."

His answer was lame. His wariness during the interview was starting to show on his face. He was having trouble putting a story together. It was time to shift the blame of these shootings onto him as well.

"One of the particular comments that you made was very troubling when they (news) were doing the Mesa shooting. You said, 'What about the guy I fu@#ing shot on 27th Avenue and Northern?'"

"No . . . I . . . That just musta been me talking sh*#. Are you sure it was me and not Sam?" I was positive, and so was he. "Well, if that was just me, I was just talking sh#* . . . I don't know . . . People say silly stuff when they're drunk. I, mean, look at Mel Gibson. They've been playing that to death. I'd been drinking . . . I've not shot at anybody anywhere."

Time for more good tidbits.

"Do you remember a conversation about the networks and the news talking about these shootings, possibly being followed or being related in other states? Do you remember that?"

Surprisingly he answered, "Yes." He could not remember the specifics, of course. "What did I say?"

"Well, it specifically says here that in a different voice you said, 'We're being copycatted, Sam.' In a higher pitched voice."

"In a different voice, that makes no sense to me."

It made no sense to me either, but the copycatting was significant. He had no answer for that comment. He was losing the battle badly. I needed a knock-out blow to hopefully get him to confess.

I didn't even preface the comment with anything; I just let him have it. "We are pioneers, Sam . . . What did you mean by that?"

"Pioneers?"

"Explain to me why you would say something like that?"

He tried to look me in the eyes, but he couldn't. His posture sank into his chair, and he dropped his head. He sat there silently for a moment, then spoke as his voice trailed off.

"I don't know . . . just pioneers, you know . . . or I don't know, just pioneers . . . We just went somewhere that nobody else has ever done before . . . so I don't know . . . We're . . . We act like we're demigods and gods . . . you know . . . it's just like joking . . . I guess other people wouldn't find it funny."

During this whole interview, I had taken a soft approach to Dale. So far he had talked his ass off. Yelling and calling him a murderous thug would shut him up. So I decided to sit there and watch. I let the camera record his actions, his demeanor. His head was down, and his body language spoke volumes. He was defeated, and he knew it. We sat there in silence. No questions, just silence.

After about a minute, he looked up and shook his head. He knew what I was waiting for, and he wasn't going to give it up.

"I don't know . . . So you guys think I'm a part of this?"

What else was there to say? Now it was my turn to act stupid.

"What do you think?"

"I think, you think I'm a part of this. I think you think Sammy and me are in this car killing everybody since May of '05. You guys are going to charge me with murder and all this other crap. I'm gonna fu#*ing go to jail, and they're gonna take my house, that's what I think."

He had it right. But that didn't mean he was going to confess. In fact, just the opposite. He became more emboldened. Over the next half an hour, I hit him with more statements from the wire. It was all just sh*# talking, according to him.

He claimed that if I wanted to know more about the shootings that I needed to talk to who was responsible, or maybe talk to Sam. He had told me everything that he could. If we were watching him like we said we were, then he knew that we hadn't seen him do anything, or he would've been picked up before this. He knew we would never let him kill anyone and stand by and watch.

He knew we had no witnesses to identify him. He even brought in sexual fantasy into the equation.

"I joke about it, but I really don't like violence. Like when I saw the older guy who'd been shot. It just about made me throw up. I don't get off on stuff like that. I didn't go home and masturbate or any crazy stuff like that. That's what sickos do . . . "

Yeah, sickos like you.

"I know you're not going to believe me because of whatever, but . . . I've been as honest with you as I can be. I've told you everything I know."

Being honest and being as *honest as you can be* are two different things. I fired another shot, just to let him know I caught that.

"That doesn't tell me that you're not involved. Being as honest as you can be tells me that you're starting to understand the ramifications of this whole thing."

I confronted him with his lies, specifically about the night of picking up Sam at the casino. This time around, he filled in the last three hours.

"Dropped him off at the . . . I went to Metro-Center, bought a couple of movies, went back to the Stardust. He was playing pool, and he said he wanted to stay there so I went home and started cleaning up. One-ish or so, Sam and I text . . . He said the casino was bad . . . went and picked him up, wasn't sleepy, drove around for a little while, came home . . . "

"Where did you drive to?"

"All over hell and back: Chandler, Gilbert, Mesa, Tempe . . . We were all over hell and back."

"What was the purpose of that?"

I already knew his answer.

"Not tired."

The lies and the minimizing of facts ran abundant. Detective Donnie Byers of Mesa PD decided to enter the interview room. I introduced Donnie as he came in, and I asked Dale if he knew where he was Sunday night, July 30th; the night Robin Blasnek was murdered in Mesa. It was perfect timing, and Detective Byers could step right into the interview since he was case agent on that murder.

Dale answered, "I don't really remember."

"Dale, I'm with Mesa police, and I'm investigating the shooting of the girl Sunday night. I just came from Mesa, and they're doing a search warrant on your apartment, your vehicle, your locker, and stuff like that. There are some things . . . I've talked to Clark here a little bit . . . you seem like a pretty nice guy. A smart guy, and here's the deal. Your buddy over there . . . I don't know if there's something wrong with this guy, but he's sitting in the room just bawling. There ain't a soul in there. He's just in there bawling."

It was a lie, but a thought-provoking tactic. If Detective Byers could get Hausner to be worried about Deiteman's demeanor, it could lead Hausner to an admission. Hausner could believe that Dieteman was getting ready to confess so he should do it first, looking better in the eyes of a jury. I've seen this work before.

Problem was Hausner wasn't buying it. Donnie took the bad cop lead. The interview turned into an interrogation.

"Listen to me, just listen to me. There's absolutely no doubt in our mind. The evidence is irrefutable. It absolutely is. You seem like a nice guy . . . sounds like maybe you got a few issues, but here's the deal. You're the one with the 410 shotgun. That's the weapon that was used in the Mesa killing. You've been told about the map that was found in your trash. Are your fingerprints gonna come back on that? Yes or no?"

"I don't know," Hausner said.

"You and I know that they're gonna come back . . . Here's another thing. My understanding is in talking to Clark that you said you haven't fired a weapon in how long?"

"Maybe a month."

Oops, bad answer. I knew where Byers was going here. The shell casing in the trash was just found.

"A month? How often do you empty your trash? You don't wait a month to empty your trash."

Hausner agreed that he didn't empty his trash once a month, more like daily. Donnie had him backpedaling, and I was enjoying watching the show.

"Inside your trash along with the map is a soda can. Inside the soda can is a 410 casing, number four shot. Which is the same ammo that was used in the Mesa shooting. Your fingerprints are on the can. Do you get what I'm coming to here? Here's how the evidence is starting to stack up. Your car has been identified as being at the scene of a shooting. You guys are interviewed at the scene of a shooting. A 410 shotgun. It's your shotgun. You said your buddy doesn't own any guns. He doesn't own a vehicle, and I'm sure that you wouldn't let him drive your vehicle twenty-eight or nine times without you knowing about it."

Hausner was nodding his head, agreeing with everything Detective Byers was saying. Yet, Dale Hausner never budged. Even when Detective Byers gave him the out and told him that he believed Dieteman was the shooter and that Dale was just the driver, he just acted ignorant.

"I'm not with him. I'm sorry. I'm telling you everything I know."

He kept ripping into Hausner. He confronted him with the wire, including the part about Sam not killing anyone. Still nothing. "We're not going away! You're not gonna walk away from this stuff. I think you think you can squirm out of this, and you can't. I didn't write this stuff down just to come in and try and fool you. It's a fact."

As I sat there and watched, I realized that Dale Hausner would never admit or confess to anything. He was smart in that way. He knew that some things could be explained away and others argued. He knew if he confessed, that could never be explained away. He'd been hit with every fact over and over, from being a shooter to a lookout, and the endless driving around on August 1st and into the morning of the 2nd. We had tried to sympathize with him about his daughter and the loss of his children, all to no avail.

Detective Byers took another shot.

"Dieteman's gonna get his opportunity. What are you gonna do when he tells us that 'I shot and he drove' or 'he drove and I shot'? What are you gonna feel like?"

"I don't know."

It was certainly a possibility, but not a guarantee Dieteman would confess. "You're screwed!" Detective Byers yelled.

Hausner, the ever confident gunman, answered, "He's not gonna say that! He's gonna say I've never been with him. I haven't been with him, ever!"

Detective Donnie Byers was fed up and excused himself from the interview with a few parting shots at Hausner's credibility.

"You need to sit here and think about it. After four or five hours, you're really not convincing."

"I understand," Dale said as Detective Byers got up to leave. "Thank you, Officer."

As the door shut, I looked at Dale Hausner and could only ponder what type of personality I was dealing with. Narcissist for sure. Sociopath, maybe psychopath? As I tried to read him, I really, truly believed that he thought he could talk his way out of this arrest. He wanted to cooperate, as long as it didn't implicate him. He believed he was the smartest guy in the room. I wasn't going to let him revel in what he thought was victory.

"I think at this point we're . . . "

"Going in circles?"

He filled in my sentence., just like many psychopaths do. They always know what the other person is thinking. It makes people believe they are smarter than they really are.

It was time to interview Sam. I had one last opinion to share.

"I think this was all about notoriety. That when the Baseline Killer got a lot of press ... these shootings stepped up! I'm a real smart guy about this stuff."

Unknowingly, Hausner nodded his head up and down confirming what I was saying.

"Yeah," was all he could muster.

CHAPTER 42

"Dieteman is ready for you," Lieutenant Benson said.

I had just sat down in the CP to munch on a cold breakfast sandwich and down a caffeine-laced drink. I was beyond exhausted. Hausner's interview had been a rollercoaster of facts, half-truths, and lies. I was dizzy, and my body ached all over. I almost surrendered and threw up the white flag. Somebody else go do this!

The interview rooms that housed Dale Hausner and Sam Dieteman were separated by about forty feet. There was no way Dieteman heard any of our conversations with Hausner, nor could Hausner hear what Sam would say. We weren't even sure if Samuel Dieteman knew that Hausner had been arrested, since he was taken outside by the dumpsters and not allowed to go back to the apartment.

As I opened the door and walked into Interview Room 4, Sam was resting until he heard the door. He sat up and tried to wake up. The time of the interview was exactly 7:39 a.m., almost eight hours after his arrest. "Morning," I said. He was still half asleep. "Yeah," Sam answered in a groggy reply. I almost hoped he would invoke his right to remain silent. I told Sam who I was and that I was the one that had him brought down. I advised him of his rights and went through all the pleasantries of trying to start a conversation with someone you've never met. I gathered all his personal information, including the facts that he was unemployed and currently living with Dale Hausner. He also confirmed that he had stayed with Dale's brother, Jeff Hausner, for four or five months before he moved in with Dale. That put him living with the Hausners since early '06, but not in '05 when the .22 caliber shootings were going on. It was possible that they shot together, but just didn't live together.

Sam was originally from Minnesota and didn't own a vehicle, all information that I already had verified through background checks. The last car he had driven was one that belonged to Jeff Hausner. So far he had not lied about anything. He also admitted to drinking last night and using "a little meth." He claimed he was not addicted to either of the substances.

I was running on fumes, and it was time to cut to the chase. I wasn't interested in us becoming chums. Dale had told me intimate personal details, and it had worn me out. I just wanted the facts from Sam, if he was going to talk at all.

"OK, do you have any idea why you're here?" I couldn't beat around the bush much less than that. Neither was Sam's answer.

"Yeah, I believe it'd be the Serial Shooter case."

If I hadn't been so tired, I would have fallen out of my chair. My next question was in rapid response, just like I had assumed that's what he would say.

"And why would you ... why would you think that?"

"Cause I think I know the guy that's been doin' it. I've been stayin' with the guy that's been doin' it."

I was told that there was a loud cheer in the monitoring room, and a bunch of high fiving going on. I couldn't hear, and neither could Sam, but the feeling that came over me in those few milliseconds of trying to process what he said was one of almost panic. I was a zombie sitting across from the man who was obviously going to spill the beans on the largest criminal case in this state. I needed to focus and wake up, or I was going to embarrass myself.

"Well, that's exactly what this is about," I said as I tried to gather my thoughts and plan my next line of questioning. "I think you know a lot about it, and that's why I'm here, to pick your brain, OK?"

Sam nodded his head up and down in agreement. For months, I had thought about what I would ask these two when they were finally caught. I couldn't just spoon-feed him the cases and have him tell me about them after I explained which one he needed to expound on. I needed Sam, which Dale refused to do, to explain each shooting to the best of his recollection. The only way to do that would be to see exactly what and how much he remembered or knew. So I opened it up with a softball question.

"If you would . . . kind of tell me how it is that you know that's what I'm investigating (The Serial Shooter Case) and you think you know the person behind it, if you would, just . . . I'm going to let you speak, so . . . "

I sounded like a blubbering idiot. I was trying to focus, but it was hard. I just wanted him to talk, and I would then ask questions based on that.

"Well, you know I'm tryin' to remember . . . when I was staying at Dale's brother Jeff's house, I had an argument with Jeff's roommate there. I packed up my stuff and left . . . and Jeff and Dale had come and picked me up walking on the road. Later, we went and got something to eat and dropped Jeff off back at his place. We was heading up . . . I don't know what the heck it was, 32nd or 44th Street, and he's like well 'sit back.' I'm like alright, why? Then the window starts going down, and he brought up this little shotgun . . . blam! . . . fired at some fat guy that was walking down the road and . . . "

That is how it began. Samuel Dieteman witnessed Dale Hausner fire a shotgun at a pedestrian walking on the sidewalk in the area of 32nd Street or 44th Street. I had several shootings in the area, but only one of a larger male; Kibili Tambadu, shot on 44th Street just north of Van Buren on May 2nd 2006. The same night Claudia Gutierrez-Cruz was murdered. It was the first time Sam was with Dale Hausner shooting civilians.

Sam verified that they were in Dale's blue Toyota Camry. Dale's car has power windows so he controlled Sam's side of the car. Sam sat back as the shotgun was removed from the backseat and then fired out Sam's passenger window. It happened sometime in May in the area of Van Buren.

Sam continued on in greater detail about this first shooting, but wouldn't mention the murder of Claudia, even when I pushed for an answer. He played ignorant.

Sam laid out for me the shootings he could remember with the most clarity. James Hodge, shot in the back from the roadway by Dale Hausner. Yes, he and Dale talked to the victim and police.

"I think he wanted to go see if he hit the guy, and then we were up there and well, we're on our way back to the car and seen the officers pulling up ... so he just flagged them down."

It was Dale's idea to go view the carnage. Dale drove and shot the twelve gauge. Sam knew what was happening, and did nothing to stop it.

Then Sam added this tidbit. "I have never driven this guy's vehicle. I don't think anybody's ever been allowed to drive his car."

Sorry, Dale. That puts you behind the wheel of every one of these shootings, in your car! It was a nice piece of information.

I clarified one fact. "It's a different gun than the one he used the first time? Do you know what caliber that was? I asked.

"410," Sam said.

The odyssey of Sam Dieteman took us through what he could remember. Each time he would mention a new shooting, I would gather the details—

what gun was used, where the shot came from, what area, and so on. He never implicated himself, but he was skipping the timeline on a lot of the shootings. He was having a hard time remembering, and I don't know if it was the fact that he was an alcoholic and drinking a lot, or the fact that he had smoked meth earlier. I could see the struggle as he strained to remember the details that I so desperately needed for him to spill out.

"When's the next time you remember being with him when he (Dale) does this same thing?"

Sam had already sunk his own boat by being there and not reporting these shootings. He would be charged as an accomplice, no matter what now.

"I don't know, probably sometime in June," Sam said. "Probably around Van Buren or something . . . It was . . . uh . . . where he handed me the gun that night and . . . alright, c'mon . . . Your turn or something . . . so we kinda freaked out then. That's when I shot high . . . "

I was told you could hear a pin drop in the monitoring room. Samuel Dieteman had just signed his death warrant. He admitted to a shooting. This now shed a different light on the interview. Up until this time, it had been Hausner driving, Hausner shooting, Hausner wanting to get out of the car and see if anyone was hit. It was a whole new ball game.

"Let's talk about this a little bit," I said. "You shot that time?"

I wanted to make sure my ears weren't deceiving me.

Sam nodded his head up and down. I could tell he wasn't proud of what he did. He looked down as he explained the details.

It was a woman walking on Van Buren, probably around 32nd Street. He fired at her with the 410 out the passenger window.

"I think there was like a hooker or something walking there."

He was sure it was a female. He stated that Hausner hated hookers, so the gun was handed to him to take her down. He fired high and claimed that he didn't hit her. He said Dale was pissed because, if they missed, he figured they would get caught. I think he felt more justified since he didn't hit her. The problem was he was talking about Diane Bein. She was shot in the back, neck, and left shoulder just like Sam described. It happened on July 1st, not in June as Sam had thought.

I broke the news to him that he did in fact hit her, although he didn't believe me. He was adamant about the gunshot missing her.

"I know cause I'm sure she kept walking."

Actually she took off running and collapsed at the motel down the road, but there was no need to punctuate the point.

"Did you do any more shooting that night?"

"I think we shot at some black guy. I think. It was in that area of town . . . I'm just not exactly sure . . . no it wasn't Van Buren . . . it was some side road or something."

Jeremy Ortiz had been shot minutes after Diane Bein on what could be considered a side road, Oak Street.

"We drove down, turned around, came back by and shot at . . . I remember hearing that guy yell or something . . . not sure if he was hit." The same 410 shotgun had been used.

He admitted to shooting at a male who was walking on a side street, somewhere in the area of 51st Avenue and Olive, but missed. He was referring to shooting at the attorney, Michael Cordrey. He fired high again, not wanting to hit anyone.

"You know, he was pissed again that I missed that guy," speaking of Dale.

He thought he had used the 410 when in fact a twelve gauge shot cup had been recovered.

It was obvious that the alcohol and meth not only blurred his memory now, but he had used these drugs on the nights of these shootings. It was surprising he could remember any of the facts. He had the most trouble with the dates, even though they had been printed in the newspaper ten times over.

When it came to the two Mesa shootings, Sam would deny being there.

"I know it was a couple of weeks ago . . . just did it . . . he had come home from work and . . . hit somebody on a bike. I was sleeping back at the house." Hausner acted alone, which was highly doubtful. "He text messaged me if I'd watch the news, and then when he got home he told me about the hit. It was in the paper . . . it was on the news. Don't remember hearing much about it or anything about it after he initially said something till I seen it coming back from Vegas."

Sam was talking, so I just kept asking, "When's the next time that something occurred?"

He searched his almost obscure brain cells for the next significant event.

"Let's see here. When we got back from Vegas, we went driving around." He was talking about the night of the surveillance. "I don't think anybody, or I know nobody got shot that night."

I was waiting to see if he spilled the last and most publicized event. The murder of Robin Blasnek. I didn't give him an open-ended question on this one. I let him know there was at least one more shooting that I knew he knew.

"The next time that there was a shooting, describe that for me if you would?"

"When the heck was that . . . when he came home and woke me up. Gosh, just a couple of days ago. When he came home and woke me up and it was on the news . . . them sayin that the lady died."

"I want you to be very specific here for me. You were sleeping, and he came and woke you up?" I imagined Detective Donnie Byers leaning up to the TV monitor, salivating at what Dieteman was about to announce. "What did he tell you?"

"It was just me . . . me and my little air mattress. He sat there. He's shaking my leg. 'Hey, Wake up! . . . The news! . . . The news! . . . And he's all happy. 'What's her name in Mesa? . . . The one who just got shot and killed the other day?'"

He denied being present even though I asked several times. His details on the murder of Robin Blasnek were sketchy at best.

But the answers of seeing it on TV opened up the door to the question of how well Sam was following the cases. Dale was obsessed, but I needed to hear from Sam the level of his commitment.

Sam admitted that Dale kept newspaper clippings of the shootings, and he obviously looked at what Dale had collected. They watched the news together, sometimes laughing at what they perceived as police bungling.

It was time to take a break. We had been at it for over an hour and a half. I needed to try to regroup and come back with some logical questions in response to his admissions. Sam needed some water and a bathroom.

I walked into the command center, and all the other case agents were either on the phone or streaming through their investigations. Their bosses who had joined us were doing the same thing. Dieteman's admissions opened the floodgates.

Lieutenant Benson came in and asked me how I was feeling. I wasn't sure how to answer. Prosecutor Vince Imbordino, who had sat through both interviews, was the most helpful. He handed me a list of questions that needed to be touched on. Of all the people there, he appeared to be the most exhausted. Prosecutors aren't use to staying up all night. His hair stood up like bed head, and his eyes were bloodshot.

I cracked open my crime book and checked my notes. Unbeknownst to me, Lieutenant Rich Benson, my boss and lead manager of this case, had heard Sam ask for not only water, but a cigarette. Obviously smoking is prohibited in the building. Nobody that I know of was ever allowed to smoke inside it. Lieutenant Benson broke the mold and told someone to get Sam a cigarette. In LT's mind he had earned it. He was also offered a breakfast sandwich.

Since Sam had only mentioned about half of the shootings, Vince Imbordino and I decided to work on shoring those cases up. I would need more details about those cases. That became the plan. I would also happen to ask if Sam knew anything about those other pesky little cases, the .22 caliber murders.

After a half-hour break, I walked into a smoked-filled interview room. I hate cigarette smoke and was choking immediately upon entry. I had no sleep in the past two days and was now gagging on cigarette smoke. As I sat down to start up the interview again, I kept choking on all the smoke. I had to stand up and open the door and try to fan the air out of the room so I could breathe. Sam got a kick out of that.

"In all these shootings, was there ever anyone else besides you and Dale present?"

Sam shook his head and answered, "No." Sam also related that no other vehicle was ever used, including Jeff Hausner's car.

As we went back through the six cases he could recall, Sam related that he did not own any guns personally. All the guns used in these crimes belonged to Dale Hausner. He listed the two 410s, the 12 gauge, but didn't know the calibers of the other shotguns.

I asked Sam about the modification and reasoning behind sawing off the butt of the single shot 410. His answer was just what I wanted to hear.

"Probably easier to carry . . . or something."

This same modified single shot 410 would be used in all the crimes. It made perfect sense. One shot from a single shot shotgun. It explained the reason only one round was fired at all the victims.

"When you guys would go out and shoot, who was taxed with putting the ammunition in and taking care of ammunition?"

"Usually Dale, cause he had a glove that he put it in with."

"What was the purpose behind that?" I already knew the answer.

"I guess so no prints . . . or something . . . "

"What would happen to the expended casing that was fired?"

"He'd usually hang on to it and throw it later." Sam said. "So it wouldn't be found in the area, I guess."

Sam went on to say that even though the gun was toted in a bag to and from the apartment, the 410 was usually laid out on the backseat, back floorboard, or by Dale's leg as he drove for easy access. The gun was now small enough that Dale could hide it, if need be.

Before I forgot or became a blubbering idiot, I decided to ask Sam what he knew about all the cases. It was obvious that he had only known Dale since early 2006, but it was worth seeing just how much he knew about things that happened it 2005.

"You've seen what's going on with this whole thing, right? You've seen the media coverage and all the hype, and you know that there's thirty some odd cases associated with this series of random shootings, right?"

Sam nodded his head in agreement.

"Did you ever take part in or ever see or ever hear about anybody else taking part in anything but a shooting where a shotgun was used?"

At least I got it out without giving away anything.

"I know he said he used to use a . . . .22."

"He used to use a .22?"

I wanted to make sure I wasn't hallucinating, so I asked Sam to verify what he just told me.

Sam nodded his head up and down, again confirming a yes answer.

"Did he say when?" I asked.

"Last year." Sam Dieteman knew and had been told personally by Dale Hausner that he was responsible for those shootings. It wasn't a smoking gun, but it was a start. "He said he got rid of that last year."

"Got rid of the gun last year?" I asked.

Sam nodded his head. I needed to know how he had come to this information.

"We were sitting around talking, and I think I was going through something in the paper or something. Just talking about they shot a bunch of cats, dogs, llamas or something."

Sam believed what Dale had told him because even though Dale was many things, he was not a liar. Even though he wasn't present, Sam was convinced Dale killed people in 2005.

I don't know for a fact whether Sam had put much thought into how this whole thing started, but right now the wheels were turning in his mind. I decided to exploit that for a moment.

"How did it come up that you guys would go out and do this? I mean, were you just sitting around eating, drinking, and just decide to do this? You know, was it something you thought about? . . . Describe it to me."

"We would go over to his brother Jeff's house, and usually have the car . . . he always had the gun with him, you know . . . and go out and do it. Usually go out to eat and after that, just driving around, and we're talking and that's when we'd see somebody out there walking around . . . alone . . . "

Sam described how they would surveil their victims, sometimes for only a short time period, to make sure that they were alone. They did it mostly by driving around, not in a fixed position. They were concerned about surveillance cameras, but not paranoid. "We didn't like go around the buildings and see if there's cameras or not . . . basically the only way I can put it is there's somebody out there by themselves . . . we just look and nobody around . . . you know . . . get 'em!"

As I sat back and listened to Sam describe their movements and target acquisitions, I realized I had made a huge mistake in profiling these two. They were not the smart, careful, calculating types that I had forewarned everyone about. They were two klutzes fumbling around in the dark, finding targets of opportunity on a whim, finding those souls out there that made their way around in the dark for whatever reason. They weren't professionals; they were just plain lucky.

I asked Sam if he had spoken to anyone about these matters, or if there was anyone else that knew. Ron Horton wasn't the answer that I got.

"Well, I know his brother knows . . . cause I talked to him . . . and he's talked about it before and . . . "

"Who has?" I asked.

"Jeff has . . . and him and Dale talked about it before, and he talked to me about it."

"OK, so Jeff knew what you guys were doing! . . . Is that what you're telling me?"

Sam nodded his head and said, "Uh hum."

Jeff Hausner, brother of Dale, roommate of Samuel Dieteman, knew everything—from Sam and Dale's exploits in 2006 to those 2005 cases. Then he dropped the bombshell.

Jeff admitted to being present during the shooting of animals in 2005, which meant, if he were present on nights when animals were killed, there were those same nights when humans were shot and killed.

For the next couple of hours, we went through the cases as best we could. I told him about the surveillance and wiretaps. He just nodded with agreement. Their reign of terror was over, and he knew it. He seemed almost relieved. He admitted that they referred to their outings as "recreational violence."

But his interviews were far from over. Detective Byers had the murder of Robin Blasnek to solve. Detective Pete Salazar from Scottsdale PD would surely want to talk to Sam about Claudia Gutierrez-Cruz.

When Detective Byers and Detective Salazar joined Sam Dieteman, they thanked him for his honesty. Yet, after watching hours of my interview, they didn't buy the minimizing or denial of his involvement, particularly when it came to the murders of Claudia Gutierrez-Cruz and Robin Blasnek.

Sam was confronted with the 410 shell casing in the trash and the wiretap conversations.

"Don't kill anyone tonight" was brought up. Why would Dale say something like that if he hadn't killed anyone?

Detective Donnie Byers went right into the two Mesa shootings, first focusing on the bicyclist. In a brilliant move, he minimized the fact that the bicyclist wasn't killed, just wounded. He got Sam to admit that he was arrested just a few hours previous to the shooting for shoplifting at a Walmart and that Dale was with him. He used my interview with Sam to get it out that they did all these shootings together, no lone wolf stuff going on here. Donnie never let him lie. He just told him he was there, and he knew it.

Sam eventually admitted that he was present and in his usual spot, the front passenger seat, for the shooting of the bicyclist and the murder of Robin Blasnek.

"Just driving around . . . we seen her . . . we just kept driving around, turning around . . . waiting for there to be no cars." Sam thought they were on Gilbert Road, but wasn't sure. "I think she was talking on her phone or something."

Robin was targeted because she was alone and looked like a "whore" to Dale Hausner. When Robin was shot, Sam said she went down and looked as if she was holding her leg.

Detective Byers had opened the questioning for Detective Salazar to intercede by informing Sam that we knew about another female that had been murdered, the one in Scottsdale, the one Sam talked to Ron Horton about.

When Pete took over the questioning, he asked Sam to think real hard about the night of May 2nd, 2006, the night he had already admitted was the first time he and Dale shot someone together.

When he was asked about shootings in Scottsdale, Sam balked. He said that at one time they targeted a rollerblader there, but that was it. Detective Salazar then produced the map and showed the pinpointed dot right on top of the murder location of Claudia Gutierrez-Cruz. Sam became nervous and started to cough. Even though I was just monitoring, I could see his body gestures changing. He was uncomfortable with this line of questioning.

Pete produced a picture of the obituary of the victim and showed that to Sam, hoping for a response, but he still got denials. Sam was mumbling his answers and not waiting for questions to be finished. He was clearly hiding something.

Detective Salazar threw Ron Horton into the mix. He told Sam that Ron had given him up, that Ron had come forward with the information about Sam shooting a woman he thought was a man. Ron had told police that Sam felt bad about killing the woman.

The detective hammered Sam, asking him to "show some remorse for the family." Do what's right and admit it. In his last volley, Detective Salazar stated, "We don't think you wanted to participate in this, but you yourself said you had too much to lose—a place to live. He had a stronghold on you; he got you to do a lot of things you normally wouldn't do."

After all of Detective Salazar's volleys, Sam finally gave in.

"I didn't try shooting her. I tried shooting at her and missing like the other people."

Problem was he was too close. Dale had spotted her and said, "Get her!" Dale handed the shotgun to Sam, and he fired. Sam thought he had missed because he never saw Claudia go down. But when they turned around and returned to where he shot her, they saw her sprawled out on the grass.

But unlike Dale Hausner, Sam Dieteman was troubled by the murder of Claudia Cruz. He had to stay drunk for weeks just to sleep at night. Even though he didn't remember telling Ron Horton about the incident, he was haunted like most individuals with a conscience.

Since Sam had confessed to murder, he came clean with the Walmart arsons as well. Dale lit the first one, and Sam lit the second one. Dale changed his shirt between the fires because it was just too loud and easily recognizable.

The cool water felt wonderful, and I snatched a paper towel from the dispenser. I also grabbed a pen and in big letters wrote the name *Jeff Hausner* on my notepad. I circled it numerous times.

Dale Hausner and Samuel Dieteman were charged with every shotgun-attempted murder and murder case that I and the other case agents had investigated, seventeen of them to be precise. They would also be charged with two counts of arson of an occupied structure.

The command post now looked like a frat house the night before finals. There were soda bottles and empty pizza boxes all over the place. Paper plates and napkins overflowed the garbage cans. The crime books were strewn all over the place, as everyone who had looked through them had left them wide open.

The police held a press briefing, announcing the capture of the Serial Shooters. We received numerous requests for interviews from all over the world. One of my old roommates, John Stallings, was the lieutenant in the Public Affairs Bureau. The PIOs informed the media that the investigators would not be talking.

Lieutenant Benson came in and announced that no one, he meant no one, was to report to work tomorrow, Saturday August 5th. We would all go home and get at least one day of rest before meeting again on Sunday.

As I readied myself to leave the building, I was assured that most of the media had moved to the jail to film the perp walk and holler questions at the two killers. I could slip out unnoticed.

When I got to my hotel room, the one I paid for and barely used, I dropped my briefcase on the floor and pulled the bed comforter off. I stripped down to my boxers and got on the bed. I put my phone next to the bed and decided not to shut it off. Someone would have to have a big set of cojones to call me right now. The room was pitch black. I love the dark curtains in hotel rooms. I didn't even turn the TV on to catch the news. I didn't care. I could see the coverage tomorrow, or the next day.

I'm not sure how long I rested, maybe one or two minutes, and then I didn't remember anything. Pure exhaustion took over, and I crashed into sleep.

My ringing cellphone startled me awake. Once again, I thought I was dreaming.

I sat up and fumbled through the dark to find and answer my phone. There was obviously no rest for the weary. "Hello," I think I said.

"Clark, it's Hugh Lockerby. I'm down at the jail, and we have a problem."

Oh, for god sakes. Can't anything go right? "What, Hugh?"

"This booking paperwork is all screwed up. Weren't there supposed to be two counts of murder listed here?" Hugh asked.

I felt like I was drunk as I was trying to rack my brain to wake up.

"Yeah, two counts of murder, fifteen counts of attempted murder, and drive-by shooting." I couldn't get out of the fog. Was that number even right?

"Well, I'm down here with the charging attorney, and they only have one murder, our Scottsdale case. Mesa's isn't here, and I can't get a hold of Donnie Byers. This commissioner says she's going to award a bond unless we can come up with the other murder charge."

"Oh, for fu#*'s sake! How many cases would she like? Maybe a couple more attempted murder charges? She obviously knows who these guys are. What's the problem?"

Hugh knew I wasn't yelling at him, just venting my frustration. He was as tired as the rest of us.

"The last I heard, Mesa was going to file their own paperwork because of the different jurisdictions. I saw Donnie with their paperwork before I cut out of the office. Isn't it there?"

"Hold on, Clark."

Hugh was checking with the administrators and law clerk types.

"OK, I think we may have found the problem. Let me call you back."

He hung up the phone. This was great. Now I get to sit here, not sleep, just hang out with my thumb up my butt, waiting to see if someone gets to bond these guys out.

After about half an hour, I called Hugh back. The paperwork had been adjusted, and there were no problems. The Serial Shooters were given no bond status. We had averted a potential crisis.

I went back to sleep, and this time I shut off my cellphone.

CHAPTER 43

August 5th started with a lousy night of sleep from the 4th. Have you ever been so tired that sleep sucks? That's how I felt, even though I must have slept at least ten hours. I checked my phone for messages and had one forwarded call.

"Hello, my name is Karen Hausner, or it used to be. I was reading the Internet and heard about the arrest of Dale Hausner and I was wondering if you could confirm if it was my ex-husband?"

In my line of work, ex-wives and ex-girlfriends are gooses that lay golden eggs. They usually have a plethora of dirt, and they're usually willing to gab. I dropped my hotel key off at the front desk and walked out into the morning heat. I had thought about heading straight home, but who was I to listen to orders? Besides, I needed to get to Dale Hausner's ex-wife before the media. I didn't want her commenting about their relationship until I had a chance to talk to her.

Police headquarters was quiet. Some of the media trucks had pulled up stakes and left, but the BLK was still out there, so they weren't going anywhere for awhile until he was caught.

As I worked my way to my cubicle, I saw the infamous blinking light on my phone working overtime. I didn't dare check messages. I grabbed my desk phone and dialed the number to Karen Hausner. It rang once, and she picked up. I hoped she hadn't been sitting there all day waiting for my phone call.

Karen made it clear that she had remarried and did not want her married name published. I could totally understand. She had changed her last name so the media had no idea how to get to her. That was good fortune for us. I asked her to narrate her history with Dale, and I was sure I would interrupt to clarify things. Over the next two hours, I was subjected to unbelievable insight into the making of a serial killer.

Karen met Dale when they worked together at a grocery store here in Phoenix. She was sixteen and in high school; he had dropped out. The year was 1990.

They started dating, and like all new romances things were great for awhile. But then Dale's personality started to show through. He was angry, even at a young age. Nothing was ever good enough. He would try to influence her away from family and friends and became over controlling. They'd been dating about one year when Dale told her that if she ever left him, he would kill her. He then changed that to say that if she ever left him, he would kill himself and let her live with the guilt.

One day, Karen saw the light and left Dale. She had enough of the constant monitoring. She left the state to be with family in Texas. Dale was introduced to a friend of theirs and ended up marrying her. Her name was Tracy, and they had a child together. Tracy was pregnant with another man's child when Dale met her. He became the stepfather to the first child, and a real father as well. Dale would call Karen in Texas every once in awhile even though he was married. He told her he had made a huge mistake in marrying Tracy. Karen still loved him, but not his ways. She finally told him to stop calling. The relationship was over.

After two years of marriage and a child, Dale and Tracy split. The first person Dale called with the news was Karen. Like a lost puppy and still in love, Karen got sucked back in by the master manipulator. He promised having a child had made him grow up. He was just a boy when they met, but now he was a man. Karen bit hook, line, and sinker. Dale sent her a plane ticket, and on the day that his divorce from Tracy was finalized, they married. Karen was more than happy to be a stepmother to Dale's boy, Jeremiah, and to Tracy's child, Donavon.

But soon the old Dale returned. At that time, both she and Dale were working at a Walgreens store in Phoenix. Dale began to steal. At first it was small things like cosmetics and personal items, but that grew into more lucrative items like booze. Karen told him to knock it off, but he couldn't help himself. It was there just for the picking.

It wasn't just stealing that worried Karen. Dale had an uncontrollable anger. She told me of a time when Dale had gone to look at a used truck in the neighborhood that he found for sale. Dale, being the smooth operator, tried to negotiate a lower price than the owner wanted. The owner refused. Dale walked away, furious. Later that night, Dale returned and torched the truck. It would not be Dale's first or last arson.

Before Dale got them both fired, Karen convinced him that she had enough of Phoenix. She wanted to start over in Texas, with or without him. Of course, it was with him. Karen was the most attractive woman Dale had ever been associated with, and he wasn't about to lose his eye candy. Besides, he was obsessed with her. No way she goes anywhere without him.

The Texas move in the summer of 1994 was good for the relationship. Their marriage flourished, and they had never gotten along better. Karen was happy because she was close to her family. Dale didn't appear to be too concerned about his family and was a well-liked son-in-law. Dale continued to get visitation with the two boys from his previous marriage.

But all the glory and love ended on one fateful night. On November 12, 1994, Dale, Karen, and the two boys were driving back to their home in Pasadena. It was late at night, and Dale had relinquished the driving to Karen. He was asleep in the front seat and the boys were in the back. Karen didn't want to drive, but Dale was insistent. She was tired, too.

Karen takes full responsibility for what happened next. She fell asleep at the wheel, and the car plunged off a bridge into a creek. Normally, it wouldn't have been so bad, but the creek had swelled with a summer storm. It was running fast and deep. Dale and Karen made it to the surface. The boys did not.

They determined the cause of death of the boys to be drowning, the manner of death an accident. Karen and Dale's relationship would never be the same.

After the accident, Dale, of course, blamed Karen. The Hausners grew apart. Dale began to cheat on her, and their relationship sank. She stayed with him because she felt a tremendous amount of guilt. The verbal abuse she took from Dale over the accident turned to physical abuse.

One evening, Dale beat Karen, and she ended up in the hospital. She's not sure why the beating occurred, just that it did. Karen's family disowned Dale. Karen forgave him.

Since Karen's family wanted nothing more to do with Dale, they decided to move back to Phoenix. But things weren't any better here. Dale continued to cheat on her and threatened her with not only physical harm, but death. He told her that he could get away with killing her because nobody would ever find her body, and that he could plead insanity if caught because he had been institutionalized as a young boy.

Dale had also confided that he had homosexual fascinations. He was having a hard time with this, as he had been raised to hate homosexuals, and he himself was purely homophobic. Karen believed that while they were married, Dale had an affair with another man. That was the last straw.

Karen filed for divorce. She began to date her current husband before she and Dale's divorce was final. They were still living together at the time. Karen figured that her relationship was over, even though she still loved him. Dale somehow found out that Karen was dating another man. He came home one night and confronted her. She was honest enough to admit the affair, and Dale went off. He grabbed his copy of the Satanic Bible and started reciting versus from it. He then dragged her, dressed only in a T-shirt and panties, kicking and screaming, to his car, claiming that if she didn't go with him, her boyfriend was dead. Once he got her inside, he drove to an area just north of Phoenix outside the city of Wickenburg.

Once there, Dale pulled out into the desert to an area he knew, one where he had gone shooting before. He produced a shotgun from the trunk, pulled her from the passenger seat, pointed the gun at her, and asked, "Where do you want it, the head or the chest?"

She never answered the question. Just then two saviors/angels came to Karen's aid. Two motorcyclists found the road they were on and drove toward them. Karen can still remember the two individual lights on the dirt bikes. Dale put the gun away and told her to get back in the car.

"It's too crowded here," he mumbled.

He then drove her back home.

Even after all these incidents: the threats, the beatings, the lies, Karen still loved him. Dale played on that. Even though they divorced, Dale wouldn't leave her alone, and Karen couldn't get over him. Maybe it was the bad boy image or the psychotic episodes. Whatever the reason, they reconciled again and even remarried.

This marriage lasted just months. Karen filed for an annulment. She knew she had to get out of Phoenix to be rid of him. She left Arizona with her new boyfriend, a man soon to be her husband. Still she kept in contact, a mistake that she now regretted horribly. She last saw him in what she believes was 2002. She finally cut all contact with him in 2003.

I asked Karen if she would agree or disagree with these adjectives describing Dale. Attention seeker, yes; no conscience, yes; illusions of grandeur, yes; thrill seeker, yes; angry, yes; felt wronged by the system, yes; and a blamer, yes.

Karen began to chuckle and asked how long I had known Dale. I told her I just met him yesterday. The adjectives I used to describe Dale Hausner, along with what Karen told me, clearly pointed to Hausner as a psychopathic killer.

Karen closed with one story that couldn't be ignored and spoke to the profile of Hausner. Dale and a friend were questioned by police for a criminal matter. Karen couldn't remember the crime. What she did remember is that Dale told her the two friends were separated, and Dale was told by police that his friend had, "ratted him out." Dale continued to deny involvement in the crime and was subsequently released from custody. He told Karen, "If you ever get in trouble with the police never admit to it; you never confess." He had learned at an early age to never admit to anything. Admitting gets you busted, and there's no manipulation or escape from an admission. He had carried that truism into adulthood.

I thanked Karen for her insight and told her I would be in touch. For now, I had what I needed.

You gotta love those scorned ex-wives.

Sunday August 6th brought a meeting of all the case agents, assistant case agents, and front line supervisors. The mood was much different than several days ago before the arrests. Lieutenant Rich Benson started off with a joke about not having to see our ugly faces every day from now on. The UC guys were ecstatic with the arrests. They could go back to their drug cases. I had other things in mind.

Although the coming week would be a blur, I had two goals. Investigate every aspect of Dale Hausner and Sam Dieteman's lives and get Jeff Hausner.

Detective Jewell never interviewed Sam Dieteman. Based on what Sam had told me, Detective Jewell decided to contact Jeff. He was brought down and interviewed. Jeff even allowed the search of his car and home for any weapons. None were found, of course. Jeff, just like his psychopathic brother, admitted to nothing. He had no idea what his brother and ex-roommate Sam Dieteman had been up too. He was as shocked as anyone.

Detective Rich Label had come to the meeting and had been able to just complete the wiretap supplements under the forty-eight hour rule. He had gotten the documents to the judge an hour before deadline. Under the trusted eye of Deputy County Attorney Laura Reckart, they had met our obligation. Losing those wiretaps would have been disastrous.

A grand jury convened on August 11, 2006, and indicted Dale Hausner and Sam Dieteman on all the charged counts. The task force needed to continue to follow up on all tips that came in on the case and clear those individual wrongly accused. It would be important down the line when the case went to court to be able to say that we followed up, and we were able to close every tip that came in. There were literally hundreds of them.

Then there were the tips that came in about Hausner and Dieteman. I followed up on most of those tips. It was incredible how people came out of the woodwork to give us information about these two men.

One of Dale's childhood friends said Dale used to stick live pigeons in the microwave and watch them cook. Another said we needed to look into other states, like Nebraska, where the Hausners had lived to see if there were any murders up there. Some of the tips led to nothing, but some of them gave more insight.

We called all of Sam's contacts and drinking buddies. They were surprised he was involved. They knew him to be a drunk, and a bar brawler, but a murderer? We phoned his family and ex-wife. Most of them were located in Minnesota. His mother and stepfather refused to talk to us. Sam was unemployed, so there was no work history.

Since Dale had worked for the City of Phoenix, getting his employment records was just a phone call away. When I reviewed his records, I immediately saw a pattern. Starting in 2005, with the first murder of Tony Mendez, Dale Hausner had a nasty habit of not showing up for work following the day of a shooting. I guess being out all night hunting will do that. He took all kinds of days off: vacation, sick, compensatory, FMLA, personal leave, you name it.

He must have realized what he was doing because he changed the pattern. In July of 2006, and up until the murder of Robin Blasnek, he went to work the next morning after a shooting. Nobody said he wasn't cunning.

Besides all the guns and ammunition found in Dale's apartment, including the sawed-off 410 shotgun, our search of his car proved productive as well. Although we didn't recover a .22 rifle, we found other incriminating items: one hundred rounds of .22 ammunition, crystal meth, news clippings, and 410 shotgun shells. The car was torn apart, and, of course, we removed the seat cushion in the backseat where we found five expended .22 shell casings. They were all Remington, just like the ones recovered from some of the animal shootings and from Timothy Tordai's scene. We even located his latex glove, used for the removal of fired casings.

I was particularly interested in the newspaper clippings. Hausner had done a good job of keeping track of the shootings. But once again he made a fatal error. The clippings he kept were from not only his escapades with Sam Dieteman in 2006, but articles dating back to 2005. Why would he have those if he wasn't involved?

One of my close friends from the Public Information Office, Connie Tyler, entered the command post and informed me that Dale Hausner had called for a press conference. He just couldn't keep quiet.

The event was broadcast, and I turned it on to watch Dale Hausner march out in front of the throngs of reporters to answer their questions. He was dressed in his jailhouse stripes, the customary wear for inmates at Maricopa County Jail. His hands were shackled to his waist as he sat down behind a table. He was back in his element, on stage for everyone to see.

When he was asked why he was holding the press conference, Dale said it was scheduled through the jail to profess his innocence. He blamed Sam Dieteman for taking his car out at night and using his guns. Dale claimed he was guilty only by association. He had no idea Sam was doing all this. When asked about the Walmart video showing him in the stores at the times of the arson, Dave said, "I was there," but he stated that he didn't have anything to do with the fires. "I'm an upstanding member of society." He said he had no violent past.

He was asked about his guns, and he said he was a "collector." He also had knives in his house which he once again referred to as "stabbing weapons." Hausner fired off answers to questions like a pro athlete that conducted interviews on a daily basis. He even got smart with one of the reporters, mocking her question as being stupid. Eleven minutes into the interview, his court-appointed attorney interrupted and told him he needed to stop the interview.

I clicked the off button on the TV remote. I could only hope that Jeff Hausner would be this foolish. Maybe he'd talked to someone, anyone, confessing that he was involved. Maybe narcissism ran rampant in the Hausner family.

It was wishful thinking.

With what sources were left, Jeff Hausner became the target of the task force. We needed to keep surveillance units attached to him. It was possible that Jeff could say something to someone or make an attempt to obtain and/or destroy evidence. If he did, we needed to be ready to pounce.

Jeff knew that too. He had become extremely paranoid. He was constantly looking over his shoulder. A man who was once predictable in his actions had become very wary of everything going on around him. Surveillance of him was nearly impossible. He hunkered down in his condo and would only come out for work or to go to a bar to get loaded.

We took the step of introducing a female UC officer into his most frequented establishment. She was perfect. He confronted her as being a cop right off the bat. She, of course, told him to "piss off" and acted as if she wanted him to leave her alone. In fact, the bar workers and patrons told Jeff to shut up, she was just a new customer looking for a nearby watering hole. That ruse was soon ended after the confrontation, and the UC female pulled out.

We interviewed some of Jeff's old acquaintances, people that called in with information on the older Hausner brother. Some of them put him with guns at the time of the 2005 murders, but nothing panned out. Every stone we turned and every friend we talked to yielded no evidence that tied Jeff to the crimes.

After about a month, it was decided, over my protest, that the UC operations on Jeff Hausner would cease. We would have to get him some other way.

It was also determined that the task force would finish whatever leads needed closing, and then it, too, would go away. Phoenix and Mesa Police's Crime Labs had completed most of the forensic work. Everyone knew this case was years away from going to trial. At this point, we needed to decide what forensic evidence needed to be examined and under which method: DNA, fingerprinting, writing analysis, or ballistic analysis.

I became responsible for all the continuing follow-up on both Sam Dieteman and Dale Hausner. I even found one of Dale's coworkers who thought he was a nice guy. That's how psychopaths work, not everyone sees them for what they are. Dale's boss was a little less enamored with Dale. He had written him up for being unexcused from work and conducted an investigation of harassment. He thought that Dale was leaving the work site during work hours, but could never catch him. Dale had also been caught selling DVDs and CDs at work, a violation of city policy.

At first, some of Dale Hausner's neighbors thought he was a pleasant guy. He generally introduced himself to them as a photographer. The neighbors reported that most conversations with Dale revolved around his sick daughter, Rebecca. Dale also made it seem like he was the only parent of the child. Nobody ever saw any women visiting the apartment.

Shortly after Dale moved in, there was a rash of tire slashings in the apartment complex. Some vehicles were hit several times. However, Dale Hausner's Camry remained untouched. Neighbors told me that Dale also became paranoid. Any knocking, banging, or loud noise sent him storming out of his abode in a rage.

Since Dale was a firebug, I decided to also research fires in and around Jeff Hausner's apartment. I ran a check through the Phoenix Fire Department and asked them to search a grid one half mile around the Jeff Hausner condo for unexplained arsons. I didn't have to look any farther than the complex.

In a year and a half time period, there were over two dozen fires—trash dumpsters, palm trees, fields, debris, you name it.

All of this information led me to believe that Dale Hausner, Jeff Hausner, and Samuel Dieteman weren't just out shooting people; they were destroying things all over the city.

How much of that was true would come to light soon.

CHAPTER 44

As I sat at my desk, rummaging through Dale Hausner's financial records, I received a phone call from a man who I refer to as the leading prosecutorial aide behind this investigation, a paralegal named Jeff Colbert.

Colbert, as I came to call him, had been at the Maricopa County Attorney's Office for six years. He was assigned to the Homicide Division and was Lead Prosecutor Vince Imbordino's righthand man. If you needed anything done, anyone contacted, or anyone questioned, Jeff Colbert knew who it was and why. He knew all the homicide detectives, good or bad, and most of the defense attorneys in town. He could tell you who was a good lawyer, a good investigator, and who was an idiot. We both shared a passion for golf. He was funny, and over the course of this case, we gave each other more crap about our prospective offices than two sewer lines running together. I got so used to talking to Colbert that every time my cellphone rang, I just answered, "What now, loser?" He would rip back with how worthless I was for not getting something done I was supposed to have already completed. We went back and forth all the time.

But the phone call I got today was good news, something I had been hoping for since the day of the arrest. Samuel Dieteman wanted to talk, and his attorney had arranged for it to happen.

It would be scheduled for September 27th.

I don't know about other jurisdictions, but in our county, if an inmate wants to talk to police and has legal representation, we usually have to enter into a contract. That contract was known as a freetalk.

In essence, it means that a person, usually someone who's in custody or looking at charges, agrees to talk about specific information that may help law enforcement. The obvious gain is two-directional. Police get information that will hopefully help their investigation, and the criminal can say that he helped. His help may garner some type of leniency, or it may clear him of some culpability. As long as the criminal tells the truth, he's not subject to any further implication in the crime. Whatever he says cannot be used against him.

The fact that Sam wanted to talk was huge. It had been over a month and half since his arrest, and his explanations were suspect. This was a chance for me to clear the air about all the cases, maybe even get some further information on how to go after Jeff Hausner.

Sam Dieteman's lead attorney was Maria Schaffer. Her co-counsel was Quinn Jolly. I had heard about Maria, but never been in a court room with her. Her reputation was excellent. I knew nothing about Quinn.

Vince Imbordino joined me at police headquarters for the interview. He had a few questions for Sam as well.

What started out as awkward turned into anything but. Sam believed that his mind was clearer today than on the day of his arrest. He now had the drugs and booze out of his system, and he had almost two months to think about everything. He felt today would be much better.

For the next several hours, Samuel Dieteman vented.

He talked about the things he, Dale, and Jeff would do together—the shootings, beat downs, arsons, criminal damages, and thefts. Sam didn't just remember the cases with Dale; he lowered the boom with something better   a stabbing.

"I think there were about four incidents of those when we were all together. I think the last time we did anything like that Jeff stabbed a guy at 75th Avenue and Thomas."

The date of the stabbing was in April, 2006. Sam went on to explain in-depth how he, Dale, and Jeff had gone out to eat. They had stopped at a store, and Jeff had been approached by a homeless man asking for money. As they all walked away, Jeff became angry. He told Dale and Sam that he was "going to do something to him." Sam tried to talk Jeff out of it. Dale walked to his car. But Jeff would not listen to reason. As Sam watched from about fifteen feet away, Jeff Hausner produced a knife and plunged it into the stomach of the homeless man. It was a knife that Jeff usually carried. There was also a witness, a skinny, blonde chick. Finally, a case we could make against Jeff Hausner. If only we could find the victim and this "blonde chick."

The term "RVing" was in fact coined by Jeff, initially based on what the three of them did together: beat and stab people, start fires, damage property. Sam used it later to describe their antics, but it was Jeff that referred to it most often. But Sam knew something none of the rest of us knew, with the exception of his attorney. Sam listened to Dale and Jeff talk about their escapades in 2005. Being off the booze and the dope, Sam's memory became very clear.

When I asked what Jeff and Dale had told him about that time, Sam, without any prompting, laid out the murder of Nathaniel Shoffner, a black male shot just off of Van Buren Street. I knew right away which case Sam was talking about, but nobody else did. It was the case I kept tucked away from the media and from the task force. I let Sam tell the story.

The murder of this black male transient occurred just off of 20th Street and Monroe. The Hausner brothers had seen a dog in the area and targeted it with their .22 rifle. Shoffner walked up on the man and the dog and startled them. There were words exchanged. Dale tried to shoot Mr. Shoffner with the .22, but it jammed. Dale then asked for the 410 shotgun from Jeff. Jeff handed it to him. Jeff and Dale argued about whether or not the 410 shotgun was going to kill anyone. Dale fired, and Shoffner went down. Sam said that the victim was holding a "beer bottle, and he shot him right through it." It was believed to be the first murder they had committed with a shotgun.

Since the story had never gotten any media coverage, there was only one way for Sam to know about this murder. He was either there, or he listened to people who were at the scene. Since it occurred in November of 2005, Sam was living with Jeff at the time and didn't even know Dale. I believed he heard the story straight from the horse's mouth.

Sam believed that Shoffner's murder was before Christmas because Jeff and Dale talked about other shootings right around that time.

"They were telling me, both, and were around Christmas . . . it was like three or four homeless kids . . . bums they said they'd shot. They said one of them was on a bus stop bench," Sam said.

We certainly had three people shot downtown just after Christmas, and we had the shooting of Reginald Remillard, who was sitting on a bus bench when he was murdered. Again, Sam placed both Jeff and Dale at these shootings. Again, the only way Sam would know about these shootings would be if he had been there, or if he had heard Jeff and Dale talk about these killings. Through these stories, Sam was nailing Dale's coffin shut and opening a big can of worms on Jeff.

In discussing their targets, Sam made this assessment: "It's more that Jeff talked about the animals than Dale. They were real proud of the horses they shot. Dale leaned more toward the hookers; Jeff wanted the bums mostly."

The weapon of choice for all these shootings: the .22 rifle.

When asked if there was anything else he could tell us, Sam offered up this little tidbit: "I remember Dale used to complain that when he had the .22 rifle, Jeff would always shoot people more than once . . . like three or four times . . . and he'd stick out the window farther so the casings I guess would fall out in the street."

Several of the animals that were shot had multiple strikes in and around them. But the humans were different, except for one. Marco Carillo, one of the murdered victims from the downtown shootings, was shot twice in the chest. He was the only victim with multiple gunshot wounds.

There was only one incident that Sam couldn't specifically remember—the shooting of Paul Patrick in front of the Jiffy Lube on Indian School Road. Paul had been shot at close range, but he was still alive. It was the same night of the Walmart arsons where video captured Dieteman and Hausner together. It was the only shooting in the series on that particular night.

Vince Imbordino asked Sam about the large quantity of unopened liquor found in Dale's car. Sam explained that all of the liquor was stolen. It was how Sam and Dale funded their lifestyle. The booze was shoplifted and sold to the highest bidder, or orders were taken and then filled. If you wanted an expensive bottle of tequila, put in an order, and they'd try to get it for you. They would also steal and sell DVDs, CDs, computer games, etc. It all went to the Hausner/ Dieteman general fund for RVing.

In our first interview, Sam had denied being involved or present in the shooting of David Perez, the young Hispanic who was shot at 27th Avenue and State Street. The particulars of this shooting were captured on the wiretap when Dale bragged about it. Now Sam owned up to being there. He described how they spotted David on 27th Avenue, then followed him down a dark side street. Dale pulled right up next to David, leveled the shotgun a foot from his head, and fired. David went down immediately. Sam assumed he died, but they never heard about it in the news. David was talking on his cellphone when he was shot.

As Sam Dieteman spoke, I could only look at him and feel dismayed. He was an articulate and semi-intelligent character. He had just gotten mixed up with the wrong duo.

But he gave me hope. Hope in nailing the one dreg out there walking around, free as the wind.

Jeff Hausner.

CHAPTER 45

The report was an aggravated assault/stabbing that occurred on April 14th, 2006. The victim was a Raymond McQueen, a forty-two-year-old transient with no known address.

Patrol officers had responded to a 911 call and found Raymond with a stab wound to the lower right abdomen on the sidewalk in front of a store. Even though Raymond was conscious, he was bleeding internally and couldn't tell the first responders anything. Sam was right about the witness and even described her perfectly: a blonde, thin chick. She was also a transient.

The problem was the female didn't actually witness the stabbing, just the aftermath of Raymond bent over holding his stomach. She did describe two subjects, both white males, fleeing to a light blue colored car. One of the white males had shoulder-length dark hair with a beard.

Raymond McQueen was transported to the hospital where surgery commenced immediately. Raymond was too severely injured to talk. The case was assigned to a detective who asked the hospital to call as soon as he was able to talk. The hospital never called, and several days later, Raymond walked away to re-enter street life.

A records check found Raymond in one of the places where transients end up, prison. He had recently been arrested for burglary from a vehicle, a felony. He had gotten hungry and had stolen some change out of the ashtray of a truck, hardly the crime of the century. Unfortunately, it wasn't his first felony. He got four-and-a-half years and was currently housed in the Department of Corrections in Florence, Arizona.

As I looked at his booking details, I found that Raymond couldn't read or write. He was indigent and had a whopping four cents on him when he checked into prison. He had been segregated from general population for some reason. He told prison investigators that he "feared for his life."

Raymond and I would meet for the first time in the Offices of the Criminal Investigation Division at Florence, a single-story dwelling used as a staging place for prison investigators. Raymond was escorted into the office wearing the usual orange inmate jumpsuit. His hands and feet were not shackled. He had a noticeable limp, and one of his eyes appeared to be physically disabled. He was not told why I was there, only that I was coming from Phoenix to talk to him.

I introduced myself. He was pleasant. I told him that I was not there to pile any more charges on him. That broke the ice a little. I could see his body language change. I was there to talk to him about the night he was stabbed. I knew that he had never been interviewed, and I wanted his side of the story. He looked mildly shocked. He thought no one cared about what happened to him.

Raymond and his girlfriend had been panhandling (begging) for money outside of a grocery store. He saw two white males exiting the store and decided to ask one of them for any spare change. He described the males as both "big guys." The male he approached told him, "Yeah, just one minute," and walked to the other male who was standing a few feet away. The two males talked. Raymond watched as the white male reached into his pocket for what he thought would be money. Raymond decided to approach him.

When he got within a few feet, the one male turned, and in a flash, Raymond felt the pain of a sharp object in his stomach. He didn't even have time to react, let alone see what it was that plunged into his abdomen. Instead of some change, Raymond got a knife in the gut. He felt the warm sensation of blood and looked down. The sweater he was wearing turned red. He turned to his girlfriend and yelled. She came rushing over. He could see the two men run away and get into a blue car parked in the parking lot. Neither of the two got into the driver's seat in the car. The person that stabbed him said nothing.

I asked Raymond if he could identify the person that stabbed him, and he said he thought he could. Of course, I was prepared for this and had just happened to put together a couple of photo line-ups for Raymond's viewing pleasure. Within a few seconds, he pointed to the picture of Jeff Hausner. He was positive that was the man that stabbed him. Raymond had spent almost three weeks in intensive care.

As we talked, Raymond had a noticeable slur to his speech. He had suffered a stroke some time back, which also made him limp. He was clearly not the ideal victim to bring in front of a jury of the defendants' peers, but he certainly wouldn't be the worst victim I had ever brought into court to testify. As we said our goodbyes, he thanked me for taking the time to look into the matter. I told him, "No, thank you." He had no idea why I was thanking him.

As I drove back to Phoenix, I realized that even with this stabbing case, I was no closer to tying Jeff to the .22 rifle murders. I was convinced he participated in those killings, and it frustrated me that I still couldn't prove it. As I drove, I thought … and thought. Eventually I hatched a plan. A long shot plan at best. It would take a stroke of luck and an accomplice, but it may be the only shot we had at getting Jeff for murder.

Jeff Hausner was arrested at his ex-wife's apartment on November 2nd, 2006, almost three months after his brother. He was transported to Phoenix Police Headquarters and placed in one of the interview rooms. Unlike his brother Dale, Jeff invoked his right to council. He was going to make us prove our case, not give it to us. He was booked on one count of Attempted 2nd Degree Murder for the stabbing of Raymond McQueen.

The arrest of Jeff Hausner brought a media swarm of publicity. His face was plastered in every newspaper in the state. Much of the attention focused on him being Dale's brother. However, it didn't take long before the media hypothesized what I already believed to be true. Jeff was a part of the series before Sam got involved. This is what we had hoped.

Even though Jeff Hausner had become a focus in the investigation, I never took my eye off of Dale and Sam. The case against them for the shotgun shootings was solid. That, coupled with the evidence gathered from the .22 shooting scenes, their M.O., and the evidence from Dale's apartment and car meant it was time to charge them with the rest of the murders and the Walmart Arsons.

On November 17, 2006 a grand jury indicted Dale Hausner with the additional crimes of Murder, Drive by Shooting, Aggravated Assault, Arson of an Occupied Structure, and Cruelty to Animals for the 2005 .22 caliber cases—thirty-five additional criminal counts.

Sam was additionally charged with one count of Conspiracy to Commit Murder for their trolling around the southeast valley on August 1st and 2nd, the Attempted Murders of David Perez and Michael Cordrey, and the Walmart Arsons.

I was still investigating other murders and shootings, all in the hopes of stacking more charges on the trio.

The Maricopa County Jail falls under the jurisdiction of the Sheriff's Office. Anything that goes on there must first be cleared by their chain of command. In order to move forward with my plan to get Jeff Hausner, I would need the backing of the County Attorney's Office. I met with Prosecutor Vince Imbordino a few days after the arrest of Jeff Hausner. We had numerous conversations about Jeff's involvement, and Vince was adamant that, in order to convict Jeff, he would need more evidence.

When I laid out my plan, Vince was less than skeptical. He thought I was nuts. But he also realized we were running out of options to get Jeff Hausner.

Vince bought off on the idea, and so did his bosses. Together with the Phoenix Police Department's backing, we contacted the Sheriff's intelligence division. It would be up to them to run the scheme. During a meeting with the Sheriff's Office intelligence division, I put forth what I believed could be a ruse to nail Jeff Hausner. I first had to lay out why I wanted to implement this course of action.

In doing all the background research on Jeff Hausner, I noted that he, like Dale, had never done any real time. But Jeff was not articulate and intelligent like Psycho Boy. He had no idea how the criminal justice system worked, let alone the jail or prison systems.

Jeff was currently held in the jail in a unit known by its acronym of SMU, Special Management Unit. This unit housed the most dangerous inmates in the county. Sam and Dale were in there. Anyone that was deemed a threat to other prisoners or correctional staff was kept there. Murderers, rapists, violent gang members all housed in the same place as they awaited court appearances or sentencing. Most, if not all of the inmates, were headed for prison.

SMU has individual cells. The inmates are not allowed any physical contact with other prisoners. They are in lockup twenty-three hours a day. Death row is easier time than here. The inmates have one hour a day out of their cell. It's called recreational time. It's spent in a small room attached to two cells known as a day room. It has a phone in it for calls, a desk and chair to sit and write, and if you decide, you can talk to the other inmate that shares the same day room. For two hours a day, at his cell or yours, you can talk with the guy housed next to you, albeit through the cell door or a small window.

It's hell, but it was perfect for what I needed. Jeff Hausner, by all reports, was an alcoholic. I was sure at this point in his incarceration he was suffering from the DTs. He was vulnerable and needed a friend, someone who could explain the justice system to him, somebody with experience.

Intelligence Deputy Monty Callahan attended this meeting. He'd been working jail intelligence for the Sheriff's Office for years. He had contact and information sheets on all the inmates, especially the ones in SMU. I asked if he just happened to have any informants housed in SMU, and if he did, were they reliable. I needed somebody hard core.

Deputy Callahan had such a person housed in SMU. He'd helped on a previous murder case. That case had wrapped up, and his information had proven to be reliable.

The subject had been in DOC for years and was a white supremacist. He knew the lingo, had the knowledge and the tattoos to prove he was legit. He would be perfect.

But there was a kicker. The informant was to know nothing of the plan. Jeff was to be placed next to him, and all the information gathered would come without any meddling by police. We did not want the informant to be considered an agent of the state. The informant would have to come forward on his own without any prompting.

So, the plan was implemented.

For now, we would all just sit back and wait to see if in fact Jeff Hausner, the cherry in the system, decided to talk to his newfound friend.

Patience had become a virtue.

In classic Hausner fashion, Dale hired a publicist in an attempt to get the PR train moving in what he thought was a favorable direction. He had been crucified and vilified in the media by politicians, police spokespersons, and the general public. In the Old West he probably would've been hung by a lynch mob before he ever got to trial. The so-called publicist was a man named David Hans Schmidt.

Schmidt was known as the "Sultan of Sleaze." His claim to fame? He secured a lucrative deal for Bill Clinton's girlfriend, Gennifer Flowers, to pose for *Penthouse* magazine. Schmidt also said that he had obtained diaries and nude pictures of other people like Paris Hilton. He lived in Arizona now and tried to keep his name front and center. There was never any downside for Schmidt. During an interview, Schmidt was bold enough to state that he expected to make a lot of money off representing the accused serial killer, Dale Hausner.

Consequently, Schmidt jumped all over the investigation and made outlandish claims of cover ups, conspiracies, and police incompetence. Dale was innocent, and the cops screwed up. He really blasted us after the arrest of Jeff Hausner.

"Why did this take so long? If Jeff was involved, he should have been arrested with Dale. These guys are just out to get the Hausners."

However, an incident that took place on December 4, 2006 proved devastating to Schmidt and Dale Hausner's few remaining allies, I have this theory about culpability and rational thinking that I have espoused for several years. I call it the "Circle of Blame." In this theory, I believe that there are four stages to the circle, all of them leading to some type of conclusion about one's own guilt.

In the first stage, blame is placed on whoever got the perpetrator caught. In Dale's mind, that would be Sam Dieteman. Sam had ratted him out, so Sam was to blame for Dale's incarceration, not his own actions.

Once they get past this stage, they go to stage two. This is where they realize that the evidence is more than just someone's statements. The case contains irrefutable facts that tie them to the crimes to which they were charged. The defendant is given all the reports and a lawyer to lay out the case against them. It's at this point that the person makes a decision to either fight the charge or look for some type of deal if one is presented. The blame now is squarely on the shoulders of the person, and they understand that. They either accept it or continue to blame others in the cycle.

If they decide to fight on, then they move to the third stage of blame: the police. This is where the person dissects the investigation, usually with their attorney, and tries to affix blame on the investigation. They look for anything to make it look like police were incompetent, lazy, or dishonest. The case is going in front of a jury to be fought out for the person's alleged injustice. If he wins, he's out. If he loses, then we move to phase four of the circle.

When the defendant is found guilty, and can no longer blame the person that gave him up, himself, or the police, they then blame their attorney. The attorney didn't do their job, they were incompetent, etc. The defendant never once takes blame for their own actions. When I heard the news about Dale Hausner's exploits on December 4th, I was firmly convinced he was in stage two of the cycle.

Dale Hausner was found in his cell, covered in pink vomit, and unresponsive from what appeared to be an attempt at suicide. Two bottles of New Day Antihistamine Allergy Caplets were found empty in his cell. No note was written. He was transported to Maricopa County Hospital in serious condition, and unfortunately survived. Dale was contacted by investigators and claimed to have ingested more than two hundred over-the-counter pills in an attempt to kill himself. He would not say why he did it.

In the meantime, the Schmidt spin machine was in full cycle mode. Dale got depressed because of the conditions that he was kept in. He now realized that this attempt at suicide was a lashing out at the system, not an admission of guilt. Dale fully expects to recover, and realizes that he made a mistake. He is now, more than ever, committed to fighting for his freedom. You just got to love these guys. They can make an 8.0 earthquake look like a fissure.

Within several months the spin machine stopped, but not because of lack of funds, or publicity, or burn out of constantly hearing about how innocent Dale Hausner was. No, it would stop because the Sultan of Sleaze, David Hans Schmidt, had problems of his own. Schmidt had attempted to blackmail actor Tom Cruise over some alleged wedding photos. He was trying to extort money out of them not to publicize the photos. Cruise apparently took offense to this and notified the authorities. Schmidt was arrested and charged accordingly. He had admitted his role and plead guilty to the charges. He was looking at ending up in prison.

As I was driving home late one night, I received a call from homicide Sergeant Mike Polumbo. Mike, a really nice guy, was one of the supervisors handling the BLK murders.

"Hey Clark, do you know a David Hans Schmidt?"

"Yeah, I know him. He's Dale Hausner's publicity hack. What's he spouted off about now?"

I knew that Schmidt must have held a news conference or said something that was going to piss me off, again. I didn't even consider the source of the call.

"Well, we just found him hanging in a closet. He's dead. Looks like he committed suicide."

I wanted to feel bad; I really did. But to be honest, Schmidt had said some ugly things about me and the investigation. So I didn't feel bad. He'd taken Dale Hausner's side for his own publicity. Now he was dead.

I could only wonder to myself if everything and everyone this case touched was cursed.

CHAPTER 46

In late November, a Silent Witness tip came in, stating that the caller, a Charisse Kane, had a husband who was currently incarcerated, but he had information regarding Dale Hausner. There was a phone number listed with an area code from Florida. I assumed it was just another jailhouse stoolie, looking to cut a deal for some information. What I got was something entirely different.

To make a long story short, John and Charisse Kane came to Arizona to run a bartending school. Dale Hausner was one of the school's graduates. In fact, Dale and John Kane had become friends after Dale had finished school. Dale was desperate for work, or so he claimed, so John would try to get him bartending gigs on a regular basis.

But there was more to the story than just a simple friendship. Dale Hausner brought cheap booze and DVDs to the bartending school to sell. He did it regularly. John knew about it and even purchased some of the stolen items.

John taught classes during the day, and Charisse managed the finances of the school. Nobody at the school, besides the teachers, knew that John and Charisse were married.

One day, Charisse received a sexual harassment complaint from one of the students. The complaint was lodged against her husband, John. Charisse took all the information down and talked to John about the complaint. John explained the incident, and no formal investigation was launched. He claimed it was a misunderstanding. The complainant would continue at the school, but she was switched to evening classes to finish her required hours. The episode upset John greatly, and he had vented about it to Dale Hausner. When he heard what had happened, Hausner was furious.

Shortly afterward, a shooting occurred at the school. A vehicle was shot up as it sat in the parking lot. The vehicle was owned by one of the students who attended the bartending school owned this vehicle. Dale told John that he had done it as retaliation against the female who filed the sexual harassment complaint. The car's owner was a student at the school, but not the one who'd filed the complaint. The real victim whose car got shot up that night had no problems with John Kane or Dale Hausner, for that matter. She was innocent, victimized by a maniac. She left the school immediately. John was not sure what happened to her.

This shooting had occurred on December, 29, 2005 at around 1900 hours (7:00 p.m). On that very same night and into the next morning, two people were shot and killed, two people wounded, and dogs had been killed. Better yet, police recovered six .22 caliber shell casings at the school parking lot.

This was an unbelievable turn of fortune in the investigation into the .22 shootings. If, in fact, ballistics science matched the shell casings from this bartending school shooting to the ones recovered from other shooting scenes, it would be the first time that someone besides Sam Dieteman could tie Dale Hausner to one of the shootings. We could reconstruct the whole bloody night rampage.

It wasn't John Kane's conscience that got the best of him. He was looking prison dead in the face. A gun and narcotics arrest had him looking at several years. If he helped us, maybe we could help him. He was an articulate, intelligent guy who got caught up in an addiction that ruined his life. His wife had left him and moved back to Florida. She was pregnant at the time of his arrest, and he had a son he'd never seen. Jail had not been all that bad for John. At least there he was clean and sober.

Like so many of these crimes in this series, there was a story behind the story.

The intended target of the shooting, the harassment complainant left the school after the shooting for personal reasons. She didn't realize that the shooting had anything to do with her complaint. She had never even heard of the Serial Shooter Case.

A phone call from the FBI brought a new twist to the case. They wanted to know why we were running computer checks on the student that owned the car that was shot up. It turns out that car belonged to a person in the Witness Protection Program. Hausner had shot up the car of a federally protected witness! The student was moved immediately out of fear of being discovered and targeted. The poor soul was whisked away from what little life had been built, all on a mistaken case of criminal damage by gunfire.

The call that I was waiting for came on December 19.

Jail intelligence Deputy Monty Callahan had been contacted by the informant. I don't know how, and I didn't ask. I just wanted to know if there was anything that we could use against Jeff.

Over the last month, Jeff Hausner had talked about the crime to which he was accused, the stabbing of Raymond McQueen. He had also talked of other things. Since Dale and Sam were also housed on the same floor, there was a lot of chatter about who did what, who was snitching on whom, and who was really to blame. The best way to get to the bottom of it all would be to pull the informant out and just talk to him. But this is no easy task.

There are few ways to get out of your cell. Everyone is in twenty-three hour lockdown. If you are pulled out of your cell, everyone up in SMU knows about it. Getting out of your cell is a big deal, and you'd better have a foolproof plan to explain yourself once you get back. Otherwise everyone will think that you are a rat. New charges, a court appearance, or a doctor's visit are good excuses that you can use.

On December 21, I would meet with a complete stranger. A person who, without even knowing it, was going to hopefully provide key information to the ongoing criminal investigation into the third serial killer in this case, Jeff Hausner.

The informant, now referred to as Rick, was brought over in his jailhouse garments. He was tall, thin, with a good build. He looked younger than his thirty-seven years. Prison had not been too tough on him. He carried all the tattoos of a white supremacist.

Since he had approached me unsolicited, I played totally ignorant. I was told by someone he knew at jail intelligence that he may have some information about a current criminal investigation that I headed. I had heard he wanted to speak to me about this matter.

Rick went through the basics of what I already knew—he was housed in SMU next to Jeff Hausner, brother of serial killer Dale. Even though they didn't share a cell, Rick educated me on the layout of their unit, and how things worked up there. I sat and listened, taking notes as if I had no idea about any of this.

Rick said Jeff was an idiot who knew nothing. He didn't even know how to operate the phone that sat outside their cells. Rick had to teach him everything. He couldn't believe how naïve Jeff was, and frankly it was a little annoying at times. He felt like he was dealing with a kindergartner. It was more than I hoped. Jeff had come to Rick with his hat in his hand, begging for instruction, for someone to show him the ropes, and help him transition.

Jeff had laid out the stabbing case against him for Rick, and Rick told him he was basically screwed because the victim had identified him. People had also witnessed the stabbing and were willing to testify against him. It seemed to Rick that Jeff was in a hopeless situation.

Jeff told Rick the victim was currently incarcerated in the State Penitentiary in Florence. Jeff was ignorant about prison life, but he had heard certain things he believed were true: you don't snitch, you need to watch your back from your enemies, and things happened in prison all the time.

So he brought his ignorance to Rick and asked a simple question. How could he get to Raymond McQueen? How could he intimidate him to drop the charges or shut him up permanently? In other words, Jeff was comfortable with murder as an option, if that was the best solution. He asked Rick if he knew anyone that could take care of his problem.

Jeff had not directly implicated himself in the Random/Serial Shooter Case, but he had said things that made Rick believe he was involved. Jeff used the words "we" and "us" when he talked about the case. Rick was smart enough to pick up on those cues. He also knew too much about some of the cases to be a casual observer.

Our conversation lasted for hours, with Rick telling me what he heard and me writing it down like it was brand new information. In essence, it was, at least as far as Jeff was concerned. I asked a few questions when there was something I didn't understand, but for the most part, Rick did all the talking. I listened.

The plan was coming together beautifully. Rick was more than happy to listen and talk to Jeff, but it wouldn't be for free. He'd heard about the reward money that had been offered, and he wanted out of jail. He had a girlfriend on the outside and a kid. He couldn't take care of them from jail, so freedom was his ultimate goal. But I needed more than Rick's word.

Rick would be given a digital recorder to capture his conversations with Jeff. The recorder could tape for seven hours, and the chip would be passed to and through Deputy Callahan. It was important for Rick not to initiate these conversations. He was not to talk to Jeff about any of the facts of Jeff's current case, the stabbing. If Jeff brought it up, so be it. However, Rick could bring up the conspiracy to murder Raymond McQueen and the serial murders whenever he wanted.

In order to tag Jeff Hausner for the conspiracy case, we would set up a ghost pen pal in prison: me. Rick would start to receive mail and correspond accordingly. We would set up an elaborate code system that only we could decipher. Jeff would be taught the code. The idea was to have Jeff contact the ghost, me, and arrange the hit on McQueen, thus we'd have the overt act needed for a conspiracy to commit murder charge. Rick had used codes for years in communicating in the joint. He knew all the ins and outs. Since inmates can't receive letters from other inmates, I had to send them in an envelope marked from somewhere in Phoenix. The envelope had a bogus name and address, but inside it was me writing him from the state prison in Florence. My code name would be RR.

Armed with his recording device, Rick left police headquarters with a purpose—one that could get him some money in his pocket and possibly freedom, or at least a reduced sentence.

Rick received the first letter on December 22nd. He was able to show Jeff Hausner his letter from his prison buddy, RR. Of course, RR had received a coded letter from Rick about looking into the possibility of killing Raymond McQueen.

Raymond McQueen would be referred to in code as *the car*. My letter to Rick stated that the car "was in good shape, and runs well." I also told Rick that I thought I could get him a "good deal on it." It would cost him a thousand dollars now and twenty-five hundred when he got out. That was the agreed-upon price to kill McQueen.

But time was starting to work against us. Jeff had become paranoid, and even though he hinted around about wanting McQueen murdered, he wasn't coming right out and saying it. Jeff also believed that his cell was bugged.

He was very careful with anything that he said. When he did say something, it was in a low voice. The digital recorder I gave Pete was state of the art, too good, as a matter of fact. It picked up everything, every clank, scream, belch of Rick or anyone else in the cell block. I could hear Rick real well because the recorder was in his cell. Jeff, however, was getting washed out with sounds of jail doors slamming, and other everyday noises.

After a couple of weeks of listening, it was obvious the recordings weren't sufficient. Rick had been privy to the conversations and heard what was said. He heard Jeff admit to being involved in the .22 caliber murders and conspiring to kill Raymond McQueen. Unfortunately, the recordings weren't clear enough to charge Jeff with anything. It wasn't like I didn't want to, but I knew ultimately that a jury would also have to be convinced of what was said. If I wasn't, they wouldn't be.

Rick was more motivated than ever. He wanted out, and he wanted Jeff prosecuted. He would get Jeff on tape, and he would convince him to pass a code to me to kill Raymond McQueen.

I had known for awhile that both Jeff and Dale Hausner were sending coded messages from jail by using word search puzzles. Since I had been monitoring their mail, they had been receiving hundreds of pages of them, all blank. They would circle different words or groups of letters to be deciphered by whoever got the word search.

To the casual observer, it would seem innocent enough. Doing word searches to pass the time made sense when you were in lockdown twenty-three hours a day. But it was an old trick I learned about years ago. You circle certain words or letters and set up a key. The person who sent the word search has the key and deciphers the code. Occasionally, it was as simple as following the circled letters to make a word or a sentence.

Sometimes I could break the codes, sometimes I couldn't. Unfortunately, the ones I broke said nothing incriminating. They were useless coded messages about some trivial crap. I became convinced that, in Dale's case, he was doing it just to test me. It was part of a larger scheme to get a different code established that I couldn't break.

While Jeff Hausner was out of his cell, I received a call from Rick. He believed that he had recorded enough for us to nail Jeff. Plus, he wanted to show me the new key code he had devised for the murder/conspiracy case. I had him removed and brought to police headquarters under the guise of a doctor's visit.

Rick first handed me the key to the code he had devised. It was built like a graph—one through ten on the top, and A through J on the side, with each box filled with letters, words, or short phrases. There were several key sheets. Each of them had to be used simultaneously. All Jeff had to do was write a series of letters or numbers, and he could spell out for me what he wanted done to poor old Raymond McQueen. Jeff was convinced that I existed since I had been sending correspondence to Rick for over a month now.

The problem appeared to be money. Jeff was having a hard time getting thirty-five hundred dollars together. He didn't want to piss me off by not paying, so he was trying to beg, borrow, or steal the money, anyway he could.

Rick and I decided to drop the price to two grand. Anything less would have seemed bogus, even for a moron like Jeff. Rick had already given him the code sheet, and the new negotiated price should not be a stumbling block anymore.

Rick and I sat and listened to the dozens of hours of taped conversations. As luck would have it, just when the conversation turned to something meaningful, it would get washed out by other noises, or we could only hear certain parts of Jeff's voice. Rick was as pissed as I was. He knew what Jeff had said, but now he got to hear it for himself. It made him want to get Jeff even more.

Rick had done everything we asked. He put himself out there and convinced Jeff that he was a stand-up guy. He groomed Jeff, taught him the ropes. He befriended a guy that he quite frankly couldn't stand. Jeff was annoying as hell, and his idiotic questions made Rick want to murder Jeff himself. He so wanted us to nail him.

In all of the recordings, there just wasn't enough. Rick knew it too. The last chance was the coded correspondence. He knew it, and so did I.

I bought Rick a McDonald's hamburger and sent him back to his cell block. He was thoroughly convinced that Jeff Hausner knew the only way to keep himself out of prison was to kill Raymond McQueen. The only way to do that was to write and pay me to do it. Good ole "RR" was just waiting for the opportunity and the cash.

I went home that night, thinking that things were not hopeless. Even though we had been thwarted by logistics that we couldn't overcome, I felt in a matter of weeks that Jeff Hausner would be facing a conspiracy to commit murder charge.

The next day, I received a phone call from Deputy Callahan. I assumed that it was good news. I assumed wrong.

While Rick had been over at police headquarters talking to me, detention officers had decided to toss his cell, a rudimentary procedure that is occasionally done in jails and prisons. The DOs toss an inmate's cell in hopes of finding contraband. They may stumble across something else to hold over the inmate's head as well.

Even though they found no contraband in Rick's cell, they did find my digital recorder under his mattress. Instead of putting it back and inquiring jail intelligence why he would have such a device, they decided to leave it out in the open.

When Jeff Hausner got his hour out of his cell, he just happened to wander over to his new best friend's digs. He saw the digital recorder.

The game was up.

As soon as Rick returned to his cell, Jeff confronted him through his door. At first, Rick denied it, but there was no getting around it. Everyone in SMU had heard he was a snitch. He was blackballed from any further conversations with anyone. He was a man that could never be trusted.

It was nobody's fault. Our dealings with Rick had been so secret that only a few of us knew about the operation. When Deputy Callahan finished telling me the story, I felt as if I had betrayed Rick. He had done everything we asked, and then some. But it was not to be. Our plan that we had kept so secret backfired on us. All our hard work and hope had been destroyed.

Rick would be moved that next day away from Jeff Hausner. But before he left, he went off on Jeff. In a letter written to me from SMU, Rick wrote that he told Jeff he had him on the recordings, admitting to everything. Jeff would be charged any day now, and there would be no plea deal for him. He had just better confess.

According to Rick, Jeff was in tears. He was scared sh#*less.

Even though no new charges were filed, Jeff Hausner decided not to fight the current one any longer. Jeff Hausner plead guilty to the Attempted Murder of Raymond McQueen. The charge was also deemed a dangerous offense, which meant that any further convictions in cases against him, by statute, would mean serious prison time.

For this case, Jeff Hausner received seven-and-a-half years in the Department of Corrections. It was the most he could get for his first conviction. It was a slap on the wrist by comparison to what I believed he had done.

Samuel Dieteman thought so as well.

CHAPTER 47

Dale Hausner's initial lawyers were removed from the case because of conflicts of interest. There had been so many victims, some with less than stellar pasts, that it was only a matter of time until it was discovered that one of them had been represented by Hausner's appointed attorneys.

So the legal representation of Dale Hausner fell to the Office of the Legal Advocate, one of three public defenders offices.

One of the biggest fallacies in the criminal legal defense world is that a top-dollar, private attorney is the way to go. The more money you pay, the better the representation. Sure there are good private criminal defense lawyers out there, and if the defendant or his family has the bucks, then you can shop for those services. But by volume and experience alone, no one can compete with the public defenders' offices. These lawyers handle ten times the cases that private lawyers handle, and their experience is unmatched. They have taken numerous cases to trial, capital murder cases in particular. These people truly are the backbone of legal defense work.

Every capital murder case that is charged in Maricopa County is assigned two defense attorneys. Ken Everett and Tim Agan were the two lucky attorneys in the Office of the Legal Advocate that were bestowed the right to represent Dale Hausner.

Ken Everett and Tim Agan were both seasoned veterans of the criminal defense world. Though I had never faced them in court, their reputations were solid. Both had tried numerous murder cases and serious felonies. Dale Hausner was lucky to have them.

Their first order of business was to dismantle our case from the very base—tear apart the ongoing criminal conspiracy and try to make the series of shootings appear to be individual criminal acts. Under Arizona Rules of Criminal Procedure, it was the State's job to prove that Dale Hausner and Samuel Dieteman committed the crimes of the Random/Serial Shooter case as "connected together in their commission and were part of a common scheme or plan." Just because the cases are similar does not automatically make them part of a common scheme or plan.

So a motion was filed to consolidate all the cases for one court proceeding. The State believed, and presented in our motion for this consolidation, that these two committed these crimes together to terrorize and frighten the community as well as for notoriety purposes. Since the time of their arrest, no further series of random shootings had occurred.

The defense challenged this theory and filed a motion to sever the cases into forty or so separate trials. They claimed that since there were no eyewitnesses that could identify the defendants and the car they used, and no DNA or ballistic matches to any of Dale's guns, that the crimes could have been committed by anyone. They were right.

The problem for the defense came in the form of the ballistic matches of the shell casings found at the sights of the different shootings. Some had been positively identified. That evidence plus the admissions of Samuel Dieteman made the case for our consolidation of the acts solid, but it wasn't a given.

To bolster our claim that the crimes were all related, the Maricopa County Attorney's Office hired a consultant to bring a psychological perspective to the case, a perspective that would come from years of being involved in the evaluation of serial killers, their personalities, their motives, their inner demons. The county went and hired the best person that I knew to bring the psychological demeanor of serial killers to light. They hired Dr. Park Dietz.

Years before, I had attended a seminar where Dr. Dietz was the keynote speaker. Educated at Cornell and John Hopkins, he holds both a psychiatric Ph.D. and an M.D. He has interviewed some of the world's most notorious serial murderers, including Jeffrey Dahmer. I was thrilled to have him on board. I had a chance to sit down and work with one of the most renowned and well respected forensic psychiatrists in the world. I couldn't wait to pick his brain. I also wanted to share some of my theories about Dale Hausner and see if Dr. Dietz agreed or disagreed with my diagnosis.

One day after reviewing one of the wiretap sessions with Dr. Dietz, I decided to ask him what I thought was a very profound and in-depth question about serial murder suspects. It pertained specifically to Dale Hausner, and what I had learned during the investigation.

"Why is it that serial murderers tend to also commit arsons of structures? What's the connection between the two?"

Dr. Dietz looked at me, paused for a second, and then answered. "Because they're destructive fu@*ers."

I looked over at Dr. Dietz as he sat in what I had assumed was deep intellectual thought. Quick with a response and not to spoil the moment, I asked, "Is that your professional opinion?"

"Yes, it is." He had a sheepish grin on his face as I looked again to see if there was something I missed. There wasn't.

What I learned about Dr. Dietz was that not only was he a brilliant criminalist, but he had a hell of a sense of humor. We traded stories about police work and his work with the FBI and other agencies. You would have never thought that he was the man so revered in the law and psychiatric community. He acted like one of us, and he loved police.

At the evidentiary hearing, Dr. Dietz testified that he was convinced that the cases were related, not only by M.O., but by psychological factors of reveling and destruction. He believed that the killing of the animals was related to a deep need to punish and cause turmoil to the owners, as well as death to the animals.

He also believed, as did I, that Dale Hausner was the leader of the two, and Samuel Dieteman the follower. That comment in the evidentiary hearing brought a cynical smile to the face of Dale Hausner, who was present in the courtroom.

Even though they brought their own psychologist in to dispute what Dr. Dietz said, the court ruled in our favor, and the cases would proceed to trial as one continuing criminal act.

Despite the failure of the severance hearing, the defense for Dale Hausner filed for the suppression of evidence. There were motions to suppress his press conference, to suppress his interview, to order the court to change venue, and in the biggest motion, to suppress the wiretaps. Dale Hausner would testify in these hearings. All the proceedings in this case were handled in the courtroom of Superior Court Judge Roland Steinle III.

Judge Steinle had been an attorney since the mid-seventies. He came from a family of lawyers. His father, his grandfather, even his brother were all law professionals. His grandfather was a State Supreme Court Justice. His father was a well respected lawyer and once represented Milwaukee crime boss Frank Balistrieri, a mob boss made famous in the movie *Casino*.

Just like his father, Judge Roland Steinle III had graduated from Marquette. He received his J.D. in 1976. Judge Steinle was in private practice for ten years, and during that time, served in the Army reserve as a Judge Advocate General. He became a public defender in Maricopa County in 1986, and then moved to the Office of Legal Advocate in 1995. There he defended the likes of the Dale Hausners of the world in capital murder cases. He became a judge in 2001 and was now sitting in judgment in this larger-than-life criminal court case.

I had heard horror stories about Judge Roland Steinle III from prosecutors in the County Attorney's office. He was a jerk, a defense's best judge. We should ask him to be removed because of his past capital punishment defense work.

What I learned over the course of the hearings and through the ultimate trials of the defendants was that Judge Steinle was a pure jurist. He followed the law and didn't mandate from the bench. He was the ultimate professional. If you go into his court, you better have your ducks in a row, or he's going to make a fool out of you. Don't argue something without having the precedent or case law to back up what you're saying. There would be no question about who was in charge in Judge Steinle's court.

As to the press conference, Hausner stated that he had no idea why he was being marched into the throngs of reporters. He had signed a waiver given to him by the Sheriff's Office stating that he had a "blanket request" by the media for an interview. Meaning that the "blanket" covered all media: TV, radio, and print.

Hausner tried to spin it, saying he thought he was getting a "blanket" for his cell because he was so cold. Even though he spouted off about Sam, his ex-wife, and his innocence, not once until his lawyer stopped the interview did Dale do anything but flap his gums.

That motion to suppress the press conference was denied.

Next the defense would claim that Dale Hausner was subjected to cold and harsh interrogational tactics. His ramblings when I questioned him and in other police interviews were coerced out of a threat to his daughter's safety, and again because he was cold and wanted a blanket. Linus would have been proud.

His motion to suppress his interview was also denied.

Judge Steinle ruled that even though there was certainly publicity in this case, the key to a change of venue is if the publicity is "so outrageous that it promises to turn the trial into a mockery, or a mere formality." When the publicity is primarily factual and noninflammatory, the standard is not met. In a rip to the defense, Judge Steinle wanted to know if they had conducted any research in the area to see if the general public had been prejudiced. They had not. They did not provide any articles or television programming to show any inflammatory statements besides Phoenix Mayor Phil Gordon calling the two shooters "monsters."

The motion for a Change of Venue was denied.

The last big hurdle for us to get over was the suppression of the emergency wiretap. This motion was vigorously fought by Deputy County Attorney Laura Reckart, the initial reviewing attorney assigned to the wiretap. Laura had now been assigned full time as the second chair to the trial for the prosecution of Dale Hausner.

Ken Everett would argue that there was no need to get an emergency wire because there was no emergency, simply stated. After the night of August 1st and into the 2nd, police had Hausner and Dieteman under constant surveillance. No emergency existed. Police could have stopped any actions by the two, thus defusing the emergency need for the wiretap. He argued that a conventional wiretap would have been more appropriate, and that in fact an emergency wiretap is unconstitutional. He stated that the State should have moved on Samuel Dieteman as early as June of 2006, when ATF first got wind of his involvement in the Walmart arsons. Had they done so, these emergency wires would not have been needed.

His most fierce argument came in the area of why the bugs were placed in the first place. It wasn't because we were worried about his client shooting anybody. It was because we were hoping to gather probable cause by listening to their conversations. Since the arrests were made within a few hours of the wiretap, the state played its hand and used the conversations as further PC to make the arrests.

Laura Reckart obviously disagreed, as did the rest of the County Attorney's Office. Judge Roland Steinle was not so simply persuaded. He asked the state to produce the one witness who made the decision to trigger the emergency wiretap, one of two men with the power to sign off on such a venture—elected County Attorney Andrew Thomas.

At first, there was push back from the Office of the County Attorney. What kind of precedent would this set? Would judges be able to drag the County

Attorney in at their beck and call to justify every decision made by his office? What would the ramifications be?

After some more legal wrangling, County Attorney Andrew Thomas testified in State v. Hausner. Thomas stated that after he was briefed by Detective Darren Udd, he felt compelled to sign the order to stop the deaths of innocent citizens. The information was clearly and convincingly spelled out to him, and he reacted accordingly. He was just one of the witnesses brought forth.

Sergeant Don Sherrard testified about the harrowing night of following the two killers through the East Valley as they *trolled* for victims. Detective Rich Lebel testified that, based on his briefings, that there was not enough information to obtain a conventional wiretap. Detective Udd testified to his briefing of the County Attorney. Lastly, I testified that if, in fact, the two had decided to shoot someone on the night of the surveillance, based on their M.O. in all the previous shootings, we could not have stopped them.

After the testimony, in a large triumph for the state, Judge Steinle ruled that the wiretaps were legally obtained. He denied the defense's motion to have them suppressed.

This decision would tear a huge hole through the defense camp of Samuel Dieteman. With the wiretap evidence being admitted in addition to his admissions, the case against Sam was virtually indefensible.

◈

I remember sitting at my desk, going through my phone messages when I heard a recording left by a woman who claimed to be Ron Horton's cousin.

Ron was sick, hospitalized with a staph infection. By the sound of her voice, it didn't appear to be too serious, but they wanted the police to know. She told me that Ron had my number. I thought it was odd for her to leave this message.

When I returned the phone call, the cousin now shared the seriousness of Ron's condition. He was in John C. Lincoln Hospital and was in a life-or-death struggle. I beat feet to the hospital. It was late in the evening, and I was told that the family did not want any more information about Ron being leaked. Apparently, some of Ron's friends had visited and released some information about Ron's condition without the family's approval.

I was there to see if my witness, the man who provided the key piece of information to the Random/Serial Shooter Task Force was going to be OK, and all I got was, "You'll have to talk to the family." I was able to ascertain that Ron had contracted MRSA. What the hell is MRSA?

After leaving the hospital, I went back to headquarters and started my research. Methicillin-resistant Staphylococcus aureus, commonly referred to as MRSA, is a bacterium that causes infections. It's a form of a staph infection. Some of us carry staph bacteria in our body and never have any real problems. It's usually spread by contact with someone that's infected or by touching objects that have bacteria on them. It's usually not serious, but in rare cases, it can be life threatening. MRSA hits people with weak immune systems the hardest. I was pretty sure after reading up about this infection that Ron would be just fine.

The next day, I received a phone call from Joyce Hart, Ron's mother and one of the sweetest persons on the face of the earth. I was glad to hear from her and expected a full confirmation on Ron's positive treatment and prognosis.

I was wrong. Ron was very ill. The doctors had been pumping antibiotics into him for days, and he was getting worse, not better. MRSA had infected his bloodstream, and Ron was basically comatose. He was given a 50/50 chance of survival.

Over the next several weeks I talked to Joyce, her husband Roger, and Ron's sisters, Tracy and Sherry, on a regular basis. They started to feel like family, and together we prayed and consoled each other, hoping that Ron could somehow pull through, that he was too important to pass, and that he had much in life left to accomplish.

On January 26th, 2008, Ron Horton passed away from the effects of MRSA. I found out that Ron had injured his arm, and that was how the staph had spread.

Although Ron's testimony was not critical to the case because Sam had confessed, it was still important to the case to put a face to the timeline of the arrests. His testimony would have locked up one of the key components of the state's case, showing that, within a week of his coming forward, arrests were made in the huge manhunt. His unexpected death was yet another tragedy of a case marked with them. This case, and the people associated with it, really were cursed.

As I sat at my desk two days after Ron's death, his mother Joyce called. She asked me if I would speak at Ron's funeral.

At first, I was hesitant. I had only known Ron for a short time. I wasn't a close friend or relative. But Ron and I had formed a bond. He had spoken highly of me, and I owed him.

"I understand if you feel uncomfortable and would rather not," Joyce said. "We just thought that you might be a good person to talk about Ron, and what he meant to this community."

With that, I jumped at the chance to speak at a hero's funeral. Of course, I would do it. It would be an honor.

The small chapel in Mesa was packed with Ron's closest friends and family. The media had been denied entrance. Ron's cousin spoke first. He told stories of Ron that had the attendees laughing. They were close, and he did a great job.

I scripted a speech for Ron that laid out our relationship—how we first met on the fateful night of July 28, 2006, in the middle of the largest criminal investigation in this state's history. How Ron had chosen the restaurant, and how I watched as he rode up on his Harley with his long hair flowing in the wind, no helmet, of course. I told them that I didn't prejudge Ron because of his tough biker look. How we sat down over a meal, Ron and I, and he first told me about his previous contact with police. I told the mourners that I tried to look surprised, which got a good laugh.

I referred to Ron as the snowball that started the avalanche, the man with the guts to come forward. I made a point to tell his friends, family, and coworkers that Ron wasn't afraid of being labeled a snitch, a rat, a tattletale. He stood above all that. Ron was a man's man, and a hero in this community.

I quoted the English novelist Graham Greene, who wrote:

Behind the complicated details of the world stand the simplicities: God is good, the grown-up man or woman knows the answer to every question. There is such a thing as truth, and justice is as measured and faultless as a clock. Our heroes are simple: they are brave, they tell the truth, they are good swordsmen and they are never in the long run really defeated (The Ministry of Fear [London: Penguin Books, 1943], 88-89).

I closed by telling everyone there that, by the grace of God, Ron didn't have a choice but to come forward. His family had instilled that into him as he grew up. Traits like class, integrity, and high moral values are passed down from your parents and entrenched in your soul by your siblings. Ron was proud of his family, and they were of him. "To his family, his relatives, his friends, I say thank you. To Ron Horton, I say, God bless, and may you rest in eternal peace."

CHAPTER 48

Over the past twenty-five years, I've gone on vacations with some lifelong friends. We used to go all the time, but with jobs and family restrictions, we have made it just an annual event. It's a guys' trip, a chance to get away for a few days, let loose, and play a little golf. A few years back, we discovered the gulf coast of Mississippi, namely Biloxi and Gulfport. This became a treasured retreat for our group, full of Vegas gaming, some really nice golf courses, and Southern hospitality.

I was sitting by the pool after a day of golf when I noticed that I had three voicemails on my city cellphone. I had taken my phone just in case of an emergency, and I knew that if I had messages that something big had come up.

The first message was from Deputy County Attorney Laura Reckart. In a quiet voice, like she was passing on some type of national secret, she told me that Samuel Dieteman's lawyers had called, and that he would be pleading guilty in court to two counts of murder and one count of conspiracy to commit murder. There had been some negotiations behind the scene for some time now.

This wasn't a total shock. Sam had no wiggle room and apparently had told his lawyers that enough was enough. He was guilty and ready to take his punishment. But the kicker was that the plea deal gave him nothing. By pleading guilty, he could still face the death penalty. A jury would be impaneled to decide his fate.

Last, but not least, as part of the plea agreement, Sam would agree to testify truthfully about all the crimes that he and Dale Hausner had committed.

The County Attorney's Office had hit the jackpot. Having one less trial would save the county thousands of dollars in trial expenditures. It also made the state's star witness one of the co-defendants. They couldn't have scripted it any better.

So on April 4, 2008, in a quiet, non-publicized hearing in front of the Honorable Judge Roland Steinle III, Samuel Dieteman knowingly and willingly agreed to the plea agreement. The media reported it after the fact. This hearing had been so hush-hush that none of the press were informed about what Sam had decided to do.

I hadn't seen or talked to Sam since September of 2006. I was totally prepared to spend the next year and a half in court, testifying at both cases. The news of the plea deal was sweet music to my ears. It was one less lengthy court trial where I would have to regurgitate all the information I knew about these crimes. It meant that I could concentrate now on Dale Hausner alone.

But Sam Dieteman had something else in mind. In a state-recorded interview, as part of his plea agreement and with his attorney present, Sam dropped another bombshell. He told of the attempted murder of another citizen. The perpetrator was none other than Jeff Hausner.

I thought we were done with Jeff, but Sam clearly wasn't. No one else had come forward with any information on Dale's brother. Deep down, I think it grated on Sam that Jeff could get away with so many murders and shootings. So two years later, Sam decided to reopen an old wound.

Somewhere in the middle of May of 2006, while Sam was still living with Jeff, he and Dale and Jeff went out cruising one night. It was one of those nights where Sam knew something was going to happen. Sam was plastered. Dale was driving his car, Sam was in the front seat, and Jeff was in the back.

They spotted a male walking alone somewhere in the area of 75th Avenue and Camelback. Sam remembered a church with a parking lot. It was going to be another routine jumping, where they'd all get out, beat the guy up, and then take off. The problem was, Sam was no good to them that night, He was too liquored up to beat anyone.

Jeff got pissed at Sam for being such a pussy and decided he would take care of the guy by himself. Dale pulled the car off of Camelback Road, and Jeff jumped out. Dale then drove back around and pulled into the church parking lot. The male was close by, still walking. Dale Hausner circled the empty parking lot and drove up to the guy. Dale got his attention and said, "Hey man, can you tell me how I get back to the 101 (freeway)?" The man started giving him directions. Jeff came up from behind and stabbed him in the back and neck two or three times. The guy dropped the soda he was drinking and ran back toward Camelback Road.

Sam assumed the victim was critically injured. When Jeff Hausner returned to the car, Sam saw the knife blade covered with blood. "Dale turned on the light and said, 'Let me see the knife.' There was blood all the way down to the knife handle."

Sam had written out a statement on legal paper of all the shootings and murders that he or the Hausners had done, except for this one. The list was long, including everything Sam knew about the .22 caliber murders. We would, of course, have an in-depth discussion on all of these cases.

But, for now, I had one more crack at the piñata. Jeff Hausner was squarely in my crosshairs once again.

His name was Timothy Davenport, a semi-employed blue-collar worker who lived with his parents in a modest home in Maryvale. His story was just like the rest.

He was out walking to a friend's house, drinking a soda, when he noticed a car drop off a passenger. He didn't think anything of it. The car then circled around and pulled in front of him. At the time, he was crossing a church parking lot at 73rd Avenue and Camelback. He was contacted by the driver and asked for directions. Before he knew it, he was stabbed multiple times. As he turned to look at his assailant, he was slashed across the face. He didn't get a look at him. After being attacked, he ran to a friend's house, who ultimately took him to the hospital.

When Timothy was contacted more than two years after the crime, he was stupefied with my interest. Like Raymond McQueen, he thought no one would care. It turned out that Timothy Davenport had watched the arrest of Dale Hausner on TV. He recognized the mugshot that was plastered all over the news. He knew it was the driver of the car that had diverted his attention so someone could stab him from behind. When Timothy saw footage of Hausner's blue Camry being towed away, he recognized the car from that night. Timothy was positive about Dale and the Camry's involvement. And you know how many people Timothy informed about his crime? Nobody! He sat on it. He never told police anything about what he had discovered.

Well, now the case would come to light. With Timothy Davenport and Samuel Dieteman's testimony, we would get to charge Jeff Hausner with another attempted murder.

It wasn't the murders I had hoped for, but it was something.

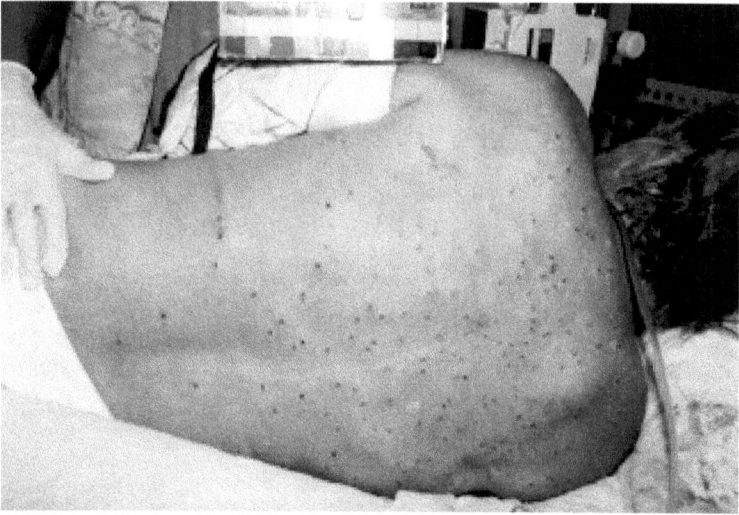

Victim James Hodge, shot in the back by Dale Hausner with a 12 gauge. Referred to in the wire taps.

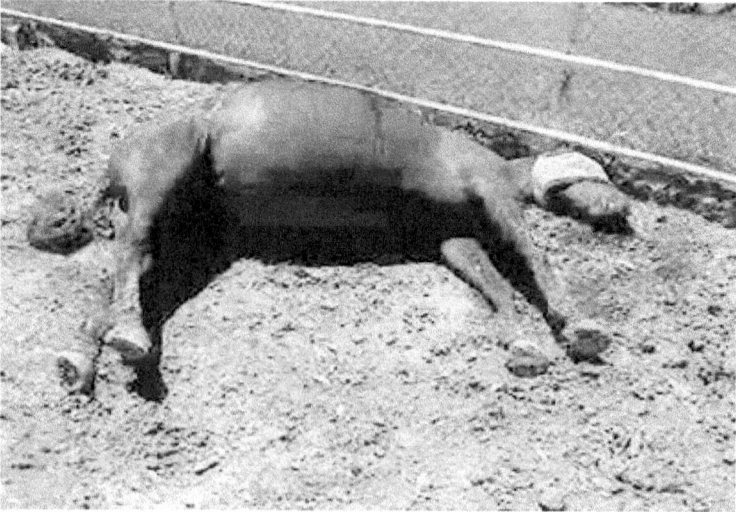

Horse "Sara Moon" shot and killed in Tolleson, Arizona. Killed with a .22 rifle.

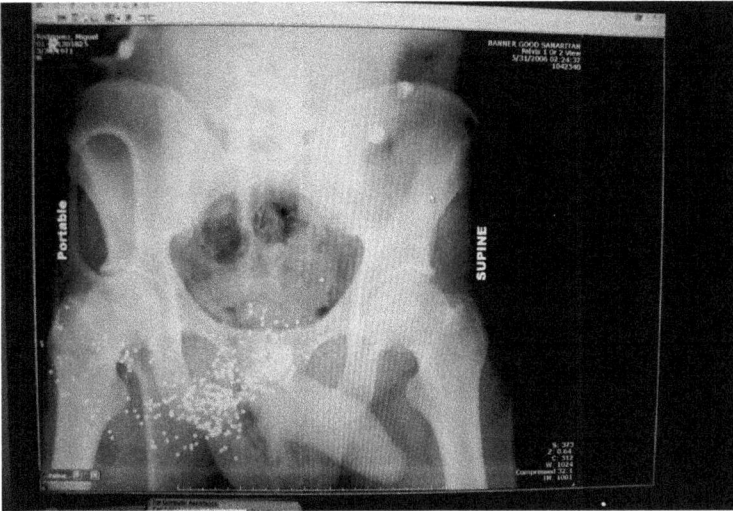

Victim two of the triple shooting, Miguel Rodriguez's x-ray. Shot from close range with all the pellets still inside.

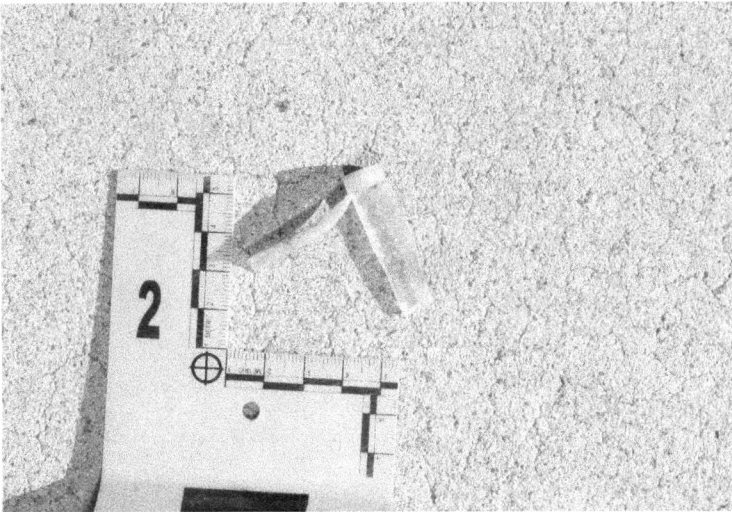

The 410 shotcup from the Ashley Armenta crime scene. She was barely hit with pellets as Dieteman aimed high to miss her.

Robyn Blasnek crime scene. Item 2 marks the 410 shotcup.

The .410 shotgun with a cartridge loose, and the black canvass bag it was carried in. Dietman sawed the butt off for better maneuverability inside the car.

.22 caliber shell casings recovered from the back seat of Hausner's Toyota Camry. Ballistically matched to other crime scenes.

One of the many buckets of ammuntion recovered at Hausner's apartment.

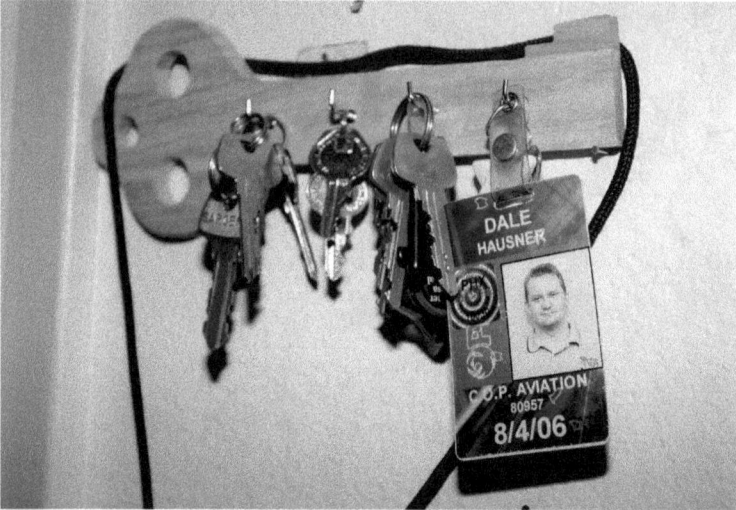

Hausner's airport ID badge. Notice the expiration date was the day of his arrest.

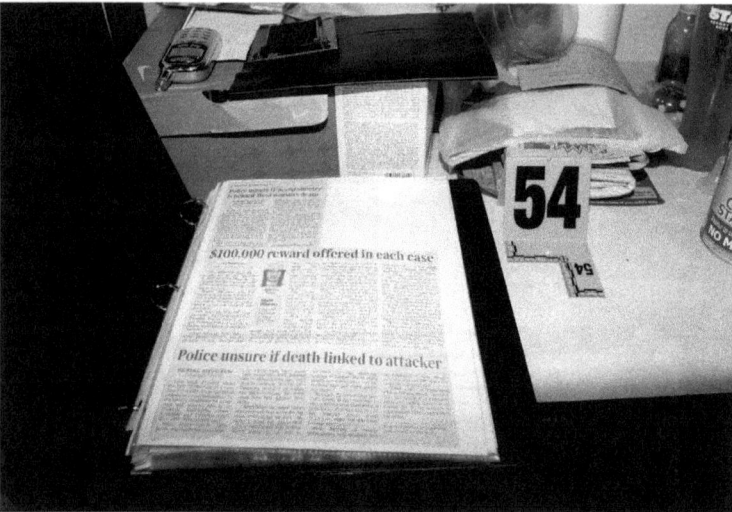

Hausner's scrapbook with numerous clippings of his and the BLK's exploits.

Joseph Roberts' bicycle that he was pushing the night of his shooting.

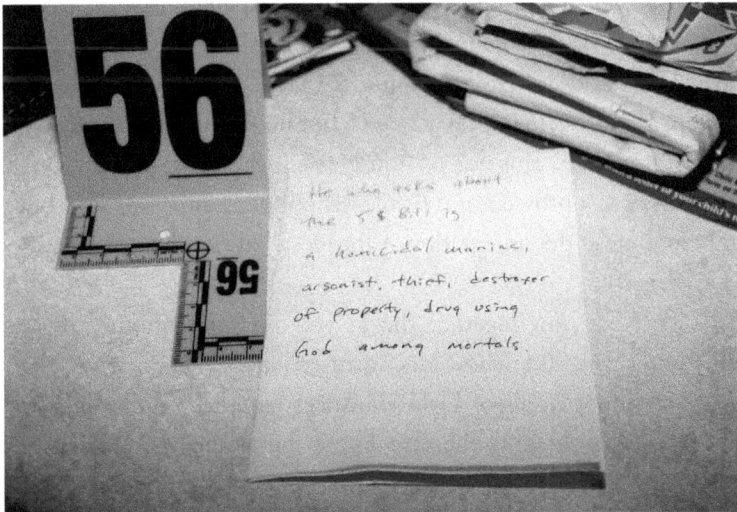

Hausner describing himself before he was arrested. He left many strange writings in and around his apartment.

CHAPTER 49

The death penalty trial of Dale Hausner commenced in September 2008. Hundreds of jurors were summoned, interviewed, and questioned. I sat through the entire process. There was little anxiety while the selection process was underway. But when the final twenty jurors were selected, some had horrified looks on their faces. Up until now, it had been amusing, but not anymore. Thanks to the Internet, these twenty people were going to sit on a jury of the largest capital murder case in Arizona history with the whole world watching.

And so on October 6, 2008, the trial of Dale Hausner began. The State was given one day to present opening remarks. Vince Imbordino addressed a packed courtroom of reporters, victims, victimized family members, and the general public.

Vince Imbordino has prosecuted over fifty death penalty cases in his illustrious thirty-two year career as a county prosecutor. His style of presentation is calm and quiet. He would even admit to jurors that sometimes he has a hard time speaking up. Vince is a man of few words, but he lets his experience in the legal system speak for itself. This was obviously the biggest case and biggest stage in his entire career as a prosecutor. His old-school demeanor was soft, but direct. Instead of looking at documentation, Vince recalled facts based on memory. He exuded experience.

Jeff Colbert had put together the PowerPoint presentation for Vince. It was well done. The slide show documented all the victims who had been shot or stabbed as a result of Dale Hausner's exploits. A map followed each slide of the victim, showing the area where the victim was injured or killed. All in all, thirty-seven people had been murdered or shot by Dale Hausner or Samuel Dieteman. The slide show also included information about the two Walmart arsons.

Over the next seven months, Vince and his co-counsel, Laura Reckart, would lay out for the jury the evidence gathered that pointed to Dale Hausner as the one responsible for these crimes: the twelve gauge and 410 shotguns recovered from Dale's apartment; all the ammunition, the map, and the shell casing found in the trash; and Dale's private collection of newspaper clippings, some dating back to 2005.

Dale's car matched the description given by several victims. Police had found .22 caliber ammunition and shell casings inside the car. They also had discovered latex gloves which, according to Sam, were used to load and unload weapons. More importantly, those shell casings found in Dale Hausner's car were positively identified to evidence recovered at the crime scenes of Timothy Tordai, Whiskey the dog, and the shooting at the bartending school.

Over one hundred witnesses would testify for the state, most of them investigators or crime lab personnel. The victims who survived provided heart-wrenching testimony. Those who died had family to speak for them.

Becky Lewis, sister of murder victim Reginald Remillard, was called to the stand to try and explain why Reggie was out sitting on a bus bench in the early morning hours of May 24, 2005. Reggie was ill and did not want to go to a clinic. Bottom line: he was shot dead in the neck on a bus bench, a place where he liked to sit and gather his thoughts.

David Estrada's mother, Rebecca, testified and related her last few days with him before he was murdered. They were planning a vacation together. She talked about how he worked construction, but had been hoping to land a job at a restaurant named Tiffany's. For three years, he had tried to get his foot in the door at the restaurant. He had obtained an interview right before he was killed. Photos of David's property found at the crime scene were shown on the courtroom screens. Rebecca recognized his guitar case and duffle bag.

Rebecca Estrada would become one of the two most recognizable victims in this trial. The other was Paul Patrick, a survivor, but mortally wounded. Rebecca was pounced on by the media every time she showed up in court. She worked full time and wanted to be in court every day, but just couldn't. When she was there, she was vocal, a rock of strength for the pursuit of justice. Paul was a bastion in court as well.

Media would filter in and out as well. Nick Martin, a reporter with the East Valley Tribune, blogged the trial in its entirety. Through his website, HeatCity.org, he gave daily updates on who testified and what of interest occurred inside the courtroom. Mike Watkiss, a local TV reporter for KTVK Channel 3, also attended the trial. Mike had been a crime reporter in the valley for a long time. As one of the most trusted faces in the media, Mike has a passion for telling it like it is and reports the news with a panache that no one can emulate. Jennifer Vogel with local Channel 12 was there every day, along with Michael Kiefer from the *Arizona Republic*, representing the print side.

A parade of dog and horse owners from the West side of Phoenix and Tolleson would sit in the seat next to Judge Roland Steinle's bench. They all related the heartache of finding their pet severely injured or dead. Some of them heard the shots fired, some only saw the aftermath. All of them were hard hit by the reality of someone killing or harming a defenseless animal. Many of them cried during their testimony, which in turn caused tearing in the jury booth and in the gallery.

Detective Ron Rock testified how he connected all the animal shootings with the murder of David Estrada. He even investigated some of the Phoenix animal shootings where the victims felt that Phoenix Police hadn't put in enough effort.

Detective Cliff Jewell testified about the downtown murders, the shootings on that fateful December night. We showed the Department of Environmental Quality video surveillance where we believed Dale Hausner drove his car four times past the corner of Adams and 10th Avenue. Since there were two cameras, I had taken the footage to Diane Meshkowitz, one of our forensic photo specialists. She put the two camera views on a DVD in a side-by-side reenactment. In this way, the jury would be able to see a six-second delay during one of the car's passes. That would be plenty of time for Dale or Jeff Hausner to come on target and murder Jose Ortis.

Veterinarians testified on how these animals suffered. Dr. Lyons and Dr. Fischione from the Medical Examiner's Officer testified about the death cases. Most, if not all of the victims, had died excruciatingly painful deaths. Deprived of oxygen, these victims drowned in their own blood, sometimes taking as long as five minutes to die.

John Kane testified about his relationship with Dale Hausner from the bartending school, how Hausner had told him about shooting the car up, and how he bragged about never being caught.

Phoenix Police Scientist Phil Wolfslagel and Lee Garrett conducted all of the examinations on the .22 caliber bullets, shell casings, and projectiles recovered from the scenes and from the bodies of the victims. Phil testified that even though the bullets were all gold plated and all had the same ballistics, except for Tony Mendez's case, there were several guns that could fire those cartridges.

But something I found in Dale Hausner's financial records made Phil's testimony even more credible. In his records, Dale had listed the purchase of a .22 caliber rifle from the pawn shop. This gun had the same rifling characteristics as the bullets recovered from these scenes. It fit the description of the .22 rifle that disappeared, the one Dale supposedly never had or had thrown away.

Mesa Police Crime Lab Criminalist Kelly Speckles testified about the fingerprint evidence. She developed and identified Dale Hausner's right index finger to the Dr. Pepper can found in the trash, which just so happened to have the expended 410 shell casing in it as well. The Phoenix Metropolitan Street Map had both Hausner's and Dieteman's fingerprints. A torn piece of paper, with a victim's name, Robin Blasnek, on it also carried the mark of Hausner's left palm print. The infamous 410 shotgun had both Hausner's and Dieteman's fingerprints on it.

With the help of Phoenix Police Firearms instructor Robert Lee, we fired dozens of rounds through both the sawed-down 410 shotgun and the twelve gauge. We fired both the guns from a car the approximate height of Dale Hausner's Toyota Camry and from five to fifty feet. The reconstruction took a whole day. My shoulder hurt so bad after firing that twelve gauge, I couldn't lift my arm for two days. The thing kicked like a mule. I could see why they switched guns and used the easier-firing 410. Later in court, I presented the evidence to the jury to corroborate Sam's testimony about who fired and where.

DNA was clearly not the strongest part of the state's case. In fact, most of it came up either eliminating Dale Hausner with no profile at all or with mixtures of profiles. The latex glove that Dale used to remove spent shell casings from the 410 shotgun proved to be the most significant piece of the state's DNA evidence. Those prints came back as a match with twelve loci. In other words, there was a one in fourteen trillion chance that this was not Dale's DNA.

Detective Rich Label testified about the Emergency Wiretap, and how it was the only way the police could get ears in the Hausner apartment and in Dale's car. Detective Label summarized and typed the wiretap conversations for a day straight after their arrests to be in compliance with the court order. But that was only part of the story.

On one of the most attended days of the trial, the prosecution played the wiretap recordings. Up until this time, people had only heard the rumors of what was on them. Prosecutor Laura Reckart led Detective Jason Buscher through the wire room, the spike mikes, the enhancements, and the countless hours he spent reviewing and editing the tapes.

I tried not to make eye contact with Hausner much during court, but I did watch his reaction to the wiretaps, especially when he referred to his victim, Robin Blasnek, as "Blastnek"; when, in front of his young daughter, he told Dieteman not to kill anyone that night; when he spoke of circling around, of watching media reports and newspaper articles; of comparing their body counts to the murders of the Baseline Killer. In the end, there wasn't a lot of testimony needed. The tapes said it all.

At this point, I had spent weeks on the stand, talking about the shotgun cases, about the reconstructions, about the task force, and about all the leads that flooded in. Without Ron Horton, I had to explain how his tip led us to Dieteman, how we followed them, wiretapped them, arrested them, and interviewed them.

Then came Sam's turn. Vince Imbordino led Sam through his past, and how he met up with the Hausner brothers. Sam talked about how he became an alcoholic and reintroduced himself to methamphetamine, courtesy of Dale. Starting with the Raymond McQueen stabbing, Sam described how he had been indoctrinated into the crime spree—starting with smaler incidents, breaking car windows, slashing of tires, setting trash dumpsters and piles of landscaping debris, such as palm fronds, grass clippings, and tree branches on fire. All of this led up to May 2, 2006, the night that would forever change Sam Dieteman's life—the night Dale Hausner shot Kibili Tambadu, and the night he murdered Claudia Gutierrez-Cruz.

Sam walked the jury through every shooting, stabbing, and arson. At first, Sam would direct his testimony towards the prosecutor, Vince Imbordino. But Vince told Sam to look and talk to the jury. From then on, Sam very seldom looked at Vince or anyone else in the courtroom. He would bow his head in shame when Vince asked him about a shooting where he had been present or where he was responsible for what happened. He would try his best to explain their overall strategy. They knew none of the victims. All were picked at random, all by themselves, with no witnesses around. He could offer no real explanation for his actions, besides his daily meth use. The testimony was convincing, and the prosecution soon rested.

Ken Everett, Dale Hausner's lead attorney, is a competent, boisterous attorney. He and co-counsel Tim Agan presented the best defense they could. Dale had given his team a day planner with an alibi for almost every night of every shooting. According to Dale, he was out with different women every night. He needed to keep track of his activities because none of the women knew about the others, and Dale wanted to keep it that way.

The defense would place the blame on Sam Dieteman. They did suggest that he might have had help from none other than Jeff Hausner. Sam pleaded guilty to the shootings. He was the initial focus of the investigation. Dale never told anyone he had committed any shootings. It was Sam who led the "secretive life." Sam was the one that lived on the west side of town, not Dale. They didn't meet up until April of 2006, well past the shootings of 2005. Who did he live with on the west side? Jeff Hausner of course. Sam was a liar and a mooch.

The .22 caliber gun had never been recovered. There were no matches of guns found to bullets, shot cups, or casings recovered. The ballistic evidence did not prove who fired the gun. Only one case had a positive identification by a victim. That was two years after the fact, after all the media sensationalism. There were no positive identifications by any witnesses either. Plus, we had multiple descriptions of cars from which the shots were fired.

Those pesky wiretaps the state thought were so compelling were just a couple of intoxicated guys sitting around, jabbering about shootings, but never admitting to anything specific. It was the same type of talk you would hear in a locker room.

There was, of course, the subtle introduction of the death of Dale Hausner's children on November 12, 1994. That day was so tough for Dale. He would never have shot the dogs Shep and Irving or murdered Nathaniel Shoffner that night. Instead he would have been grieving and visiting his children's gravesite.

Dale Hausner was a boxing commentator who had allegedly been on Showtime, HBO, ESPN, and other local stations. He had his own boxing show, was a skilled boxing photographer, and a part-time bartender. He had a full-time job working at the airport and a sick daughter that he cared for dearly. Don't focus on Dale; focus on the guy that is setting him up: Sam Dieteman.

During Sam's cross-examination, Ken Everett tried to paint Sam as a murdering liar, a thug who had a violent past. Sam didn't disagree with the murdering part; he couldn't. It was the truth. But Sam didn't waver on his facts.

He never saw Dale Hausner with a .22 caliber rifle, but Jeff had one. Sam was the only State's witness to any crime. Why should a jury believe a murderer? But Sam was credible.

Insignificant witness after witness came to the stand, called by the defense, to try to stop the carnage. None of them really mattered.

I felt that it was a given that Dale Hausner would testify no matter what his attorneys advised. It was too big of a stage, too great of an opportunity for him to pass on. After all, he was a showman. His psychopathic personality would take over. He would think he could schmooze a jury into believing anything that he wanted them to believe.

I was, of course, right. On February 2, 2009, Dale Hausner took the stand in his own defense. In total, he would spend six days on the stand, spinning a web of deceit that would make Ted Bundy proud.

He talked of his family, daughter, and his own upbringing. Since being in jail, he had received a diploma in Christian Science, a pathetic attempt to garner some religious empathy. He talked about the loss of his boy and his stepson. He talked about his marriages, and where he lived since moving to the Phoenix area as a small boy. He talked about his employment as a boxing photographer, bartender, talk show host, and janitor. He admitted he wasn't the most stable or hardest worker by any means.

Then he went into denial mode. He never murdered anyone. He was never present when anyone was murdered. He owned animals. He would never shoot one. In 2005 and 2006, he only knew of the shootings through the media. The articles he saved were from 2006 only. The 2005 ones belonged to Sam Dieteman. He was only an interested observer. Oh, and by the way, he has never been *convicted* of a felony.

He denied that he used his Toyota Camry for these crimes, including the arsons. To the best of his knowledge, his vehicle was never used for anything but transportation to and from work. He had conveniently lost a set of keys to the car and had never found them. He had no idea why the shell casings were found in his backseat, unless of course somebody planted them there. And the latex gloves that Sam testified Dale had used to load and unload his weapon after a shooting? Dale used those gloves in his work as a janitor.

Dale testified that he destroyed the .22 caliber gun a week after he bought it at the pawn shop. He had tried to fire it twice in the desert, and both times it jammed. The pawn shop wouldn't take it back, so there was only one responsible thing to do. It was broken up by him and Brother Jeff, placed in two different trash dumpsters.

Hausner had no idea how this testimony and many other statements would come back to bite him hard. That's what psychopaths seldom understand. When they think they are fooling everyone with their lies, half-truths, and innuendos, sooner or later they forget what they said.

His big hammer, the day planner with all his women dates, was written mostly in pencil. All entries we believed made after his arrest. You see, inmates are not allowed to have pens in Madison Jail.

Dale Hausner was a lady's man, the Hugh Hefner of the janitorial world. So we called them all to testify. His ex-wife, the mother of his child, the supposed girlfriends. All of them poked holes in his story. They testified about what a lying scum bag he was.

Through his testimony, Dale Hausner gave us an opportunity to bring in evidence that had previously, as a late discovery submission, been disallowed. But now we would be able to use Dale's cellphone records to disprove what he had said on the stand.

When Dale Hausner testified that he was here or there at a particular time, we could show that the cellphone records put him right on top of some of the shootings and near the others. The cell tracking showed his movements throughout the valley as he weaved his way to shooting locations. It was the last nail in the coffin.

In her closing arguments, Prosecutor Laura Rechart masterfully put it all together. She went through the cases one by one. She again described all the mountains of evidence, played some of the wiretaps, and ripped Hausner about his testimony. Laura mocked his day planner and penciled in notes and codes. "His alibis turned in to ali-lies," Laura fired off. Regarding those cellphone records that wouldn't have been admitted without his arrogant testimony, she could only say, "Gotcha."

On February 26, the case of the State Versus Dale Hausner was given to the jury, a group slimmed down from the original twenty to just twelve. It was sad for some of them to have sat through the last seven months and not be picked for the final panel. Judge Steinle thanked them dearly, and told them that he couldn't believe after this lengthy period of time that we didn't lose a single juror.

It would take two weeks of deliberation before the jury brought back verdicts on all eighty-seven counts of murder, attempted murder, aggravated assault, drive-by shooting, arson, and cruelty to animals. They had been able to reach a decision on every count.

I arrived at the courthouse about an hour early that day. I had one of the worst headaches I had ever experienced. I'm sure it was stress induced. No matter how much you work, no matter how hard you try to piece things together, no matter how simple you make it, you still have twelve inexperienced people sitting there in judgment. Can you really expect them to comprehend it all, especially a case this size? Did they hear all the key testimony? Were you and the other witnesses believable and credible?

Judge Roland Steinle, the man who sat in the courtroom all of these months, could not be present for the reading of the verdicts. He was ill. The presiding judge of the criminal court called the court to order. He asked if the jury had reached a verdict. The foreperson stood and advised that they had. The verdict was handed to the judge. He went through each count then handed them to Linda, the bailiff.

The murders of Mr. Mendez and Mr. Remillard were read first: not guilty. For the aggravated assault of Barbara Whitmer, whose dog was killed while they were out walking: not guilty. For the count of cruelty to animals on the night Nathaniel Shoffner was murdered: not guilty.

I, for one, did not panic. There was a chance that we could lose every .22 caliber shooting case that didn't have a shell casing tied to it. As I sat at the prosecution table, I knew that those first two murders were the toughest to prove. I had predicted acquittal for Reginald Remillard's murder. I was not shocked at the not guilty verdict in the Tony Mendez case.

Then the avalanche of doom landed on the defense. Guilty after guilty after guilty. In total, Dale Shawn Hausner was found guilty of eighty counts of murder, attempted murder, drive-by shooting, and cruelty to animals. Oh, and yes, guilty of the arsons too.

◈

Dale Hausner presented no mitigation on his behalf in the death penalty phase of the case, just more diatribe. Allocution is the right to speak directly to the jury about what someone has done. It is a right of law. In Hausner's case, it was befitting. It was his final stage, his last hoorah, and his last pulpit from which to speak. He once again was in charge of his life, and nobody was going to tell him what to do.

Hausner took control immediately upon the jury being seated in the box. They had convicted him of six murders and countless other shootings, but he was a law-abiding citizen. He, of course, disagreed with their decision. He took the time to tell everyone, specifically me, that he hoped police did a better job in the future of catching serial murderers—not him of course, but others. It never should have taken fifteen months to find the culprits.

"It didn't, jackass, just two for me," I thought to myself.

He let everyone know that the Hausner name will now be bantered around like Bundy. He's sorry for that, or so he claimed. He didn't want his family to suffer. He was sorry for putting them through all this. He apologized for the deaths and shootings without accepting any responsibility. It must have been Sam ... Jeff ... and/or the one-armed man.

Listening to him made me physically ill. If one of the victims or family members had jumped the courtroom dividers, like many of those courtroom video attacks I've seen on TV, I wouldn't have stopped them. He needed the sh#* kicked out of him, and I could only hope someone when would do it when he got to prison.

He finished in typical Hausner fashion. He threw a twist into his final words, a twist only those who know nothing about psychopaths would understand. He asked to be given death. At this time, only juries can issue the death penalty.

You see, by asking for death, Dale Hausner controlled his own fate. He could later say that he asked for it, and therefore he got that penalty, if the jury took him at his word. I believe he asked for it *not* to get death. He assumed the jury despised him, his remarks, his antics enough to warrant death. But, if they despised him enough, they might do just the opposite of what he asked. Either way, he could say that he won. The control freak came out one last time.

The jury took little time to decide that he needed to die. Dale Hausner lost even though he won. With that verdict, he would be moved to Arizona's Death Row.

CHAPTER 50

The trial of Jeff Hausner would take place before Sam Dieteman's death penalty trial commenced. Sam had signed on to help in all the prosecutions of the Hausner brothers. We needed to get Jeff Hausner out of the way just in case death was dropped on Sam's head.

There was media present to follow Jeff's trial, but it was nothing like the circus that had followed Dale. Jeff, unlike his twisted brother, would not be testifying on his own behalf. He was much too smart for that. His lawyer, Leo Valverde, was an excellent attorney. A well mannered, impeccably dressed litigator, Leo would never have allowed himself to be subjected to the same absurdity that Dale's attorneys endured. Jeff Hausner would make us prove the case against him, not imploding himself on the stand.

Prosecutor Laura Reckart, fresh off the Dale Hausner victory, tried the case alone. There were only a few witnesses to call for the state, and I would sit through the trial with her.

Timothy Davenport took the stand and told a jury of his peers how he had left his house and was en route to another friend's house on this fateful evening. He had purchased a soda and took off walking along dangerous Camelback Road. He saw Dale Hausner's light-blue Camry pull onto a side street next to the church and stop. He saw one guy get out of the car. Then he watched the car pull into the church parking lot, circle around him, and come to a stop. The driver was none other than the serial murderer Dale Hausner. Dale engaged him in small talk as the unknown assailant snuck up from behind him and stabbed him multiple times. He couldn't identify the stabber. He tried to turn and look. That movement cost him a permanent scar on his face. There was little doubt that Timothy was the victim of a horrific, random act of violence. But who perpetrated this cowardly act?

Once again, Sam Dieteman would be the star witness. Sam would testify that he sat in the front seat of Dale's car as he watched the events unfold. Sam was supposed to go beat or kill Timothy that night, but he was too drunk. Jeff had called Sam names for being too cowardly to attack that night. Just as he had for me on several occasions, Sam Dieteman laid out the entire event for the jury. More importantly, it matched how Timothy Davenport had described the random attack.

I was then called to the stand to talk about how I first became aware of the case. Again, there was no way anyone could have known that I would even be able to find the case, let alone find the victim and get his story. Sam was definitely present, and so were Dale and Jeff Hausner.

The defense called no witnesses. They certainly weren't going to call convicted serial murderer Dale Hausner to the stand to counter Sam Dieteman's testimony. Leo Valverde's defense was simple. Attack the credibility of Sam Dieteman, convicted murderer, awaiting a sentencing of life or death, and try to convince the jury that Sam was the attacker, not Jeff. Jeff was not present. He was at his condo.

The trial lasted just one week. The jury deliberated for one day. As we walked to court to hear what the jury had decided, Laura asked me if I was ready for a not guilty verdict. As we walked the long, narrow second floor passage that connects the County Attorney's Office with the Central Court Building I told her to have a little faith. Jeff Hausner had been able to skate on all the 2005 murders even though I believed he had been an accomplice. I felt we had a good chance, and I trusted the jury to make the right call.

Judge Roland Steinle once again had sat over the proceedings of the case. He called the court to order. "Have you reached a verdict?" The foreman responded they had.

I watched as Annie the bailiff took the verdict to Judge Steinle, and he looked it over. It was then read to the court.

"We the jury, in the above and entitled action find the defendant, Jeff Hausner, guilty of the charge of Attempted Murder."

I looked at Laura and whispered, "Ye of little faith."

From the prosecution table, she turned and looked at me through her glasses. I could see an ever so slight upward turning of the corners of her mouth. She had done it. Prosecution 2, Hausners 0.

I sat and watched as two deputies escorted Jeff past the prosecutors table and out of the courtroom. We looked at each other for a brief moment. He said nothing and neither did I, although I wanted too. My look said it all.

"Gotcha you murderous fu*#!"

Jeff Hausner was sentenced to eighteen years for the attempted murder of Timothy Davenport. That combined with his seven and half years for the stabbing of Raymond McQueen gives him over twenty five years in the big house. I can live with that.

Now there was just one more piece of the puzzle to finish. The death penalty trial of one Samuel John Dieteman.

CHAPTER 51

Over the last two years, I had grown fond of Samuel Dieteman's lawyers, Maria Schaffer and Quinn Jolly. I appreciated their work. They had been instrumental in preparing Dieteman for testimony in the Hausner trials, pointing out possible conflicts in the cases, all in an attempt to save Sam's life. There was no doubt Sam had made poor choices. Clearly he was a grown man capable of saying no and walking away, but the Hausner brothers had ruined his life. Their influence, their grooming had put Sam in the position he faced in his upcoming trial—life imprisonment or death.

Sam was the star witness, and sometimes star witnesses get breaks. That was not the case for Sam. He had killed, maimed, and wounded. A plea bargain had been signed, and the prosecution was obligated to follow it. Anything else would have been a fraud upon the court. I, as lead investigator, was to follow the same rules of any court proceeding. Tell the truth no matter how painful it might seem. We had to paint Sam as a thrill-seeking braggart, a man who, like Dale, had reveled in the fame of terrifying the community, a man captured in recordings poking fun at the media, at police, and at the dead. This was all true.

The defense had to find sympathetic jurors, those that could see beyond what Sam Dieteman had done and act mercifully towards him—a man who had gunned down several innocent human beings; a man who stood lookout while his partner killed and maimed others; a man who knew for months and told no one about his co-conspirators, murderers well beyond the time he knew them. This jury would need to be able to see Sam as a father, a husband, a son, a man who helped convict those same co-conspirators.

Jury selection took just over a week. The trial would commence in July 2009. Just as in Dale's case, the jury would need to hear it all. In doing so, the prosecution would only call a few witnesses. We need not return to the crimes of 2005, the ones to which Sam only had knowledge. We would deal with the summer of 2006, the time when Sam rode shotgun, no pun intended, and, with his partner's prodding, fired at will of his own and of his partner's prodding.

The state would call Detective Pete Salazar of Scottsdale PD to lay out the murder of Claudia Gutierrez-Cruz. The one murder where Sam pulled the trigger. Detective Donnie Byers of Mesa PD would lay out the murder of Robin Blasnek. I would present the sixteen other shotgun cases surrounding Sam Dieteman where he either fired or sat with a watchful eye. Detective Jason Buscher would present the wiretaps.

For the defense, the mitigation part of this case would provide the media with all the sound bites that it would need to keep the news ratings high. It would take the most time, bring the most compelling of witnesses, including yours truly. For the first time in my twenty-one year career, I would be called as a direct witness for the defense.

I told the jury of fifteen that Sam Dieteman had been a highly corroborated witness for the state. He had confessed to the shootings he partook in, helped with identifying the assailants, both Jeff and Dale Hausner, and in the other shootings and stabbings. Sam was the only reason we were able to put Jeff Hausner behind bars. Sam had given me the background information I needed to tie a bow on Random/Serial Shooter package. What's more, Sam was not a serial murderer, not by law enforcement, academia, or criminal law statutes. He had committed, in essence, only two murders, and three was the threshold for serial murder status. I had no idea how important that statement would later become.

During cross-examination by Vince Imbordino, who told me later he relished going after me on the stand (the bastard), it was brought out that Sam never once walked away. Never once did he notify the police about what was going on. It was, in fact, Sam heard chuckling and yukking it up on the wiretaps about gunning down a Guardian Angel. It was Sam who talked about shooting people as they "walked away," giving him that "extra couple of seconds to aim." Yes, Sam Dieteman had only been responsible for two deaths, but there could have been many more.

To lay the groundwork for what life behind prison walls would be for Sam, the defense called Arizona State Prison Warden Carson McWilliams. A thirty-one year veteran in the wars of prison stays, he would testify about Sam's new digs, the place where, whether he lived or died, he would spend the rest of his days. It was not a pretty picture.

Next the defense would call the mother of Samuel Dieteman, Mary, to the stand. At fifty-four years old, she looked weathered and torn. Sam was her only child, her baby. As she fought back tears, she said Sam was, "the best thing that ever happened to her."

Sam had no real father, so he spent most of his childhood being watched by his grandfather. They grew up mostly in trailer parks. She did admit to moving around a lot while Sam was a child, mostly back and forth between Arizona and Minnesota. She remarried once and then was quickly divorced. Soon after that, she ended up in a physically abusive relationship. Sam was a part of this environment. According to Mary, Sam was locked out of their apartment one night when he was ten years old. The boyfriend told Mary that Sam was staying at a friend's house, when in fact he spent the night bundled up on the outside porch. Guns were pointed at the two of them. Sam would soon be sent back to Minnesota to evade further threats and abuse.

Sam became a troubled teenager, stealing petty items and getting caught. He forged Mary's checks, and she prosecuted him. Then, when he was fourteen, Sam became a father. His girlfriend, Dorothy, three years his senior, gave birth to a baby girl. Sam was too immature to be saddled with fatherhood. He and Dorothy would separate and reunite. Dorothy had another child with another man, but Sam grew to love this baby just like his own.

As an adult, Sam worked with Mary's new husband, John. John introduced Sam into the world of electrical science. John trained Sam as an electrician, and Sam made good money. He liked his new skill set.

But in 2001, Sam's wife filed for divorce.

"He was nothing without those girls," Dorothy testified through tears at his trial.

Sam began drinking and stopped going to work. At the time, he was living with John and Mary. When he became a freeloader, they soon gave him the boot.

Mary last saw Sam for three days in July, 2006. His daughters came out for a visit. Sam spent those days trying to make up for the lost years. This would be the first and only time that Mary would meet Dale Hausner.

"He took pictures of Sam and the girls," she recalled.

The next time Mary would see Sam, he was on CNN, handcuffed and walking into jail. Her life and Sam's daughter's lives were now destroyed by a summer of random recreational violence. According to Mary, his girls cry all the time about it.

Barbara Bumpus, the mitigation specialist, had put in a year or more of research on the life of Samuel John Dieteman. Barb is paid to look at all the facets of her client's life, good and bad. When it comes to a capital case, it is usually bad. It usually starts with family. For Sam, it is a story that I believe was filled with the heartache of youth lost, youth taken, and youth destroyed.

Barb interviewed his school counselor who said that Sam would usually arrive at school, alone, wearing a black jacket or sweatshirt with the hood pulled over his head. He was an outcast. Sam had no friends and was not social. When all of Sam's school records were amassed, he had been moved from one school to another twenty-two times during his elementary years. Sometimes he had transferred to as many as three different schools in one year.

Sam's daughters, Rachelle and Danielle provided heartbreaking video testimony. Rachelle had just become a mother, which made Sam a grandfather at the ripe old age of thirty-four. Rachelle and Danielle had not seen their father for five years, from 2001 to 2006. They loved their dad. They described him as fun and caring.

When the girls received the phone call about the arrest of their father for murder, they were heartbroken. Not their dad, not the one who used to make them laugh and tickle them. He couldn't be the monster, the serial killer that everyone said he was, not the dad they knew. All they wanted was their dad to live, the one they knew from childhood, not the one accused and facing the death penalty. Tears flowed in the jury box and in the gallery.

Ron Horton's sister, Tracy Whittenburger, was called to discuss the impact of Sam's arrest on Ron. Tracy wrote him asking him how he felt about Ron turning him in. Sam had written her back. It appeared as though Sam had forgiven Ron, even praised him for having the guts to come forward. That meant a lot to the Horton family.

The last witness in the case would be none other than Sam Dieteman himself. He apologized to the jury for them being there. He wished that they didn't have to sit in judgment for his atrocious acts. He understood completely if they gave him the death penalty, but he didn't ask for it.

Sam talked about the Hausner influence and the effects of alcohol and meth use on his mindset. He then said for the first time that he did not blame anyone else. He was sitting in front of them because *he* made poor choices. Yes, the Hausners were there, but he should have walked away from them. When Maria Schaffer asked Sam how he felt about Dale and Jeff Hausner, you could have heard a pin drop in the courtroom. I half expected a rage-filled, expletive-laden oratory on what a lowlife Dale was and still is. But in a quiet, unapologetic way, Sam said, "I feel sorry for him for having no feelings." The student had become the teacher. As far as Jeff goes, he was "disappointed."

All Sam really wanted was to shield his family from any further disgrace. "They are victims in this as well," he stated. He read a poem he had written to his daughter which told of better times and better things to come. He loved his children. He realized the pain and suffering he had caused them. Sam apologized to the victims, the court, and the jury for what he had done. In his last substantial statement to the jury, Sam told them, "Don't regret your decision, whatever that might be. I apologize for putting you in this position. It is my fault."

Can a man attain redemption, or is there a limit? Sam had lived up to his part of the plea agreement. Was that enough to save his life? After all, he had killed, maimed, terrified, and ruined countless lives. Could twelve people see past all his misdeeds and save his life? Did the destruction he caused sit too heavy, like a thick fog in the middle of the night, to render anything but death?

All of us would find out after only a couple of days of deliberation. I knew that the decision would come back quickly or at least within a short time period. There was only one thing to decide. Let him live, or give him death.

Judge Steinle asked for the jury to enter the courtroom. We all stood as the jury filled the box. I could see tears streaming down one of the female jurors faces.

"Have you reached a unanimous decision?" Judge Steinle asked.

A male juror stood and replied that they had. I tried to get a read on the jury, but they all sat there in stunned silence. Had the proceedings overwhelmed them? Judge Steinle took the decision and read it silently to himself. He then handed it to the court clerk, Julie, to read aloud.

Two decisions had to be made. Sam could receive death for either the murder of Claudia Gutierrez Cruz or Robin Blasnek. Or he could receive life with no possibility of parole for either of their murders.

"In the murder of Claudia Gutierrez Cruz . . . a sentence of life. In the murder of Robin Blasnek . . . a sentence of life."

I can't describe how I felt after the verdicts were read. I believe that I would have had the same indescribable feeling had he been given a death sentence. As I look back on it now, I can only describe a feeling of closure for me. As I sat at the prosecution table, I made eye contact with one of the male jurors after the verdict was read. He was trying to get a read on me, as our eyes met. I simply nodded. He smiled slightly and nodded back.

After the sentencing, Sam was led from the court to a holding cell for transportation back to jail, and ultimately to prison. There were six armed deputies surrounding Sam's tiny holding cell when I walked back toward them. I wanted to talk to Sam one last time.

As I opened the secure door to the cell, I took a seat on the cement bench at the back of the cell. It was cold, just like a cell block should be. Sam looked up at me without any real expression.

I took a deep breath and asked, "Well, how are you feeling?"

With the same pathetic shake of his head, he took a low tone of voice and answered. "I'm in shock, Detective. I really didn't expect to live."

"Yeah, I can understand that. But, Sam, for some reason they saw your life as something worth saving. From here on out, it is up to you to make it something, as much as you can. Keep your nose clean, and maybe somewhere along the line if you get access to other inmates, you can be a positive influence in their lives."

Sam nodded his head. "You know, Detective, maybe I could make them see that my life was ruined by being an idiot and by poor choices. Maybe I can change just one person's outlook. Maybe I can help someone see that acknowledging what they did, and not making excuses for what they did, helps in the healing process, not only for themselves but the victims as well."

"You're a grandfather and a father, you know. You need to try to help your kids get through this. That was painful in court listening to your children. They obviously love you, so be there for them."

Sam eyes started to well up. I had said enough.

As I got up and looked back at Sam one last time, I was reminded of all the victims of these horrible crimes. I had to say one last thing.

"Hey Sam, if a victim or their family reaches out to you for an explanation, try to give one, would you? As painful as it might be for you, it's more painful for them to live with what happened."

Sam looked up and nodded his head up and down. "I will, Detective. You take care of yourself."

Like all things in life, however, relief and closure is never long lived. There would be more deaths and one more near death associated with the Random/

Serial Shooter Case. One that no one could've ever expected. A near death so close, and so real, that it would change the way many people looked at the investigation. It would also make this investigator, for the first time in my life, step back and take a look at the big picture.

CHAPTER 52

After the trials ended, I went through my first round of interviews. Since I had never spoken directly to the media, I asked that Sergeant Andy Hill be present for the sit-downs. Although I could clearly take care of myself, it was possible that a question may pose a problem in regards to sensitivity or political issues that surrounded the case. I could count on Andy to deflect these questions.

The first interview was with Mike Watkiss of local TV station KTVK channel three and Michael Kiefer of the *Arizona Republic.* Both of these men had spent countless hours inside and outside of the courtroom. They had interviewed civilian witnesses, victims that had survived, and family members of dead victims. I knew that any question they asked would be well thought out and probative.

For the first time, I was able to relate some of the insight into both Dale Hausner and Samuel Dieteman. It was important to distinguish the two as being polar opposites: Hausner the psychopath and Dieteman the follower. For three years, I had investigated this case, and I found it easy to navigate the conversation about their identities.

Mike Watkiss wanted to know if the convictions in the cases brought closure to me. I answered that I hoped so, not just for my sake, but for all the victims and those families affected by this terrible ordeal. What I know for certain is that there is no closure for a family of a lost loved one or someone so mortally wounded they can't take care of themselves. Closure is an overrated word.

Lead prosecutor Vince Imbordino and I also sat down with the other local media outlets after the conclusion of the trial. Vince did most of the talking, and for both of us it was a good way to end it.

Nick Martin, who had been employed by the *Mesa Tribune* during the trial, had another angle on the proceedings. He approached me after the trial about what he called "The Third Man." He was referring to Jeff Hausner, the man I believe responsible for initially grooming Sam Dieteman and passing him off to his brother Dale. To me, this interview was one last shot at trying to pin the 2005 murders on Jeff. In my heart of hearts, I know he was his brother's keeper during those events. Like 2006, 2005 was not a one-man job. Nick and I sat down for a long chat.

Nick's article was published in *Phoenix Magazine*. I had hoped that this last ditch effort where I laid out the case against Jeff Hausner, would startle someone's memory, maybe convince a Hausner family member or anyone to come forward and provide a lead that put Jeff in the car with his brother Dale for just one murder.

Unfortunately, as well received as the article was, no leads came from it. It appears as though I would have to live with Jeff Hausner's sentence: twenty-five years for attempting to murder Timothy Davenport and Raymond McQueen.

◈

After all was said and done, I took a brief respite from work. The year-long back to-back-to-back trials had worn me out. It was time to relax a bit.

On December 12, I was playing a two-day golf tournament in a men's club that I had joined several years ago. It was the first day of the tourney, and things were looking great. I came within an inch of a hole-in-one, and I was striking the ball solid.

On the tenth hole, I started to feel a pinching sensation in my back. Over the next eight holes, the pain grew worse. After my round, I was driving to Mesa to watch my daughter in a soccer tournament when I realized that I must have blown a disc in my back. Instead of going to the tournament, I drove myself to Mercy Gilbert Hospital. I have a high pain tolerance and have been an athlete my whole life. As much time as I spend at hospitals doing follow-ups on victims, it is the last place I would want to go.

As I walked up to the check-in line at the ER, I told the admitting nurse that I had severe back and now chest pain, plus pain radiating down both of my arms. Within fifty minutes, I was in surgery. I was having a massive heart attack and didn't even know it. I was on the table with people scrambling all around me, and I realized that I was probably going to die. I decided not to fight it. Even though I didn't want to go, I was ready. The curse of the Random/

Serial Shooter case was about to take another victim. I don't remember anything after that. No white light, no relatives who passed, nothing.

Modern science and my commitment to staying in excellent shape saved my life. I had a completely blocked artery caused undoubtedly by the stress of this case.

When I tell people the story of finishing my round of golf, driving to the hospital, and checking myself in, they look at me as though I'm an idiot. Here's the deal. I have never had any symptoms of heart disease. My HDL is 30, and my blood pressure is usually 100/65. My triglycerides are almost zero, and I exercise almost every day. I've never smoked and barely drink. That family history of heart disease that seems to be passed down generation after generation and kills numerous Americans . . . is not part of my legacy.

So knowing all that, why on earth would I ever think I was having a heart attack?

In the meantime, I am alive and well. I refuse to let this case or anyone associated with it kill me. And in the end, I'd like to think that justice prevailed.

EPILOGUE

Many people ask why it took so long for me to write and publish this book. There are several reasons. First, the manuscript initially contained over a thousand pages. That preliminary draft included all the murders, shootings, arsons, and criminal damage that we believed these three individuals were involved in. Ultimately, I removed the murders and shootings that we could not charge them with in court, hoping that someday someone would come forward with information to solve those cases. Unfortunately, we just didn't have enough evidence to get a conviction on some of the homicides and shootings. The arsons and criminal damage cases were too frequent and immense.

Second, at one time or another, over three hundred people had taken part in this investigation, including investigators, officers, agents, and lab technicians. I tried to mention almost all of them, but it became overwhelming to account for everyone. The story started getting lost, so I needed time to determine what information and details had to stay and what had to go.

Third, until June of 2018, I was actively investigating homicides. I felt that it would have been a distraction for this book to be published while I was working cases for the City of Phoenix and helping other jurisdictions with their cases. I wanted to spend all my time looking for murderers.

Over the years, information about the victims continued to come in. Some of the victims who lived after being shot, later passed away, including Miguel Rodriguez, Diane Bein, Darryl Davies, and Paul Patrick. Those were just the people who passed away as of my retirement. All inquiries I received were from medical examiners across the country performing autopsies to determine the cause of death of these victims. In Miguel's case, the autopsy was performed across the border. The shootings were all a contributing factor to these people's deaths, and definitively the cause of death in the case of Miguel and Paul. Miguel never made it to trial to testify; he died after convictions were obtained. Paul, the ever-present stalwart in this case, experienced several strokes and passed away in 2019.

Dale Shaun Hausner took his own life by over-dosing on allergy medicine while sitting on death row in 2013. He had sent out some letters in the end taking very little responsibility for his actions, but clearly wanting to be put to death. In fact, he had been fast tracked to die by lethal injection before he took his own life. The ultimate psychopath, he remained in control of his own fate to the very end.

ABOUT THE AUTHOR

Detective Clark Schwartzkopf (retired) served for over thirty years in the Phoenix Police Department. He works as a consultant in serial murder cases, unsolved and cold case homicides, school threats and violence, and risk/threat assessments of public figures. He earned a BS in Business Economics, an MS in Counseling from Northern Arizona University, and an MEd in Domestic Preparedness from Grand Canyon University.

He has taught courses in terrorism at Grand Canyon University, has presented to numerous investigators and TV media over the years, and has taught and coordinated training for homicide detectives. He has also trained school personnel on best practices to deal with school violence. Detective Schwartzkopf was awarded investigator of the year in 2010 and decorated dozens of times for his work in violent crime investigation. He is now moving into the area of corporate investigations and crime scene reconstruction and security.

**For more information on the case, please go to
www.randomrving.com**

Royalties from the book launch of Random Recreational Violence will go to the "100 Club of Arizona" 100club.org. Founded in 1968, the mission of the 100 Club is "to provide financial assistance to families of first responders who are seriously injured or killed in the line of duty and provide resources to enhance their safety and welfare."

www.ingramcontent.com/pod-product-compliance
Lightning Source LLC
Chambersburg PA
CBHW060303030426
42336CB00011B/914